The
Plant-Powered
Dog

Unleash the healing powers of a whole-food plant-based diet to help your canine companion enjoy a healthier, longer life

Diana Laverdure-Dunetz, MS

with W. Jean Dodds, DVM

Dogwise™ Publishing

Wenatchee, Washington U.S.A.

The Plant-Powered Dog

Unleash the healing powers of a whole-food plant-based diet to help your canine companion enjoy a healthier, longer life

Diana Laverdure-Dunetz, MS
W. Jean Dodds, DVM

Dogwise Publishing
A Division of Direct Book Service, Inc.
403 South Mission Street, Wenatchee, Washington 98801
1-509-663-9115, 1-800-776-2665
www.dogwisepublishing.com / info@dogwisepublishing.com
© 2022 Diana Laverdure-Dunetz and W. Jean Dodds

Interior: Lindsay Davisson
Cover design: Jesús Cordero

Limits of Liability and Disclaimer of Warranty
The authors and publisher shall not be liable in the event of incidental or consequential damages in connection with, or arising out of, the furnishing, performance, or use of the instructions and suggestions contained in this book. This publication contains the opinions and ideas of its authors. It is intended to provide helpful and informative material on the subjects addressed in the publication. It is sold with the understanding that the authors and publisher are not engaging in rendering veterinary, medical, health, nutrition or any other kind of personal or professional services in the book. The reader should consult his or her veterinarian, medical, health, nutrition or other competent professional before adopting any of the suggestions in this book or drawing inferences from it. The authors and publisher specifically disclaim all responsibility for any liability, loss or risk, personal or otherwise, which is incurred as a consequence, directly or indirectly, of the use and application of any of the contents of this book.

Library of Congress Cataloging-in-Publication Data
Names: Laverdure, Diana, 1965- author. | Dodds, W. Jean, author.
Title: The plant-powered dog : unleash the healing powers of a whole-food
    plant-based diet to help your canine companion enjoy a healthier, longer
    life / Diana Laverdure-Dunetz, MS with W. Jean Dodds, DVM.
Description: Wenatchee : Dogwise Publishing, [2022] | Includes
    bibliographical references and index.
Identifiers: LCCN 2022036071 (print) | LCCN 2022036072 (ebook) | ISBN
    9781617813306 (paperback) | ISBN 9781617813313 (ebook)
Subjects: LCSH: Dogs--Food. | Dogs--Nutrition. | Vegetarianism.
Classification: LCC SF427.4 .L38 2022 (print) | LCC SF427.4 (ebook) | DDC
    636.7/0852--dc23/eng/20220829
LC record available at https://lccn.loc.gov/2022036071
LC ebook record available at https://lccn.loc.gov/2022036072

ISBN: 9781617813306   Printed in the U.S.A.

More Praise for

The Plant-Powered Dog

It's wonderful that people love their dogs so much. But it's ironic that many people are needlessly subjecting other animals to horrible cruelty and violence to feed their dogs. *The Plant-Powered Dog* offers a kinder—and healthier—alternative. This eye-opening book guides readers step-by-step in transitioning their dogs to a nutritious plant-based diet and reveals the connection between animal ingredients and canine chronic diseases. Read it and you will realize that the road to optimum health for companion dogs is also the compassionate road.

Gene Baur, President of Farm Sanctuary and author of *Farm Sanctuary: Changing Hearts and Minds about Animals and Food and Living the Farm Sanctuary Life*

The *Plant-Powered Dog* addresses the doubts, breaks through the myths, and leaves every human who loves a dog with a choice that is scientifically solid and ethically unassailable.

Victoria Moran, author *Main Street Vegan*, director Main Street Vegan Academy

Dedication

This book is for the leaders, the trailblazers and the visionaries who speak out for the voiceless. It is for those who know that all life is precious and that all animals deserve peace, love and kindness. It is for the fearless warriors bucking a cruel and antiquated system and for the quietly curious who are willing to discover new and exciting possibilities. It is for everyone who understands that the path to raising vibrantly healthy dogs is paved with compassion for all living beings, respect for our beautiful planet and hope for future generations.

This book is for you.

Diana also dedicates this book to her parents, Alan and Betty Falk. You raised me to stand up for what I believe in and to leave this world a better place than I found it. You are not here in body to see it, but you are here in spirit, and I'm sure you approve. And to my husband, Rodney. In the face of your own overwhelming adversity, you have taught me to be strong and that it's never too late to make a positive difference.

Jean also dedicates this book to her much-loved husband and partner, Charles Berman, who has thankfully overcome health issues recently. Also, we are blessed to have faithful family, friends and supporters worldwide that have stood by us during these stressful times.

Table of Contents

Preface 1

Introduction 4

Part 1: Steps to Raising a Thriving Plant-Based Dog **8**

Chapter 1. A Review of Nutritional Science 9

Chapter 2. The Facts About Plant-Based Diets 26

Chapter 3. Setting Yourself Up For Success 47

Chapter 4. Essential Nutritional Components 56

Chapter 5. Comprehensive Ingredients Guide......................................76

Chapter 6. Building Recipes 123

Chapter 7. Overcoming Obstacles 169

Part 2: Plant-Based Diet Solutions for Common Canine Chronic Diseases....... 180

Chapter 8. Plant-Based Diet Solutions For Cancer 181

Chapter 9. Plant-Based Diet Solutions For Diabetes..........................212

Chapter 10. Plant-Based Diet Solutions For Food Intolerances 225

Chapter 11. Plant-Based Diet Solutions For Chronic Kidney Disease 233

Chapter 12. Plant-Based Diet Solutions For Gastrointestinal Disorders........249

Final Thoughts 268

Appendix...269

Resources..291

Cited Works..300

About the Authors..365

Acknowledgments

Many talented, supportive and inspired people came together to make this book possible. We are grateful to all of them. We'd like to thank Larry Woodward of Dogwise Publishing. Without him, this book would have forever remained merely the seed of an exciting idea. Larry, you enabled it to sprout and grow within these pages. When we approached you with the concept for a plant-based dog nutrition book, you believed in our vision. Moreover, you believed in us. You believed in our ability to bring this vision to life and to deliver an original and significant work that would disrupt outdated beliefs on the optimum diet for modern companion dogs. We hope we delivered, and we also know that the final product is so much better because of your wise editorial guidance.

We would also like to thank the entire team at Dogwise Publishing. As always, you shepherded us kindly and patiently through every step of the publishing process. This is a family-based business in every sense of the word. You have, as always, made us feel a part of that family.

Thank you also to all the researchers who have brought—and continue to bring—new information to light regarding the benefits and applications of plant-based dog nutrition. This book would not be possible without your dedication to advancing scientific knowledge and your recognition of an evolving world paradigm.

We also owe a deep debt of gratitude to all those special people dedicated to helping their animal companions, themselves and our world stay safe and healthy. You made this book possible. Thank you for being there, for trusting us, and for opening your minds to facts and science.

Diana would like to thank some special people who have influenced her life and career. Thank you to everyone in the veterinary community who participated in my 2019 Plant-Powered Dog Food Summit, which served as the genesis of my journey along the path toward a compassionate and healthy way of nourishing our canine companions: Drs. Jennifer Coates, Jean Dodds, Andrew Knight, Armaiti May, Marybeth Minter, Richard Pitcairn, Margo Roman, Erika Sullivan, Lorelei Wakefield and Ernie Ward. Thank you not just for myself, but on behalf of all the animals your work has spared—and continues to spare—from a life of cruelty and misery.

Diana would also like to give a special shout-out to Dr. Ernie Ward. While globe-trotting to educate others throughout the world, you took time from your insanely busy schedule to provide invaluable feedback based on your extensive veterinary nutrition expertise. This book is better because of your input. You rock!

And a big thank you to Lindsay Rubin Carvalho. You were always ready and willing to bounce ideas off, offer your expertise in the dog food space and provide moral support. It was nice to know you were available on the other end of the computer or phone line with a fresh new perspective and a virtual smile.

Our most heartfelt thank you goes to our husbands—Diana's husband Rodney and Jean's husband Charles. Thank you for your support in everything we do. You are true partners in every sense of the word.

We hope we didn't forget anybody. If we did, we apologize. Please know that we are most grateful to you.

Preface
An Enlightening Plant-Based Journey

"I think I need to quit my canine nutrition practice." It was 2017 when I (Diana) sadly uttered those words to my husband, Rodney. I loved creating fresh-food recipes for dogs. I'd spent three and a half years studying for a Master of Animal Science degree and had invested more than a decade building a rewarding canine nutrition consultancy and fresh-food formulation career. Things were going great, but I just couldn't do it any longer. I'd been vegetarian for many years, but after learning more about the egg and dairy industries, I'd made the leap to veganism. Except, I felt like a fraud. How could I even call myself vegan when I was packing pound after pound of animal ingredients into my clients' recipes?

That's when I decided to quit the business I loved. It wasn't an easy decision, but it felt like the only one. Despite my education and years of experience, I had never questioned whether dogs needed to eat animal ingredients to be healthy. I just accepted it as a fact. After all, weren't dogs wolves? And didn't wolves need meat? And weren't all these experts out there online talking about 'species appropriate' diets?

There seemed to be no other option for me. Harming any animal in any way—including feeding companion dogs—just no longer felt right. But I also refused to harm my canine clients. So, there it was. I kept coming back to the same 'solution'—walk away from my canine nutrition practice.

But when I revealed this decision to my husband, his response shocked me. "Why don't you do your own research and see if dogs can be healthy on plant-based diets?"

I had a degree and experience in the field, but that thought had never crossed my mind. Do my own research? What research could there possibly be? Weren't the facts just known?

I realize now that I had been too close to the situation. I had been following the same 'experts' shouting the same myths. And it seemed like the louder they shouted their message, the more everyone (including myself) believed them. I didn't even hold space in my mind that there could be an alternative. My husband, however, didn't have any bias. He wasn't in the industry. He just looked at it from what now seems like the obvious angle. "Do your own research."

Thankfully, I heeded his advice. I started with the obvious—social media outreach. This led me to an introduction and conversation with Professor Andrew Knight,

Veterinary Professor of Animal Welfare at the University of Winchester Centre for Animal Welfare in Hampshire, England. Professor Knight has written around 150 academic and 80 popular publications as well as presenting many YouTube videos on a variety of animal welfare issues, including plant-based companion animal diets. Professor Knight gave freely of his time, information and resources, and he shocked me with some disturbing facts about animal ingredients in pet foods that I had not previously known. My eyes began to open. Or, I should say, they began to pop open.

Next, I had the immense pleasure of speaking with Dr. Richard Pitcairn and his wife, Susan Pitcairn, MS. Dr. Pitcairn has been a leading force in the field of holistic veterinary medicine for more than four decades. Throughout those many years, he has witnessed chronic diseases in companion dogs and cats skyrocket so alarmingly that in the fourth edition of their book, *Dr. Pitcairn's Complete Guide to Natural Health for Dogs & Cats,* he and Susan advocate for the switch to a plant-based diet. The Pitcairns introduced me to the word "bioaccumulation." It changed my life, and I'll be forever grateful to them for that and so much more.

But my research didn't stop there. Not by a long shot. In fact, it led me to assemble some of the most respected minds in veterinary nutrition for the Plant-Powered Dog Food Summit, the first online summit dedicated to plant-based dog nutrition, which streamed online in March 2019. For a year, I sent videographers all over the world, from Australia to Arizona, to interview experts and learn what they knew about the health dangers of animal ingredients and the health benefits of plant-based foods for dogs. I also dove deep into the latest scientific research papers—many of which are cited in this book.

The knowledge I gained from my research and from the Plant-Powered Dog Food Summit was life-changing. I learned that not only can dogs thrive on a well-balanced plant-based diet, but that it might just be the key to health and longevity for our canine companions. I was excited! I was also prepared to take my recipe consultancy and formulation practice in a new direction—one centered on a 100% whole-food plant-based approach to canine nutrition.

I must admit that while I felt great about this transition, I also didn't think I'd attract much business. After all, canine nutrition is a pretty niche business. But a *plant-based* canine nutritionist? Let's just say that I wasn't waiting for the email inquiries to light up my computer screen!

Boy, was I ever wrong. Query after query started popping up, and before I knew it, I had more business than I could handle.

I loved passing along the information I had learned to my clients, teaching them about the dangers of animal ingredients and how their dogs could live long and healthy lives on a cruelty-free plant-based diet. Most were new clients, but some were clients for whom I had previously formulated meat-based diets and were now returning for plant-based recipes. Suddenly, I had the best of both worlds. I could help my canine clients achieve optimum health without ever harming another animal.

I was also connecting more deeply with my clients because I had travelled the same road they were on and had experienced the same emotions. The only time I had handled meat during the previous decade was to feed my dog, Chase, who passed away in 2018. Discovering that I would not need to compromise my values or my dog's health when it came time to welcome our next canine family member was like winning the lottery. And helping my clients discover that same freedom was like winning the lottery every day. Canine nutrition was fun again!

Since that time, I have had the pleasure of working with compassionate, caring dog lovers from all over the world to address a wide variety of chronic canine health conditions with a plant-based diet. But still something nagged at me. No matter how hard I worked, I could only reach a limited number of people within the scope of my nutrition practice. And I wanted to spread the word about the health benefits of plant-based dog diets to *millions* of people!

The solution was as clear as a blank page on my computer screen. *Write a book.*

The choice of co-author was obvious—Dr. Jean Dodds. As an expert in multiple areas of holistic canine medicine, including food intolerances, nutrition, inflammation, autoimmune disorders and vaccinosis, Jean has spent a career spanning more than 50 years helping to improve the health and longevity of companion dogs. And as a vegetarian for many decades, she understands the impact that diet has on all animals, our environment, ourselves and future generations. Happily, Jean jumped on board, excited to spread the word about the healing powers of plant foods for dogs.

This book reflects the latest research in the fields of canine and human nutrition, as well as the realities of a rapidly changing world. The information on these pages may be difficult for many people to digest. It will likely even anger the die-hards who cling to the myth that dogs are carnivores as if they are hanging on to a life preserver on a sinking ship. And the animal agriculture and meat-based mass market commercial pet food industries certainly don't want this information made public knowledge.

But we want you to hear what science has to say. After that, you need to decide for yourself what to feed your dog. But at least you'll decide based on facts and not myths. That's what I did, and it's the best decision I've ever made, for my clients' dogs and my own plant-based pup, Moo, who my husband and I adopted from Vietnam in September 2019.

I was once ready to give up my canine nutrition practice, but thanks to my husband, I did my research and realized that I didn't have to compromise my values to help dogs live long and healthy lives. Jean agrees with me, as does her vegetarian husband, Charles.

We hope that as you read this book you, too, will agree. We also hope that you will enjoy the freedom from purchasing and handling animal products and that your beloved canine companions will reap the many health benefits associated with consuming a well-balanced plant-based diet.

Introduction

A lot has changed since the publication of our previous book, *Canine Nutrigenomics: The New Science of Feeding Your Dog for Optimum Health,* back in 2015. Researchers have uncovered exciting new scientific discoveries regarding diet and health for people and companion animals. Documentaries and undercover investigations have revealed many disturbing issues regarding the animal agriculture and seafood industries, including animal welfare concerns, the environmental impact of raising huge numbers of livestock and the consequences to marine life and our oceans. We have also faced a global pandemic, teaching us that how we interact with other species affects not only their welfare, but also our own.

These are serious matters, but they're also an invitation to think and act in new and exciting ways. They are an opportunity to shift our individual and cultural perspectives from a 'me first' to a 'we're all in this together' view—with 'all' being humans, animals and the Earth.

As Sir Paul McCartney stated, "We have a responsibility to act now to minimize our impact on this planet—for our children and future generations who will inherit what we leave behind."

We wholeheartedly agree. And we're excited because everywhere we look, we see this happening. It's happening because it's becoming evident that plant-based diets can be healthier for both people and our canine companions. At the same time, plant-based diets spare land and ocean animals, reduce environmental impact and help decrease global warming.

People everywhere are excited about these benefits and they are expressing this excitement with their purchasing decisions. In 2019, sales of plant-based foods grew by 11% to more than $4.9 billion, while total US retail food sales grew by just 2% during that time. And between 2017 and 2019, the plant-based foods sector increased by $2 billion, growing nearly 28% a year in that time period (The Good Food Institute, 2019). The plant-based pet food sector is also expected to boom from $3.8 billion in 2021 to $6.5 billion by 2028 (Research and Markets, 2021).

Companies are responding to the growing demand for plant-based foods with innovative new products that seem to spring up almost weekly. The demand is so high that plant-forward foods are overtaking store shelves. You no longer need to seek out a specialty store to discover a huge variety of plant-based items. Now, they're offered everywhere from fast-food drive-throughs to local grocery store chains and big box retailers.

We are inspired by the scientists, innovators and entrepreneurs who are coming together to create positive change in the human and pet food sectors. Thanks to them, we can choose from an abundance of compassionate foods that not only delight the palate, but that we can feel good about consuming and feeding to our canine companions.

We're also inspired by people like you: people who are making more conscious eating and living choices for themselves and who are interested in doing the same for their four-legged family members. A 2019 study out of the University of Guelph in Ontario, Canada, surveyed 3,673 dog and cat caretakers to determine their attitudes and feeding practices. The survey revealed that 35% of those who did not already feed their dog or cat a plant-based or vegan diet were interested in doing so (Dodd et al., 2019).

What a fantastic time we are living in! We are at the dawn of a new era of compassion and respect toward the Earth and all beings who share it with us. And this new era is powered by plants.

Many people question whether a plant-based diet really provides adequate nutrients. For that answer, we point to the growing number of world-class athletes who embrace a plant-based lifestyle, including tennis greats Venus Williams and Novak Djokovic, Formula 1 world champion Lewis Hamilton (whose Bulldog, Roscoe, is also plant-powered), ultramarathoner Scott Jurek and world-record holding powerlifter Patrik Baboumian.

Given the success of plant-based diets for people, you might wonder if our canine companions can also benefit. Can dogs really thrive—and feel satisfied—munching solely on plants? The more that researchers delve into these questions, the more it becomes clear that the answer is a resounding, "Yes!"

New studies continue to emerge supporting the health benefits of nutritionally-sound plant-based diets for dogs. One such study compared caretaker-reported perceptions of health for dogs fed plant-based versus meat-based diets in the United States and Canada. Data was collected for 1,189 dogs, including 665 who consumed strictly meat-based diets and 339 being fed strictly plant-based for an average of three years. Those feeding a plant-based diet had more positive perceptions of their dogs' health than those feeding a meat-based diet, including fewer reported health disorders per dog. Specifically, plant-based dogs were less likely to suffer from ocular (eye), gastro-intestinal and hepatic (liver) disorders than the meat-fed dogs. But perhaps the most astounding finding was that *the plant-based dogs reportedly lived one-and-a-half years longer than their meat-fed counterparts* (Dodd et al., 2022).

But what about fun-time at mealtime? Can dogs feel excited and satisfied consuming plant-based foods? For the answer, researchers from the University of Winchester in England surveyed thousands of dog (and cat) caretakers on a variety of factors regarding their companion animals' food-oriented behaviors, health and welfare. The study, which involved 2,308 dogs (and 1,135 cats), revealed that those consuming nutritionally balanced plant-based diets for at least one year were just as eager eaters and just as healthy as those fed meat-based diets (Knight & Satchell, 2021).

This research is exciting, and it's also just the tip of the iceberg. You'll be discovering a lot more fascinating—and likely shocking—science throughout this book.

You may also have questions of your own, such as, "Isn't my dog a carnivore?" or "Can my dog get enough nutrition from plants?" or "How can I create my own nutrient-dense plant-based recipes?" or "What about plant-based nutrition for chronic health conditions?" or even "How do I address my dog's plant-based diet with my veterinarian?" We'll answer these questions—and many more—as we move forward.

Get ready to join us on an exciting journey that will change the way you think about feeding your canine companion. In the following pages, we'll call upon the latest scientific research to reveal why feeding a well-balanced plant-based diet to modern companion dogs may just be the missing link to optimum health and longevity.

We'll also lead you beyond the world of theoretical knowledge and into the world of *action*. For this purpose, we've segmented the book into two parts.

Part 1: Steps to Raising a Thriving Plant-Based Dog. The seven chapters in Part 1 will guide you through the process of transitioning your dog to a well-balanced plant-based diet. The information in each chapter builds upon the previous so that you are taking logical action steps toward your dog's nutritional goals. Chapter 1 lays the groundwork for this exciting journey with an in-depth review of the latest nutritional science, including new advances detailing the relationship between diet, inflammation and disease. In Chapter 2, we will debunk common myths about the nutritional needs of dogs and present the research-based facts. Chapter 3 will show you how to set you and your dog up for success on your plant-based journey. Chapter 4 details the six essential nutrients comprising your dog's diet, while Chapter 5 provides a comprehensive ingredients guide. In Chapter 6, you will discover how to use the proprietary Recipe-Builder Pie and Recipe Creation Chart, along with our recommended supplementation, to design your own 'almost complete and balanced' recipes for your dog. This chapter also includes information on evaluating commercial plant-based dog foods and relevant laboratory testing. Chapter 7 rounds out this section with tips and tricks to overcome the most common obstacles you might encounter along this dietary journey.

Part 2: Plant-Based Diet Solutions for Common Canine Chronic Diseases. The five chapters in Part 2 dive into a plant-based approach for some of the most common chronic health conditions seen in modern companion dogs. Chapter 8 takes a deep dive into the diet-related causes of cancer, how to protect your dog and the top research-based ingredients to help prevent and reverse this terrible disease. We will also provide a science-backed discussion of the popular ketogenic diet. Chapter 9 provides nutritional solutions for dogs suffering from diabetes, while Chapter 10 tackles the common issue of food intolerances. In Chapter 11, you will get an eye-opening look at causes and dietary approaches for chronic kidney disease. Chapter 12 wraps up this section with plant-based solutions for common gastrointestinal disorders.

In the **Appendix,** you'll find 10 delicious supplemental recipes. Some are designed as tasty treats, while others make perfect sides, toppers or occasional meals. All are packed with nutrients to support your four-legged friend's optimum health.

A comprehensive **Resources** section will assist you with your dog's plant-based journey, including where you can purchase the foods and supplements that we discuss throughout the book.

The **Cited Works** section at the end of the book houses a complete list of the scientific studies we cite. They are grouped according to the corresponding chapter and alphabetized by the first listed author's last name to make locating them quick and easy. You'll notice that this section is long! The reason is that scientific evidence is important. When you feed your dog a plant-based diet, we want you to have the knowledge and confidence that you're doing so not based upon our opinion, but on the latest research.

New words or phrases that might be unfamiliar to you are introduced in **bold** print with the definition just after. This will help you to learn new terms quickly and to refer back to them for a refresher whenever necessary.

Consider this book as your partner along your journey to raising a thriving plant-based dog. With each step, you'll further build your knowledge and confidence. And, since each chapter builds on the one before, we encourage you to use this book much as you would a GPS system in your car. Let it guide you toward your long-range destination while in the short-term steering you clear of potholes, bumps and roadblocks. Follow it one step at a time and before you know it, you'll be navigating the world of plant-based dog nutrition as smoothly as Venus Williams glides across the tennis court—like a true champion.

We thank you for embracing this new and exciting approach to canine nutrition. Together, we can help our beloved dogs live longer, healthier lives while creating a more peaceful, compassionate and vibrant world for all beings.

Peace, plants & paws,

Diana Laverdure-Dunetz, MS

W. Jean Dodds, DVM

Part 1
Steps to Raising a Thriving Plant-Based Dog

Nothing can bring you peace but yourself. Nothing can bring you peace but the triumph of principles.

- Ralph Waldo Emerson

Chapter 1
A Review of Nutritional Science

"It's all in the genes." These were the first words of the first chapter of our previous book, *Canine Nutrigenomics: The New Science of Feeding Your Dog for Optimum Health,* which was published in 2015. Back then, we set out to dispel the myth that our health—and the health of our companion dogs—is primarily predetermined by our **genes** (short sections of DNA, or genetic code) that we inherit from our ancestors.

At first glance, it might appear freeing to believe we're at the mercy of the genetic hand we've been dealt. It reminds us of the famous song, *Que Sera, Sera,* meaning, "Whatever will be, will be." After all, we may as well eat whatever we want and live however we please if our health outcome is beyond our control. But in reality, this mindset strips us of our freedom—namely, the freedom to make beneficial diet and lifestyle choices that will help stack the deck in favor of us living a long and healthy life. This is true for us and our canine companions.

Whether or not a person or animal will suffer from one or more chronic diseases really depends on three main factors:

1. Our inherited genes
2. **Epigenetic factors** (environmental influences that change how our genes behave without changing our DNA) (CDC, 2022) and
3. The interaction between our genes and epigenetic factors

Our bodies are made up of trillions of cells, and each of these cells contains our genes. Our genes serve as the instruction manuals for cells to make new proteins, which perform different 'jobs' in the body (e.g., enzymes, insulin, antibodies, transcription factors) (National Human Genome Research Institute, 2019; Science Learning Hub, 2022). We each have a unique set of genes—except for identical twins. Identical twins have the same DNA, the same genetic code. Because of this, it makes sense that they would suffer from the same chronic diseases. But this isn't the case. Studies of identical twins have proven that the influence of genetics on chronic disease is modest. And do you know which type of chronic disease has the lowest genetic correlation? *Cancer!* (Rappaport, 2016).

In fact, genetics is shown to account for just 8.26% of cancers in people. This means that epigenetic factors—including diet, lifestyle and exposure to toxins—account for more than 90% of cancer risk. A study titled *Genetic Factors Are Not the Major Causes of Chronic Disease* shows that exposures—and not genetics—account for the greatest risk for all common chronic diseases. There were only two chronic diseases where genetics accounted for more than 40% of risk: autoimmune thyroiditis (42%) and asthma (49%) (Dodds & Laverdure, 2011; Rappaport, 2016).

This is powerful information because it means that we have far more control over our health destiny—and that of our canine companions—than we ever thought possible.

New advances in nutrigenomics

In *Canine Nutrigenomics*, we introduced the concept of **nutrigenomics** (nutrition + genomics), which is the study of how nutritional ingredients affect health at the cellular level by influencing **gene expression,** the way our genes behave. Nutrigenomics is a fast-moving scientific field. When we completed that book, we knew that fascinating and thought-provoking discoveries would continue to emerge. Here, we're excited to advance the concept of nutrigenomics by drawing upon exciting *new* research that you can use to optimize your dog's health—and your own.

Let's begin our journey with a recap of some key nutrigenomics concepts. This will give you a solid foundation for understanding how epigenetic factors such as the foods you put in your dog's bowl (and on your own plate) regulate gene expression to help promote either optimum health or chronic disease.

Many diseases, one root cause

At first glance, chronic health conditions such as arthritis, obesity, cancer, gastrointestinal disorders, endocrine disorders, autoimmune diseases, kidney and liver disorders, and heart disease appear to affect different bodily systems and stem from different physiological mechanisms. But as practitioners of Traditional Chinese Medicine (TCM) and other Eastern forms of healing have known for thousands of years, the body isn't made up of isolated parts. Like a precisely calibrated clock, people and animals are an intricate web of systems working together and cooperatively as a symbiotic whole (hence the term "holistic" medicine).

Just as our bodies function holistically, there is also a holistic root cause linking the vast array of chronic diseases that plague millions of people and companion animals in our modern society. That root cause is **cellular inflammation,** or inflammation at the cellular level. Under normal circumstances, cellular inflammation isn't a bad thing; it's the body's normal immune response to an **antigen,** which is any substance that the body considers to be a foreign invader. The invader can take many forms, including:

- External injuries, such as a scrape, bruise or splinter
- Pathogens that invade the body, such as bacteria, fungi or viruses
- Chemicals and toxins
  (InformedHealth.org, 2018)

When an antigen attacks, the body jumps into action to defend itself. The tissues release **immune cells,** white blood cells that rush in to immobilize or eradicate the antigen. These immune cells release a variety of substances known as inflammatory mediators, such as histamine, eicosanoids, proinflammatory cytokines and macrophages. The inflammatory mediators prevent further inflammation and help with tissue healing and regeneration (Abdulkhaleq et al., 2018; InformedHealth.org, 2018).

There are two types of inflammation:

Acute cellular inflammation is a temporary inflammatory state triggered by a specific event (e.g., trauma or infection). It gets bad fast, but it also gets better quickly—from just a few hours to a few weeks. Acute inflammation has a beginning, middle and end. Once the immune system neutralizes the offender and heals the affected area, the inflammation subsides and the body returns to its previous state of **homeostasis,** or balance (Harvard Medical School, 2020; Pahwa et al., 2020).

Chronic inflammation occurs when the normal acute inflammatory process becomes disrupted. This type of inflammation creates a vicious inflammatory cycle because it leads to cellular oxidative stress (OS) and the production of Reactive Oxygen Species (ROS), such as free radicals (Dodds, 2016; Dodds & Callewaert, 2016; Dodds, 2019). ROS perpetuate the body's inflammatory response because they send signals that tell cells to ramp up the production and release of proinflammatory cytokines. Think of it like the movie Groundhog Day, with Bill Murray. Every morning at the same time, Murray's character woke up to the same song on the alarm clock, met the same people and acted out the same scenarios. When he eventually realized he needed to change his own behavior, he was finally able to break this repetitive cycle and move the clock forward to a new day. It's the same with chronic inflammation. Even though the immune cells have finished their job, they are stuck in a continuous loop, repeating their attack. But with no pathogen to fight, the cells target healthy tissues and organs. The result is a long-term inflammatory state that waxes and wanes for months, years or even an entire lifetime (Dodds, 2016; Dodds & Callewaert, 2016; Harvard Medical School, 2020). This type of prolonged OS damages or destroys cells and tissues, produces **dysbiosis** (disruption in the homeostasis of the gut microflora) and leads to cancer and other chronic inflammatory diseases (Dodds, 2016; Li et al., 2016; Dodds, 2019).

Here is the shocking part that many people don't realize: *Diet is a key risk factor of chronic inflammation in both people and companion animals* (Dodds, 2016; Dodds & Callewaert, 2016; WHO, 2020).

It is possible to suffer from chronic cellular inflammation and not even know it. That's because we can't see cellular inflammation like we can see the outward inflammation of a cut or bruise. It's only when the systemic inflammatory fire simmering deep within us rages so out of control that outward signs start to manifest. This is true of people and animals.

Sadly, the first symptom of chronic cellular inflammation is often chronic disease, such as one of the following:

- Allergies

- Arthritis

- Autoimmune diseases

- Cancer
- Cardiovascular disease
- Cognitive issues
- Chronic kidney disease
- Periodontal disease and gingivitis
- Diabetes
- Gastrointestinal disorders
- Kidney disease
- Liver disease
- Lung disease
- Obesity
- Skin and coat disorders
- Urinary tract disorders

Just how serious a problem is chronic cellular inflammation? Take a look:

- Chronic inflammatory diseases are the leading cause of death in people (Pahwa et al., 2020).
- In the United States, six in 10 people (60%) suffer from a chronic disease and four in 10 (40%) suffer from two or more chronic diseases (CDC, 2020).
- Three out of five people (60%) worldwide die from chronic inflammatory diseases such as obesity, heart disease, chronic lung disease, cognitive disease, chronic kidney disease, diabetes and cancer (CDC, 2020; Pahwa et al., 2020).
- According to the World Health Organization (WHO), chronic diseases pose the biggest threat to human health (Pahwa et al., 2020).
- In the United States, chronic inflammatory diseases are expected to rise over the next 30 years (Pahwa et al., 2020).

As a society, we're inflicting the vast majority of chronic diseases on ourselves through poor diet and lifestyle choices. And this unsettling trend doesn't only affect humans. The story is just as grim for our canine companions. *Chronic diseases are skyrocketing in companion dogs.*

Chew on these troubling facts:

- Approximately *six million* new cases of cancer are diagnosed in dogs (and cats) each year. According to the Veterinary Cancer Society, cancer is the leading cause of death in almost half of dogs (47%), especially those over 10 years of age (and 32% of cats). Dogs get cancer at about the same rate as people, and they suffer from more types of cancer than any other type of companion animal (FETCH a Cure, 2020).
- Diabetes in dogs increased by 79.7% from 2006 to 2016 (compared to 18.1% in cats during that same time) (Banfield Pet Hospital, 2016).

- In 2018, 55.8% of dogs (and 59.5% of cats) were classified as overweight or obese (APOP, 2019).

- Osteoarthritis (OA) in dogs has increased by 66% over the past 10 years (and 150% in cats) (Banfield Pet Hospital, 2019). More than 20% of dogs over the age of 10 are affected by OA.

- The NutriScan saliva-based food intolerance test has identified an alarming number of food sensitivities among dogs (and cats). Close to nine thousand Nutriscan tests performed to date since January 2012 indicate that almost 70% of dogs have shown a sensitivity to one or more ingredients, with *all of those dogs testing intolerant to at least one animal or fish ingredient* (Dodds, 2017/2018; Dodds, 2019; Dodds, 2019a).

- Of 478 dogs tested via Hemopet's CellBio assay between May 2019 and August 2020, 52% (248) had positive (elevated) levels of **isoprostane**, prostaglandin-like compounds formed in the cells by the reaction of free radicals with arachidonic acid. Elevated isoprostane levels indicate the presence of systemic oxidative stress and inflammation (Dodds, 2016; Dodds & Callewaert, 2016; Dodds, 2019).

It's no coincidence that staggering numbers of modern companion dogs suffer from one or more chronic inflammatory diseases. Our canine companions have fallen victim to the same lifestyle-related conditions that are skyrocketing among people living in developed societies. As a culture, we and our companion animals are overfed and undernourished, and we are all travelling down the same dangerous inflammatory path.

In 2017, researchers from the Research Institute of Biomedical and Health Sciences at Las Palmas de Gran Canaria University in Las Palmas, Spain and from the Department of Animal Medicine and Surgery at the Universidad Autónoma de Barcelona in Barcelona, Spain, evaluated the relationship between obesity and obesity-related metabolic dysfunction (ORMD) in 93 dogs aged two to 14.7 years and their human families living in an obesity-prone area of Spain. The team found that obesity and ORMD in companion dogs was higher in this region and directly correlated to obesity in their human caretakers (Montoya-Alonso et al., 2017).

The researchers discovered that:

- 78% of the overweight/obese people also had overweight/obese dogs.

- *All* the dogs diagnosed with ORMD lived with overweight/obese people.

- 40.9% of the dogs were obese, 40.9% had **hypertension** (high blood pressure), 20.4% had fasting **hypertriglyceridemia** (elevated blood triglycerides), 20.4% had fasting **hypercholesterolemia** (high cholesterol) and 5.4% had fasting **hyperglycemia** (high blood sugar).

(Montoya-Alonso et al., 2017)

The message is clear. We not only share our homes with our dogs; we also share many of our poor dietary choices. And our beloved canine companions are paying the price with their health.

Fortunately, emerging research shows that it doesn't have to be that way. In the largest dog health study to date, researchers collected data on 2,536 dogs fed a conventional meat (1,370 = 54%), raw meat (830 = 33%) or vegan (336 = 13%) diet for at least one year. The authors examined seven general indicators of ill health: 1) unusual numbers of veterinary visits, 2) medication use, 3) progression onto a therapeutic diet after initial maintenance on a vegan or meat-based diet, 4) guardian opinion of health status, 5) predicted veterinary assessment of health status, 6) percentage of unwell dogs and 7) number of health disorders per unwell dog. They also considered the prevalence of 22 of the most common canine health disorders. The percentages of dogs in each dietary group reported to have suffered from health disorders were 49% (conventional meat), 43% (raw meat) and 36% (vegan). Based on the results of this and other studies, the authors concluded that:

> *Accordingly, when considering health outcomes in conjunction with dietary hazards, the pooled evidence to date from our study, and others in this field, indicates that the healthiest and least hazardous dietary choices for dogs, among conventional, raw meat and vegan diets, are nutritionally sound vegan diets (Knight et al., 2022, pp. 29).*

Fighting inflammation with diet and lifestyle

Let's unpack two seemingly contradictory facts:

1. Most chronic diseases have a genetic basis (that is, they start in the genes).
2. Most risk for acquiring a chronic disease comes from epigenetic factors such as exposure to environmental influences (e.g., diet, lifestyle, toxins, chemicals, drugs, vaccines), not from the genes we inherit.

If most chronic diseases start in the genes, then how can we possibly have so much control over our health and the health of our canine companions by changing our environmental exposures? After all, people and animals can't change their genetic code. The DNA we are born with remains with us throughout our lives.

To see how this works, let's back up a bit for a little genomic primer.

Together, all the genes in an organism are known as the **genome**. It's currently estimated that there are 19,996 protein-coding genes in the human genome (Zimmer, 2021), while the canine genome contains about 22,182 protein-coding genes (Halo et al., 2021). You can think of genes as the architects that design our bodies. Just like an architect draws up plans for a building, genes provide the blueprint that determines how our bodies are built. In short, genes make proteins, proteins make cells and cells make us (and our dogs) who we are (Mullis et al., 2022). But here is the fascinating part: Not all genes make proteins all the time in all the cells. They also do not all make the same types and amounts of proteins. Via the process of gene expression, certain genes in cells can be turned on (activated), meaning that they produce proteins, while others are turned off (suppressed) and don't make proteins (Dodds & Laverdure, 2015).

Gene expression determines what happens inside of cells and what type of jobs they perform. We're all born with **stem cells,** unspecialized cells that can become anything. Then, based on gene expression, the cells specialize; some become skin cells, while others become organ cells, muscle cells, brain cells, blood cells or other types of cells.

Genes determine an organism's **phenotype**, which are observable characteristics ranging from body shape and size to eye and hair color, right down to the little freckle on your nose (or wherever it is!). Your dog's genes determine characteristics including breed, tail and ear shape, eye color and coat color and texture. Genes also determine who we are on the *inside*, such as our blood type, hormone levels and any genetic predispositions to disease.

Gene expression also determines whether cells become healthy or diseased.

This means that by changing the way our genes express, we can influence whether or not our cells will manifest disease—even if there is an underlying genetic predisposition. We can influence gene expression through messages we send to the **epigenome**, which is a layer of chemical compounds that surrounds our DNA. By 'tagging' cells via chemical reactions, the epigenome sends instructions to genes, telling them whether to activate (make proteins) or suppress (not make proteins), as well as which proteins to make (National Human Genome Research Institute, 2012; Dodds & Laverdure, 2015). In other words, the epigenome controls gene expression.

It makes sense, then, that positively influencing the epigenome is the key to fighting inflammation and creating optimum health. But how can we influence the epigenome? This is the really cool part.

The epigenome communicates with epigenetic factors in our environment, such as diet and lifestyle.

Think of the epigenome like circuit breakers in your home and epigenetic factors like switches. By flipping various switches up or down (activating or suppressing the circuit breakers), you can control which areas of your home have power and which don't. The circuitry behind the breakers (the genetic code) remains the same. But turning the breakers on or off (via environmental changes) determines whether you have the power to watch TV, cook dinner and take a hot shower, or whether your home is plunged into darkness.

So, while you can't change the genes you or your dog were born with, by flipping epigenetic switches you can directly influence the way these genes behave (express).

For example, your dog might have been born with a genetic predisposition for diabetes mellitus; but that doesn't mean he is doomed to get that disease. By nourishing him with foods that send healthy epigenetic messages and tell his genes to express in a way that protects his cells, you can keep him healthy and disease-free—and he'll never be the wiser!

Even in cases of chronic diseases, cells have a remarkable ability to repair, regenerate and renew—if you send the right nutritional messages to the epigenome:

- Feeding a diet rich in foods that tell the epigenome to initiate healthy gene expression
- Reducing or removing foods that send harmful messages to the epigenome and cause unhealthy gene expression

(Dodds, 2020)

Now, here is the really exciting part:

The more research that is done in the field of epigenetics, the more we learn that a plant-based diet is superior for promoting optimum gene expression, disease prevention and longevity.

Throughout this book, we'll show you how to send healthy epigenetic messages to your dog's genome with a nutrient-dense, well-balanced plant-based diet.

Epigenetics and the gut microbiome

One of the epigenetic connections between health and disease that we'll talk a lot about focuses on the collection of bacteria that live in the gut, primarily in the **colon** (large intestine). These bacteria are part of a diverse and complex community of **microbes** (the others are fungi, protozoa and viruses) that reside in and on the body, including the gut, mouth, skin and genitals. As a group, these organisms are called **microbiota**. Just like cells, microbiota have their own genetic code. The genetic code for all the microbiota in an organism is called the **microbiome** (Qin & Wade, 2018; Bulsiewicz, 2020; Dodds, 2020; Kavli Foundation, 2020).

More than 1,000 different species of microbes live in your dog's gut (and your own)—far more than any other part of the body. And get this. *The microbiome of all the microbiota in your dog's body has more than 150 times the number of genes than his cellular genome* (Simpson et al., 2002).

This means that your dog is *mostly* microbes!

As fetuses, dogs and people have sterile guts, but immediately after we are born, microbes move in and begin colonizing us. Most of them take up residence on the mucosal surface of the intestinal lining, known as the **gut-associated lymphoid tissue (GALT)**. The GALT is the largest immune organ in the body, making up 70% of our entire immune system. In fact, the GALT microflora is so important that it is called the 'forgotten organ' (O'Hara & Shanahan, 2006).

Beneficial bacteria that live in the gut promote health to the host (you and your dog) in many ways, including:

- Helping produce anti-inflammatory compounds
- Creating **short-chain fatty acids (SCFAs)**, beneficial byproducts of bacterial fermentation
- Preserving the integrity of the intestinal epithelial tissue barrier
- Producing and metabolizing vitamins and trace minerals
- Protecting the body from infection
- Regulating digestion by controlling intestinal mobility

  (Mondo et al., 2019)

Pathogenic microbes, or bad bacteria, also live in the gut and vie with good bacteria for top spot. Even healthy microbiomes have some bad bacteria, but an excessive amount creates dysbiosis, which as we previously mentioned is an unbalanced gut microbiome. Dysbiosis creates inflammation in the GALT, lowers immune function and results in 'leaky gut.' Normally, the cells that make up the GALT are packed closely together, forming tight junctions that create a barrier between the gut and internal systems. When the GALT lining is compromised, these cells separate, creating openings that cause the lining of the gut to become more permeable, or 'leaky.' A leaky gut is like a wide-open door with a big welcome sign for antigens (those nasty foreign invaders). These unwanted guests waltz right through the openings in the epithelial lining of the GALT and cross over into the bloodstream. When this happens, the immune system jumps into action, creating chronic cellular inflammation and making us (and our canine companions) vulnerable to a whole host of immune-mediated diseases (Bulsiewicz, 2020).

Researchers are just beginning to understand the complexities of the gut microbiome, but scientific trends are already emerging. One of these trends involves the epigenetic connection between environmental factors, the microbiome and chronic inflammatory diseases.

Here is how it works:

- Environmental factors like diet and lifestyle send epigenetic messages to the gut microbiome.
- Based on these environmental messages, the gut microbiome produces bioactive metabolites that communicate with the host's cells, both in the gut and throughout the body.
- These metabolites 'speak' to the cells and alter gene expression through DNA methylation and histone modification.

(Dodds & Laverdure, 2015; Qin & Wade, 2018)

In other words, the microbiome communicates with our epigenome to alter gene expression and create either a state of health or inflammation (Qin & Wade, 2018).

An unbalanced gut microbiome can lead to a whole host of chronic inflammatory diseases, including:

- Asthma
- Diabetes mellitus
- Colorectal cancer
- Crohn's disease
- Eczema
- Food allergies
- Guillain-Barre syndrome
- Kawasaki disease
- Multiple sclerosis
- Lupus

- Metabolic syndrome
- Non-alcoholic fatty liver disease
- Obesity
- Rheumatoid arthritis
- Sjogren's syndrome
- Ulcerative colitis

(Qin & Wade, 2018; Bulsiewicz, 2020)

The good news is that beneficial gut bacteria love to munch on a variety of plant foods. In the coming pages, we'll divulge these gut-friendly foods and show you how to use a plant-based diet to help promote a vibrant gut microbiome and optimum health for your best friend.

Toxins and the microbiome

Toxins send unhealthy epigenetic messages that disrupt the gut microbiome and lead to a variety of chronic inflammatory diseases.

The cycle looks like this:

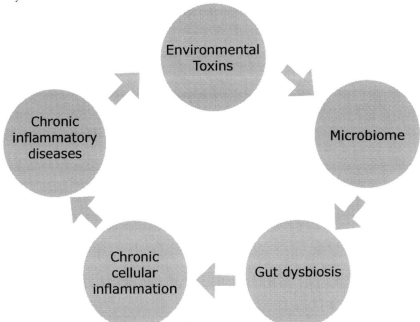

There is no getting around it. The modern world is a toxic world, and dogs are particularly vulnerable. They eat and roll in grass sprayed with pesticides, herbicides and other poisons. They drink puddles containing toxic runoff. They lick floors cleaned with chemical products. Their bodies absorb toxic flea and tick oral and 'spot on' treatments. Over-vaccination further stresses their immune systems. These are just some of the environmental hazards that tax our dogs' bodies daily.

Much of the toxic exposure in our environments is out of our control, but there is one major type of toxin that we can consciously manage—*dietary toxins.*

We'll discuss the role of toxins in specific disease processes later, but for now it's important to point out that *the lower down on the food chain you and your dog eat, the fewer toxins you ingest.* This is because of **bioaccumulation**, which refers to the build-up of toxins in the fatty tissues of animals.

Bioaccumulation works like this:

- Plants absorb low levels of toxins from the environment, such as the soil and sea water.

- Small animals or fish eat the plants and absorb the toxins, storing them in their fatty tissues.

- Larger animals or fish consume the smaller ones, further concentrating the toxins in their bodies.

- Those at the top of the food chain—such as dogs and people—eat the larger animals or fish and are exposed to the highest doses of accumulated chemicals.

  (McDougall, 2010; Pitcairn & Pitcairn, 2017)

Toxins that bioaccumulate in food animals include:

- Antibiotics, antimicrobials and other drugs, including penicillin, tetracycline and furamazone

- Bacterial toxins, including cyanotoxins from blue-green algae

- Environmental chemicals such as fluoride and chlorine

- Natural and synthetic growth hormones, including estradiol, progesterone, testosterone, zeranol, melengestrol and trenbolone

- Heavy metals, including arsenic, aluminum, lead and mercury

- Polychlorinated biphenyls (PCBs)

- Persistent organic pollutants, such as dioxins

- Pesticides, herbicides and fungicides, including glyphosate

  (National Research Council [US] Committee on Drug Use in Food Animals, 1999; McDougall, 2010; Ferrão-Filho & Kozlowsky-Suzuki, 2011; Pitcairn & Pitcairn, 2017)

This list includes just a small sampling of the toxins that bioaccumulate in the tissues of food animals. Most of us try to protect our dogs from environmental toxins, *yet the largest exposure is dietary.*

Noted physician, author and nutrition expert Dr. John McDougall points out that 89% to 99% of chemicals found in our bodies come from meat, eggs, fish and dairy products (McDougall, 2010; Pitcairn & Pitcairn, 2017). That's virtually all of them!

And guess who, as a group, consumes massive amounts of these animal products: *our canine companions*.

Bioaccumulated toxins in food animals pose serious health consequences to those who consume them, including toxicity to the gastrointestinal tract, liver, nervous system and skin, as well as antibacterial resistant infections, behavioral modifications and cancer (Shryock, 1999; Ferrão-Filho & Kozlowsky-Suzuki, 2011; CDC, 2018).

Fortunately, you can dramatically reduce your dog's toxic exposure by feeding him ingredients low on the food chain—*plants*.

Meat and the microbiome

You might have read articles online citing studies that a raw meat diet alters the canine microbiome in a way that creates greater gut microbiota diversity and richness. What you may not have read is that these studies compared *unprocessed* raw meat-based diets with *processed* mass-market commercial diets comprised predominantly of extruded kibble (Kim et al., 2017; Sandri et al., 2017; Schmidt et al., 2018). We do not find it surprising that an unprocessed diet of any sort would result in greater microbial diversity and richness when compared to a commercial kibble or even canned food. As one major study comparing the gut microbiota of dogs fed raw meat diets to extruded kibble diets notes:

> *These differences might be due to differences in the way the two diet types were manufactured and differences in the main ingredients of the two diets. Generally, commercial feeds contain controlled nutrients and controlled microorganisms, because they undergo formal manufacturing processes, including compression through high temperature and high pressure and microbial monitoring. However, natural diets do not go through any manufacturing process and are fed to dogs as raw, so that more nutrients and microorganisms in the natural habitat are absorbed into the gut of the dog* (Kim et al., 2017, pp. 8).

The study authors acknowledge that a natural and unprocessed diet is much more likely to benefit the gut microbiome than one that is highly processed, including processing to control microorganisms. In addition, all the raw meat diets in this study (Kim et al., 2017) contained comparable levels of macronutrients (proteins, fats, carbohydrates) regardless of the type of meat fed, while the macronutrient levels of the kibble diet differed from the meat diets (Schmidt et al., 2018). Differences in macronutrient levels alone can account for significant changes to the gut microbiota.

As one study reports:

> *However, for dogs, the kingdom of origin of the ingredients seems to be less important than the overall macronutrient composition. Extruded diets with similar macronutrient contents, but prepared exclusively with vegetable sources of protein, do not seem to significantly alter the microbiome of dogs when compared to traditional (mixed animal and vegetable) extruded diets* (Pilla & Suchodolski, 2020, pp. 3).

In other words, dogs need to get the proper levels of macronutrients (proteins, carbohydrates and fats), *but they do not need to get them from animal products*.

In fact, shifting from an animal protein-based diet to a vegetable protein-based diet can beneficially alter the gut microbiome of dogs suffering from food-responsive dysbiosis. A 2018 study published in the *Journal of Veterinary Internal Medicine* looked at the effect of an animal protein-free (APFD) extruded diet on the fecal microbiota of dogs with food responsive enteropathy (FRE) and on healthy dogs (HC) (Bresciani et al., 2018). The macronutrient composition of the diet used in the study was similar to typically available commercial dry adult maintenance diets. Ten dogs diagnosed with FRE and 14 healthy dogs received the corn-based diet for 60 days. (The diet contained animal fat, but not animal protein). At baseline, the fecal microbiota of the FRE dogs differed significantly from the healthy dogs. So, what happened at the end of the trial? In the researchers' own words:

> *Our results suggest that, in FRE dogs, treatment with the APFD led to a partial recovery of the fecal microbiota by significantly increasing microbiota richness, which was significantly closer to a healthy microbiota after the treatment. In contrast, no changes were detected in the fecal microbiota of HC dogs fed the same APFD* (Bresciani et al., 2018, pp. 1903).

These findings are significant for several reasons:

- Prior to adopting a diet free of animal proteins, the FRE dogs suffered from unhealthy microbiomes.

- The microbiomes of the FRE dogs *significantly* improved after just 60 days on the vegetable protein-based diet, becoming much more like the microbiomes of the healthy dogs.

- The healthy dogs suffered no negative shifts in microbiota from the vegetable protein-based diet.

The researchers also noted that it was not the nutritional composition of the diet, but the diet itself, that produced the beneficial effects:

> *We therefore conclude that the fecal microbiota of FRE dogs changed after the dietary trial, not directly because of the composition of the APFD, but because the diet promoted recovery from the disease. Recovery from disease was a strong driver to change the microbiota composition. This hypothesis is supported by the fact that the APFD did not drive any changes in the fecal microbiota of HC dogs* (Bresciani et al., 2018, pp. 1908-1909).

Interestingly, plant-based diets could potentially become an important nutritional treatment for dogs with certain types of dysbiosis.

A 2019 study published in *Environmental Biology* compared the gut microbial DNA of domestic dogs with wild wolves and humans (Alessandri et al., 2019). The study also analyzed how the dogs' gut microbiota were affected by consuming either a balanced commercial diet higher in fiber (3%) and carbohydrates (30%) or a BARF (Bones and Raw Food) diet. The results were very different to earlier studies comparing a commercial diet with a fresh raw food diet. Let's take a look:

- The gut microbiota of the dogs consuming the commercial food showed a higher level of complexity than the BARF group.

- At the phylum level, beneficial Bacteroidetes decreased in dogs fed the BARF diet.
- Prevotella 9, Faecalibacterium and Sutterella significantly decreased in the BARF group compared to the commercially fed group. (Faecalibacterium is a commensal species shown to possess anti-inflammatory properties and to promote a healthy gut microbiota in people.)

(Alessandri et al., 2019)

According to the researchers:

In this context, the reduction of Faecalibacterium spp. in the BARF group indicates that a meat-based diet is less protective against inflammatory activity in the canine gut (Alesssandri et al., 2019, pp. 1334).

Since gut inflammation is correlated to systemic inflammation in the body that can trigger a variety of chronic inflammatory diseases, the fact that "a meat-based diet is less protective against inflammatory activity in the canine gut" is vitally important information.

So, what do we make of the persistent chatter touting the benefits of raw-meat-and-bone diets (RMBDs) on the canine gut microbiome? We think this statement from a 2020 review article published in *Frontiers in Microbiology* sums it up well:

Based on the available evidence to date, research on RMBDs does not show clear benefit on the gut microbiome and may increase the risk of pathogen exposure (Wernimont et al., 2020, pp. 8).

Kingston's microbiome gets a boost with plants

Kingston, a six-year-old American pit bull terrier mix, started out life with a lot stacked against him. At only about seven weeks old, he was abandoned at a shelter with two broken legs and a broken hip. In spite of a number of surgeries, one of Kingston's legs remains a few inches shorter and he suffers from permanent degenerative spinal deterioration. Given his physical disabilities, the last thing that Kingston needed was additional health issues. However, in June 2021, he suffered from a serious gastrointestinal flare-up and his 'dad,' Sam, rushed him to the veterinary emergency room. A biopsy and ultrasound confirmed that at just four years old, Kingston suffered from severe Inflammatory Bowel Disease (IBD). Likely due to the lack of colostrum as a puppy paired with the extensive antibiotics during that same time, Kingston was also diagnosed with a severe microbiome deficiency.

For several years, Kingston could not hold down food and would often vomit several times per day. The specialists told Sam that Kingston would most likely need to take prednisone for the rest of his life. However, Sam was determined to manage the IBD and to control any flare ups with diet and a fecal transplant. As he said, "Keeping Kingston's IBD symptoms at bay is of the utmost important."

To complement Kingston's oral fecal transplant supplementation, Sam reached out to Diana for a custom-formulated plant-based diet. After a lengthy intake and discussion with Sam regarding Kingston's health conditions, Diana created a special recipe to address Kingston's IBD, help stimulate a healthy microbiome and address his systemic inflammation.

After three months on Diana's recipe, Sam reported that, "Kingston is doing great on his diet! His symptoms have subsided, and he has not had any flare ups! He has his energy back and his bowel movements appear much healthier. He also hasn't vomited in a long time, which is all tremendous!"

This poor boy got off to a rough start, but thanks to Sam's wonderful care and Diana's microbiome-friendly plant-based diet, Kingston can look forward to a bright and healthy future.

You'll discover more fascinating revelations about the evolution of the canine microbiome in the next chapter. And throughout this book, we'll talk about ways to enhance the health of your dog's gut microbiome using the power of a whole-foods, plant-based diet. As you read on, it's great to know that this information can benefit you, as well!

New realities invite a new approach

Just as nutritional research continues to evolve, so does the current state of the world. Today, we face global challenges that we could not possibly have foreseen just a few years ago. Humanity is at a crossroads, and the path we choose will determine not only our own future, but the future of all beings and the planet we call home.

We know that you want your dog to live a long, healthy life. We want that, too. That is why this book focuses on the health benefits of feeding your dog a nutrient-dense, well-balanced plant-based diet. We could spend an entire book talking about the environmental and animal welfare benefits of eating plants, but many other people have already covered these issues eloquently and in detail, and we want to offer a fresh approach. But if you'd like to dive deeper into how adopting a plant-based lifestyle for you and your dog will help end the suffering of other species and save our planet, we highly encourage it. We've included a list of documentaries in the Resources section for this purpose.

If you're reading this book, you may already be aware to some extent of the horrors endured by food animals and the environmental devastation caused by the animal agriculture and fishing industries. And you've probably come across information about the questionable practices of the mass-market commercial pet food industry and some of the unseemly ingredients that end up in pet foods.

Today, we face global challenges that will decide the future of all species on this planet—our own included.

We wrote much of this book during the height of a devastating global pandemic known as Covid-19, an infectious disease caused by a newly discovered type of coronavirus called SARS-CoV-2. This virus was first identified in a wet market—a group of stalls that sell and slaughter live animals of all kinds on site. These places are called wet markets partly because of the blood, innards, scales and other parts of the animals whose slaughtered remains permeate the floors of the stalls. These sentient animals often exist in filthy conditions and often die of disease. The close proximity of these animals to each other and to the people who frequent wet markets make them breeding grounds for disease (Animal Equality, 2020; Maron, 2020).

And while Covid-19 has spotlighted the dangers of global transmission of infectious diseases, we are still trying to rationalize that literally billions of animals continue to suffer in the shadows, being born into an existence plagued by poor nutrition, inhumane practices and diseases that ultimately lead to slaughter typically at the hands of large industrial meat production facilities. The people who work in this industry also suffer from the risks and stress involved.

The infection rate for Covid-19 was found to be five times higher in slaughterhouses and meat processing facilities than in the general population. Outbreaks of the infection from these facilities has occurred around the world—including the United States, Germany, Ireland, France, the Netherlands, Spain, Italy and the United Kingdom (Slow Food, 2020).

At the time of this writing, hundreds of millions of people worldwide have been infected with the virus that causes Covid-19 and more than six million people have died (Worldometer, 2022). Humans are being forced to face the reality of their own actions. When we try to dominate nature, we all lose.

Here are some things to consider when you're deciding what to feed your family, both two-legged and four:

- Worldwide, more than 70 billion land animals are killed each year for food production (Sanders, 2018).
- Between 37 billion and 120 billion farmed fish and a trillion wild fish are killed each year (Zampa, 2018).
- One quarter of global gas emissions comes from food—half from animal products, and half of those from beef and lamb (Poore & Nemecek, 2018).
- We are currently in the midst of the Earth's sixth mass extinction, brought about by human overconsumption, including high-density animal production (Ceballos et al., 2020).

In their research article published in June 2020 by the *Proceedings of the National Academy of Sciences*, noted ecologist and conservationist, Gerardo Ceballos of the Universidad Nacional Autonoma de Mexico and his colleagues from Stanford University and the Missouri Botanical Garden, sent a chilling message regarding the current mass animal extinctions:

> *The ongoing sixth mass extinction may be the most serious environmental threat to the persistence of civilization, because it is irreversible. Thousands of populations of critically endangered vertebrate animal species have been lost in a century, indicating that the sixth mass extinction is human caused and accelerating. The acceleration of the extinction crisis is certain because of the still fast growth in human numbers and consumption rates. In*

addition, species are links in ecosystems, and, as they fall out, the species they interact with are likely to go also. In the regions where disappearing species are concentrated, regional biodiversity collapses are likely occurring. Our results reemphasize the extreme urgency of taking massive global actions to save humanity's crucial life-support systems (Ceballos et al., 2020, pp. 13596).

The human species represents just 0.01% of all living beings on Earth, yet our over-consumption has resulted in the loss of half the plants and 83% of all wild animals on the planet (Carrington, 2018). At the same time, billions of animals are bred and kept as livestock.

With so many animals bred and killed for food and an environment on the brink of devastation, the problem can seem overwhelming. You might wonder how as one person with perhaps one dog you can make a difference, but we assure you that you absolutely can.

According to the *Vegan Calculator* (2018), the average person consuming a plant-based diet saves the life of one farm animal per day. Now think about a typical dog, who eats meat every day at every meal—and lots of it. When you transition your dog to a plant-based diet, you have the potential to save thousands of land and sea animals over your dog's lifetime. We don't know any other scenario where saving animals is so easy!

The same is true for the environment. Purchasing pasture-raised beef simply is not the answer. According to a 2018 study published in the journal Science, even beef cattle raised on natural pastures produce six times more greenhouse gases and use 36 times more land than plant protein production (Carrington, 2018a; Poore & Nemecek, 2018). Joseph Poore from the University of Oxford in the United Kingdom, who led the research, told *The Guardian* that, "A vegan diet is probably the single biggest way to reduce your impact on planet Earth, not just greenhouse gases, but global acidification, eutrophication, land use and water use" (*The Guardian*, 2018). You'll discover more about the environmental impact of your dog's diet in the Chapter 3 Sidebar, "Green dogs help save the planet."

The best part is that you don't have to choose between your dog's health and compassion for all animals and our planet. In the following pages, we'll reveal how plant foods nourish your dog's cells and microbiome, fight inflammation and help protect your canine companion from chronic diseases.

Are you ready for more? Let's move forward!

Chapter 2
The Facts About
Plant-Based Diets

Today, vegetarianism and veganism are rising rapidly, thanks to increasing awareness of what constitutes a healthy diet, along with an evolving respect for other species and our planet. What once seemed 'impossible' is now happening, with companies like Burger King leading the way. The formerly meat-focused company now offers a variety of plant-based options such as the Impossible Whopper in the U.S., the Plant Based Whopper in Singapore, the Veggie King burger in France and the Rebel Whopper, Vegan Royale chicken-style sandwich and vegan nuggets in the UK. In March 2022, the company made an astonishing move when it turned its flagship London restaurant fully vegan for one month. Burger King has also pledged to make half of its menu meat-free by 2030 (Pointing, 2022; Webber, 2022).

This is great news, but there's a long way to go. There are still millions of skeptics out there, and the powerful livestock, dairy and seafood industries continue to wield their powerful resources trying to convince consumers that going plant-based is fraught with danger. But the tide of public opinion is turning for three main reasons:

- More and more people (and their dogs) are thriving eating nutritious plant-based foods.
- People are becoming conscious of how their actions affect other species and the planet.
- There are significant environmental and climate-change issues that result from using livestock as food sources. Methane is released into the atmosphere and retained in significant quantities. This adds to global warming trends, as does deforestation to make way for new livestock grazing lands, since carbon-absorbing trees are removed.

Even so, you may still be confused or skeptical about feeding your dog a plant-based diet, due to the massive amount of misinformation—and even disinformation—that circulates online and in some books. It's understandable, so in this chapter we'll present the scientific facts and address some of the most common questions we hear about plant-based dog nutrition.

Modern dogs are *omnivores*, not carnivores

The pet food industry has done a fantastic job of feeding us the greatest myth of all related to dog nutrition—that the sweet ball of fur curled next to us on the couch is really a wolf in dog's clothing and therefore needs to eat meat to thrive. The truth is that modern domestic dogs, while sharing some characteristics with wolves, genomically evolved along a different path that has resulted in some important similarities to humans with respect to key genes related to digestion, metabolism, neurological processes and chronic diseases such as cancer. This close genomic relationship likely came about because domestic dogs and people have been cohabitating in close quarters and sharing many of the same food resources for thousands of years (Sriskantharajah, 2018).

A 2014 study published in *Animal Genetics* illustrates a significant genomic evolution. Researchers from Uppsala University in Sweden found that dogs have evolved to digest starch more efficiently than wolves, evidenced by an increased number of pancreatic amylase (AMY2B) genes as compared to their wolf ancestors. The researchers discovered that:

> *High amylase activity in dogs is associated with a drastic increase in copy numbers of the gene coding for pancreatic amylase, AMY2B, that likely allowed dogs to thrive on a relatively starch-rich diet during early dog domestication.... Pancreatic amylase (AMY2B) serves as the first step in the digestion of starch to glucose in the small intestine (Mocharla et al., 1990) by catalyzing the breakdown of starch to oligosaccharides maltose and maltriose. Axelsson et al. (2013) specifically demonstrated that selection had acted on a series of duplication events to favor the accumulation of additional copies of AMY2B, resulting in an average sevenfold copy number increase in dogs relative to in wolves, and that this increase corresponds to higher pancreatic AMY2B expression as well as higher serum amylase activity* (Arendt et al., 2014, pp. 716).

Companion dogs also possess many other traits that distinguish them from nutritional carnivores, including:

- Dogs can convert plant-based beta-carotene (also known as provitamin A) to retinol, the pure form of vitamin A. Carnivores cannot make this conversion and must obtain retinol from animal sources.

- Dogs can convert linoleic acid (LA), an essential omega-6 fatty acid found in plant-based sources, to arachidonic acid (AA). Carnivores lack the enzymes necessary to make this conversion.

- A dog's requirement for the essential amino acid arginine falls between a cat and a rat, which is consistent with dogs having evolved eating an omnivorous diet.

- Dogs can convert the essential amino acid tryptophan to niacin, as can humans. Cats cannot make this conversion and must consume preformed niacin from food or supplements.

- Dogs can synthesize taurine, so it is not considered an essential amino acid, however, cats cannot, due to the lack of enzymes necessary in this process (more on dogs and taurine shortly).

- Dogs can digest almost 100% of the carbohydrates they consume.

  (Lewis et al., 2000; Ball et al., 2007; Case et al., 2011; McDonald et al., 2011)

Evidence indicates that dogs accompanied immigrant farmers during the Neolithic expansion from the Near East into Europe about 10,000 years ago. These agricultural farmers replaced the local hunter-gatherer populations and introduced new crops to Europe, including wheat, barley, peas, broad beans and lentils (Colledge & Conolly, 2007; Morgane et al., 2018). Given that dogs have been munching on grains and legumes since the Neolithic age, we believe it's time to rethink the term 'species-appropriate diet' to reference plant foods rather than animal-based foods!

In the largest study of its kind to date, Anders Bergström from the Francis Crick Institute in London and his colleagues sequenced the genomes of 27 ancient dogs living as far back as 11,000 years. They were shocked to discover that *five different types of ancient dogs* had already spread through Europe, Asia, the Americas and Siberia at that time. Based on this ancient breed diversity, which would take a great deal of time to develop, the authors believe that the genetic history of dogs may date well before 11,000 years—all the way back to the Stone Age. They also found that all the dog lineages shared one common ancestor—a "single ancient, now-extinct wolf population"—and that dogs have genomically evolved largely independent of their wolf relatives, "…with limited gene flow from wolves since domestication…." Interestingly, the reverse is not true: the authors found that there has been "substantial dog-to-wolf gene flow" (Bergström et al., 2020; Luntz, 2020; Wells, 2020). Given these findings, perhaps wolves are becoming genomically more like dogs!

The similarity between dogs and humans does not end at the cellular level. It goes even deeper—*all the way down to our microbiomes.* If you've ever felt a 'gut' connection to your dog, there's a good reason!

We previously mentioned a 2019 study published in *Environmental Biology* that compared the gut microbial DNA of domestic dogs with wild wolves and humans. The researchers analyzed 169 fecal samples from 51 different dog breeds, six fecal samples from grey wolves and 79 fecal samples from healthy human adults using sophisticated microbial gene sequencing technology. They discovered that modern dogs have *lost* six bacterial genera typical of the wolf core microbiota. At the same time, dogs have *gained* five taxa that are present in the human core gut microbiota. Moreover, there were no significant differences based on the breed of dog (Alessandri et al., 2019).

The researchers concluded that:

> *Altogether, the metagenomic investigations presented in this study revealed that, while maintaining common characteristics with its wild relative in terms of taxonomic composition and metabolic potential, the domesticated canine gut microbiota has been extensively shaped by artificial selection, altered diet and close contact with humans* (Alessandri et al., 2019, pp. 1339).

Another interesting study took place in 2018. Luis Pedro Coelho from the European Molecular Biology Laboratory in Heidelberg Germany and his colleagues extracted the DNA from multiple stool samples of 64 dogs (32 Labrador retrievers and 32 Beagles). Half of the dogs were lean/normal weight, while the other half were overweight/obese. The researchers created a gut microbial gene catalog containing 1,247,405 genes and compared it with previously published microbial gene catalogs of pigs, mice and humans. They discovered that at the phylum level (made up predominantly of Firmicutes, Bacteroidetes, Proteobacteria, Actinobacteria, and Fusobacteria), the canine gut microbiome shares a 63% overlap with the human microbiome, compared to only a 20% overlap between humans and mice and a 33% overlap between humans and pigs (Coelho et al., 2018).

In their study published in the journal *Microbiome*, Coelho and his team wrote:

> *As microbial gut strains are host-specific, this similarity cannot be explained solely by direct transmission between dogs and humans. Rather, it must be a function of similar physiology and lifestyle* (Coelho et al., 2018, pp. 4-5).

In other words, dogs and humans have lived together for thousands of years. We've dined together for thousands of years. And our microbiomes have evolved together for thousands of years.

Coelho and his colleagues also wanted to see how diet would affect the dogs' gut microbiomes. They fed their canine subjects the same baseline diet for four weeks, after which they randomly divided the dogs into two groups. One group received a high-protein/low carbohydrate (HPLC) diet, while the other group was given a lower-protein/higher-carbohydrate (LPHC) food. They found that the high-protein diet significantly changed the microbiomes of the overweight/obese dogs, but not of the lean dogs, *echoing the same results found in humans* (Coelho et al., 2018).

According to the researchers:

> *The structural and functional similarity of the dog microbiome to the human one implies that, as human studies are predictive of results in dogs, dog studies may be predictive of results in humans. Thus, dog studies provide a double benefit: for dogs directly and for their potential to generalize to humans* (Coelho et al., 2018, pp. 7).

We see that dogs and people are microbially similar enough that each species can benefit from research on the other. This is advantageous all around because people and dogs share many of the same chronic lifestyle-related diseases, and both species suffer from an obesity epidemic. We'll be talking a lot more about this throughout the book.

Omnivore does *not* mean herbivore

Occasionally, we receive comments from people lambasting us that "dogs are not herbivores!" It's important to set the record straight here. An **herbivore** is "any animal that eats only plants" (Oxford Learner's Dictionaries, 2020). Examples of herbivores are horses, cows, elephants, goats and rabbits. Typically, herbivores cannot digest meat.

Of course, we are not calling dogs herbivores, any more than we are claiming that people are herbivores. We are saying (and proving) that dogs, like people, are *not* nutritional carnivores; they are **omnivores**, which is "an organism that can feed on both plant and animal sources" (Biology Dictionary, 2020).

As an article published in the *British Journal of Nutrition* clearly states: "Although it shares many anatomical and metabolic characteristics with the cat, the domestic dog is metabolically more omnivorous and can digest, absorb and metabolize a considerable amount of dietary carbohydrates" (Deng & Swanson, 2015). As we have shown here and in the previous chapter, both the genomes and microbiomes of dogs have epigenetically evolved over thousands (and perhaps tens of thousands) of years in parallel with their human companions.

Most people have no problem accepting that modern dogs have evolved behaviorally—after all, we wouldn't invite a wolf to snuggle with us in bed! Now, it's finally time to hop on the evolutionary biology train and accept that dogs have also evolved physiologically and metabolically. We must once and for all let go of the myth that modern dogs are nutritional carnivores and accept the fact that they have evolved into omnivores who can thrive on a nutritiously balanced diet of plant-based ingredients.

Plant-based dogs *can* get plenty of protein

"Where do you get your protein? The same place your 'protein' gets theirs."

- Anonymous

If you follow a plant-based lifestyle, you've no doubt heard the "Where do you get your protein?" question more times than you can count. Cultural biases in favor of animal products are no accident; they are the carefully designed result of decades of marketing and lobbying by the powerful meat and dairy industries—in the United States, Europe and elsewhere. In 2019, the U.S. dairy industry spent $7.9 million to hire government lobbying firms, while the U.S. meat industry spent $4.6 million (Center for Responsive Politics, 2020; Center for Responsive Politics, 2020a). Since the animal agriculture industry is closely connected to the pet food industry, these strategies also influence pet food marketing messages and consumer beliefs about what type of food is best for companion dogs.

Despite all the money and power of these special interest groups, consumers are ready for a change. As we mentioned in the Introduction, demand for plant-based human and pet foods is skyrocketing. There is just no denying it: Plant-based nutrition is not a fad, for ourselves or our canine companions. It is the healthy, sustainable diet of the future.

Now, let's look at the facts about dogs and protein.

To help us out, we'll introduce our (imaginary) canine friend, Benji, who we've decided is a four-year-old, 22-pound neutered male Beagle of average activity level (We hope you like the name Benji because we'll be referring to him a lot throughout the book!). As a healthy adult dog, Benji is nutritionally at a maintenance stage.

Using a little math wizardry that we will detail in Chapter 6, we've determined that Benji needs to consume about 600 Calories per day to maintain his weight and that he requires a minimum of 27 grams of protein daily.

Side note: Now is a good time to explain why we capitalize the C in Calories throughout the book. A Calorie with an uppercase C is known as a 'large calorie,' which refers to 1,000 'small calories.' A Calorie is the same as a kilocalorie ('kilo' means 'thousand') or kcal, which is the energy value you will commonly find on commercial pet food packages. Calories are typically used in reference to fresh-food diets for people and animals, so that is what we use throughout this book.

The following chart shows the Calories, protein, fat and glycemic load of some popular plant-based foods.

Sample Nutrient Composition Chart

Food	Amount	Total Protein (grams)	Calories	Total Fat (g)	Est. Glycemic Load
Tempeh, cooked	100 g (3.5 oz)	18.2	196	11.4	5
Lentils, boiled	1 cup	17.9	230	0.8	13
White beans, boiled	1 cup	17.4	249	0.6	18
Adzuki beans, boiled	1 cup	17.3	294	0.2	21
Split peas, boiled	1 cup	16.3	231	0.8	13
Small white beans, boiled	1 cup	16.1	254	1.1	15
Pinto beans, boiled	1 cup	15.4	245	1.1	15
Kidney beans, boiled	1 cup	15.3	225	0.9	15
Pink beans, boiled	1 cup	15.3	252	0.8	20
Black beans, boiled	1 cup	15.2	227	0.9	14
Navy beans, boiled	1 cup	15	255	1.1	15
Great northern beans, boiled	1 cup	14.7	209	0.8	13
Chickpeas (garbanzo beans), boiled	1 cup	14.5	269	4.2	17
Broad beans (fava beans), boiled	1 cup	12.9	187	0.7	13
Tofu, firm	½ cup (126 g)	10.3	88.2	5.3	1
Quinoa, cooked	1 cup	8.1	222	3.6	18

(Source: NutritionData, 2020)

By combining ingredients from our chart, we can create a wide variety of options to meet and exceed Benji's daily RDA of 27 grams of protein. Here are just a few examples:

- 3.5 oz tempeh (18.2 g protein, 196 Calories) + 3/4 cup cooked lentils (13.4 g protein, 173 Calories) = 31.6 g protein and 369 Calories
- 1 cup cooked chickpeas (14.5 g protein, 269 Calories) + 1/2 cup cooked adzuki beans (8.7 g protein, 147 Calories) + 1.75 oz tempeh (9 g protein, 98 Calories) = 32.2 g protein and 514 Calories

- 1 cup firm tofu (20.6 g protein, 176 Calories) + 1 cup cooked fava beans (12.9 g protein, 187 Calories) = 33.5 g protein and 363 Calories
- 1/2 cup cooked split peas (8.2 g protein, 116 Calories) + 1/2 cup cooked kidney beans (7.7 g protein, 113 Calories) + 3/4 cup cooked white beans (13 g protein, 187 Calories) = 29 g protein and 416 Calories

The plant-based combinations we can use to achieve Benji's daily RDA for protein are almost endless; you are limited only by your imagination. And with all of these delicious options, Benji certainly will not get bored with his meals!

What about amino acids?

Dogs and people don't just need protein. They need **amino acids**, which are the building blocks of protein. We'll talk more about amino acids in Chapter 4. Critics of plant-based dog nutrition often claim that dogs need animal proteins because they are considered 'complete proteins,' meaning that they provide the correct ratio of all 10 essential amino acids that dogs must get from diet. Most plant proteins, on the other hand, aren't complete proteins because they either lack an essential amino acid or don't contain them all in sufficient quantities. Soy is an exception. It contains all the essential amino acids that dogs need and so is considered a complete protein.

Meat-feeding advocates use the complete protein argument as a scare tactic. Of course, you wouldn't rely on feeding your dog one type of plant protein as the sole source of his dietary amino acids, any more than a meat feeder would expect their dog to get all the nutrients he needs from just a hunk of meat. Neither option would be nutritionally balanced.

This is where thoughtful ingredient combining comes into play. When you provide your dog with a variety of plant-based proteins from legumes, grains, seeds and nuts, he will receive all the essential amino acids he needs to thrive over the course of days, weeks, months and years.

As The Ohio State University Veterinary Medical Center website says:

As long as the diet has the proper balance of available amino acids, whether they come from plant or animal sources does not make any difference to the nutritional health of the pet (OSU, n.d.).

Go Buckeyes!

Can dogs consume *too much* protein?

The Association of American Feed Control Official's (AAFCO) minimum protein recommendation for adult dogs at maintenance is 18% or 45 grams per 1,000 Calories, but many pet food companies create foods with *double* that amount—a whopping 36% protein and 90 grams per 1,000 Calories (Case, 2021). Some companies even produce foods with *more than 60% protein* (Ephraim et al., 2020). The prevailing opinion when it comes to dog nutrition seems to be, "the more protein the better."

But once a dog's requirements for total protein and individual amino acids have been met and even exceeded, is it prudent to keep piling on more and more protein? Or is it possible for dogs to get *too much* protein? Some researchers are using **metabolomics**, which is the emerging scientific field of analyzing metabolites in the body, to answer this question.

Just as an organism has a genome, which is the sum of all its genes, it also has a **metabolome**, which is the sum of all the metabolites in the organism (Gaynor, 2017). Metabolites are found in bodily fluids and tissues and can be used as markers of an individual's biological status. For example, changes in metabolite status can be used as early markers for certain diseases. It is estimated that there are 3,000 to 5,000 detectable metabolites in the human body, so metabolomics can provide groundbreaking insight into an individual's health at the metabolic level (Gowda et al., 2008).

A 2020 study published in the journal *Toxins* used metabolomics to look at dietary protein and dog health. Thirty healthy adult dogs (15 male and 15 female) were rotated on a low (18.99%), medium (25.34%) or high (45.77%) protein diet each for 90 days. The foods consisted of "high quality" (90% digestible) dried chicken and soy protein. The dogs' metabolite levels and microbial composition were analyzed after each 90-day feeding period (Ephraim et al., 2020).

The researchers found that:

- The high-protein food created significant increases in uremic toxins associated with kidney disease and inflammation, including the harmful postbiotics indole sulfates and p-Cresol (more on these in Chapter 11).

- The high-protein food resulted in significantly *lower* levels of beneficial anti-inflammatory metabolites, including sarcosine, dimethylglycine, and betaine.

- Fecal pH increased during consumption of the medium and high-protein foods, with the highest fecal pH associated with the food highest in protein.

- Fecal levels of harmful indole metabolites significantly increased on the high protein food, while levels of beneficial indoles significantly decreased.

- Several changes in the microbiome indicated a benefit of the lower-protein food. Dogs who consumed the high-protein food had a lower abundance of the microbial species *Collinsella*, which is also lower in dogs suffering from acute diarrhea or IBD (Suchodolski et al., 2012). Dogs consuming the lower-protein food had increased abundance of *Faecalibacterium prausnitzii*, a bacterium that produces the beneficial short-chain fatty acid (SCFA) butyrate and is associated with decreased inflammation (Martín et al., 2017). Humans with Crohn's disease (Sokol et al., 2008) and irritable bowel syndrome (Rajilić-Stojanović et al., 2011) have lower levels of this species.

    (Ephraim et al., 2020)

The study authors concluded that long-term consumption of high-protein food increases metabolites associated with kidney dysfunction, inflammation and proteolysis (the breakdown of proteins into smaller peptides or amino acids) (Ephraim et al., 2020).

Like the authors, we believe that more studies into the effects of high-protein diets on canine health are warranted. In the meantime, as the researchers note, "The optimal ranges of protein for healthy adult dogs are not known" (Ephraim et al., 2020, pp. 1).

Why, then, does the myth that 'more protein equals better health' continue in the dog food industry and among many consumers and veterinary professionals? We're not sure, but we can hazard a guess. It appears that savvy pet food manufacturers and marketers (maybe the same ones responsible for the 'dogs are wolves' myth) discovered that 'protein' was a catchword that resonated with consumers, and they ran with it. But the cost to our dogs' long-term health remains to be seen.

The dogs in the study did remain visibly healthy for the duration; however, they were only monitored for 90 days. This illustrates the important role of scientific disciplines such as metabolomics and genomics. The ability to identify deep inward changes in the body—such as metabolites and gene expression—can potentially warn of impending disease long before outward clinical signs manifest. This explains why identifying metabolic and genomic markers for diseases such as cancer, kidney disease, diabetes and Parkinson's disease continues to be of utmost importance within the scientific and medical communities. Diagnosing these serious illnesses as early as possible could mean the difference between life and death.

So, you see, dogs don't need excessively high levels of dietary protein. In fact, it's possible that too much protein can be *harmful*. Yes, you want to be sure you're feeding ample protein that provides all the essential amino acids your dog needs. But beyond that, there's no need to get carried away or stressed out about it.

Plant-based equals lower fat

Protein-rich plant foods are also typically lower in fat than animal proteins. Lower fat means fewer Calories because fat contains more than twice the number of Calories as protein and carbohydrates for the same amount of food. Feeding your dog nutrient-rich, lower-Calorie foods enables him to eat more and feel more satiated without packing on the pounds. This is super important because obesity is a major contributor to cellular inflammation, chronic inflammatory diseases and shorter lifespan in dogs (ScienceDaily, 2019).

A large observational study of 50,787 companion dogs who visited Banfield Pet Hospital's nationwide clinics between April 1994 and September 2015 found that overweight dogs live up to *two-and-a-half years less* than normal weight dogs (ScienceDaily, 2019). Keeping your dog fit and trim is vital to helping him live a long, healthy life, and feeding him a diet that is *nutrient-dense* while not *Calorie-dense* is the best way to accomplish that goal.

Not only can a plant protein-based diet help keep dogs from becoming overweight; it can also improve metabolic status during weight loss and possibly even result in greater weight loss compared to meat-based diets. A study published in the *Journal of Obesity & Weight Loss Therapy* found that after four weeks on a black bean or navy bean weight loss diet, overweight dogs had improved serum cholesterol, triglycerides, high-density lipoprotein (HDL) and low-density lipoprotein (LDL) compared to dogs fed a nutritionally comparable pork and bonemeal-based weight-loss diet (the control diet). Serum blood urea nitrogen (BUN) was also decreased in the navy bean group, while alkaline phosphatase (ALP) was decreased in the black bean group compared to the control diet (Forster et al., 2012).

The authors concluded that:

> *Beans are an effective staple food ingredient and a quality protein source during weight loss and these results suggest that consuming a diet with high dry bean intake improves lipid profiles along with other metabolic biomarkers when compared to a non-bean caloric restricted diet alone* (Forster et al., 2012, pp. 6).

In addition to the metabolic benefits, the bean-eating dogs also trended toward greater weight loss than the dogs on the meat-based control diet. While four weeks was likely not long enough to show statistically significant changes in weight loss between the groups, the researchers speculated that a longer time on the diets might result in a greater difference, as has been reported in people (Hermsdorff et al., 2011; Forster et al., 2012). Given these results, they recommended "further explorations of the effects of dry bean consumption for chronic disease prevention, and regulation of lipid metabolism with weight loss" (Forster et al., 2012, pp. 6).

Note the mention of *chronic disease prevention* in the previous quote. As the researchers pointed out in their study, beans are associated with a whole host of health benefits, including increased longevity (Darmadi-Blackberry, 2004), reduced risk of heart disease (Anderson & Major 2002) and diabetes (Jiménez-Cruz et al., 2006; Helmstädter, 2010) and decreased risk of multiple types of cancer, including colon (Hughes et al., 1997; Hangen & Bennink, 2002), mammary (Thompson et al., 2008), upper digestive tract and stomach (Aune et al., 2009) and prostate (Key et al., 1997).

When your dog meets his protein requirements with fewer Calories, there's also more room left in his bowl for other health-boosting foods such as leafy-green, yellow-orange and cruciferous vegetables. These antioxidant and phytochemical-rich nutritional powerhouses fight inflammation, defend against cellular oxidation and protect against chronic inflammatory diseases such as cancer (more on diet and cancer in Chapter 8).

Another bonus of meeting your dog's protein needs with disease-fighting, low fat/low Calorie plant foods is that you have more room in their diet for *healthy fats* found in certain seeds and nuts. Health-boosting seeds and nuts provide essential fatty acids, amino acids and a wide variety of trace minerals. Compare that to animal-based saturated fats, which store bioaccumulated toxins that contribute to chronic inflammatory diseases such as cancer. In Chapter 5, we'll dive into detail regarding the healthy fats we recommend for your dog's diet.

If you review our ingredient/protein chart once again, you'll notice that we also included the **glycemic load (GL)** of each ingredient. GL measures two important effects an ingredient has on blood sugar: 1) how *quickly* the ingredient causes blood sugar to rise after consumed, and 2) how *much* glucose per serving the ingredient sends into the bloodstream, indicating how high the blood sugar will rise (Harvard Medical School, 2020). GL is one way to track a carbohydrate's quality and can be especially useful for diabetic dogs and people. It's recommended to keep daily GL under 100, which as you can see is easy to do with protein-rich plant foods. By comparison, one cup of unbleached all-purpose white flour has a GL of 66. In addition, the white flour provides 'empty Calories,' lacking the vital nutrients found in high-quality plant-based proteins.

Many people still buy into the myth that carbohydrates are bad; however, you can't lump all carbohydrates together any more than you can lump all fats together. If we did that, we would avoid all fats because of dangerous fats such as hydrogenated oils.

We'll dive deeper into each food group later in the book, but for now we want to point out that your dog can get all the protein he needs—and more—without consuming animal products.

What about digestibility?

At this point you might be thinking, "But hold on. Certainly, plant proteins are inferior because they are less digestible." Let's take a look.

A study published in the *Journal of Animal Science* compared a diet containing 25% cooked navy bean powder (by weight) with a control diet of comparable macro- and micronutrient content. The researchers wanted to find out if the bean-based food was just as safe, palatable and digestible (for both energy and nutrients) as the control food. Twenty-one healthy companion male and female dogs of a variety of breeds participated in the 28-day randomized, blinded, placebo-controlled study, meaning that not even the researchers knew which food the dogs were eating (Forster et al., 2012a).

So, what did they discover? At the end of the study, *"No differences were observed between the two groups"* (Forster et al., 2012a, pp. 2631).

- The bean-eating dogs experienced no increase in flatulence or significant changes in stool consistency.
- The dogs found the bean-based diet to be palatable.
- The bean-based diet was digestible across a variety of breeds.
- There was no change in clinical laboratory markers, including complete blood counts (CBC), blood biochemical profiles and urinalysis in either group.

In their own words:

> *These results indicate that cooked navy bean powder can be safely included as a major food ingredient in canine diet formulations and provide a novel quality protein source, and its use warrants further investigation as a functional food for chronic disease control and prevention* (Forster et al., 2012a, pp. 2631).

Once again, we find that not only are legumes safe, palatable and digestible for dogs, but that they are also recommended as a **functional food**, which is a food that contains health benefits beyond providing basic nutrition such as vitamins and minerals (Hasler, 2002). Given the skyrocketing cases of chronic diseases in modern dogs, our canine companions could certainly use all the functional nutrition they can get!

Let's dive even deeper and look at the effect of cooked navy beans on the canine microbiome. In a study published in the journal *PLoS ONE*, researchers at the Colorado State University Veterinary Teaching Hospital's Animal Cancer Center recruited 21 clinically healthy male and female companion dogs of various breeds between the ages of two to seven to participate in a randomized, double-blinded, placebo-controlled study. Eleven of the dogs received a control diet containing 0% cooked navy beans, while the remaining 10 dogs were fed a nutritionally comparable diet made up of 25% cooked navy bean powder. Using sophisticated gene sequencing technology, the researchers analyzed the dogs' fecal microbiomes before and after the four-week feeding trial (Kerr et al., 2013). They concluded that:

> *No negative alterations of microbial populations occurred following cooked navy bean intake in dogs, indicating that bean powders may be a viable protein and fiber source for commercial pet foods* (Kerr et al., 2013, pp. 1).

Another study published in the *Journal of Animal Science* analyzed the digestibility and stool quality of dogs fed a kibble made from various types of soy compared with a poultry meal kibble (Clapper et al., 2001). The authors concluded that:

> *Results of the current study and previous work in our laboratory agree that, at the terminal ileum, soy protein fractions are equal to or superior to animal protein by-products* (Clapper et al., 2001, pp. 1531).

A more recent study looked at the digestibility and acceptability of legumes and yeast as novel dietary protein sources in extruded dog food. Ten adult dogs were randomly assigned to consume one of five diet formulations using either: 1) garbanzo beans, 2) green lentils, 3) peanut flour, 4) dried yeast or 5) poultry by-product meal as the primary protein source. The dogs were fed their assigned formulation for 14 days (Reilly et al., 2021). Blood and fecal analyses during and at the end of the trial showed that:

- The dogs readily accepted the high-legume diets (40% for garbanzo beans and green lentils and 30% for peanut flour) and dry yeast (30%).
- Serum chemistry and CBC analyses reflected normal values for healthy adult dogs.
- The legume and yeast-based diets had no negative effects on the dogs' fecal quality.
- All the diets were well digested.
- *The legume and yeast-based diets benefited the dogs' microbiota*, producing greater concentrations of short-chain fatty acids (SCFAs) than dogs fed the poultry by-product meal formulation.

(Reilly et al., 2021)

These findings led the authors to conclude that:

> *Inclusion of these novel, plant-based, protein sources showed no detrimental effects on nutrient digestibility or fecal characteristics and represent viable protein sources in canine diets that can produce beneficial shifts in fecal metabolites* (Reilly et al., 2021, pp. 1).

We do want to mention a small, short-term feeding study conducted on eight dogs for seven days. The study found that extruded diets high in fiber and resistant starch (amylose) from legumes decreased macronutrient and sulfur-containing amino acid (cysteine, methionine and taurine) digestibility compared to a rice-based diet. However, the authors noted that at the end of the feeding trial, all the dogs' plasma levels of these amino acids were within normal range. They also pointed out that the legume-based extruded diets produced a low glycemic response, which could help reduce the risk of diabetes mellitus (Quilliam et al., 2021). The bottom line? Based on the evidence, the researchers determined that:

> *This study showed promising effects of grain-free, pulse-based diets that could be utilized for the improvement of health in dogs* (Quilliam et al., 2021, pp. 8).

Scientific research illustrates that dogs readily accept and efficiently digest plant-based proteins, that these proteins benefit the gut microbiome and that they can help prevent and manage canine chronic diseases. We could continue citing human and animal studies showing the disease-fighting benefits of legumes (Shi et al., 2004; Venn & Mann, 2004; Villegas et al., 2008; Gupta et al., 2010; Zhou et al., 2010; Kerr et al., 2013). And we've already begun demonstrating the immense health risks, including cancer, of consuming a diet rich in bioaccumulated toxins (more on this to come).

Which type of protein would you rather feed your dog: health-boosting plant-based proteins that respect all animals and the environment; or animal-based proteins that contain harmful bioaccumulated toxins, unnecessary fat and Calories and that contribute to massive animal suffering and environmental devastation? Now we know where the expression, "It's a no-brainer" comes from.

High-performance dogs *can* thrive on plants

Many people are concerned that a plant-based diet cannot fulfill all the nutritional needs of their canine athlete. To address this concern, let's start with a quick assessment:

- Does your dog compete in athletic events, such as agility trials, disc dog competitions or obedience trials?
- Is he a police dog, military, herding or search-and-rescue dog?
- Does he perform assistance or service tasks for the disabled?
- Does he jog or hike numerous times per week?

If you answered "yes" to any of these questions, then you likely live with a canine athlete. However, if your dog simply enjoys long strolls, the occasional romp on the beach or an invigorating weekend hike, he doesn't qualify as an athlete for the purpose of this discussion. This distinction is important because if you overestimate your dog's energy needs, you run the risk of overfeeding Calories and he could end up overweight. And as we've already mentioned, overweight dogs are at greater risk of chronic diseases and reduced lifespan.

The greater concern with modern companion dogs is not whether their diet can keep up with their activity level, but whether their activity level can keep up with their diet.

We have an epidemic of canine obesity and chronic illness because dogs are overfed and under-exercised, not over-exercised and underfed.

True canine athletes, however, do benefit from targeted nutrition to support their high-performance lifestyles. Can a plant-based diet give them everything they need?

One of the reasons for writing this book is because our own knowledge and perspective have evolved and shifted over the years. There was a time when we promoted meat-based diets for canine athletes because that was the best information we had. We now realize that this is not necessary. Like all dogs, *canine athletes need nutrients, not specific ingredients*, and they can get all these nutrients from a well-balanced plant-based diet.

Look at all the human athletes who have adopted a plant-based diet in recent years. Just a few years ago, it would have seemed incomprehensible that football players, power lifters, gold-medal Olympians and other elite competitors could fuel their muscular bodies, strength and endurance with plants. Now, this is no longer unusual. Not only do these world-class athletes state over and over that they *feel* better since giving up meat and dairy—they also credit their diets as a large part of their *performance* success.

Novak Djokovic is currently the number one ranked tennis player in the world—and plant-based. Djokovic gives so much credit to his plant-based lifestyle that he even served as a producer of *The Game Changers*, a 2018 documentary discussing the science behind plant-based eating for maximum athletic performance.

Djokovic is not alone. Here are just a few testaments from meatless elite athletes:

Dusan Dudas – Bodybuilding champion:

> *Vegetables like kale, spinach and broccoli, nuts, seeds and grains can provide the building blocks for a strong and powerful physique.*

James Lightning Wilks – Former professional mixed martial artist:

> *I spent over 1,000 hours looking at peer reviewed medical science and realized that a plant-based diet is superior and optimal for health and athletic performance.*

Carl Lewis – Nine-time Olympic track and field gold medal winner, Olympic silver medal winner, 10-time World Championship medal winner:

> *I've found that a person does not need protein from meat to be a successful athlete. In fact, my best year of track competition was the first year I ate a vegan diet.*

Robert Cheeke – Champion bodybuilder and author:

> *I definitely have more energy, an easier digestion, increased metabolism, and much reduced recovery time after workouts. I have less inflammation, can train harder and faster, and my heart and joints are much healthier—there is really nothing negative I can think of as being a vegan athlete.*

Patrik Baboumian – Powerlifting world-record holder and winner of *Germany's Strongest Man*:

> *Don't listen to those self-proclaimed nutrition gurus and the supplement industry trying to tell you that you need meat, eggs and dairy to get enough protein. There are plenty of plant-based protein sources and your body is going to thank you for stopping feeding it with dead food.*

(McGee, 2020; Plantastic Life, 2020)

These competitors realize that they can feel better, perform better and do better for the world by eating a plant-based diet—and you can take that same approach with your canine athlete. Of course, we are not claiming that high-performance dogs have the same nutritional requirements as their more sedentary counterparts. Athleticism certainly places greater demands on the body that must be met with appropriate nutritional adjustments. But while it's tempting to lump all athletic dogs into one dietary group, that simply isn't practical. Nutritional needs vary based on the type of activity.

There are three systems from which the body draws energy during exercise:

Adenosine triphosphate–creatine phosphate (ATP-CP) system (also called the phosphagen system or one enzyme system). This system uses adenosine triphosphate (ATP) and creatine phosphate (CP), which are stored in the muscles. It fuels the body for very short periods—about five to 20 seconds—or just enough for one high-intensity vertical jump.

Glycolytic energy system. This system takes over when the ATP-CP system stops and supplies energy from five to 20 seconds and up to about two minutes. It uses the process of glycolysis to convert glucose from carbohydrates into ATP (energy). It's used in lower-intensity strength and power activities.

Oxidative energy system. This system is the most complex and takes over where glycolysis leaves off, after about two minutes of exercise. The oxidative system is an aerobic system, meaning that it uses oxygen to convert substrates into energy. The oxidative system provides the long, slow energy burn needed to fuel endurance activities, such as long-distance running (Gillette, 1999; Heffernan, 2012; Dodds & Laverdure, 2015).

The body gets its energy from three dietary sources: carbohydrates, proteins and fats. All forms of high-intensity exercise benefit from increased dietary protein to facilitate tissue repair. In one study, sled dogs fed a diet containing 28% protein showed a decline in hematocrit (packed red blood cells), but those fed a diet containing 32% or greater of protein did not (Hill, 1998). However, whether a higher percentage of dietary carbohydrates or fat is required depends upon the type of activity and which energy system the body is using.

Dogs who engage in strength or power activities such as sprinting, Frisbee competition, military training and dock diving will typically require a diet higher in carbohydrates to fuel glycolysis, however if the dog repeats these short bursts of activity, his body will eventually begin using the oxidative system and he'll require a balance of energy sources from carbohydrates, protein and fat (Gillette, 1999).

Dogs who partake in long-range endurance activities draw on the oxidative energy system and need a higher percentage of dietary fat to delay the negative effects of fatigue (Gillette, 1999). Sled dogs thrive on a high-fat diet (>50% of the energy) (Hill, 1998), along with high protein.

However, protein needs appear to vary, and excessive levels are not always beneficial (where have we heard that before?). One study showed that racing Greyhounds performed better on a higher fat/higher protein diet containing 32% fat and 25% protein compared with a lower fat/lower protein diet containing 25% and 21% protein (Hill et al., 2000). However, another study found that Greyhounds ran slightly slower (0.18 seconds) when fed a high protein (37%)/low carbohydrate (30%) diet compared to a diet containing moderate protein (24%) and high carbohydrates (43%) when the diet contained the same level of fat (33%) (Hill et al., 2001).

The bottom line is that high-performance dogs require specialized dietary regimens based on the type of exercise; however, these diets *do not* need to contain animal ingredients. A 2009 study published in the *Journal of British Nutrition* compared blood samples of 12 Siberian husky sled dogs. Half the dogs consumed a commercial meat-based diet recommended for active dogs, while the other half received a meat-free diet formulated to a comparable nutritional analysis. The main protein source in the meat-based diet consisted of poultry meal (43% pre-extrusion), while a combination of fine soybean meal and corn gluten made up 43% (pre-extrusion) of the meat-free diet. The dogs exclusively ate their assigned diet throughout the 16-week Australian sled-dog racing season, including 10 weeks of competitive racing. Researchers collected the dogs' blood samples at weeks 0, 3, 8 and 16 and conducted veterinary health checks at weeks 0, 8 and 16. The blood results for all dogs, regardless of diet type, remained within normal range throughout the study and the attending veterinarian deemed them all to be in excellent physical condition (Brown et al., 2009). The authors concluded that:

> *The present study is the first to demonstrate that a carefully balanced meat-free diet can maintain normal haematological values in exercising dogs* (Brown et al., 2009, pp. 1318).

In addition to physically thriving, the plant-fed dogs readily accepted and consumed the meat-free diet, demonstrating no issues with the food's palatability (Brown et al., 2009). These results once again refute the myth that dogs turn up their noses at plant-based cuisine. (Note that we do *not* condone dog racing of any kind.)

The bottom line is that, just like some of the highest-performing human athletes in the world who fuel their bodies with plants, your athletic dog needs a proper balance of nutrients, *not* animal ingredients.

Plant-based diets should *not* be blamed for canine DCM

In July 2018, the U.S. Food & Drug Administration's (FDA) Center for Veterinary Medicine created a panic among the pet food industry and consumers when it issued its first of three advisories regarding a possible association between diet and non-hereditary canine **dilated cardiomyopathy (DCM)**, a type of heart disease in dogs. The FDA's investigation of this issue has focused primarily on grain-free diets featuring non-soy legumes (e.g., peas, lentils and chickpeas) as well as potatoes as the main ingredients. The investigation launched after the FDA began receiving increased reports from veterinarians regarding cases of DCM in dogs consuming these diets (U.S. FDA, 2019; Solomon, 2020; U.S. FDA, 2021).

Not surprisingly, the media has paid a lot of attention to—and often sensationalized—this topic. Given the seriousness of DCM and the confusing information that has been released by various entities, we understand that many people are concerned about feeding diets rich in legumes and potatoes—including plant-based diets—to their canine companions. To help better understand the issue, let's take a closer look at DCM and what we currently know regarding its origins and relationship to diet.

What is DCM?

DCM is a potentially fatal heart condition that involves enlargement of one or more heart chambers. It typically starts in the left ventricle, which is the lower left chamber, but it can progress to the right ventricle and the upper two chambers. When the heart enlarges, it becomes weak and thin and cannot contract properly to pump blood. Eventually, fluid builds up in the lungs and body, causing congestive heart failure and dangerously high blood pressure (Cedars Sinai, 2021; Dodds, 2021).

How common is DCM in dogs?

DCM is the second most common type of heart disease affecting companion dogs. Genetics is the most common cause, with more than 50% of dogs in some breeds affected, such as Doberman Pinschers (Calvert et al., 2000; Martin et al., 2009; Wess et al., 2010; Smith et al., 2021; Yamka, 2021). According to the American Veterinary Medical Association, about 77 million companion dogs live in the United States (AVMA, 2019). Published studies on the rates of DCM incidence indicate that at least 308,000 to 1,001,000 dogs in the U.S. have DCM at any given time. These numbers include dogs with DCM resulting from *any* cause, including genetics (McCauley et al., 2020).

How many cases of DCM have been reported to the FDA?

As of September 2020, veterinarians had reported about 2,000 suspected cases of DCM to the FDA, of which about 1,100 (55%) ended up meeting the case definition for DCM. This does not refer to 1,100 instances of diet-related DCM; the number represents cases resulting from any cause, including genetics. The other approximately 900 reported cases (45%) turned out to be other types of unrelated heart disease (Solomon, 2020; Yamka, 2021).

What causes canine DCM?

Based on current research, it appears likely that canine DCM results from not one, but multiple potential risk factors that come together in certain dogs. These include, but are not limited to:

- Age
- Cardiotoxins

- Chronic tachycardia
- Dietary factors (See following section)
- Gender
- Genetic predisposition to DCM
- Genetic predisposition to chronic malabsorptive gastrointestinal disease
- Genetic predisposition to low taurine and/or low carnitine
- Heat processing
- Hypothyroidism
- Infectious causes, such as myocarditis
- Metabolism

   (Johnston, 2020; McCauley et al., 2020)

As we already mentioned, genetic predisposition is by far the most common cause, with the following breeds most at risk:

- Doberman Pinschers
- Great Danes
- Boxers
- American Cocker Spaniels

   (Dukes-McEwan et al., 2003)

Other breeds with a higher reported incidence of DCM are:

- Bulldogs
- Golden Retrievers
- Saint Bernards
- Airedale Terriers
- Newfoundlands
- Scottish Deerhounds
- English Cocker Spaniels

   (Backus et al., 2003; Bélanger et al., 2005; Backus et al., 2006; Meurs, 2010; Vollmar et al., 2013).

Diet-related risk factors for DCM in dogs

Nutritional factors can contribute to DCM, just as diet and lifestyle play an important role in all chronic diseases, including cancer. Many dietary factors can potentially contribute to DCM in dogs, including:

- **Insufficient dietary protein:** These diets may lack the amino acids necessary for taurine and carnitine synthesis.

- **Low sulfur-containing amino acids:** These are amino acids that are necessary to synthesize taurine and carnitine. (Methionine and cysteine are the two amino acids necessary to synthesize taurine, while lysine and methionine are necessary to synthesize carnitine).

- **Fiber such as beet pulp:** Excessive fiber may decrease the digestion of protein and amino acids and lead to a deficiency in sulfur-containing amino acids and thus in taurine and carnitine.

- **Heavy metals:** Heavy metals such as arsenic, cadmium and mercury in pet foods might also play a role in canine diet-related DCM. Taurine detoxifies heavy metals, which means that taurine that would otherwise be used for other functions is depleted during detoxification, resulting in deficiencies.

- **Nutrient deficiencies:** Numerous nutrient deficiencies can lead to heart disease, including DCM. We already mentioned deficiencies in protein and sulfur-containing amino acids. Other possible deficiencies include carnitine, potassium, choline, thiamine (vitamin B1), copper, vitamin E and selenium.

- **Taurine deficiency:** Taurine deficiency has been associated with DCM.

(McCauley et al., 2020)

Popularity of grain-free diets

In 2018, grain-free diets comprised up to 44% of dog food formulations in certain U.S. markets. This means that *tens of millions* of dogs in the U.S. have been consuming and thriving on these diets (Brooks, 2020).

A new study at the time of this writing further supports the safety of grain-free diets, finding no correlation between rates of canine DCM and the skyrocketing growth of grain-free pet food sales. The study retrospectively polled veterinary cardiologists across the U.S. to determine the incidences of canine DCM diagnosed between 2000 and 2019. Data was provided for as many years as were available (a range of one to 20 years, with an average of 8.1 years). Information was received on a total of 68,297 canine cardiology cases diagnosed by veterinary cardiology referral hospitals during that time. The incidence rate of DCM ranged from 2.53% to 5.65%, with an average rate of 3.9%. During that same time, popularity of grain-free pet foods soared, growing from $900 million in 2011 (the first year that grain-free pet food sales were recorded) to $5.4 billion in 2019 (Quest et al., 2022). Based on their findings, the authors concluded that:

> *There was no significant correlation between the national DCM incidence rate or the individual breed groups* ($P > 0.05$) in relation to the grain-free pet food sales (Quest et al., 2022, pp. 1).

We also find it interesting that the diet-related DCM scare appears confined to the United States (Yamka, 2021). Currently, nobody knows why this is the case (and we are not aware of anyone who is trying to find out). However, due to differences in how U.S. and foreign governments regulate toxic substances, dogs who live in the U.S. are likely subjected to many more environmental chemicals (see Chapter 8) than their canine counterparts across the globe. In fact, a veterinary group responsible for sounding the diet-related DCM alarm have stated that "…DCM can also occur secondary to environmental causes such as direct toxins (e.g., alcohol, chemotherapeutic agents, antibiotics, heavy metals) …" (Smith et al., 2021, pp. 1). And as we just mentioned, taurine detoxifies heavy metals, which can lead to deficiencies. It makes sense, then, that if dogs in the U.S. accumulate more toxins in their bodies due to environmental exposures, they'd also be more susceptible to taurine deficiency and DCM. This is just a theory, but we think it's important to investigate why dogs residing in the U.S. appear especially susceptible to diet-related DCM.

Breaking news: FDA ends DCM updates

Shortly before going to print, we received extraordinary news. On December 23, 2022, the FDA announced that it would *cease* releasing further public updates on the potential link between certain types of diets and canine DCM. The FDA cited a lack of "meaningful new scientific information" as the reason for this decision. The FDA also acknowledged that reported cases of DCM "do not supply sufficient data to establish a causal relationship with reported product(s)." There's more good news: reported cases of canine DCM declined significantly between 2020–2022 compared to 2018–2020 (U.S. FDA, 2022; Wall, 2022). We hope this latest information will help end unfounded public panic and put this important issue into its proper perspective.

No dog should perish from DCM. However, we must remember that even after years of investigation, the prevailing scientific opinion is that DCM is a rare and multifactorial condition. In Chapter 6, we will discuss our recommended supplementation to accompany plant-based diets. These additions include taurine, l-carnitine, omega-3 fatty acids, B-vitamins and supplement mixes that contain methionine, antioxidants and other essential nutrients for cardiac and general health.

A plant-based diet helps keep Wesley's heart happy

Weighing in at just over eight pounds, Wesley is a small dog with a big heart—literally. On January 26, 2021, the 13-year-old Chihuahua mix suffered congestive heart failure (CHF). Wesley's cardiologist ordered tests that revealed Wesley has an enlarged heart with a bulge in the region of the left atrium (upper left chamber). This sweet boy was diagnosed with chronic degenerative valvular disease, Stage C, indicating that Wesley is symptomatic and suffers from current or past signs of heart failure. Due to Wesley's leaky valves, his heart was unable to properly pump blood to his body. Instead, blood backed up into the vessels of his lungs, causing fluid to accumulate and resulting in his CHF episode.

Also known as endocardiosis, chronic degenerative valvular disease makes up about 75% of all canine heart diseases. Given the seriousness of the condition, Wesley's cardiologist recommended that he be treated with the proper medications and diet to help control the disease and prolong his life.

The goal of Wesley's cardiologist and his 'dad,' Andrew, was to keep Wesley out of CHF and symptom-free for as long as possible. For Andrew, it was also important that Wesley enjoy a good quality of life. Knowing the heart-healthy benefits of a plant-based diet, Andrew contacted Diana in

February 2021 for a custom-formulated cardiac support recipe. After diving deep into Wesley's individual health situation and dietary requirements, Diana created a special recipe to meet all his nutritional needs and support his optimum heart health.

At the time of this writing, we're thrilled to report that Wesley's heart size continues to remain stable, and he has had no additional episodes of CHF. Given the seriousness of Wesley's condition and the guarded prognosis for dogs with Stage C endocardiosis, his cardiologist is very pleased. So is Andrew.

"I'm so happy with how Wesley is doing on his plant-based cardiac diet," he says. "While Wesley's condition is degenerative, by providing him with optimum nutrition to support his heart, along with the proper medications, I feel good knowing that he will have the best chance to live his life to the fullest."

We hope that you found these scientific facts about the nutritional needs of dogs informative. Now, let's dive into our first action step and start setting yourself—and your canine companion—up for success on your plant-based journey.

Chapter 3
Setting Yourself Up For Success

You've digested a lot of important information so far. Now, it's time to set your plant-based plan into action. Our mission is to give you the tools to create success with your dog's new dietary regimen, and to do this we're going to proceed logically and incrementally down the plant-based path. By the end of our journey, you'll have the knowledge and confidence to feed your dog to thrive on a nutrient-dense, well-balanced plant-based diet.

This chapter is all about laying the proper groundwork, both for yourself and your canine companion. After all, this is a major—and important—life step you're both taking. Preparation is key to success and setting yourself up for success is what this chapter is all about. Here, you'll find our Seven Step Action Plan that you can begin implementing today to move you and your dog toward your plant-based goals.

Action Step 1: Discover your 'why'

Have you ever made changes to your own diet? Perhaps at some point you wanted to drop a few pounds or just adopt a healthier lifestyle. Maybe your doctor noticed your glucose or cholesterol numbers inching upward and recommended nutritional modifications to help you avoid prescription medications. Whether we're changing our diet, our job or our hometown, there's typically an underlying motivator—a reason that inspires and propels us toward our desired outcome. This motivator is our 'why.' Identifying a strong 'why' fuels our zeal and keeps us energized to reach our goals, even when the going gets tough.

Let's face it; you're going to encounter some obstacles and resistance along the way toward your goal of transitioning your dog to a plant-based diet. There will be times when you feel tired, or unmotivated, or someone will come along and challenge you for your choices. Without knowing why you've chosen this path, you're much more likely to steer off the road when you encounter bumps. But when you understand why reaching your destination matters, you'll have the motivation and determination to stay focused.

Here are some possible 'whys' to get you started. Feel free to take ownership of any and all that apply to you. You can also grab a notebook or your favorite tech device and jot down your own reasons for transitioning your dog to a plant-based lifestyle.

1. **Animal welfare.** For many people, their dog's diet is the last holdout to their vegan lifestyle. We've had many vegans tell us how they feel disgusted when they handle meat to feed their dog, and they're thrilled when they discover that this is no longer necessary. As we discussed in Chapter 1, you can potentially save thousands of farm animals just by transitioning one dog from a meat-based to a plant-based diet. Compassion towards all living beings is a noble reason to stop feeding animal products to your dog, and this 'why' will fuel your commitment even during stressful times.

2. **Environmental impact.** Scientists have warned that time is running out to save our planet. Forest fires, deforestation, greenhouse gases, mass species extinctions and other environmental crises threaten the Earth's future and the future of generations to come. Rather than seek out new planets to inhabit, why not focus on saving the beautiful one we already call home? When you feed your dog plant-based, you'll have a direct and lasting impact to help our planet survive, regenerate and renew. (See 'Green' dogs below.)

3. **Manage and reverse chronic illness.** If there's one thing that we all want, it's to keep our beloved canine companions healthy and happy for as long as possible. If your dog currently suffers from a chronic disease, you want to do everything in your power to help him achieve better health. Eliminating unnecessary toxins from his diet will enable his body to focus its energy where it belongs—sending healing messages to his cells—rather than constantly fighting to protect itself from a barrage of foreign invaders.

4. **Prevent chronic disease.** If your dog is currently healthy, now's the time to make positive changes that will prevent future disease. When you eliminate animal products from his diet, you'll also eliminate the dangerous toxins that bioaccumulate in animal tissues—toxins that send unhealthy epigenetic messages to the genome and microbiome, triggering oxidative stress and inflammation that can lead to a whole host of chronic diseases down the line.

5. **Cultural or religious beliefs.** The United States is known as a meat-eating culture, with famous fast-food commercials proclaiming, "Where's the beef?" and "We have the meats." But it's not like that everywhere. Many faiths, such as Seventh Day Adventists, Hindus, Buddhists and Jains consume vegetarian or vegan diets (Patience, 2016). Some religions even consider animals as sacred, and in countries such as India and Ethiopia, people focus their meals on grains, legumes, fruits and vegetables. If your culture or religion discourages or prohibits eating animals, rest assured that you can feed your canine companion to thrive within the parameters of your beliefs.

6. **Human health.** We hope that when you read this, your life and the lives of your loved ones are back to a more normal state in coping with the terrible COVID-19 pandemic. If this pandemic has made one thing perfectly clear, it's that humans are not immune from the consequences of our own behavior. As we write this, global interest in plant-based products is soaring. We hope that if there is a silver lining to this tragic situation, it's that people will continue to decrease their dependence on animal products—for our own health as well as the health of all animals and the environment.

'Green' dogs help save the planet

How much can one dog's consumption of animal products contribute to our planet's current environmental crisis? More than you might think. A professor at the University of California, Los Angeles figured out that dogs (and cats) make up 25% to 30% of the environmental impact of meat consumption in the United States. In fact, if dogs and cats had their own country, it would rank fifth in global meat consumption.

Here are just a few ways that animal agriculture harms the environment:

- Every second, one to two acres of rainforest are destroyed for animal agriculture.
- Livestock raised for meat, dairy and eggs create 14.5% of all global greenhouse gas emissions.
- Meat-eating dogs and cats are responsible for the production of about 64 tons of carbon dioxide per year. This is equal to about a year's worth of driving 13.6 million cars.
- Producing just one pound of meat uses 13 pounds of grain and 2,500 gallons of water.
- Every gallon of milk produced requires 1,000 gallons of water.
- It takes 477 gallons of water to produce one pound of eggs.
- Almost half (45%) of all the Earth's land is used for livestock production.
- Every meal that contains meat results in the loss of 55 square feet of rain forest.
- Deforestation is the major cause of animal extinction.

    (Hewitt, 2017; Brown, 2019)

The good news is that your dog can play an important role in helping solve our planet's environmental crisis. Switching your dog to a plant-based diet can drastically reduce the demand for food animals over time because raising them will no longer be profitable. This in turn will reduce deforestation and greenhouse gas emissions, helping to rebalance our ecosystem and save other animal species from extinction. It will also free up natural resources such as crops and fresh water so they can be used where they are most needed—to feed the millions of hungry people throughout the world.

Action Step 2: Assess your dog's current status

Now that you know your 'why' for transitioning your dog to a plant-based diet, it's time to evaluate his current health and lifestyle status. After all, even the best GPS system can't guide you toward your desired destination unless it knows your starting point.

Once again, grab your trusty notebook, computer, smart phone, etc. and jot down your answers to the following questions:

My dog is a(n):

- Puppy (small or medium breed)
- Puppy (large or giant breed)
- Adult (healthy)
- Adult (with a chronic condition)
- Senior (healthy)
- Senior (with a chronic condition)

My dog's activity level is:

- Sedentary
- Moderate activity
- High activity

My dog's weight is:

- Ideal
- Underweight
- Overweight

My dog's eating habits are:

- Finicky
- Normal
- Robust

If my dog has current health issues, will they need to be addressed with the new diet? Examples include:

- Adrenal disease
- Arthritis, bone and skeletal disease
- Cancer
- Chronic kidney disease
- Diabetes mellitus
- Food sensitivities
- Gastrointestinal issues
- Liver disease
- Obesity
- Pancreatic disease
- Parathyroid disease
- Skin and coat disease
- Thyroid disease

Please take the time to assess your dog's starting point accurately and honestly. Your responses will help guide you with creating your goals in the next Action Step.

Action Step 3: Write down your goals

Now, review your assessment results from Step 2 to help you identify specific goals you'd like to achieve by changing your dog's diet. Perhaps you want to:

- Decrease or abolish medications
- Eliminate problematic food ingredients
- Help your dog lose weight
- Improve your dog's dental health
- Improve skin and coat health
- Increase energy and stamina
- Optimize your dog's gastrointestinal health
- Promote longevity
- Relieve pain or discomfort associated with a current health condition

These are all valid goals, and you might have others. Once again, we encourage you to grab a notebook or your favorite tech device and write down your goals. Unlike your 'why,' which is your internal motivation for changing your dog's diet, your goals should be SMART:

- Specific
- Measurable
- Achievable
- Relevant
- Time-based

  (Mind Tools, n.d.)

You'll recall our dog, Benji, who we introduced back in Chapter 2. Let's pretend that Benji needs to shed a few pounds. We would not want to write as our goal, "I want Benji to lose weight" because that is too vague, cannot be specifically measured and has no time reference attached to it. Instead, we would want our goal to look something like, "I want Benji to lose three pounds by March 12." You can make any goal a SMART goal. For example, the goal, "I want Benji to have more energy" is unclear and difficult to track. Instead, make it SMART with something like, "I want Benji to easily be able to hike three miles with me by September 15."

Having clearly defined objectives that are reasonable, relevant, achievable and time-sensitive promotes clarity and provides structure. This makes it more likely that you will attain your desired outcome. And, when you go back and review your goals (which you should do often), you'll easily be able to tell whether you are on track or need to adjust your plan.

Action Step 4: Consider your situation

Have you ever set a New Year's resolution, only to find that by February (or sooner) you've broken it? If so, you're not alone. One of the main reasons people give up on achieving their goals is that they fail to account for factors in their lives that can get in the way. If you want to lose 20 pounds but travel half of every month for work, requiring you to eat a lot of airport and fast food, your weight loss game plan will need to accommodate this reality. Perhaps you'll need to adjust your timeline, pack healthy snacks and portable meals, or research restaurant menus before arriving at your destination.

In our experience, these are the most important lifestyle factors to consider when it comes to managing your dog's diet:

Work schedule. Do you work from home or at an office? If you work at an office, do you work long hours? Do you arrive home exhausted, barely able to put your own meal on the table? If your work life dominates your time, you'll want to prepare your dog's meals in bulk, so you can easily remove each day's portion from the freezer or refrigerator, let it come to room temperature and serve with minimal effort. You'll also want to keep a stock of high-quality commercial vegan dog food on hand for those times when opening a can or bag is about as much energy as you can muster. We'll offer guidance on how to select commercial vegan dog food in Chapter 6.

Travel schedule. Do you travel a lot? If yes, is there someone else in your household who stays with your dog, or do you board him at a facility? If you have support from other family members, you'll need to instruct them on meal preparation, feeding schedule, supplement additions, etc. If this person is unable or unwilling to prepare and feed your fresh-food recipe while you're away, you should have an appropriate vegan commercial food available to fill the gaps during this time. The same holds true if you board your dog, along with feeding instructions for the staff.

Physical condition. Do you suffer from arthritis, neurological or other health issues that limit your mobility? If you answered yes to this question, intensive prep-work for a home-prepared diet might not make sense—or even be possible—for you. In this situation, selecting a commercial vegan product that you can top off with dog-friendly whole foods could offer the perfect combination of ease and freshness.

Finances. Is cost an important factor when selecting your dog's food? Don't worry if you answered "yes" to this question. You don't have to drain your wallet to feed your dog a high-quality plant-based diet, either fresh or commercial. If you're on a budget (which many of us are), you'll find tips and tricks for saving dough on your dog's greens in Chapter 7.

Evaluating your lifestyle is an important step in achieving success with your dog's plant-based diet. Remember that the A in SMART goals stands for Achievable. When you recognize any potential roadblocks before beginning your journey, you can either eliminate them in advance or work around them, increasing your likelihood of staying on course.

Action Step 5: Schedule a veterinary visit

Medical doctors advise patients to undergo a checkup and lab work prior to beginning a new diet or exercise regimen, and the same recommendations hold true for our canine companions. The following should be performed before your dog begins any new nutritional plan:

- Full physical examination
- Blood chemistry profile
- Complete Blood Count (CBC) test with differential
- Thyroid Profile Panel

We will discuss more about these health checks in Chapter 6. You might also consider one or both of the following tests depending upon your dog's individual health situation:

NutriScan Saliva-Based Food Intolerance Test. This patented test uses a small sample of your dog's saliva to analyze reactions to 24 common food antigens. If your dog suffers from gastrointestinal issues, itchy skin, chronic yeast infections or other signs of food sensitivity, NutriScan will provide specific results as to which foods are safe to eat, and which should be avoided. (See Chapter 10 and Resources.)

CellBIO. By measuring the level of the biolipid isoprostane in your dog's saliva, CellBIO can detect the presence or predisposition to oxidative damage in cells caused by inflammation, infection, periodontal disease, obesity and even cancer. This patented test works both in dogs currently suffering from a chronic health issue as well as in clinically healthy dogs to help predict future oxidative damage at the cellular level. (See Resources.)

Remember, it's important that you complete your dog's physical exam and relevant laboratory work *before* beginning any new diet. You'll need this information as a baseline for future comparisons.

Action Step 6: Consider your options

When transitioning your dog to a plant-based diet, you might wonder if it's better to follow recipes formulated by a canine nutritionist than to create them yourself. Engaging the services of a professional canine nutritionist is a financial investment and it may be difficult to know in advance if it's the right move for you. Here are some things to consider:

Does your dog suffer from a chronic health condition? If your dog suffers from one or more chronic health issues, you should consider calling in professional nutrition assistance. Certain medical disorders require detailed dietary specifications to ensure your dog receives all the nutrients he needs to best address his specific issue and overall health. Such conditions include chronic kidney disease, diabetes, gastrointestinal disorders, liver disease, pancreatitis, seizures, thyroid disease and urinary tract stones, among others.

Do you feel more confident following a trusted recipe? If you want to take the guesswork out of your dog's diet, working with a qualified canine nutritionist might be right for you. This way, all you have to do is follow the recipe, including adding the specific recommended supplements, and you're good to go. The problem is that recipes online and in books may not be properly formulated, nor are they geared for your dog's individual needs. Having a recipe that is custom balanced for your dog can alleviate a lot of time and stress.

Do you want to provide a lot of variety? A recipe from a canine nutritionist is like a commercial diet. It's formulated to be 'complete and balanced,' and you must follow the recipe exactly to ensure your dog receives the proper nutrient levels. If you prefer to change the ingredients in your dog's diet often, a custom recipe may not be the best option for you.

Is your dog finicky? If your dog is a picky eater, working with a canine nutritionist is probably not a good idea. Substituting ingredients because your dog doesn't like them will change the balance of the recipe, resulting in a formula that is no longer guaranteed nutritionally balanced.

Are you on a tight budget? There is an initial investment in working with a canine nutritionist that needs to be taken into consideration. It's up to you to decide whether the investment makes sense for your budget. Diana offers a complimentary 15-minute phone consultation to help you decide if working with a canine nutritionist is the right decision for you and your dog. (See Resources.) Bear in mind that you don't need to make this decision right away. You can decide at any time to invest in a custom recipe; you can even rotate it in with your own meals that you'll learn how to create in Chapter 6.

Action Step 7: Address your veterinarian

Many people are uncomfortable discussing their dog's plant-based diet with their veterinarian due to a lack of support or feeling judged. This is unfortunate and reflects the issue that veterinarians are frequently not up to date on the latest scientific information regarding canine nutrition. This can also be upsetting and frustrating for you as the client. If you find yourself in this situation, you have two choices: 1) find another veterinarian who is supportive of your dietary decision, or 2) work calmly with your current veterinarian to the best of your ability.

It's tempting to want to avoid conflicts by not discussing your feeding choices with your veterinarian. We urge against taking that approach. Your dog's diet is a crucial part of his overall healthcare plan. If your veterinarian is unaware of your dog's nutrition, she won't have all the information necessary to best help your canine companion.

Sometimes, there's enough good in your veterinary relationship that it's worth working through this uncomfortable situation. At other times, this issue is a tipping point, signaling that it's time to move on.

You may be thinking, "I'll never find a vegan veterinarian near me." It would be wonderful if you could find such a person, but the good news is that it's not necessary. All you really need is a veterinary partner who will respect and support your decision to feed your dog a plant-based diet.

What's the best way to find such a person? There are a few things you can do to narrow your quest:

Pick up the phone. We recommend selecting several veterinary clinics within a reasonable distance from your home, calling them, explaining your situation and asking their stance on plant-based diets for dogs. If the receptionist doesn't know the answer, ask them to find out and get back to you. Or, better yet, see if they offer a free phone or in-person veterinary consultation.

Get social. Many larger cities and metropolitan areas have their own vegan groups on social media platforms like Facebook, and people in these groups are usually more than happy to offer advice. You may find out that someone has already done the legwork for you.

Ask a professional. For help finding the right veterinarian, you can call or email the American Holistic Veterinary Medicine Association (AHVMA). The AHVMA also offers a listing of integrative veterinarians via their free VetFinder online tool. The Veterinary Association for the Protection of Animals (VAPA) also offers information on vegan veterinarians. (See Resources.)

Whether you decide to form a new veterinary relationship or forge ahead with your current one, we urge you to stand firm against misinformation and pressure. Stay strong in your principles and follow the science presented in this book. You could even give a copy to your veterinarian!

Chapter 4
Essential Nutritional
Components

You've come a long way in your journey to raising a thriving plant-based dog. So far, you've discovered that inflammation is the common root cause of chronic disease and that by changing epigenetic factors (e.g., diet) you can send healthy messages to your dog's cells so that his gene's express for health rather than disease. You've learned that modern companion dogs have genomically and microbially evolved from their wolf ancestors over thousands (or perhaps tens of thousands) of years into omnivores capable of thriving on a well-balanced plant-based diet. You've learned to separate myths from facts regarding plant-based dog nutrition. You've even completed action steps to set you and your dog up for success as we continue to move forward in this exciting process. We also hope that you've scheduled your dog's physical examination and baseline lab work. (If you haven't already done so, please do that now before proceeding any further.)

In the next step along our journey, we're now going to dive into the six most important nutritional components of your dog's plant-based diet:

- **Carbohydrates**
- **Fats**
- **Proteins**
- **Vitamins**
- **Minerals**
- **Water**

(Case et al., 2011; McDonald et al., 2011)

You'll discover what each one is, why it matters for your dog's health and the specific applications in plant-based diets. This information lays the foundation for understanding how to select specific ingredients based on their nutrient profile, which we'll talk about in the next chapter. It also underscores the importance of integrating appropriate supplementation into the diet to ensure that it's well-rounded, which we'll cover in Chapter 6 when we build recipes.

Carbohydrates

Carbohydrates are molecules made up of individual glucose (sugar) units that are linked together into chains of varying lengths. Along with fats and proteins, carbohydrates are known as **macronutrients** because they supply energy (four Calories per gram) to the body.

You've probably heard the terms **simple sugars** and **complex carbohydrates**. This refers to the number of glucose units that make up the carbohydrate chain. Simple sugars (also called simple carbohydrates) contain just one or two sugar units, while complex carbohydrates (starches and fiber) contain three or more glucose units.

There are two categories of simple carbohydrates:

Monosaccharides
- Contain one glucose unit.
- Glucose, fructose and galactose are the three monosaccharides.
- They are readily absorbed by the body as energy because they cannot be broken down into smaller units.

Disaccharides
- Contain two connected single sugar units, or monosaccharides.
- Sucrose (table sugar), lactose (from dairy) and maltose are the three disaccharides.
- High fructose corn syrup is a manmade disaccharide (which we strongly recommend avoiding).

There are also two categories of complex carbohydrates:

Oligosaccharides (contain three to 10 connected monosaccharides)
- These include fructooligosaccharides (FOS), mannan oligosaccharides (MOS) and galactooligosaccharides (GOS). (See more on prebiotics in Chapter 12 on FOS and MOS.)
- Most **prebiotics** (non-digestible carbohydrates that are fermented by the gastrointestinal microbiota and thus convey health benefits to the host) are oligosaccharides. Note that while traditionally only polysaccharides were considered as dietary fiber, oligosaccharides are now also included as fiber based on their physiological effects (Slavin, 2013). (More on prebiotics in the section, "Prebiotic fibers: The microbiome's best friend?")

Polysaccharides (contain more than 10 monosaccharide units)
- Starches and fiber are polysaccharides.
- These are broken down and absorbed more slowly by the body than simple carbohydrates.

Many people think of sugar as bad and unhealthy. We often hear statements like, "Sugar causes obesity!" or "Sugar causes cancer!" But this view is far too simplified. All carbohydrates contain sugar and some of the healthiest foods on the planet contain simple sugars. Berries, for example, are some of these healthy foods and contain fructose and glucose. The key is that *fresh, whole fruits* also contain lots of fiber. The fiber insulates the sugar, slowing down the rate at which it is absorbed by the body and thus avoiding rapid glucose spikes (Egan, 2013). Avoid processed fruit juices, however, as these have been stripped of their fiber. Naturally pureed whole fruit juices with their fiber, such as found in smoothies, are fine. (See the Appendix for a Protein Superfood Smoothie recipe your dog will love!)

We never want to feed our canine companions refined carbohydrates such as white flour or processed foods containing added sugars, such as sugary cereals, cookies or other treats. These foods are largely devoid of nutrients, create rapid spikes in blood sugar and are associated with a variety of health risks, including obesity, cardiovascular disease and chronic inflammation. Complex carbohydrates, on the other hand, are packed with health-promoting vitamins, minerals, antioxidants and **phytochemicals**, natural compounds produced by plants that contribute to their color, taste and smell (Harvard Medical School, 2019). These types of carbohydrates provide powerful disease-fighting protection and are the ones you'll turn to when building your dog's whole-food plant-based recipes in Chapter 6.

Why carbohydrates matter

Carbohydrates often get a bad rap in the dog nutrition world. People claim that dogs don't need dietary carbohydrates because dogs can synthesize glucose (the primary form of energy used by the body) from fats and proteins, assuming that adequate fat and protein are present in the diet (Case et al., 2011). (Note that pregnancy and lactation are special situations.)

This is a shame because a wide variety of complex carbohydrates—known as **functional carbohydrates**—offer benefits far beyond their ability to provide energy. If we deny our dogs functional carbohydrates, we also deny them nutrients that are scientifically proven to benefit the gut microbiome and protect against a wide variety of chronic inflammatory diseases, including destroying cancerous tumor cells.

Functional carbohydrates promote optimum health

There's a reason that health experts advise us to "eat all the colors of the rainbow." Those beautiful plant hues—deep reds, blues and purples of berries, vibrant oranges and yellows of peppers and carrots, gorgeous greens of dark leafy veggies—are not only visually stunning, they're also full of health-promoting properties. As we just mentioned, complex carbohydrates from plant foods are packed with vitamins, minerals, antioxidants and phytochemicals that convey amazing health benefits to those who consume them. There are more than 5,000 phytochemicals. Some of the most well-known include:

- **Anthocyanins**, pigments that give red, blue and purple fruits and veggies their vibrant colors

- **Carotenoids**, found in yellow-orange plant foods

- **Flavonoids** in foods like apples, berries and soybeans

- **Lutein** and **zeaxanthin** in dark leafy greens

- **Quercetin** in plants such as berries, cherries, broccoli and citrus

(Harvard Medical School, 2019)

You might recall our discussion of Reactive Oxygen Species (ROS), including free radicals, from Chapter 1. Excessive levels of ROS in the body trigger chronic systemic inflammation and a variety of chronic inflammatory diseases, including asthma, atherosclerosis, biological aging, cancer, degenerative eye disease, diabetes, inflammatory joint disease, neuro-degenerative diseases and senile dementia (Florence, 1995; Uttara et al., 2009; Dodds, 2016; Dodds & Callewaert, 2016). Certain phytochemicals such as polyphenols and carotenoids act as **antioxidants**, substances that defend cells from oxidative damage caused by ROS.

Phytochemicals are currently being studied for their potential ability to protect against cancer via multiple pathways, including promoting **apoptosis** (cancer cell death), fighting inflammation, blocking **angiogenesis** (formation of new blood vessels that deliver oxygen and nutrients to tumors) and eradicating carcinogens before they can develop into cancer (Collins, 2015).

Functional carbs are filled with fiber

Just hearing the word fiber can cause a yawn. After all, fiber isn't the sexiest topic. But fiber is essential to health, and most of us—including our dogs—don't get enough of it. Many veterinarians that promote a plant-based diet believe that dogs raised on high-meat/low-fiber diets—especially raw-meat-and-bone diets (RMBDs)—are perpetually constipated. Some meat feeders even boast that their dogs' poop is small and hard, but ouch! Is that really a good thing?

The current preference for small poop likely originates from the belief that fecal matter consists mainly of food. And, of course, we don't want to see large pieces of undigested food in our dog's stool. But the food that goes in their mouths is just a nominal percentage of what comes out the other end. Fecal material in dogs and people is made up of about 75% water and 25% solid matter (Encyclopedia Britannica, 2015; Ackland, 2018). Of the 25% solid matter in people (and presumably in dogs), about 30% is made up of indigestible food matter, while about another 30% consists of bacteria and other microbes (dead and alive). The rest is comprised of cholesterol and other fats, inorganic substances such as calcium phosphate and iron phosphate and a small amount (2% to 3%) of protein. Other waste material includes cellular debris, bilirubin and dead leukocytes (The Editors of Encyclopedia Britannica, 2015).

As you can see, expelling feces is a vital part of cleansing the body. When dogs must strain to pass hard, tiny 'marbles' of feces, this constipation also impacts (literally) their anal glands and rectal mucosa. We've worked with dogs who regularly needed to have their anal glands expressed; but once they transitioned to a plant-based diet, the fiber naturally resolved the issue.

Let's look at some of the special properties of fiber.

Fiber is a type of carbohydrate (plus lignan) found in the cell walls of plants, including fruits, vegetables, whole grains, nuts, beans and seeds. Like all carbohydrates, fiber is made up of chains of glucose molecules. Animals and humans lack the digestive enzymes to break down the bonds in fiber, so it passes through the stomach and small intestine largely intact. When fiber reaches the large intestine (colon), it becomes food for the bacteria in the gut microbiome. The bacteria 'eat' (i.e., metabolize) and digest the fiber. This digestive process is known as **fermentation** (Eswaran, Muir & Chey, 2013). You'll discover a lot about microbial fermentation as we move forward.

Fiber is typically classified by two factors:

1. **Solubility** (ability to dissolve in water)
2. **Fermentability** (the rate at which it's metabolized by gut bacteria)

Soluble fiber dissolves in liquid (think psyllium powder). As it travels through the gastrointestinal tract, soluble fiber attracts and absorbs water, swelling into a gel-like substance that slows down digestive transit time. Since soluble fiber absorbs excess water in the colon, it's often used to help control diarrhea or loose stool. Soluble fibers tend to be highly fermented by colonic bacteria.

Insoluble fiber (roughage) does not dissolve in liquid and passes through the GI tract largely intact. Insoluble fiber adds bulk to the stool and speeds up the passage of food and waste through the digestive system. Insoluble fiber is less fermentable than soluble fiber (cellulose fiber is non-fermentable).

Most foods contain a combination of soluble and insoluble fiber, with one type dominating. Both soluble and insoluble fiber offer a variety of health benefits, including:

- Controlling large-bowel diarrhea (soluble)
- Helping optimize weight by providing a low-calorie feeling of fullness (soluble and insoluble)
- Lowering cholesterol by attaching to it in the digestive tract and removing it from the body (soluble)
- Managing diabetes mellitus by slowing the absorption of sugar into the bloodstream (soluble)
- Optimizing colon health and reducing the risk of colon cancer (soluble and insoluble)
- Promoting a healthy gut microbiome (soluble)
- Reducing constipation and straining (insoluble)

Since fiber isn't digested and absorbed into the bloodstream, it provides only two Calories per gram (half the Calories of non-fibrous carbohydrates) (EUFIC, 2012).

Prebiotic fibers: The microbiome's best friend?

Prebiotic fibers are fermentable fibers that convey so much benefit to the gut microbiome they have earned the title of functional fibers (Slavin, 2013). Prebiotic fibers specifically target and benefit the good bacteria in the colon, helping them to thrive and proliferate. When the good gut bacteria digest prebiotics, the bacterial metabolism (fermentation) that takes place produces beneficial metabolites called **postbiotics**, which include short-chain fatty acids (SCFAs) (butyrate, acetate and propionate). Butyrate is considered the most important SCFA with a host of health benefits, including preventing colon cancer, decreasing chronic inflammation in the skin and elsewhere, providing a feeling of fullness, strengthening the intestinal epithelial barrier, decreasing oxidative stress and serving as an energy source for colonocytes (epithelial cells in the colon) (Donadelli et al., 2019; Marsden, 2020). SCFAs are also shown to have antitumor and antimicrobial effects and to reduce the risk of inflammatory diseases, including diabetes and heart disease (Tan et al., 2014). They may also benefit individuals with Irritable Bowel Syndrome (IBS) (Silk et al., 2009).

Benefits of prebiotics include:
- Increase populations of the beneficial bacteria *Bifidobacteria* and *Lactobacilli*
- Decrease pathogenic bacteria, such as *Salmonella* and *Clostridia*
- Promote a strong immune system
- Strengthen the gut barrier

    (Hand et al., 2010; Carlson et al., 2018)

Prebiotic foods must meet three criteria:
1. Resistant to GI acidity, breakdown by digestive enzymes and gastric absorption
2. Fermentable by intestinal bacteria
3. Specifically target and benefit beneficial intestinal bacteria

    (Gibson et al., 1994)

Most prebiotics are classified as fermentable fibers, including **beta-glucans** (soluble fibers found in the cell walls of certain types of cereal grains, mushrooms, yeasts and algae), fructooligosaccharides (FOS), oligofructose, inulin, mannan oligosaccharides (MOS), pectin and guar gum, among others (Carlson et al., 2018; Suchodolski, 2020). However, certain non-fibrous ingredients that reach the large intestine for fermentation also meet the criteria for prebiotics, including polyphenols (a type of phytochemical), linoleic acid (LA) (an essential omega-6 fatty acid) and resistant starch (Gibson et al., 2010; Wernimont et al., 2020).

The type of fiber that will be most beneficial depends on the individual. Healthy dogs should eat a combination of both types to reap the full benefits. Dogs suffering from large bowel diarrhea will benefit more from soluble fiber (think canned pumpkin, sweet potatoes and psyllium powder), whereas insoluble fiber (e.g., bran) helps 'move things along' for dogs with constipation.

We'll talk more about the role of fiber for gastrointestinal disease in Chapter 12.

Fats

Fats are molecules made up of smaller units called fatty acids. Like carbohydrates and proteins, fats are macronutrients because they supply the body with energy (Calories). Fats are a type of lipid that are solid at room temperature (e.g., animal fat, coconut oil). Oils, which are the other type of lipid, are liquid at room temperature (e.g., olive oil, sunflower oil). Fats are the most energy-dense macronutrient, supplying nine Calories per gram, or more than twice as many Calories as carbohydrates and proteins

(Hand et al., 2010). For this reason, high-fat diets also equal high-Calorie diets, so monitoring your dog's fat intake is an important part of ensuring that she does not become overweight or obese.

Why fats matter

Fats are necessary for life and serve many important functions in the body, including:

- Acting as chemical messengers to send signals from cell to cell
- Enabling normal growth and development
- Insulating and protecting the body from cold
- Promoting healthy skin and coat
- Providing structure to cell membranes
- Serving as precursors to the formation of **eicosanoids**, compounds that play an important role in pain, fever, inflammation and blood clotting
- Supplying and storing energy
- Supplying essential omega-6 and omega-3 essential fatty acids (EFAs)
- Transporting and enabling absorption of fat-soluble vitamins (A, D, E and K)

    (Hand et al., 2010; Case et al., 2011; Mandal, 2012; Marsden, 2020)

Fats are classified into two main categories based on their chemical structure: saturated and unsaturated.

Saturated fats are solid at room temperature. They are mainly found in animal foods, such as meat, poultry and dairy. Certain plant foods, such as coconut and palm oils, also contain saturated fats. We'll discuss our newest recommendations regarding coconut oil shortly. We urge you to avoid giving your dog palm oil. In addition to contributing to global deforestation, a 2021 study found that consumption of dietary palmitic acid, a saturated fatty acid prevalent in palm oil, promoted the spread of oral carcinomas and melanoma in mice (Pascual et al., 2021). Since palm oil is commonly found in processed foods, this is just one more reason to nourish yourself and your dog with a fresh, whole-food plant-based diet.

Unsaturated fats are liquid at room temperature and are mostly found in plant foods. Fish can also contain unsaturated fats. There are two types of unsaturated fats:

- **Monounsaturated fats** are liquid at room temperature and solid when they are refrigerated, due to their chemical structure. These include avocado, olive, peanut and canola oils and nuts such as almonds, hazelnuts and pecans.
- **Polyunsaturated fats** are liquid at room temperature and remain liquid even when you refrigerate them. These include oils such as flaxseed, corn, soybean and sunflower as well as walnuts and certain fatty fish, including salmon and tuna. There are two types of polyunsaturated fats:
    - **Omega-6 fatty acids:** Linoleic acid (LA) and arachidonic acid (AA)
    - **Omega-3 fatty acids:** Alpha-linolenic acid (ALA), eicosapentaenoic acid (EPA) and docosahexaenoic acid (DHA) (WebMD, 2020)

Essential fatty acids (EFAs)

Essential fatty acids (EFAs) are fatty acids that an organism cannot synthesize and so must obtain from dietary sources. Dogs need both omega-3 and omega-6 fatty acids to thrive and deficiencies in either type can lead to serious health problems. For example, LA is essential for skin health due to its role in maintaining the skin's epidermal moisture barrier. DHA is a major component of cell membranes and neurological tissues and is required for normal neurological, brain and eye development in fetuses and puppies (Case et al., 2011). The National Research Council (NRC) considers LA, ALA and EPA + DHA to be essential for both puppies and adult dogs, while AA is considered essential only for puppies (NRC, 2006).

While EFAs are necessary for health, the Standard American Diet (SAD)—and what we refer to as the Standard American Dog Diet (SADD)—typically provide a significant imbalance in the ratio of omega-6 to omega-3 fatty acids. Dogs and people typically consume far too many omega-6s, which are found in abundance in processed foods, and too few omega-3s, which are found in healthy oils such as hemp seed and flaxseed (ALA), as well as in marine sources (EPA/DHA). This is a problem because omega-6 fatty acids—particularly AA—promote inflammation in the body when consumed at high levels, and inflammation triggers chronic inflammatory diseases. On the other hand, omega-3 fatty acids regulate cellular metabolic functions and gene expression in a manner that reduces inflammation (Deckelbaum et al., 2006).

Many people think they can satisfy their dog's requirement for EPA and DHA by feeding them flaxseed oil. Flaxseed is rich in ALA, but it does not contain EPA or DHA. Neither people nor dogs efficiently convert ALA to EPA, and conversion of ALA to DHA is even more restricted (Gerster, 1998; Dunbar et al., 2010; Stoeckel et al., 2011; Turner, 2022). Therefore, EPA and DHA should be consumed directly from marine sources. This is important because EPA and DHA are shown to benefit a variety of health conditions, including cardiovascular disease, cognitive function, inflammatory skin disorders, neurological health and renal disease (Chandler, 2015; Marsden, 2020). We'll dive deeper into the best sources of EPA and DHA in Chapter 5.

Applications of fats in plant-based diets

As we already mentioned, fat is the most energy-dense macronutrient, providing more than twice the Calories of protein and carbohydrates. Plant-based diets are by nature lower in Calories because the primary ingredients—legumes, whole grains, vegetables and fruits—are nutrient-dense but not fat-dense. (We recommend that you refer to the plant-based protein chart in Chapter 2, which illustrates this point.) This is great news because obesity has reached epidemic levels among modern dogs (and cats). Obesity is a leading trigger for inflammation and chronic inflammatory diseases (Dodds, 2016). A plant-based diet is a great way for our canine companions to receive all the nutrients they need to thrive *and* enjoy ample amounts of food without over-consuming Calories and packing on the pounds.

Multiple studies on humans and animals have also found that high-fat diets adversely affect the gut microbiome and intestinal health (Shen, 2014). An article published in *Frontiers in Microbiology Research* looked at the effects of diet on the gut microbiomes of dogs and cats. According to the authors, "…the pro-inflammatory nature of dietary fat may influence microbiome composition….." and they called for further research on the topic (Wernimont et al., 2020, pp. 8-9).

Other studies show that when dogs are kept at a normal weight, higher-fat diets do not negatively affect the gut microbiota (Moinard et al., 2020; Schauf et al., 2018). But, as we've said, higher-fat diets are associated with higher-Calorie diets, and there is an epidemic of obesity among modern companion dogs. And this is where the trouble may really lie.

A study published in *Frontiers in Veterinary Science* explored how a high-fat diet fed at a maintenance-Calorie level versus a high-Calorie level affected the dogs' microbiota, intestinal barrier and physiology. In the eight-week study, 24 dogs were separated into two groups. One group of eight dogs consumed a high-fat diet (HFD) (63% of daily Calories) at 100% of their maintenance energy requirements, while the other 16 dogs ate the same HFD, but at 150% of their normal energy requirements. After just eight weeks, the dogs consuming the high-Calorie HFD had "significantly higher" body weight and body composition scores than the dogs fed the same diet at maintenance Calories. The overweight dogs also experienced other health effects (Moinard et al., 2020). The authors concluded that, "Microbiota diversity was reduced only in the case of a HFD in excess and this was associated with greater changes in microbiota composition and a decrease in insulin sensitivity compared to the same diet fed at maintenance levels" (Moinard et al., 2020, pp. 12).

Fat is also low in nutritional value. Dr. Joel Fuhrman created the Aggregate Nutrient Density Index (ANDI), which scores foods according to how many nutrients they provide per Calorie. The ANDI ranks foods on a scale of one to 1,000 based on 34 different nutritional criteria, with the most nutrient-dense foods scoring 1,000 (Fuhrman, 2017; Pitcairn & Pitcairn, 2017).

Leafy greens earn the highest ANDI ranking, with kale, collard greens, mustard greens, watercress and Swiss chard scoring 1,000. We'd expect 'empty calorie' ingredients such as cola (ranking 1), corn chips (7) and white bread (9) to rank at the bottom of the scale, but you may be surprised to learn that foods commonly touted as healthy also score low, including salmon (34), eggs (31), chicken breast (24) and 85% lean ground beef (21). Bear in mind that these rankings are not based on a biased opinion; they are the result of complex scientific calculations based on the formula $H=N/C$ (Health = Nutrients/Calories) (Fuhrman, 2017; Pitcairn & Pitcairn, 2017).

The ANDI scale not only provides insight into the nutrient density of foods, but also into the nutrient density *in the body's tissues*. This makes sense, since "we are what we eat." If we eat nutrient-dense foods, then our tissues will absorb more nutrients and become nutrient-dense. This promotes a strong immune system and helps our bodies (and our dogs' bodies) more efficiently eliminate toxins and initiate cellular repair mechanisms that protect us from chronic diseases (Fuhrman, 2017).

Perhaps the most troubling aspect of high-fat diets commonly consumed by modern companion dogs is the bioaccumulation of toxins that build up in the fatty tissues of food animals. These toxins are then transferred to dogs or people who consume those animals, sending dangerous epigenetic signals to the genome and microbiome. We'll talk more about bioaccumulated toxins and chronic diseases in Part 2.

We're not claiming that all fat is bad or that all dogs should be on low-fat diets. On the contrary, fat is essential to health and dogs efficiently metabolize fat for energy. Some dogs require higher-fat diets, such as puppies, pregnant and lactating females, canine athletes and those with certain health conditions, such as chronic kidney disease. But we believe that optimum health comes from feeding the *right types* of fats.

Again, animal fats contain bioaccumulated toxins that lead to a variety of negative health effects. Plant-based fats, on the other hand, provide all the nutritional benefits (and more) without the toxic buildup. In fact, EFAs found in plant-based ingredients such as healthy oils, nuts and seeds can function as prebiotics and positively alter the gut microbiome. For example, when gut microbes metabolize linoleic acid (LA), the essential omega-6 fatty acid, they produce postbiotics that protect the epithelial cells of the gums against bacteria that promote periodontal disease (Yamada et al., 2018).

Proteins

Proteins are complex molecules made up of smaller units called amino acids that are linked together to form peptides. Like carbohydrates and fats, proteins are macronutrients because they are capable of supplying energy to the body (four Calories per gram). As we discussed in Chapter 2 (See "What about amino acids?" on page 32), dogs and other mammals require amino acids, which are smaller structural units made up of varying chemical compositions. Amino acids are known as the building blocks of protein because when amino acids connect, they form proteins. The type of protein, and its function, depend upon the chemical properties of its amino acids (University of Arizona, 2003).

Like fatty acids, amino acids are either essential or non-essential. **Essential amino acids** are those that the body cannot synthesize in large enough quantities to meet its requirements and so must come from the diet. **Non-essential amino acids** are just as important in their functions; however, these can be synthesized by the body and so it's not necessary to obtain them from food (Hand et al., 2010; Case et al., 2011).

Dogs require 22 different amino acids to build proteins. Ten of these are essential:

- Arginine
- Histidine
- Isoleucine
- Leucine
- Lysine
- Methionine
- Phenylalanine
- Threonine
- Tryptophan
- Valine

Adult humans require nine essential amino acids. The difference between dogs and people is arginine. Arginine is considered essential for young people, but not for adults (University of Arizona, 2003). As we pointed out in Chapter 2, "The dog has a requirement for arginine intermediate between the cat and the rat, which is consistent with the dog having an omnivorous diet during its evolution" (Morris, 1985, pp. 524).

Why proteins matter

Proteins are essential for life. Among other vital functions, proteins:

- Act as antibodies that protect the body against viruses and bacteria
- Carry out nearly every cellular function critical to life
- Connect and support muscles, bones, tendons, ligaments, blood vessels, organs and cartilage
- Deliver oxygen and other molecules to every cell in the body
- Heal wounds
- Hold skin and other parts of the body together
- Provide structural support to cells and allow the body to move
- Serve as enzymes that carry out almost every chemical reaction that occurs in cells
- Supply the body with energy
- Repair muscles and tissues
- Regulate blood glucose levels
- Supply nitrogen for the body to synthesize other nitrogen-containing compounds and non-essential amino acids
- Transport and store nutrients
- Bind to and transport other molecules, including drugs (albumin)

  (Case et al., 2011; Aminoacid-studies.com, 2020; MedlinePlus, 2020)

Applications of protein in plant-based diets

Animal products are commonly thought of as higher-quality proteins for dogs because they are viewed as complete proteins, meaning that a single ingredient may contain all of the essential amino acids. The plant world also offers all of the essential amino acids required by dogs and people—we just need to focus on providing a variety of foods to attain the proper balance (which we'll soon show is not difficult). In fact, soy turns out to have an amino acid profile similar to meat (Danks, 2014).

Digestibility is also a common concern, and in Chapter 2 we quashed the myth that dogs cannot efficiently digest plant-based proteins. But you may be surprised to discover that wheat gluten (which we don't typically recommend due to the potential for food intolerances) is 97% to 99% digestible by dogs. This is even more digestible than beef at 80% to 97% (Danks, 2014)!

Plant proteins can also outperform animal proteins for dogs with a variety of health conditions, including food intolerances, allergic dermatitis, gastrointestinal disease, exocrine pancreatic insufficiency (EPI), renal disease and those at risk of hepatic encephalopathy (HE) due to liver disease, damage or shunts (Danks, 2014).

We also want to point out that dogs cannot be lumped into one group when it comes to their protein needs. Just as with fat, protein requirements vary according to the individual's health, breed, age, lifestyle and other factors. Even adult dogs at maintenance respond differently, with some dogs enjoying higher-protein diets and others becoming hyperactive or agitated on them.

Vitamins

Vitamins are organic compounds (they contain carbon) that the body requires in small quantities to live and thrive. Mammals must obtain vitamins from food since our bodies can't make enough of them to survive. For dogs, the exception is vitamin C. Unlike people, dogs can synthesize vitamin C in sufficient quantities and so the NRC and AAFCO do not consider it an essential nutrient (one that must come from food). However, we still find that companion dogs benefit from the extra antioxidant power of dietary vitamin C in order to cope with the stresses associated with certain health conditions and the effects of living in a toxic world.

Vitamins fall into two classes:

Fat soluble. The four fat-soluble vitamins are A, D, E and K. Fat-soluble vitamins become homogenous when mixed with fat and are stored in the body's fat tissues. They require dietary fat to aid in their absorption (one of the reasons that dietary fat is important). Since fat-soluble vitamins are stored in fatty tissues, they are more likely to reach toxic levels than water-soluble vitamins (Hand et al., 2010; Medline Plus, 2020a).

Water soluble. The nine water-soluble vitamins are B1 (thiamine), B2 (riboflavin), B3 (niacin), B5 (pantothenic acid), B6 (pyridoxine), B7 (biotin), folate (folic acid), B12 (cobalamin) and C. Water-soluble vitamins are actively absorbed, meaning that if the body doesn't readily use them, they are excreted in the urine. Since water-soluble vitamins don't accumulate in the tissues, they're less likely to cause toxicity than fat-soluble vitamins. (Vitamin B12 is the exception and can be stored in the liver for many years.) Choline does not meet all the characteristics of a vitamin; however, it is commonly considered to be a member of the B vitamins (Hand et al., 2010; Medline Plus, 2020a).

Why vitamins matter

Our dogs' bodies (and our own) rely on vitamins for many critical functions, including:

- Building strong teeth, bones, soft tissues, mucus membranes and skin
- Maintaining a healthy nervous system and brain
- Making hormones
- Metabolizing food
- Promoting normal growth and development
- Protecting cells from free radical damage
  (MedlinePlus, 2020a)

Every vitamin plays a unique role that enables the body to survive and thrive.

Applications of vitamins in plant-based diets

Some people think that dogs can't get enough vitamins (and minerals) on a plant-based diet. However, we find that *all* home-prepared recipes require supplementation, regardless of whether they contain animal ingredients. Multiple analyses of home-prepared meat-based diets for dogs have found shortages in nutrients that can cause severe health problems, including vitamins A and D and the minerals calcium, potassium, iodine, zinc and copper (Dillitzer et al., 2011, Pedrinelli et al., 2017; Pedrinelli et al., 2019).

Of course, it's always best to obtain vitamins and minerals from fresh foods, but we find that supplementation of home prepared plant-based diets is important to help ensure dogs receive their required levels. One reason is the realities of the world in which we live. No matter how healthy and fresh our food, crops grown today do not contain the nutritional value they once did. Intense agricultural practices over the past few decades have led to deforestation, climate change and the decimation of entire ecosystems. New breeds of crops designed to grow bigger and faster, resist pests and withhold greater amounts of pesticides and herbicides are stripping the soil of its nutrients. A study published in December 2004 in the *Journal of the American College of Nutrition* compared the U.S. Department of Agriculture's nutritional data for 43 different fruits and vegetables from 1950 and 1999. The minerals calcium, phosphorus and iron all showed "reliable declines" during that period, along with protein, riboflavin (vitamin B2) and vitamin C (Scheer & Moss, 2011). Supplementation helps to offset environmental factors that are beyond our control.

Some nutritionists advocate simply tossing a human multi-vitamin/mineral into your dog's homemade meals, but we disagree with this approach. For starters, human multivitamins typically contain far higher levels of vitamin D than is recommended for dogs, and excessive vitamin D can build up over time and lead to toxicity. On top of that, multi-vitamins typically contain vitamin D as cholecalciferol (D3), which is often sourced from lamb's wool and is therefore not vegan. Vegan human supplements use ergocalciferol (D2) or plant-based vitamin D3; however, we still find that these typically provide excessive levels for dogs.

Many people are interested in using whole-food human supplements to balance their dog's diet. While we love the premise of a supplement made from whole foods, extreme caution must be used when selecting a whole-food supplement intended for human use, as these can contain ingredients that are harmful to dogs, such as extracts from grapes, onions or inappropriately high levels of medicinal herbs.

We'll provide our supplement recommendations in Chapter 6.

Minerals

Minerals are naturally occurring **inorganic solids** (they do not contain a carbon-hydrogen bond) that are made up of **chemical elements** (substances made of only one type of atom). Some minerals are made from only one chemical element, while others are compounds of two or more chemical elements (atoms) combined in various proportions. The types of chemical elements, their proportions and the way they are put together determine everything about the mineral, including its shape, color and radiance (Oxford University Museum of Natural History, 2006).

You may recall when you were in school studying the Periodic Table of the Elements with its arrangement of all the chemical elements and their abbreviations. If so, this will help you to understand minerals. For example, copper is a chemical element with the symbol Cu, which is number 29 on the Periodic Table; the chemical element iron (Fe) is number 26; calcium (Ca) is number 20 and so forth. Picturing minerals as chemical elements like this can help us to demystify them and have a better understanding of their role both in geology and in health.

As of November 2018, there were 5,400 minerals recognized by the International Mineralogical Association (Mineralogical Society of America, 2020). But don't worry because you don't have to—and shouldn't try to—include them all in your dog's diet! Currently, the NRC and AAFCO recognize six macrominerals and six microminerals (also called trace minerals) as essential minerals for dogs (NRC, 2006; AAFCO, 2021). **Essential minerals** are those that the body must obtain from diet. **Macrominerals** are those that are required by the body in greater amounts, while **microminerals** are needed in smaller amounts, but are equally important for health.

Essential macrominerals for dogs:
- Calcium
- Chloride
- Magnesium
- Phosphorus
- Potassium
- Sodium

Essential microminerals for dogs:
- Copper
- Iodine
- Iron
- Manganese
- Selenium
- Zinc

Fun Fact: Ice is a mineral...sometimes
As we mentioned, a mineral must possess certain qualities, including being inorganic, naturally occurring and solid. Water is an inorganic substance because it doesn't contain carbon (H_2O = hydrogen + oxygen). But water is liquid, not solid, so it flunks the mineral test. Ice, on the other hand, is both inorganic and solid and so it is classified as a mineral... under certain circumstances. Can you think of when ice wouldn't be a mineral based on the definition? When it's made in a freezer! Remember that minerals

must occur naturally. So, snow and ice (including icicles that hang from your roofline) are considered minerals, but ice cubes made in your freezer aren't. Now, that's *cool!*

(Mineralogical Society of America, 2020)

Why minerals matter

Essential minerals are just that—essential to life. Each mineral has a particular role to play to ensure the body works properly. Functions of minerals include:

- Balancing the water content of cells
- Enabling red blood cells to carry oxygen throughout the body
- Forming the structure of bones and teeth
- Helping control nerve and muscle function
- Making hormones and promoting normal hormone function
- Regulating blood pressure and heartbeat
- Supporting normal growth and development

(Lawson, 2016)

Vitamins and minerals work synergistically, and deficiencies or excesses in one can cause imbalances in others. For example, too much calcium can block the uptake of other minerals, while selenium and vitamin E have a mutual sparing effect, where an increased level of either one reduces the requirement for the other (Hand et al., 2010). Getting the proper amount of minerals is important because too little can cause severe health problems (and even death), while excessive levels can lead to toxicity.

Applications of minerals in plant-based diets

You may have read articles online about how plants aren't a good source of many minerals and how plant-based minerals aren't as well absorbed as those from animal products. We're here to tell you what science says, and once again it's good news for plant-based pups.

In 2019, researchers compared the digestibility of macro- and micronutrients in dogs fed heavily animal-based and vegetable-based diets (neither diet was exclusively animal or vegetable). The results, which were reported in the *Journal of Animal Science*, "… demonstrate that a vegetable ingredient-based diet can match or exceed the digestibility of nutrients when compared with an animal-based ingredient diet" (Cargo-Froom et al., 2019, pp. 1017). Not only were the nutrients from the plant-based diet equally digestible in all cases; some of the minerals (magnesium, zinc and manganese) were *more* digestible.

Let's do a myth-busting session regarding minerals in animal versus plant-based foods.

Myth: Dairy is the best source of calcium. In Chapter 2, we touched on the dairy industry's aggressive marketing and lobbying campaigns. A great example of their success is reflected in our culture's almost obsessive connection between dairy and calcium. Given the dairy industry's not-so-subtle message that we'll all crumble from brittle bones if we don't drink milk, you may be surprised to discover that 100 grams (3.5 ounces) of whole milk contains 113 mg calcium. The same amount of raw kale delivers a whopping 254 mg of calcium, or more than twice as much (MyFoodData, n.d.). Dairy is also difficult for dogs to digest and is a major source of food intolerances. In humans, consumption of dairy has been associated with a whole host of health problems, including autism, autoimmune disorders, diabetes and heart disease (Woodford, 2009). Green leafy vegetables, on the other hand, offer a cornucopia of antioxidants and phytochemicals along with calcium. So, skip the inflammatory dairy and go green instead.

Myth: Red meat is the best source of iron. Once again, this myth just doesn't hold up. When we compare the iron content of various meat-based and plant-based foods based on a 100-gram (3.5 ounce) serving, we find that a broiled ground beef patty (93% lean) contains 2.8 mg of iron, while cooked lentils contain 3.3 mg. Pan-fried beef liver has 6.2 grams, while roasted squash and pumpkin seeds boast a whopping 8.1 grams (MyFoodData, n.d.). Meat contains heme iron, while plants contain non-heme iron. Heme iron from red meat is commonly touted as higher quality than non-heme iron because it's more readily absorbed by the body. But what you don't often hear (likely due to the powerful meat lobby), is that high intake of heme from red meat is associated with a variety of serious chronic diseases, including cancer. According to a 2014 review article published in the journal *Nutrients*:

Studies have shown that an increased risk of several types of cancer is associated with diets high in red meat. On the contrary, consumption of substantial amounts of green vegetables is associated with decreased risk of colon cancer, likely because vegetables contain low levels of heme iron (Hooda et al., 2014, pp. 1085).

The article also discusses how heme 'feeds' cancer cells:

Inhibition of heme synthesis or mitochondrial function preferentially suppresses cancer cell proliferation, colony formation and cell migration. These results demonstrated that heme availability is significantly increased in cancer cells and tumors, which leads to elevated production of hemoproteins, resulting in intensified oxygen consumption and cellular energy production for fueling cancer cell progression. This provides a unifying mechanism for heme function in promoting cancer progression (Hooda et al., 2014, pp. 1090).

Multiple studies have documented the relationship between high consumption of red meat, heme iron and chronic diseases, including cardiovascular disease, Type 2 diabetes and cancer (Czerwonka & Tokarz, 2017). Check out a few disturbing highlights quoted directly from a 2017 article titled, "Iron in red meat – friend or foe":

- High consumption of red meat increases the risk of cancers, diabetes and cardiovascular diseases.

- High levels of iron in the body can increase the risk of Type 2 diabetes.

- High heme iron consumption is associated with increased risk of cancers.

(Czerwonka & Tokarz, 2017)

You're probably thinking that this article appeared in a pro-vegan or vegetarian publication. You may be surprised to learn that it was published in the journal *Meat Science!* It appears that even the meat industry is aware of the health hazards of its own product. This scenario is eerily familiar to the decades-long tobacco industry cover-up regarding the link between smoking and lung cancer.

Sadly, cancer is rampant among companion dogs (and cats). Six million new cases of cancer are diagnosed each year in dogs (and a similar number in cats) (National Cancer Institute, n.d.). According to the American Animal Hospital Association (AAHA), the number is likely even higher, as not all dogs receive regular medical care or a definitive cancer diagnosis (AAHA, 2020). And the Veterinary Cancer Society estimates that one in four dogs will develop cancer at some point, including close to half of all dogs over the age of 10 (Veterinary Cancer Society, 2020).

While we have no way of knowing for certain at this time, we wonder about a possible relationship between the epidemic of canine cancer and the trend of feeding diets high in red meat and heme iron to companion dogs.

Myth: You need to get zinc by eating animals. While oysters contain more zinc than any other food, we don't find them a highly-palatable ingredient for dogs—or for the person needing to slip the slimy mollusks into their dog's food. Fortunately, that's not necessary because half of the top 10 foods highest in zinc are plant foods: tofu (#4), hemp seeds (#6), lentils (#7), oatmeal (#9) and shitake mushrooms (#10) (Whitbread, 2020). And, while beef chuck took the #2 spot behind oysters, a six-year, multi-ethnic cohort study of 5,285 people showed that zinc and heme from red meat was associated with increased risk of cardiovascular disease and metabolic syndrome (de Oliveira Otto et al., 2012).

Water

Water is a substance made up of three atoms—two hydrogen and one oxygen (hence the name H2O). It is the only natural substance on Earth that can take on all three physical states—liquid, solid, and gas. Water is also unique because it's less dense as a solid than liquid, which is why ice floats. Pure water has a neutral pH of 7 (USGS, n.d.).

Why it matters

Water is arguably the most essential nutrient because its deprivation will cause death more rapidly than any other nutrient deficiency. Vitamin and mineral deficiencies can take weeks, months or even years to manifest and we can go without food for about three weeks; but we can only survive for a few days without water. After that, the body will stop working properly, organs will shut down and death will occur (Hand et al., 2010; MNT, 2019).

The body relies on water for just about every function, including:

- Beginning the digestive process by making saliva to break down food
- Cushioning the nervous system and organs
- Dissolving and transporting nutrients to the cells

- Flushing waste products from the body
- Helping digest protein, fat and carbohydrates through hydrolysis
- Keeping the skin elastic
- Lubricating the joints
- Maintaining the body's proper pH balance
- Moisturizing the eyes, nose, mouth, lungs and mucus membranes
- Regulating body temperature
- Removing toxins from cells
- Transporting oxygen throughout the body

(Hand et al., 2010; MNT, 2019)

Dogs require more water per day than any other nutrient. That's no surprise, since water makes up about 56% of an adult dog's body weight (73% of lean body mass) (Hand et al., 2010). How much water a dog needs will vary according to several factors, including metabolic needs, stress, body surface area, lactation, environmental temperature, activity level, lifestyle, health status, diet and individual water loss. In general, adult dogs at a maintenance stage require about the same amount of water per day, in milliliters (ml), as their daily energy requirements (Hand et al., 2010). This means that our dog, Benji, who consumes 600 Calories per day, should drink about 600 ml (20 fluid ounces) of water daily.

Dogs typically self-regulate their water intake, but if you're concerned that your dog isn't drinking enough (or is drinking too much), you can easily measure his daily drinking level in a few simple steps:

1. Calculate his daily water requirement (in milliliters) in the same way you would calculate his daily energy requirement (see Chapter 6).

2. Add the calculated amount of water in milliliters (or converted to ounces) into a fluid measuring cup and pour it into his bowl (making sure he doesn't have access to any other water sources).

3. If he drinks all the water during the day, measure out more and add it to his bowl, being sure to include the additional amount when calculating his daily intake.

4. Measure and add more water to his bowl during the day as necessary (be sure to never let the water bowl run dry).

5. At the end of the day, pour any water remaining in his bowl back into the empty measuring cup and subtract that amount from the total amount given to determine the daily water intake.

(Adapted from Hand et al., 2010)

You can also assess whether your dog is drinking enough water by checking his urine. Simply bring a collection cup with you on your walk and hold it under the urine stream. Clear or light-yellow urine indicates proper hydration, while very yellow or dark urine means he needs to drink more. Very yellow, dark or cloudy urine can also signal a medical condition such as a urinary tract infection. If your dog's urine is off color and he's drinking a normal amount of water, you should bring a sample to your veterinarian. She might also perform a cystocentesis, a procedure in which a needle is inserted directly into the bladder through the abdominal wall and urine is extracted directly into a syringe. This procedure results in a more sterile sample.

Some dogs resist drinking water even when it's mixed into their food. In these cases, one trick is to dip a small cloth into fresh water or dog-safe veggie broth and place it in the side of the mouth at the back of the jaw. Your dog will chew on the cloth to try and remove it, swallowing the liquid in the process.

Applications of water in plant-based diets

If you're switching your dog from a kibble-based diet to a fresh-food plant-based diet, you'll likely notice his water consumption decrease. This is because daily water requirements can be satisfied by water in food as well as liquid water (Hand et al., 2010). Vegetables are very high in water content (often more than 90%) (Whitbread, 2020a), while kibble is only about 10% to 15% water.

Dogs should always have free access to fresh, clean water. But for seemingly such a simple nutrient, there are a lot of water choices out there. From tap to reverse osmosis, you may wonder which type is best. Fortunately, we've 'distilled' it all down for you and given our 'water pick.' Let's take a look.

Tap water. While it might be tempting to fill your dog's bowl with tap water, we advise against this because tap water can be riddled with contaminants. The Environmental Working Group has identified 316 different pollutants in tap water across the United States (EWG, 2009), including industrial chemicals, pesticides, metals, pharmaceuticals, bacteria, viruses, protozoan, parasites, volatile organic compounds, radiological contaminants, sewer overflows and wastewater (EPA, 2016; CDC, 2014).

Distilled water. Distilled water is also not a safe long-term hydration choice. While distilled water is pure, the distillation process removes all of the water's beneficial minerals. Studies in animals show that consuming distilled water results in a variety of adverse health effects, including a negative balance of sodium and chloride in the blood, lower volumes of red blood cells, increased secretion of cortisol and adverse changes to the kidneys, including atrophy of the glomeruli. These changes were not affected even when nutritionally adequate diets were fed (Kozisek, n.d.).

Bottled water. Many people prefer bottled water for themselves and their dogs, but at nearly 2,000 times the cost of tap water (Boesler, 2013), this can get expensive. Bottled water also poses a serious environmental issue: Americans use three million plastic water bottles *every hour* and recycle fewer than 30% (The 5 Gyres Institute, 2017). Bottled water may also not be as pure as the companies that sell it would like us to believe. The EWG has discovered contaminants in popular brands of U.S. bottled water at comparable levels to the nation's most polluted tap water systems: The include fertilizer, pharmaceuticals, arsenic, radioactive isotopes and industrial chemicals (EWG, 2008). Plastic water bottles may also contain bisphenol-a (BPA), an industrial chemical that can seep into the water and is associated with a variety of health risks (Bauer, 2017).

Filtered water. We prefer filtered tap water, which is tap water that has been run through a filter to remove impurities. There's a filtration option for just about everyone, ranging from simple countertop and faucet-mounted filters to more complicated reverse-osmosis and whole-house filtration systems. We recommend beginning your filtration search with an online visit to the EWG's National Drinking Water Database. (See Resources.) Simply enter your zip code, select your utility and get instant access to your water quality report provided by your state's water officials. You can also call your water utility company for a copy of its Consumer Confidence Report (CCR), an annual report detailing all contaminants present in your local water supply. Once you know what's in your water, you can select a filtration system targeted to address the specific contaminant issues. Before you know it, you'll have a cost-effective and abundant supply of pure drinking water for both your two and four-legged family members.

Now that you understand the benefits of each key nutrient and its applications in plant-based diets, let's move ahead and dive into the *specific ingredients* we recommend for creating your dog's recipes.

Chapter 5
Comprehensive Ingredients Guide

By now, you're probably excited and ready to begin building your recipes. But there's one more piece of the plant-powered puzzle to complete first. Before you get into the kitchen, we want you to have a thorough understanding of the specific ingredients that will comprise your dog's plant-based meals. The more you know about your ingredient options, the more prepared you'll be when it comes to combining foods in your recipes for maximum nutritional impact.

In this chapter, we're going to explore the ingredients that you need to know about to feed your dog a plant-based diet and to create nutrient-dense home-prepared recipes. You're going to discover an exciting variety of food choices and their health benefits, so you can begin to see how they fit into your dog's overall nutrition plan. We'll also cover common concerns about some ingredients so you can decide if they're appropriate for your dog's individual situation. You'll even find purchasing and preparation recommendations, along with our Pro Tips, to help you unlock the most taste and nutrition from each ingredient.

To keep it all neatly organized, we've grouped each of the foods into larger categories:

- **Legumes**
- **Starches**
- **Non-starchy vegetables and fruits**
- **Nuts**
- **Seeds**
- **Oils**
- **Add-ons**

This organization method will enable you to quickly refer to a food when you have a question, want to refresh your memory or are deciding which ingredients to mix and match as you create your recipes. At the end of the chapter, you'll find a list of dietary toxins because knowing which foods are harmful for dogs is just as important as knowing which ones are beneficial.

We recommend taking an interactive approach to this chapter. As you move through it, feel free to highlight the foods that most interest you from each category. Then, jot them down to create your initial plant-based shopping list. And remember to start slowly, with a few key items. This way, you can experiment with which ingredients work best for your dog. And, you'll have plenty of room to discover new items as you become an expert canine chef.

Legumes

Legumes are plants that produce a pod with fruit or seeds inside. Types of legumes include beans, lentils and peas. Peanuts are also legumes, but due to their high fat content, we consider them an occasional treat rather than a dietary staple. It should come as no surprise that legumes take the top spot in our plant-powered diet plan. They're packed with protein, fiber, vitamins, minerals, antioxidants and phytochemicals. And as we've already pointed out, researchers are beginning to discover their potential as a functional food for dogs.

Legumes are plant-based protein powerhouses, but their benefits don't end there. They're also loaded with health-promoting, disease-fighting nutrients, including:

- Antioxidants and phytochemicals, including anthocyanins (found in dark-colored legumes such as red and black beans and lentils), flavan-3-ols, isoflavones (found most abundantly in soy) and quercetin
- Soluble and insoluble fiber
- Vitamins and minerals, including B vitamins, iron, copper, magnesium, manganese, zinc, and phosphorus

Types of legumes

There are many different types of legumes, each with a unique texture and flavor profile to tantalize your dog's taste buds. Here are the major categories:

Beans

- These include adzuki, black, cannellini, chickpeas, fava, green, Great Northern, kidney, lima, mung, navy, pink, pinto, soy and white.
- These types of beans are consumed *without* their pods.
- They are typically sold dried or canned.

Fresh beans and peas

- These include haricots verts, English peas, fava, flat runner, long, sugar snap, string beans, snow peas, soy and yellow wax.
- Fresh beans are typically sold *in* their pods.
- These beans and peas are typically purchased fresh or frozen (not dried). Some beans, such as soybeans and fava beans, are sold either as fresh beans in their pods or without the pods, as dried or canned beans. The pods of soybeans and fava beans are inedible, and the beans must be removed from them once cooked. Fresh soybeans are also referred to in Japanese cooking as edamame.

(Cook's Country, 2008)

Lentils (See "Types of lentils" for more information)

- These include red, yellow, green, Puy and black beluga.
- Lentils are named from the Latin word for 'lens' because they look like little lenses.
- They are typically sold dried or canned.

  (Sorrells, 2019)

Southern Peas (also called cowpeas)

- These include black-eyed peas, cream peas, crowder peas, field peas, lady peas, purple hull and zipper.
- Despite their name, Southern Peas are beans, not peas.
- Black-eyed peas are the most well-known Southern Peas. They are dried and sold throughout the country.

  (Castle, 2019)

Split peas

- These are a type of green or yellow field pea that is grown for the purpose of drying.
- After drying, the skin is removed, and the pea is split in half.
- Green split peas are sweeter than the yellow variety.

  (Smith, 2019)

Tofu, tempeh

- Tofu, also known as bean curd, is made from coagulating soy milk (made from dried soybeans) to separate the curds from the whey. The curds are then pressed into white blocks of varying firmness. Tofu is typically not fermented (Rogers, 2020). It has a bland, mild flavor.
- Tempeh is a dense block made from fermented cooked soybeans; however, other grains or beans can also be used. Tempeh has a strong, pungent flavor.
- Tofu and tempeh are excellent sources of plant-based protein. Soy is a possible GMO crop, so purchase only organic, non-GMO tofu and tempeh. (See "The scoop on soy" and "Anti-nutrients in plant foods" later in this chapter for information about plant-based estrogens in soy.)

Types of lentils

Lentils boast an excellent total protein and amino acid profile. And since they take far less time to cook than their bean cousins, lentils do not require soaking. Unless your dog suffers from an intolerance to lentils or peas (these foods cross-react), you will find that these little legumes make a great staple in your recipes. But choosing lentils can be confusing. If you've ever perused the legume section of your grocery or health food store, you have likely noticed several different lentil varieties on the shelves.

Brown lentils are a very common and inexpensive type of lentil. They have a mild, earthy flavor and retain their firm shape and texture when cooked. Brown lentils are often used in soups and substituted for meat in plant-based meatloaf, burgers or Shepherd's pie. They take about 25 to 30 minutes to cook.

Green lentils are also commonly found in grocery stores. They are similar to brown lentils, but have a firmer texture and a mild, peppery flavor. Green lentils take a long time to cook—about 45 minutes—and remain firm after cooking. Since they hold their shape and texture so well, they are often used in salads or as a side dish.

Puy lentils are a type of green lentil that get their name from the area in France where they're harvested. They are small and have a slate-grey/green color with speckles. Because Puy lentils have been grown in the same region for more than 2,000 years, they're certified and protected under the French AOC (Appellation d'Origine Contrôlée) designation. For this reason, Puy lentils tend to be the most expensive lentil variety. They have a peppery flavor and remain firm after cooking. They also have a thick skin and therefore the longest cooking time of all lentil varieties—about 45 to 50 minutes.

Red lentils are small, round and bright orange in color. They are often called 'split' lentils because their seed coat has been removed and they have been split in half. Because split lentils are much less dense than other varieties, their cooking time is much shorter—about 15 to 20 minutes. Red lentils turn creamy and mushy when cooked, making them perfect for soupy dishes, such as Indian dal, as well as for purees and stews. They have a mild, sweet flavor.

Yellow lentils also become creamy when cooked and are often used in Indian dishes such as dal, curries, stews and purees. They are a bright yellow color and cook in about 20 minutes. The pigeon pea is a yellow lentil also known as arhar dal or split toor (tuvar) dal. It originated in the Eastern part of peninsular India.

Black beluga lentils are a tiny lentil that get their name from their resemblance to beluga caviar. They are harder to find than other lentil varieties. They have a full-bodied, earthy flavor and a meaty texture that retain their shape after cooking, making them perfect for lentil salads. Black beluga lentils are the most nutritious of all lentil varieties; they are packed with anthocyanins, a phytochemical and antioxidant found in purple and blue plant foods. They cook in about 25 minutes.

(Helpots, 2013; Weg, 2017; Delany, 2018; Fincher, 2020; Geertsema, 2020; Simply-Healthy, 2020; Zeratsky, 2020)

As you can see, there are many types of nutritious lentils to choose from. So, which one(s) do we recommend? The black beluga might seem like the obvious choice because of its exceptional nutritional value. But remember that digestibility is also key. Since the black beluga remains quite firm when cooked, we recommend them with the caveat to mash or puree prior to serving. But we know that ease and time spent in the kitchen are also a consideration when preparing recipes.

So, our overall winners for taste, texture and time are the red and yellow varieties. They create a nice stew-like meal suitable for large and small dogs, as well as older dogs with dental issues and those with sensitive stomachs. If you prefer to bake your dog's recipe, we recommend brown lentils, which will hold up well but are not as firm as the other types listed.

The scoop on soy

We'd be remiss if we didn't address 'the elephant in the room'—or, rather, 'the soybean in the room.' The poor soybean. What a bad rap it has gotten. Could it be that the meat and dairy industries are concerned that soy products are muscling in on their territory? Despite the best efforts of these lobbying and marketing powerhouses, sales of plant-based milks, such as soymilk, are skyrocketing. Based on data through 2019, an astounding 41% of households purchase plant-based milk. At the same time, sales of cow's milk remained flat (Chiorando, 2020). And the rise in popularity of soy-based burgers, hot dogs, sausages and other plant-based meat alternatives proves that consumers are becoming more aware of issues surrounding animal products and are seeking more compassionate, sustainable options.

The tide is clearly turning away from animal products, and the powers-that-be are noticing. This is evident by heated attempts from the National Milk Producers Federation (NMPF) to prevent soy and other plant-based milks from using the term 'milk.' Apparently, the NMPF believes consumers will be confused that a beverage made from plants comes from cows! And in February 2017, the dairy industry launched Februdairy to go head-to-head with Veganuary (which encourages people to go vegan for the month of January). Februdairy is a social media campaign designed to increase the popularity and sales of animal-based dairy. During the month of February, people are encouraged to post positive dairy-related content using the hashtag #Februdairy. Likely to the irritation of Big Dairy, the vegan community also uses the #Februdairy hashtag—to expose the horrors of the dairy industry (Dolan, 2021).

Could the anti-soy war (and much of the research, which is funded by special interest groups), boil down to protecting the profits of these influential industries? Let's see how the major concerns about soy stack up to scientific scrutiny:

Concern: Soy isoflavones mimic estrogen and increase the risk of cancer

Fact: Research shows that soy *protects* against many types of cancers, including those of the breast, colon and prostate. As the Mayo Clinic points out, studies show that women who consume diets rich in soy throughout their lives have a *reduced* risk of breast cancer (Zeratsky, 2020a). And according to the American Institute for Cancer research, isoflavones in soy activate genes that slow the growth of cancer cells and create apoptosis (cancer cell death). Isoflavones may also boost the body's ability to fight oxidative damage to cells and repair DNA, producing even greater anti-cancer benefits (Collins, 2019).

Studies linking soy to cancer were originally conducted in rats and mice. However, as science has progressed, we now realize that rodents metabolize isoflavones differently from other species, including humans and dogs. This means that consuming soy doesn't result in the same high levels of isoflavones in our blood—and our canine companions' blood—that it does in those research animals (Robbins, 2010; Collins, 2019).

World-famous nutrition author John Robbins cites numerous population studies showing the anti-cancer benefits of soy:

- The 25-year Okinawa Centenarian Study sponsored by the Japanese Ministry of Health concluded that high soy consumption was a major protective factor against hormone-dependent cancers—including breast, prostate, ovarian and colon—in the elder population.

- The Japan Public Health Center Study found that areas with the highest rates of soy consumption had the lowest rates of cancer.

- A study in the British medical journal *Lancet* found that women who consumed more flavonoids (such as isoflavones in soy) had a lower risk of breast cancer than women who consumed fewer flavonoid-rich foods.

- A 2003 study in the *Journal of the National Cancer Institute* showed that women who consumed a lot of soy reduced their cancer risk by 54% compared to women who ate little soy.

  (Robbins, 2010)

In fact, flavonoids such as soy isoflavones are such powerful anti-cancer compounds that they're currently being studied for use as synthetic drugs for cancer treatment. A 2020 article in the journal *Nutrients* concluded that:

> *Numerous studies have shown their strong positive activities in reducing inflammation, modulating immune response, and supporting and restoring the normal functions of cells. Flavonoids exert a wide range of anticancer effects and, therefore, they could serve as potential compounds for further studies on the development of novel cancer chemopreventive agents and on understanding their detailed mechanisms of action* (Kopustinskiene et al., 2020, pp. 14).

Dogs can also reap the anti-cancer benefits of soy. At North Carolina State University, researchers found that the isoflavone genistein from soy killed canine lymphoid cells in a laboratory (PetFoodIndustry.com, 2009).

One more bonus? Flavonoids are shown to create beneficial changes in the gut microbiota that could further help protect against cancer at the cellular level (Kopustinskiene et al., 2020). We'll raise a glass of soy milk to that!

Concern: Soy is a leading source of food intolerances for dogs
Fact: Thousands of NutriScan saliva-based food intolerance tests show that the top five sources of food sensitivities in dogs are:

- White-colored fish (or their oils)
- Turkey
- Corn
- Egg
- Soy

Aha! So, soy is indeed number five on this list. But let's unpack this statistic for a moment. The NutriScan test determines food intolerances by measuring a dog's IgA and IgM antibody reactions to specific ingredients (more on that in Chapter 10). But NutriScan cannot identify the source, or the quality, of the ingredients being tested. And what type of soy do you think most dogs consume on a regular basis? We predict that the soy dominating most canine diets originates from genetically modified (GMO) soybeans used in mass-market commercial pet foods.

GMO soy is designed to be highly resistant to pesticides and herbicides such as RoundUp (glyphosate), the weed killer from Monsanto (now Bayer). According to a memorandum from the Environmental Protection Agency (EPA), about 280 million pounds of RoundUp are applied to an average of 298 million acres of farmland every year (EPA, 2019). *That's almost one million pounds of RoundUp per acre of crop.* And while Monsanto continues to defend RoundUp, in 2015 the International Agency for Research on Cancer (IARC), an arm of the World Health Organization (WHO), formally classified RoundUp as a "probable carcinogen." In response, many countries have enacted national legislation to ban glyphosate at some level—but so far, the United States is not among them.

You'd think that once a product has earned the disastrous label of "probable carcinogen," it could no longer be sold. Sadly, that's not the case. RoundUp and generic glyphosate products are still on store shelves across the U.S. They are also everywhere in our environment. And the more these products are sprayed on crops, the more resistant the crops and the weeds become, and the more they're sprayed. It's a toxic vicious cycle and Bayer knows it. To get rid of its RoundUp headache, in June 2020, the company agreed to pay between $10.1 and $10.9 *billion*, resolving about 125,000 filed and unfiled claims. Unfiled claims? That's right. Not only is Bayer paying people who have already been stricken with cancer reportedly due to RoundUp; they're also budgeting for *future claims*—all while continuing to sell this known carcinogen (Melgar, 2020).

Our bodies (dogs and people alike) are designed to protect and defend against foreign invaders, including toxins. Given that, we are not surprised that GMO soy found in mass-market commercial dog foods is a leading cause of food intolerances.

So, yes, we strongly advise against feeding GMO soy to your dog. But don't deny him the health benefits of fresh, organic, non-GMO soy foods such as tofu, tempeh and edamame.

And if your dog has been exposed to commercial soy-based pet foods, we recommend the NutriScan test. This way, you can ensure he's not currently suffering from a soy-based food intolerance before starting fresh (with fresh organic soy, that is!).

Concern: Soy causes hypothyroidism (low thyroid function)

Fact: We've pointed our fingers at soy as a goitrogenic food (one that lowers thyroid function) in our previous two books. And, yes, we are extra cautious about giving soy to hypothyroid dogs. This is because soy isoflavones suppress thyroid peroxidase (TPO), an enzyme produced in the thyroid gland. TPO helps the thyroid gland turn dietary iodine into the thyroid hormones triiodothyronine (T3) and thyroxine (T4).

But there is good news. A 2003 study on healthy post-menopausal women showed that soy does not lower thyroid function if dietary intake of iodine is normal. In other words, soy is only shown to harm the thyroid when the diet is also deficient in iodine (Robb-Nicholson, 2006; Robbins, 2010). And you can easily remedy this issue by adding a little bit of iodized salt or seaweed to your dog's recipes. Please remember, however, that too much iodine is as harmful as too little. (See "Commonsense kelp cautions" in Chapter 8 for more on iodine.)

Does this mean that we recommend adding a lot of soy to your dog's diet if he's already suffering from low thyroid function? No, we don't. Some dogs with underactive thyroids suffer from Hashimoto's disease, a heritable autoimmune disorder in which the body attacks the thyroid gland. In these cases, we want to avoid anything that could potentially worsen the situation.

But if your dog has a healthy functioning thyroid and gets adequate, appropriate amounts of iodine, organic soy is a high-quality source of protein and other nutrients. (Also see "Anti-nutrients in plant foods" later in this chapter.)

What's the best type of tofu?

Do you ever go into a panic when picking out tofu at the grocery store? The dizzying array of varieties is enough to induce tofu terror. Here are some of the common types:

- Silken
- Soft
- Medium
- Firm
- Extra Firm
- Super Firm
- Sprouted

And that's just what's available in the refrigerated section. There's also tofu that comes in a Tetra Pak box. This type of tofu is shelf-stable (i.e., needs no refrigeration) and is typically found in the Asian foods aisle. Mori-Nu is a common brand found on U.S. store shelves.

Non-silken tofu is known simply as 'regular tofu,' while silken tofu is appropriately termed 'silken.' But the confusion doesn't stop there. Even within the silken category, you can find different types, including soft, firm, extra firm and light firm (Mori-Nu, 2021).

Fortunately, choosing tofu is not as complicated as it seems. The different tofu types simply reflect the product's water content. Firmer tofu indicates that more water has been pressed out during processing. You might have noticed this phenomenon if you've used a tofu press (or wrapped your tofu in a clean cloth and placed a heavy pan on top for about a half hour). After the excess water's been removed, your tofu block is firmer than it was when you removed it from the package. It makes sense that as the water content of tofu decreases, the nutrient density increases. So, as you move up in firmness, the tofu will contain more Calories, fat and protein (Han, 2020).

So, which type of tofu is best? We prefer firmer varieties, which pack the most protein power. The texture you select also comes down to your (and your dog's) taste preferences and the dish you're making. Silken and soft varieties go well in creamy foods, such as dips, sauces, smoothies and custards, while firmer varieties make a great substitute for meat.

We also love the additional benefits of **sprouted tofu**, which is made from soybeans that have been germinated for a few days so that a little sprout forms. If you're concerned about anti-nutrients, then sprouted tofu is the way to go because sprouting significantly reduces these compounds. (See "Anti-nutrients in plant foods.") A study published in the *Journal of Food Science and Technology* found that tofu made from sprouted soybeans contained 81% less trypsin inhibitor and 56% less phytic acid across all varieties. Sprouted tofu also boasted a better nutrient profile than its unsprouted counterpart, with 13% more protein and 12% less fat (Murugkar, 2014).

If you live with a picky dog, it's also good to know that tofu taste testers preferred the flavor and mouthfeel of sprouted tofu. The same study found that although tofu made from sprouted seeds ranked higher on a whiteness index, the tofu strength was about 43% less than unsprouted varieties (Murugkar, 2014). While this study was conducted with people, dogs who prefer milder flavors will likely concur.

By the way, sprouted soy milk also beat its unsprouted counterpart in all areas, with 73% less trypsin inhibitor and 59% less phytic acid, as well as 7% more protein and 24% less fat (Murugkar, 2014). But since we've yet to find pure sprouted soy milk on store shelves, those of us looking for these added benefits in liquid form will have to make it ourselves.

You can use sprouted tofu just as you would unsprouted types in your recipes. Simply select the texture that best serves your needs and you're good to go.

A bounty of beans

It's easy to get stuck in a rut eating the same few types of beans that we find at the local grocery store. No offense to the common kidney and black beans, but there is a whole world of lesser-known heirloom beans out there ready to be explored and savored—by you and your dog. Heirloom beans come from seeds that have been passed down from generation to generation, often within the same family. They are developed for their distinct characteristics, including striking color patterns, a beefy looking flesh and rich flavor. Heirloom beans are open pollinated, meaning that the seeds are pollinated by natural means such as wind, insects or birds. Beans from open-pollinated seeds will remain true to type year after year; when you plant the seeds, you will always get the exact same bean.

Heirloom beans purchased from specialty purveyors are usually fresher than those found in grocery stores. This is because they're typically sold the same year of harvest or within two years. On the other hand, dried beans can linger on grocery stores shelves for many years.

Heirloom beans tend to have interesting names that reflect the bean's family, culture of origin, geographic location or physical characteristics. The following are just a few unique heirloom bean varieties that both you and your dog can enjoy:

- Anasazi
- Appaloosa
- Borlotti
- Buckeye
- Christmas Lima
- Cranberry
- Eye of the Goat
- Rebosero
- Royal Corona
- Scarlett Runner
- Vaquero
- Yellow Eye

You can find heirloom beans at specialty purveyors. (See Resources.) Since they come with a heftier price tag than standard supermarket varieties, you may want to include them as a special occasion treat rather than a pantry staple. And don't worry if heirloom beans don't fit into your budget at all. While they can add interest to your dog's dining experience (and your own), the more popular and wallet-friendly varieties are just as nutritious.

Pro tips for cooking dried beans

Store them properly. For optimum freshness, remove dried beans from their original packaging. Pick out any broken beans or rocks and transfer to an airtight food-safe glass storage container. Store in a cool, dark place for up to a year. Got older beans that you'd like to use? Try adding 1/4 teaspoon of baking soda per pound of beans during cooking to help soften them (Huffstetler, 2020).

Soak them before cooking. Add dried beans to a large bowl and immerse them in cold water, making sure that the water rises at least two inches higher than the beans (remember that the beans will expand during soaking). Leave the bowl uncovered and soak the beans overnight, or for at least eight hours. Drain and rinse prior to cooking. Short on time? You can use the 'quick soak' method. Place the beans in a large pot and add water, covering the beans by at least three inches. (Six cups of water for each pound/two cups of beans should do the trick.) Heat the water until boiling. Boil for two to three minutes, remove the pot from the heat, cover and let sit for one hour. Drain, rinse and your beans are ready to cook (Hanneman & Colgrove, n.d; Watson, 2020). You do not need to soak lentils prior to cooking.

Cook them like a pro. If you have time to spare, you can cook your dried beans on the stove top. Add pre-soaked beans to a large pot and cover with fresh cool water—about three cups per one cup of soaked beans. (Be sure *not* to use your bean-soaking water.) Bring to a boil, reduce the heat, cover and simmer until the beans are tender (typically 45 minutes to two hours). The following are approximate cooking times for different types of beans. Bear in mind, however, that cooking times will vary depending upon the freshness of the beans, your geographic elevation and other factors. We recommend periodically testing your beans for tenderness throughout the cooking process by removing a bean and mashing it with a fork.

- Black beans: 60 to 90 minutes
- Great Northern beans: 45 to 60 minutes
- Kidney beans: 90 to 120 minutes
- Navy beans: 90 to 120 minutes
- Pinto beans: 90 to 120 minutes

    (Hanneman & Colgrove, n.d)

If you're in a hurry, you can reduce your bean-cooking time by using a pressure cooker or InstantPot. (See Chapter 7.) However, do not cook legumes in a slow cooker because this method does not deactivate the lectin toxins that are present in raw beans.

Reduce gas. "Beans, beans, the musical fruit, the more you eat them, the more you toot…." You've likely heard this funny little tune before, which refers to the potential gas-producing qualities of beans and the resulting 'music' created by those who eat them. And while we want our canine companions to gain the health benefits of beans, we would prefer to avoid the musical accompaniment. The irony is that oligosaccharides, prebiotic fibers that we already discussed feed the microbiome, also produce gas during fermentation. Fortunately, pre-soaking your beans, even when using a pressure cooker, will help to reduce gas by drawing out the oligosaccharides. We also recommend changing the water a couple of times during the soaking process. This is because when the gas-producing compounds release into the soaking water, the beans wade in that same water. Changing the water during the soaking process provides a fresh, gas-free environment for the beans (The Bean Institute, 2020). If your dog still 'toots,' check out Chapter 7 for more gas-busting strategies.

Starches

Starch often gets a bad reputation in the United States and other Western countries that heavily consume animal ingredients. As we discussed in Chapter 4, starches are non-fibrous polysaccharides—complex carbohydrates that contain 10 or more glucose units linked together. Certain vegetables, grains and legumes fall under the category of starches.

DNA analysis shows that dogs have genomically evolved to digest starches over thousands of years. But as we emphasize throughout this book, you want to be mindful of selecting the most nutrient-dense ingredients within each dietary category. After all, French fries are starches, but we certainly don't advocate feeding them to your dog (or to yourself, for that matter).

Let's look at some of the more common starches and a few benefits of each, along with some starches we recommend avoiding. To keep things organized, we've broken down this category into four sub-categories:

- Legumes
- Root vegetables
- Winter squashes
- Grains and pseudo-grains

Starch type: legumes

Please refer to the discussion of legumes in the previous section.

Starch type: root vegetables

From a culinary perspective, root vegetables are those that grow underground and have leafy greens that grow above ground. Root vegetables have been an integral part of South American and Asian diets for thousands of years. They are credited with helping fight a variety of chronic inflammatory diseases, including cancer, diabetes and heart disease. A study by the European Prospective Investigation into Cancer showed that people who ate the most root vegetables reduced their risk of diabetes by 13% compared with those who ate the least (Westcott, 2018). Root vegetables can also make an excellent addition to weight-loss diets because they provide a longer-lasting feeling of satiety than non-starchy vegetables or refined grains.

Types of root vegetables

Here are some of our favorite root vegetables and a brief rundown of their benefits:

Beetroot

- Rich in betalains, red and yellow plant pigments that provide antioxidant and anti-inflammatory benefits
- Good source of nutrients, including Vitamin C, folate, magnesium and potassium

  (Cleveland Clinic, 2020)

Carrot (also classified as a non-starchy vegetable)

- High in carotenoids, which are phytochemicals that act as antioxidants
- Contains falcarinol, a natural pesticide with anti-cancer properties

  (University of Newcastle Upon Tyne, 2005)

Celeriac (celery root)

- Excellent source of vitamins B, C and K and minerals phosphorus, potassium and manganese
- Low in Calories and carbohydrates

  (Dolson, 2020)

Jerusalem artichoke (sunchoke)

- Contains inulin, a prebiotic that benefits gut health
- Good source of vitamin C and iron

   (Del Coro, 2020)

Jicama

- Contains inulin
- Good source of vitamins and minerals, including B1, B2, B5, B6, antioxidants C and E and minerals zinc, copper, calcium, phosphorus

   (Robbins, 2019)

Parsnip

- Good source of vitamin C, potassium and folate
- Provides anti-inflammatory and anti-fungal properties

   (Henne, 2013)

Rutabaga

- Contains glucosinolates, sulfur-containing anti-cancer compounds
- Rich in a variety of nutrients, including antioxidant carotenoids, vitamins B, C and K and minerals manganese, potassium, phosphorus, magnesium, calcium, iron and zinc

   (Staughton, 2020)

Sweet potato

- Considered a superfood due to the high level of nutrients
- Rich in carotenoids and antioxidant vitamins A and C, along with B vitamins and minerals such as calcium, iron, magnesium, phosphorus, potassium and zinc

   (WebMD, 2019)

White potato

- Contains a variety of nutrients, including vitamins B6 and C, potassium, magnesium, phosphorus, iron and zinc
- Provides gut-friendly resistant starch (See "Cold potatoes" in Chapter 9.)

   (King & Slavin, 2013)

Yam

- Provides a variety of nutrients; however, contains much less vitamin A than sweet potatoes
- Higher in Calories, starchier and drier than sweet potatoes

   (Note that yams sold in grocery stores are almost always sweet potatoes. Be aware that yams can be toxic if consumed raw.)

   (Brown, 2020)

Health benefits of root vegetables

As a food group, root vegetables offer many health benefits, including:

- Rich in vitamins, minerals, antioxidants and phytochemicals
- Excellent source of sustained energy from complex carbohydrates
- Relatively low glycemic load due to high fiber content, so they won't rapidly raise blood sugar levels
- Deliver a longer-term feeling of fullness than simple carbohydrates or non-starchy vegetables
- Great alternative to gluten-containing grains

A note on corn

While corn is not a root vegetable, it is classified as a starch. Corn offers a variety of nutrients, including B vitamins, zinc, magnesium, copper, iron and manganese as well as lutein and zeaxanthin, two carotenoids that support eye health (Mayo Clinic, 2018). However, we advise against regularly feeding corn to your dog because it is:

- A common source of food intolerances
- Difficult to digest
- Possibly genetically modified (GMO) (unless organic)

There is one corn caveat. *Organic, plain, air-popped popcorn* can make an excellent low-fat and low-calorie treat for your canine companion. If you're making a batch of popcorn for yourself, remove some for your dog *before* adding any fats or seasonings, which can be harmful to your canine companion. And *never* feed corn on the cob, which can lodge in your dog's throat and cause choking or even death.

Starch type: winter squashes

Think outside the can (of pumpkin, that is) and treat your dog to a wonderful world of winter squash. The amazing nutritional profile, delicious flavors and varied textures make winter squash an excellent addition to your canine's cuisine. While each type of winter squash has its own unique nutritional profile, all winter squashes are rich in the important antioxidants beta carotene and vitamin C, along with vitamin B6 (folate), magnesium and potassium (Harvard School of Public Health, 2021).

As omnivores, dogs can convert plant-based beta carotene into vitamin A, an antioxidant that provides a powerful health punch, including fighting cancer and improving eye health. And beta carotene is safe even in high doses, whereas consuming too much pre-formed vitamin A (Retinol) can result in serious health consequences such as dizziness, nausea and even death. Vitamin A toxicity during pregnancy can also cause birth defects in offspring (NIH, 2021).

Types of winter squashes

Popular types of winter squashes include:

- Acorn
- Banana

- Buttercup
- Butternut
- Carnival
- Delicata
- Hubbard
- Kabocha
- Spaghetti
- Sugar pumpkin
- Sweet dumpling
- Turban

Pro tips for winter squashes

Slash your squash-prep time. Tired of fighting with your winter squash when trying to peel and cut it? You don't have to! You can bake your winter squash *whole* and dramatically cut down on the time and effort (not to mention the possibility of severing a finger trying to cut a tough squash in half). Butternut squash comes out especially delicious when prepared in this manner. Just clean and pat dry your squash, place it on a baking sheet and make a couple of slits in the rind using the tip of a sharp straight-edge knife. Bake in the oven at 350 degrees Fahrenheit (180 degrees C) for about 1 1/2 hours or until the skin has turned a light brown and you can easily pierce through the squash with a sharp knife (Oliver, 2022). (Note that baking times will vary based on the type and size of the squash and your oven.) Let cool until ready to handle, cut in half, remove the seeds and scoop out the flesh for use in your dog's recipes. Yes, this is a game-changer!

Chop spaghetti squash. As the name implies, the flesh of spaghetti squash separates into thin, noodle-like strands when you run a fork through it. These strands are long and fibrous, which can create a choking hazard for your dog. For this reason, we recommend chopping spaghetti squash strands into short pieces or running them through a food processor prior to serving.

Create a nutritious icing. To naturally kick up the sweetness and nutrition of your home-made dog treats, try frosting them with squash or pumpkin icing. Mix equal parts of cooked, mashed squash or pumpkin with unsweetened plant-based milk (organic almond, cashew, oat or soy work well). Spread or pipe onto cooled treats. You can even add additional dog-friendly flavors to your icing, such as a sprinkling of turmeric, Ceylon cinnamon or freeze-dried berry powder. (Avoid strawberry unless you know your dog is not allergic to this ingredient.)

Starch type: grains and pseudo-grains

If Shakespeare had been a dog enthusiast, his famous line, "To be, or not to be, that is the question" might have instead been, "To include grains in your dog's diet, or not to include grains in your dog's diet, that is the question." This debate continues fervently within the veterinary and dog nutrition worlds. Anti-grainers argue that dogs don't require grains and that they serve as little more than dietary fillers. Pro-grainers fear that grain-free diets may contribute to cases of dilated cardiomyopathy (DCM) in some dogs. (See Chapter 2 for more on diet-related DCM.)

We fall into neither the pro-grain nor the anti grain group for the simple reason that dogs are individuals. We've worked with many dogs who have benefited greatly from dietary grains. Other dogs seem to show sensitivity to most grains and should not consume them.

If your dog is not intolerant to grains, we see nothing wrong with including them in his diet. In fact, many grains are extremely nutritious, including ancient **pseudo-grains** such as amaranth, buckwheat and quinoa. Pseudo-grains look and cook like cereal grains, but they come from the seeds of broadleaf plants rather than the seeds of grasses. These are even considered **superfoods**, which is a popularized term referring to foods with superior nutrient density.

The key to using grains is selecting the right type. You've probably noticed by now that this is true of every food group. Therefore, when we talk about meeting nutritional goals, we must look beyond just the numbers. By this, we mean that two dogs can receive 'complete and balanced' diets that hit the mark with the proper levels of macro- and micronutrients. But one of those dogs can get these nutrients via a whole-food diet rich in functional, anti-inflammatory foods, while the other consumes a pro-inflammatory diet. We'll talk a lot more about this in Part 2, when we dive into the relationship between food and specific health conditions.

Recommended grains

The following grains and pseudo-grains offer superior nutritional profiles and health benefits:

Amaranth

- Amaranth is a pseudo grain with a superb protein and amino acid profile that shares qualities of both a cereal and a legume, making it nutritionally similar to rice and beans. It is high in the amino acids lysine and methionine, which is unusual for a grain. Amaranth is credited with many health benefits including immune-boosting, antitumor, anti-allergic and antioxidant, as well as reducing blood glucose levels (Caselato-Sousa & Amaya-Farfán, 2012).
- It contains a protein peptide similar to lunasin found in soy, which is credited for anti-cancer and anti-inflammatory benefits (Silva-Sánchez et al., 2008).

Buckwheat

- Buckwheat is a pseudo-grain known as a superfood due to its many reported health benefits, including antioxidant, anti-inflammatory, anticancer, antidiabetic, cholesterol reduction, neuroprotection and prebiotic effects.
- It contains a variety of beneficial bioactive compounds, including D-chiro-inositol, rutin and quercetin (Giménez-Bastida & Zieliński, 2015).

Millet

- Millet is an ancient grain rich in **phenolic compounds**, phytonutrients with powerful antioxidant and metal chelating properties (Chandrasekara & Shahidi, 2010).

- It is an excellent source of many important nutrients, including vitamin B, magnesium, manganese, phosphorus and iron, as well as the sulphur-containing amino acids methionine and cysteine (which are used by the body to make taurine). It is also an alkaline-forming food and acts as a prebiotic (Sarita & Singh, 2016). On the other hand, millet should be avoided if your dog has low thyroid disorder.

Oat (purchase certified gluten-free only)

- Oat contains beta-glucans with functional properties, including stimulating the immune system, protecting against infectious diseases and cancer and helping control glucose levels (El Khoury et al., 2012).

- It is rich in minerals, including phosphorus, thiamine, magnesium and zinc (Harvard School of Public Health, 2021a).

Quinoa

- Quinoa is a pseudo-grain rich in protein and amino acids.

- It is packed with a variety of vitamins and minerals, including thiamin (B1), folate, manganese, phosphorus and magnesium (Harvard School of Public Health, 2021b).

Sorghum

- Sorghum is an ancient grain that serves as a functional food. It is rich in phenolic compounds with antioxidant, anti-inflammatory, anti-cancer, diabetes-prevention and weight-control benefits.

- It provides a wide variety of vitamins and minerals, including vitamins A, B complex (pyridoxine, riboflavin, and thiamin), D, E, and K along with the minerals potassium, phosphorus, magnesium, and zinc (Xiong et al., 2019).

Teff

- Teff is an ancient Ethiopian grain that is gluten-free and rich in many nutrients including calcium, manganese, phosphorus, iron, copper, thiamin (B1) and vitamin C (which is typically not found in grains) (Patel, 2016).

- It contains about 20 to 40% **resistant starch**, a type of starch that behaves like soluble fiber because it resists digestion in the gastrointestinal tract and passes into the colon, where it is fermented by gut bacteria. Teff also acts as a prebiotic, stabilizes blood sugar levels, increases micronutrient absorption and improves bowel health (Nugent, 2005).

Wild rice

- Not really rice, wild rice is actually a type of gluten-free aquatic grass that grows in streams, rivers or lakes.

- It offers a wide variety of health benefits, including alkaline forming, aids digestion, anti-inflammatory, arsenic-free, supports a healthy nervous system and is rich in antioxidants and manganese (McClees, 2015).

Grains to avoid

The following grains should be avoided because they contain gluten, which can trigger reactions in sensitive individuals, including those with gastrointestinal disorders and autoimmune conditions.

- **Couscous** (tiny balls of pasta made from durum wheat semolina)
- **Oats** that are not labeled 'gluten free'
- **Rye**
- **Wheat** (includes bulgur, durum, farro, kamut, semolina and spelt)
- **Triticale** (a cross between wheat and rye)

Grains to limit

The following grains may be included in the diet if fed sparingly:

Barley

- If your dog does not suffer from gluten-intolerance or a condition triggered or worsened by gluten, he may benefit from barley's health-promoting properties. While barley contains gluten, it is also rich in beta-glucans, the fermentable soluble fiber found in oats, yeast, mushrooms and seaweed. Beta-glucans are shown to possess a variety of bioactive properties and health benefits, including producing SCFAs, stabilizing blood sugar levels, preventing and treating metabolic syndrome, and protecting against infectious diseases and cancer (Brown & Gordon, 2003; El Khoury et al., 2012).

Brown rice

- Brown rice is a whole grain and therefore more nutritious than white rice. However, it can be difficult to digest for many dogs, especially those with gastrointestinal issues. Brown rice and brown rice products have also been shown to contain about 80% more inorganic arsenic than white rice, as the arsenic accumulates in the rice's outer layers. Purchasing organic brown rice does not lower the amount of arsenic absorbed by the rice (Consumer Reports, 2014).

White rice

- White rice is bland and so is often recommended in cases of acute gastrointestinal flare-ups. However, it is a refined carbohydrate with little nutritional value. It is also high on the glycemic index and so should not be fed long term. White rice also contains arsenic, although at much lower levels than brown rice. (Tip: Plain rice cakes can be used as treats, especially for overweight dogs.)

Pro tips for grains and pseudo-grains

Treat your dog to amaranth porridge. Cooked amaranth has a pudding-like consistency and nutty sweetness, making it a perfect healthy breakfast porridge. Kick up the nutrition by mixing in some berries. Avoid overcooking amaranth, as it will turn gummy.

Watch the thyroid. Avoid serving millet to dogs with hypothyroidism (low thyroid disorder), as millet can impair thyroid function even when iodine intake is adequate (Harris, 2012). Use plenty of water when cooking millet as it quadruples in size!

Start the day out right. Serve your dog a warm bowl of oatmeal topped with berries or other dog-safe fruit and a swirl of almond or cashew butter for a nutritious and satisfying breakfast. Steel cut oats rank lower on the glycemic index than rolled oats, meaning that they create a slower rise in blood sugar and create a greater feeling of fullness. However, they are also thicker and may be more difficult for your dog to digest.

Make it light. Quinoa comes in white, red or black varieties. We recommend white (which is actually closer to tan) quinoa. It has a lighter texture and cooks up fluffier than the red or black types, making it easier to digest.

Pop up a tasty treat. Pop sorghum over a hot, oil-free skillet and offer it to your dog as a nutritious corn-free popped treat. You can also mix it into home-made cookie dough prior to baking in place of nuts.

Whip up some puppy pancakes. Treat your pup—and yourself—to some superfood teff pancakes. Top with dog-safe berries or sliced banana and a dollop of unsweetened plant-based yogurt (e.g., coconut, almond, cashew, soy) for a drool-worthy breakfast.

Go wild. Substitute wild rice for regular rice in your dog's dishes to pump up the taste and nutritional value.

Non-starchy vegetables and fruits

The plant world is bursting with so many phytochemical-rich veggies and fruits that we could spend an entire book just writing about their benefits. Instead, we thought it would be fun to go behind the colors and talk about why each one is important—and then provide you with a few key foods to try out in each color category. This way, you can experiment as you help your dog 'eat the rainbow'—and reap the health benefits!

You'll recall from Chapter 4 that phytochemicals are natural pigments produced by plants ('phyto' means plant) that contribute to the plant's color, flavor and odor. They are biologically active compounds, which means that they serve a purpose, such as protecting the plant from insect predation, pathogens and diseases. Phytochemicals also convey health benefits to those who consume them.

As we previously mentioned, it's estimated that there are more than 5,000 phytochemicals. Scientists are just beginning to uncover their disease-fighting properties, including:

- Benefiting heart health
- Boosting the immune system
- Defending against free radicals and cellular oxidation
- Fighting inflammation
- Increasing longevity

- Lowering cholesterol and blood pressure
- Promoting healthy vision
- Protecting against chronic inflammatory diseases, including cancer

Behind the colors

There are five color categories of plant foods based on their phytochemical content:

- Red
- Orange/Yellow
- Green
- Blue/Purple
- Brown/White

Red. Red-pigmented fruits and vegetables are rich in lycopene and anthocyanins. Lycopene is a carotenoid with strong antioxidant properties. Human and animal studies point to a variety of beneficial bioactivities of lycopene, including anti-cancer, antibiotic, anti-inflammatory and antioxidative. Lycopene is also shown to protect the heart and stimulate the immune system (Mendel, 2013). Anthocyanins are a group of antioxidant compounds in the flavonoid family, which are part of a larger group of phytochemicals called polyphenols. Anthocyanins are shown to protect against several types of cancers, reduce the risk of cardiovascular disease, decrease obesity and diabetes, reduce inflammation, increase cognitive performance and protect against neurodegenerative diseases, including Parkinson's disease and Alzheimer's disease (Li et al., 2017).

Orange/Yellow. Orange and yellow fruits and vegetables boast high levels of carotenoids, including alpha-carotene, beta-carotene and beta-cryptoxanthin. These antioxidant compounds are referred to as 'pro-vitamin A' because people and dogs can convert them into pre-formed vitamin A (Retinol). Carotenoids possess anti-inflammatory, anti-cancer, immune-boosting and cardio-protective properties. Lutein and zeaxanthin (non-pro-vitamin A carotenoids) are plentiful in the retina and important nutrients for eye health. Studies show that higher intake of lutein and zeaxanthin reduces the risk of age-related macular degeneration (Cooperstone & Schwartz, 2016).

Green. The dominant pigment in green plant foods comes courtesy of chlorophyll, one of the most important compounds on Earth. Plants use chlorophyll to capture and convert sunlight into the energy they need to grow. This process, called **photosynthesis**, results in the release of oxygen into the air, which is necessary for humans and other mammals to sustain life. Animal studies have shown that chlorophyll may slow and prevent the growth of cancer (Adams, 2019). Green plant foods are also packed with disease-fighting phytochemicals, including carotenoids, isothiocyanates and indoles. Dark leafy greens, such as kale and spinach, are rich in vitamins and minerals including vitamins A, C, E and K, calcium, iron, magnesium and potassium. They are also an excellent source of folate, a B vitamin that protects against cancer by controlling the repair and methylation of DNA (Yan, 2016). Isothiocyanates are phytochemicals that exert an anti-cancer effect on the epigenome by inhibiting cancer cell proliferation and inducing apoptosis (Hardy & Tollefsbol, 2011). **Sulforaphane** is an isothiocyanate produced when glucoraphanin, a sulfur-containing glucosinolate found in cruciferous vegetables, comes in contact with the enzyme myrosinase. This happens when the plant is damaged, such as by chopping or chewing. Sulforaphane has been shown in laboratory tests to stimulate enzymes in the body that detoxify carcinogens before they have the chance to damage cells. Broccoli sprouts contain the highest level of glucosinolates per serving of any vegetable (Magee, 2007). (See Chapter 8.)

How to prepare green veggies

If you're like many of us, then as a child you pushed a lot of mushy, olive/grey-colored vegetables around on your plate (or snuck them to your dog!). These overcooked veggies not only looked and tasted unappetizing; they were also deficient in many key nutrients, including chlorophyll. That's because chlorophyll is destroyed by heat and acid. Here's a brief rundown of the science behind what happens when you cook greens:

1. Raw veggies contain gases trapped between the plant's cells, slightly clouding our view of the cell's vivid green chlorophyll pigment.

2. When the veggies begin to cook, heat starts to break down the cell wall, causing the gas to expand and escape. The chlorophyll now becomes easier to see and the veggies turn more vibrant.

3. As cooking continues, heat further breaks down the cell walls, causing the release of organic acids. When this happens, the chemical structure of the chlorophyll is changed. The magnesium atom that's normally at the center of every chlorophyll molecule breaks away and is replaced by hydrogen atoms.

4. This change in chemical structure destroys the chlorophyll and causes the vegetables to turn from bright green to a dull, greyish green.

(Glass, 2007; Compound Interest, 2017)

What's the best way to maximize the level of chlorophyll in green veggies? Serve them raw. Just be sure to give them a good chop or whiz them in a food processor or blender for enhanced digestion.

If you do want to cook them, the trick is to do it quickly. The recommended time is not more than five to seven minutes, which isn't long enough to break down the plant's cell walls (Compound Interest, 2017). We recommend steaming rather than boiling, since many of the nutrients are tossed out along with the boiling water.

Chlorophyll isn't the only nutrient lost by overcooking greens. Earlier, we mentioned that chopping raw cruciferous vegetables releases myrosinase, an enzyme that breaks down glucosinolates into the anti-cancer compound sulforaphane. Well, guess what destroys myrosinase? Heat. Avoid cooking your cruciferous vegetables too soon after chopping them or you'll reduce the power of myrosinase. If this happens, sulforaphane won't form and you'll miss out on all that anti-cancer goodness (Compound Interest, 2017).

Blue/Purple. Like their red cousins, blue and purple plant foods obtain their pigments from anthocyanins and so have the same benefits. Anthocyanins possess powerful antioxidant activity, and their ability to scavenge free radicals enables them to play an important role in blocking a number of disease pathways. Anthocyanin pigments appear redder in acidic conditions and bluer in alkaline conditions.

Brown/White. White, cream and pale-yellow fruits and vegetables are rich in anthoxanthins, antioxidant compounds in the flavonoid category of plant polyphenols. Flavone, apigenin, luteolin, kaempferol and quercetin are five anthoxanthins that have demonstrated potential as a natural therapy for Alzheimer's disease (Pate et al., 2018). Flavonoid compounds convey many health benefits, including defending the body against inflammation (including gastrointestinal inflammation), helping manage diabetes by increasing the release of insulin and regenerating pancreatic beta cells (Mohan & Nandhakumar, 2014) and fighting cancer via multiple pathways, including inducing apoptosis and blocking proliferation of cancer cells (Kopustinskiene et al., 2020). Allicin, a compound in white foods such as garlic, provides powerful antimicrobial effects and has been shown to inhibit certain bacteria, viruses and yeasts. Sulforaphane produced from cauliflower and other cruciferous vegetables (discussed earlier) is a phytochemical with potent anti-cancer properties. (See Chapter 8.)

Pro tips for non-starchy vegetables and fruits

Freeze them for fun. Frozen fruits such as berries, watermelon, banana and cantaloupe make a refreshing summertime treat for dogs.

Enhance absorption. Carotenoids are lipophilic, meaning that they dissolve in lipids or fats. To enhance their absorption, serve carotenoid-rich fruits and veggies along with one of our recommended oils.

Reduce goitrogens. Cruciferous vegetables are goitrogenic foods that can further hinder thyroid function in dogs suffering from low thyroid disorder. Cooking greatly reduces the goitrogenic qualities, making these healthy foods safe to serve in moderation to hypothyroid dogs. (See "Anti-nutrients in plant foods" later in this chapter for more information.)

Maximize nutrients. To optimize phytonutrient levels, serve veggies raw, lightly steamed or cooked in a pressure cooker (such as InstantPot).

Try our recommendations to give your dog a colorful blast of delicious health-boosting phytochemicals. And remember to experiment on your own, too!

Dog-friendly veggies and fruits by color

Red	Orange/Yellow	Green	Blue/Purple	Brown/White
Beets	Cantaloupe	Broccoli	Blackberries	Cauliflower
Cranberries	Carrots	Collard greens	Blueberries	Bananas
Raspberries	Golden beets	Green apples	Purple asparagus	Garlic (in small amounts and no onions)
Red apples	Orange and yellow bell peppers	Green beans	Purple cabbage	Mushrooms (cultivated only, not wild)
Red bell peppers	Sweet potatoes	Kale	Purple carrots	Parsnips
Strawberries (if no allergy exists)	Winter squash	Spinach	Purple cauliflower	Potatoes
Watermelon	Yellow summer squash	Zucchini	Purple sweet potatoes	Turnips

Nuts

One of the most common questions we get is, "Can my dog eat nuts?" There are no shortages of opinions on the Web about this topic, so it's no wonder many people are puzzled. We are here to clear up this confusion, and to hopefully keep you from 'going nuts' trying to figure it all out. Let's take a closer look at the pros and cons of feeding your dog nuts and our recommendations for including them in your dog's diet. *(Please note that you should never give your dog macadamia nuts or black walnuts, as they are toxic to dogs.)*

Pros

Nuts are a great source of plant-based protein, fiber and other nutrients. While they are fatty, they're low in saturated fat and rich in unsaturated fats, including alpha-linolenic acid (ALA), an essential omega-3 fatty acid. As we've discussed, omega-3s play an important role in reducing inflammation and creating a more optimum ratio of dietary omega-6 to omega-3 fatty acids. Walnuts are exceptionally high in omega-3s, delivering 2,565 mg per ounce. This whopping omega-3 level even beats out hemp seeds, which offer 2,264 mg per ounce (Harvard Medical School, 2017). (Again, be sure *never* to give your dog black walnuts, which are toxic to dogs. The common English walnut is a safe variety.)

Nuts also provide a variety of vitamins and minerals, including folic acid, niacin and vitamin B6 and minerals such as magnesium, copper, zinc, selenium, phosphorus and potassium (Brufau et al., 2006). They're also an excellent source of antioxidants, including vitamin E and polyphenols. Almonds are especially high in vitamin E.

Blanched almonds boast 6.9 mg vitamin E per ounce and 2.2 mg per tablespoon (NutritionData, 2018). To put that into perspective, the NRC's RDA of vitamin E for adult dogs at a maintenance stage is 7.5 mg per 1,000 Calories. Our 22-pound dog Benji consumes 600 Calories per day, so his RDA for vitamin E is 4.5 mg (7.5 x 600 = 4,500 ÷ 1,000 = 4.5). This means that Benji can meet virtually his entire RDA for vitamin E by consuming just two tablespoons per day of almonds, which provide 4.4 mg.

Studies show that almonds and walnuts protect cells from oxidation caused by free radicals (Jalali-Khanabadi et al., 2010; Haddad et al., 2014). According to one randomized controlled study, subjects who ate walnuts were better able to fend off free radicals than those who ate fish (Hudthagosol et al., 2012). That's a lot of antioxidant power packed into a small space!

Walnuts also benefit the microbiome, thanks to their high levels of ellagitannins and ellagic acid. Trials in people show that eating walnuts every day for a few weeks increases populations of gut bacteria associated with health-promoting benefits (AICR, 2020).

Cashews are another nut that offer interesting health benefits, including:

- Lowest in Calories of all commonly consumed nuts
- Second lowest in fat (behind pistachios)
- Among the highest in total protein
- Free from an abrasive skin that could cause irritation or choking

  (Brufau et al., 2006)

Nuts can also:

- Control diabetes by increasing levels of the hormone glucagon-like peptide 1, which is involved in controlling glucose and insulin levels
- Help prevent blood clots
- Improve blood flow by relaxing constricted arteries
- Optimize good and bad cholesterol levels
- Prevent heart arrythmias
- Reduce inflammation associated with heart disease

  (Harvard Medical School, 2017; Mayo Clinic, 2019)

Consuming nuts may even increase life span. In 2013, Dr. Frank Hu, professor of nutrition and epidemiology at the Harvard T.H. Chan School of Public Health and his colleagues from Harvard University analyzed data from 120,000 participants in the 30-year Nurses' Health Study and Physicians' Health Study. Participants answered diet-related questions at the beginning of their studies in the 1980s and every two to four years for the following 30 years. The people who ate nuts were 20% less likely to have died during the 30-year period, and the more nuts they ate, the lower their death risk. According to Dr. Hu, "We found that people who ate nuts every day lived longer, healthier lives than people who didn't eat nuts" (Harvard Medical School, 2017).

Since domestic dogs and humans share a parallel evolution in genes related to diges-tion and metabolism, this study could have interesting implications regarding possible health benefits of nuts for dogs.

Given all of this positive nut news, you may wonder why you wouldn't want to feed them to your dog. Let's check out potential issues to see if nuts are really all they're cracked up to be.

Cons

The cons of nuts can be boiled down to three main factors:

High in fat. Yes, we just said that nuts are loaded with good fat, but it's still fat. And as you now know, more fat means more Calories. So, nuts are not the most efficient food choice for dogs who need to shed weight, are sedentary or prone to weight gain. Excess fat consumption can also trigger acute and smoldering pancreatitis, which is a concern for all dogs.

Choking hazard. As you've likely discovered, dogs are not the most genteel spe-cies when it comes to chewing their food. Combine this with the fact that nuts are just the right size to lodge in the windpipe and you have a possible recipe for a choking disaster.

Toxic when moldy. Moldy nuts can contain dangerous **aflatoxins**, highly toxic mycotoxins that can lead to serious neurological issues, including seizures or even death. You should never feed your dog any type of nut that you suspect is spoiled or moldy.

Our dish on nuts

Nuts are high in fat and Calories. However, they're also an excellent source of anti-inflammatory fats, protein, fiber, antioxidants and phytochemicals that are scientifi-cally shown to fight free radical damage in cells, improve the gut microbiome and help prevent disease (AICR, 2020). For this reason, we believe that, in *appropriate quantities*, certain types of nuts are a nutritious and beneficial food for dogs. Nuts and nut but-ters can be integrated as part of the total fat content of your dog's diet. (See Chapter 6 for fat guidelines.)

The nutty facts about soaking nuts

If you eat a lot of nuts, you probably follow the common advice to soak them first. This seems logical, considering the slew of online articles describ-ing how soaking 'activates' raw nuts, meaning that it increases digestibility and decreases anti-nutrients such as phytates and lectins. (See "Anti-nutri-ents in plant foods" for more information.)

But do claims about the benefits of soaking nuts really hold water? Research-ers of an eight-week human study published in the *European Journal of Nutrition* gave 76 nut-eating volunteers four different varieties of almonds: 1) whole unsoaked, 2) whole soaked, 3) sliced unsoaked and 4) sliced soaked. The volunteers consumed 30 grams of each variety for 12 days and rated factors such as overall enjoyment and severity of gastrointestinal symptoms. Phytate concentrations of all four nut groups were also measured using high-performance liquid chromatography (Taylor et al., 2018).

All the nuts were deemed acceptable taste-wise, however there were a couple of surprising findings:

- The *soaked* whole nuts caused *significantly more flatulence* than the unsoaked whole nuts.
- The phytate concentrations were *higher* in the *whole soaked* almonds than the whole unsoaked almonds.

So, what did the authors conclude?
> *This research supports previous results suggesting nuts, including different forms, are an acceptable food. They are also well tolerated gastrointestinally, but soaking does not improve gastrointestinal tolerance or acceptance as claimed in the lay literature* (Taylor et al., 2018, pp. 2771).

In 2020, researchers dived even deeper into the soaking waters. This study compared the effects of different types of soaking on phytate levels and mineral concentrations of whole and chopped almonds, hazelnuts, peanuts and walnuts. The methods used were: 1) raw (unsoaked), 2) soaked for 12 hours in salt solution, 3) soaked for four hours in salt solution and 4) soaked for 12 hours in water. As in the previous study, the phytate concentration of each nut type was analyzed using high-performance liquid chromatography, while minerals were measured using inductively coupled plasma mass spectrometry (Kumari et al., 2020). These researchers also cracked open some surprising findings:

- Overall, the *soaked* nuts had *lower* mineral concentrations than the raw nuts. This was especially true for chopped nuts.
- Soaking did not improve phytate to mineral ratios of the nuts.

  (Kumari et al., 2020)

The authors concluded that:
> *This research does not support claims that 'activating' nuts results in greater nutrient bioavailability* (Kumari et al., 2020, pp. 1).

So, there you have it. Research shows that soaking nuts is another nutritional myth not supported by science. We still love the creamy, silky texture that soaked nuts add to many recipes, though!

Important Note: These studies refer only to soaking nuts. As we already discussed, soaking beans and grains is beneficial.

Pro tips for nuts

Avoid a choking hazard. Grind nuts in a spice or coffee grinder or opt instead for store-bought or homemade nut butters. (See "Choose wisely.")

Create a flavor boost. Sprinkle ground nuts or a dollop of nut butter over your dog's meal to add a surprising boost of flavor.

Choose wisely. Always select single-ingredient nut butters that are free from added oil, salt or sweetener. Or, better yet, make your own. If you're using store-bought, be sure it's free from the artificial sweetener Xylitol, which is toxic for dogs.

Whip up some nut milk. Toss one cup cashews (soaked for one hour) with four cups filtered water in a high-powered blender and blend on high until smooth. We love cashew milk because there's no straining required. You can also use almonds (soaked for eight hours). Use the same nut-to-water proportion and be sure to strain with a fine-mesh strainer or nut milk bag after blending. (Note that while we already showed that soaking does not decrease anti-nutrients, it does soften the nuts for a creamier milk.)

Be aware of Brazil nuts. Brazil nuts are extremely high in selenium (68 to 91 mcg per nut), which in excessively high doses can cause severe health problems, including nervous system issues, tremors, difficulty breathing, kidney failure and heart failure. For this reason, we recommend feeding no more than 1/2 Brazil nut per 40 pounds of a dog's body weight daily.

Treat peanuts like nuts. While peanuts are technically a legume, their nutritional profile is closer to nuts, so treat them as such in your dog's diet.

Say no to mold. Always purchase fresh nuts. Store in an airtight glass container away from heat and light and toss unused portions after a couple of months. Storing nuts in the refrigerator or freezer won't harm the taste and will keep them fresher longer.

Avoid toxic types. Again, never feed your dog macadamia nuts or black walnuts, which are toxic for dogs.

Seeds

Seeds are the plant kingdom's tiny miracles—the result of a complex fertilization process that begins when flowers are pollinated. By producing and spreading seeds, plants keep their population alive. Each tiny seed contains the embryo of what will eventually become an entire plant. This embryo is encased within a protective outer coating, along with some food to nourish it. As the embryo grows, roots sprout from one end and stems from the other. A plant is born.

Because seeds contain the building blocks of entire plants, they are nutritional power-houses. Seeds are rich in fiber, protein, essential fatty acids and many important vitamins, minerals and antioxidants. Adding seeds to your dog's diet can help supercharge her health. Your dog will love them, and she won't even know they're good for her!

Let's look at some of the health benefits of our five favorite seeds.

Hemp seeds

Remember those cool braided hemp bracelets you made in camp as a kid? The fiber comes from the cannabis plant, which also produces dietary hemp. Hemp is one of the oldest domesticated crops and a superfood. Because they contain a tough outer shell, hemp seeds are commonly sold hulled as 'hemp hearts.' They have a mild, nutty flavor and are bursting with nutrition, including:

Protein powerhouse

- Hemp seeds excel in both the quantity and quality of protein. Protein provides about 23% of the Calories in hemp seeds, compared with about 13% in chia seeds and 14% in flaxseeds (MyFoodData, n.d.). The amino acid quality is comparable to other high-quality proteins, including soy and casein from dairy. The two main proteins in hemp seeds are globulin (edestin) and albumin, which are also the major proteins found in blood plasma (Donsky et al., 2013; Wang & Xiong, 2019).

Rich in essential fatty acids

- Hemp hearts are an excellent source of the essential fatty acids LA (omega-6) and ALA (omega-3). The omega-6 to omega-3 fatty acid ratio is about 3:1, which is rare in nature and considered optimal for fighting inflammation and protecting against chronic inflammatory diseases such as arthritis, autoimmune disorders, heart disease and cancer. Hemp seeds also provide **gamma-linolenic acid (GLA)** (Donsky et al., 2013), an anti-inflammatory omega-6 fatty acid often used to treat chronic skin conditions in dogs. (We'll discuss GLA in greater detail when we talk about oils).

Packed with vitamins and minerals

- Hemp hearts provide a variety of vitamins and minerals, including B vitamins, copper, manganese, magnesium, phosphorus, zinc and iron (Wang & Xiong, 2019).

Highly digestible

- Protein from hemp hearts is up to 97.5% digestible, compared with 97.6% for casein (milk) protein (Wang & Xiong, 2019). This is good news for dogs with sensitive stomachs.

Low allergen

- Hemp seeds are a low-allergen food (Wang & Xiong, 2019), making them the perfect dietary addition for dogs with food intolerances.

You might have come across an AAFCO position paper calling for more research into the use of hemp products in pet foods (AAFCO, 2021). Please note that AAFCO's concern arises out of the unknown health effects of psychotropic cannabinoids, which are *not* present in dietary hemp seeds sold at your local grocery store. Dietary hemp comes from a different strain of cannabis plant than marijuana and contains no psychotropic properties. So, don't worry. Your dog will get happy eating hemp hearts, but she won't get high!

Since hemp hearts are tiny and easy to digest, they do not need to be ground prior to serving them to your dog.

Flaxseeds

Flax is another ancient crop that has been used for thousands of years as both a textile and a superfood. In fact, the word 'linen' comes from the flax plant's Latin name, *Linum usitatissimum*. Flaxseeds were first cultivated around 3000 BCE and have been prized throughout history for their health benefits. Hippocrates recommended flaxseeds to patients with abdominal pains. In the eighth century, the French Emperor Charlemagne prized flaxseeds so much that he passed a law requiring his subjects to consume them! What got Hippocrates and Charlemagne so revved up about flaxseeds? They are:

High in ALA (essential omega-3 fatty acid)

- One tablespoon of flaxseeds contains a whopping 6.7 grams of ALA, which supports a healthy heart, blocks the growth of tumor cells and helps prevent chronic inflammatory diseases (Donsky et al., 2013).

Rich in lignans

- Lignans in flaxseeds are phytoestrogens, natural plant chemicals that act as antioxidants and mimic estrogen in the body. Lignans have been found to protect against a variety of cancers, particularly breast, colon and prostate (Donsky et al., 2013). Flax lignans are also used as a natural method to lower the hormone estradiol in dogs with Cushing's disease.

Full of fiber

- The soluble and insoluble fibers in flaxseeds help promote healthy digestion, control weight gain by creating a feeling of fullness, stabilize blood sugar levels and lower cholesterol.

Great for skin and coat health

- A 2001 study of 18 healthy dogs showed that one-month supplementation with either flaxseeds or sunflower seeds resulted in a temporary improvement of skin and coat health (Reese et al., 2001).

- Flaxseeds have a tough outer shell that must be broken down to release the nutrients. Purchase ground flaxseeds, also called flax meal, or grind them yourself in a spice or coffee grinder. Store flaxseeds in the refrigerator and replace them every couple of months, as they quickly go rancid.

Chia seeds

Chia seeds come from *Salvia hispanica*, a flowering desert plant in the mint family. Chia was first cultivated around 3,500 BCE in Mexico and Guatemala and was an important part of the diet of many ancient cultures, including the Aztecs and Mayans. The Mayans believed that chia seeds contain supernatural powers. In Mayan, chia means 'strength.'

Like hemp and flaxseeds, chia seeds are rich in essential fatty acids, antioxidants and fiber that support optimum health. Benefits of chia seeds include:

Improve weight loss

- A study out of the University of Toronto in Canada found that people with Type 2 diabetes who consumed about one-third cup of chia seeds per day for six months lost eight times more weight (four pounds compared to one-half pound) than those who ate oat bran and inulin fiber. Moreover, the type of fat lost by the chia eaters was visceral fat, a dangerous type of fat that accumulates around organs and is linked to insulin resistance and hardening of the arteries (Vuksan et al., 2016; Oldfield, 2017). (Note that we always want to adjust human amounts appropriately for our canine companions.)

Packed with omega-3s

- Sixty percent (59.8%) of the fatty acids in chia seeds are made up of the essential omega-3 fatty acid ALA (Ciftci et al., 2012).

Reduce inflammation

- The Canadian study in people with Type 2 diabetes also found that consuming chia seeds daily reduced C-reactive protein, a blood marker for inflammation, by about 40% (Vuksan et al., 2016; Oldfield, 2017).

Provide satiety

- Chia seeds have an amazing sponge-like quality and are able to soak up about 10 times their weight in water. When mixed with liquid, the seeds expand and form into a gel, providing a feeling of fullness without adding extra Calories.

Nutrient rich

- Chia seeds are high in several minerals, including calcium, copper, iron, magnesium and zinc.

When shopping for chia seeds, you might notice black and white varieties. The black seeds are slightly smaller, but there is no significant nutritional difference between the two. Chia seeds do not need to be ground before eating. However, because they expand when mixed with liquid, we recommend pre-soaking them at a ratio of four parts liquid to one part chia seeds for at least 20 minutes prior to serving.

Pumpkin seeds

You've probably fed pureed pumpkin to your dog at some point to aid in digestion, but pumpkin's real health jewels extend far beyond what's scooped out of a can; they are stored in the seeds of the fruit. In recent years, research into the therapeutic benefits of pumpkin seeds has gained popularity in the scientific community in the fields of chemistry, biology, pharmacology and health, with a focus on their nutraceutical compounds. To date, three primary aspects of pumpkin seeds have gained the most attention for their health-promoting potential—fatty acids, phytoestrogens and tocopherol (Lestari & Meiyanto, 2018).

Research shows that pumpkin seeds contain powerful biological activity with a variety of potential therapeutic benefits, including:

Antioxidant power

- Carotenoids and vitamin E scavenge free radicals and inhibit lipoxygenase (oxidation of lipids that leads to free radicals) (Xanthopoulou et al., 2009).

Anti-cancer properties

- Pumpkin seeds contain lignans, which are shown to reduce cancer risk, including gastric, prostate, breast, lung and colorectal (Stevenson et al., 2007; Lelley et al., 2009; Nesaretnam et al., 2007).

Eye health benefits

- Lutein found in pumpkin seeds may reduce the risk of age-related macular degeneration (Lelley et al., 2009).

Help ease arthritis

- Pumpkin seeds may serve as a natural therapy for arthritis due to their ability to reduce free radicals (Fahim et al., 1995).

You might have heard pumpkin seeds also referred to as *pepitas*, which in Spanish means 'little squash.' Pepitas are often used to describe pumpkin seeds that have had the hard white hull removed, but this isn't correct. Pepitas are actually a type of seed that grows shell-free inside of hull-less pumpkins (Slagle, 2019)! These tender green seeds are far easier to digest and so are the type we recommend giving to your dog. Grind before serving to further increase digestibility.

Sunflower seeds

If you think sunflower seeds are just for the birds, think again. The seeds of the sunflower plant *(Helianthus annuus)* are rich in nutrients shown to aid in fighting bacterial and fungal infections and a variety of chronic inflammatory conditions, including cardiovascular diseases, skin diseases and even cancers (Nandha et al., 2014).

Benefits of sunflower seeds include:

Heart-healthy

- Phytosterols, also called plant sterols, are molecules found naturally in the cell membranes of plants. In humans, phytosterols are credited with supporting heart health by blocking the absorption of cholesterol (Phillips et al., 2005; Ramprasath & Awad, 2015).

Anti-cancer impact

- Animal studies have demonstrated that phytosterols can protect against cancers of the breast, prostate, lung, liver, stomach and ovary (Phillips et al., 2005; Ramprasath & Awad, 2015).

Fight free radicals

- Sunflower seeds are rich in selenium and vitamin E, antioxidants that protect cells from oxidative damage caused by free radicals. In this way, sunflower seeds help protect against inflammation, protect the heart and fight tumor growth (Nandha et al., 2014).

Packed with nutrients

- In addition to providing vitamin E, sunflower seeds are a good source of niacin, pyridoxine, pantothenic acid and folic acid, as well as calcium, copper, iron, magnesium, manganese, selenium, phosphorus, potassium, sodium and zinc.

Promote skin health

- As with flaxseeds, dogs who consumed sunflower seeds for one month showed a concurrent improvement in skin and hair coat (Rees et al., 2001). In humans, the topical application of sunflower oil improved skin hydration with no negative side effects. Treatment with topical olive oil, on the other hand, significantly damaged the integrity of the skin barrier, potentially worsening atopic dermatitis (Danby et al., 2013).

There is no natural shell-free pepita version of sunflower seeds, so be sure to purchase pre-shelled seeds. Grind before serving to improve digestion.

Pro tips for seeds

Mix them up. Feed a variety of seeds to your dog to provide the full array of benefits. Sprinkle them on meals, bake them into treats, mix into nut butter or combine with oatmeal for a nutritional boost.

Do an egg swap. Swap chia or ground flaxseeds for eggs in your fresh-baked treats. Mix one tablespoon of ground flax meal or chia seeds with three tablespoons of water per egg. Let thicken for 15 minutes before incorporating into your recipe.

Make puppy pudding. Whip up a tasty and nutritious chia pudding. Stir four tablespoons of chia seeds into one cup unsweetened dog-friendly plant-based milk (organic cashew, almond, or soy milk works well). Add two teaspoons maple syrup (optional). Stir, let rest for a few minutes and stir again. Cover and refrigerate overnight. Stir again before portioning. Kick it up with your favorite dog-friendly fruit. Store in a closed container in the refrigerator for up to four days.

Go organic. Opt for organic seeds whenever possible. Conventional seeds may be sprayed with pesticides, herbicides, fungicides, insecticides and chemical fertilizers—all of which you want to avoid giving your dog.

Watch the tummy. When feeding seeds to your dog, remember not to give too much of a good thing, which could cause gastric upset.

Oils

We find that people typically make the following mistakes when giving their dog dietary oil:

- Not understanding the purpose
- Adding too many different types
- Adding the wrong types
- Giving too much or too little

These mistakes can potentially trigger an attack of acute pancreatitis (when adding too much) and can even result in long-term chronic inflammation by creating an imbalance of omega-6 to omega-3 fatty acids (when adding the wrong types). In this section, we'll give you the skinny on dietary oils so that you can use them confidently and with purpose. We will also divulge which types of oils to avoid.

Vegetable oils are made up of a combination of different types of fats: saturated, monounsaturated and polyunsaturated. The predominant type depends upon the oil (e.g., coconut, palm and palm kernel oils are highest in saturated fat). Oils are 100% fat (14 g per tablespoon), so they don't contain protein or carbohydrates. They are also not a good source of vitamins or minerals (except potentially vitamin E). Their primary benefits derive from the important role dietary fats play as part of a healthy diet, including:

- Helping the body absorb fat-soluble vitamins
- Increasing the bioavailability of beta-carotene consumed from vegetables
- Providing essential omega-3 and omega-6 fatty acids
- Potentially serving as a source of vitamin E (certain oils only, such as wheat germ, hazelnut and almond)
- Supporting healthy cell structure, brain and nerve function
- Supplying energy-dense Calories

Oils or seeds: Which are best?

As you just discovered, seeds provide a combination of fat, protein, carbohydrates and fiber along with a variety of vitamins, minerals, antioxidants and phytochemicals. They are also an excellent source of essential omega-3 and omega-6 fatty acids. Oils, on the other hand, are pretty much pure fat. Certain oils contain antioxidants, such as vitamin E, but they don't provide protein, carbohydrates or fiber and they are not a valid source of vitamins and minerals your dog needs to thrive. In addition, over-feeding oils can drive down the nutrient density of your recipes. For this reason, when building recipes for adult dogs at a maintenance stage, we recommend replacing at least part of the oil with seeds whenever possible.

The following chart compares Calories and a few key nutrients contained in the seed and oil forms of flax and hemp.

Flax and Hemp Seeds vs. Oils Nutrient Comparison Chart

Food	Amount	Calories	Fat (g)	Pro-tein (g)	Cal-cium (mg)	Mag-nesium (mg)	Potas-sium (mg)	Iron (mg)
Flaxseeds (whole)	1 TB/10 g	55	4.3	2	26	40	84	0.6
Flaxseed oil	1 TB/14 g	120	13.6	0	0	0	0	0
Hemp hearts	1 TB/10 g	55	4.9	3	7	70	120	0.8
Hemp seed oil (Humming Hemp cold pressed/ extra virgin)	1 TB/15 g	120	13	0	0	0	0	0

(Source: MyFoodData, n.d.-a; MyFoodData, n.d.-b; MyNetDiary, 2021)

In looking at this chart, which do you think will provide your dog with more complete nourishment: seeds or oils? Seeds, of course!

There are, as always, exceptions to the rule. You might want to opt for oils over seeds—or in addition to seeds—if your dog:

- Experiences a lack of appetite due to illness (requiring more Calories with less volume of food)
- Is a high-performance dog
- Needs to gain weight
- Suffers from intestinal issues that prevent proper digestion of seeds

As you can see from the chart, seeds contain about half the Calories of oils and far less fat, so you'll need to take this into account when building your recipes. For your convenience, Chapter 6 contains a comprehensive Ingredients Reference Chart that includes the Calories and fat of different types of oils, seeds and nut butters.

Phytoplankton/Microalgae oil

To recap, the three types of essential omega-3 fatty acids for adult dogs are: alpha-linolenic acid (ALA), eicosapentaenoic acid (EPA) and docosahexaenoic acid (DHA). (Note that linoleic acid, or LA, is an essential omega-6 fatty acid). We've already discussed the many benefits of ALA and foods that provide them, but you might recall that ALA is not an adequate substitute for EPA and DHA. This is because dogs cannot efficiently convert ALA to EPA or DHA, so they must get these essential omega-3 fatty acids directly from their diet.

When we think of sources of EPA and DHA, it's natural to think of fish oil because this is the ingredient used in most supplements. But harvesting fish for their oil comes with a steep environmental and ethical cost: decimating our oceans' ecosystems and destroying marine life.

Anchovies, herring and menhaden are the main fish sources of EPA and DHA. These small, oily fish live in a layer of the open ocean called the pelagic zone, where they play a critical role in transferring energy originating from the sun to large predatory fish. The cycle begins with phytoplankton (microscopic marine algae), which float in the upper part of the ocean. Like land plants, phytoplankton feed on sunlight. The sunlight penetrates the water, transferring its energy to the phytoplankton, which then process it into energy via photosynthesis. The small fish then eat the phytoplankton and in turn are eaten by larger fish. Removing the middleman from this process—in this case the small fish—disrupts the entire system of energy transfer, leaving larger fish without their primary food and energy source. As these delicate ecosystems collapse, the populations of larger fish that rely on them also collapse (Gross, T., 2018). In other words, by using anchovies, herring and menhaden fish as supplement ingredients, we are literally creating an oceanic famine.

Krill, another pelagic species, has become the new 'in vogue' ingredient for EPA and DHA supplements, but sadly decimation of krill carries the same disastrous consequences. Krill are tiny crustaceans that float in huge swarms. The most common species live in the open oceans around Antarctica, where they serve as a critical part of the food chain. Krill also feed on phytoplankton that bloom in the waters and are in turn eaten by larger predators, including whales, seals, penguins, albatross, squid and other fish species. Just as with anchovies, herring and menhaden, destroying the krill population devastates all the species that rely on them as their primary energy source (Oceana, n.d.). According to the website Krill Facts, "Without krill there would be no fuel to the engine that runs the Earth's marine ecosystems—more directly without krill, most of the life forms in the Antarctic would disappear" (Krill Facts, n.d.).

Fortunately, there is a nutritious, sustainable and cruelty-free alternative for dietary EPA and DHA that goes right to the original source: the phytoplankton, or microalgae. Algae-based lipids have even been shown to contain a higher percentage of omega-3 fatty acids (43.97%) by molecular weight than fish oil (33.75%) (Conchillo et al., 2006).

You may be thinking, "That sounds great, but what about bioavailability? Fish and krill oil must be more bioavailable than algae oil." Well, hold on because we have a revelation for you. It's summed up very well in this article published in the journal Biotechnology Advances:

> Specifically, marine phytoplankton and other single-cell algae are the main producers of omega-3 PUFAs, particularly EPA and DHA, and represent the basis of the food web for all aquatic creatures (Randall et al., 1990). Humans obtain omega-3 PUFAs through multiple levels of this food web: microalgae, which are directly used for food products or as animal feed; fish, which consume phytoplankton directly or eat other animals that feed on phytoplankton; and livestock, which are fed meal produced from various organisms in the food web (Borowitzka, 1997). In essence, phytoplankton are the origin of the majority of our omega-3 PUFAs (Kang, 2011, pp. 2).

Did you catch that? Phytoplankton, or microalgae, are the *original* source of EPA and DHA. The primary reason that fish and other species provide these omega-3s is because they consume the algae.

Since the use of microalgae oil is just gaining in popularity, more research is needed on its benefits, but the results are already promising. A 2008 study of 32 healthy men and women aged 20 to 65 showed that DHA from microalgae-based capsules was nutritionally equivalent to cooked salmon (Arterburn et al., 2008). A 2015 study showed that mice given DHA from microalgae oil showed improved memory function (Xu et al., 2015).

Just like land crops, microalgae are a renewable resource. In fact, microalgae grow 10 times faster than land crops and require only one-tenth of the land to produce the same amount of crop. A bonus is that growing microalgae benefits the environment rather than harming it (Winwood, 2013; Kite-Powell, 2018). We look forward to the day when phytoplankton are the sustainable source for supplemental EPA and DHA, leaving our oceans, and their precious biospheres, in harmony as nature intended.

In Chapter 6, we'll provide the recommended dosing of EPA + DHA for healthy adult dogs at maintenance, while in Chapter 11 you'll find the recommended dosing for dogs with chronic kidney disease. (See Resources for products.)

Other oils

Here's a rundown of a few other common oils with our recommendations regarding their usage:

Coconut oil

When we wrote our previous book, *Canine Nutrigenomics*, we touted coconut oil as a superfood. Since that time, coconut oil has come under additional scrutiny and once again it's the focus of debate. Is coconut oil healthy or not? Let's take a closer look at the latest evidence.

For years, coconut oil was considered unhealthy because it is made up of about 90% saturated fat—higher than butter (about 64%), beef fat (40%) and even lard (40%) (Willett, 2018). Consuming a lot of saturated fat raises bad cholesterol levels in people, which can lead to clogged arteries and heart disease. (Note that controlling dietary saturated fat intake is more important for people than for dogs, because dogs don't suffer from the same cholesterol-related cardiac issues.)

Eventually, the coconut oil tide turned, and it gained favor among health enthusiasts. The reason is that although coconut oil is a saturated fat, it's made up mainly of lauric acid, which is a medium-chain fatty acid, also called a medium-chain triglyceride (MCT). Short, medium and long-chain fatty acids are grouped by the number of carbon atoms in their chain. In general terms, short-chain fatty acids (SCFAs) are defined as having fewer than six carbon atoms, MCTs contain 6 to 12 carbon atoms and long-chain fatty acids (LCFAs) have 13 to 21 carbon atoms (Brown, 2020).

Coconut oil contains five main types of MCTs (the abbreviation after each name indicates the number of carbon atoms):

- Caproic acid (C6)
- Caprylic acid (C8)
- Capric acid (C10)
- Lauric acid (C12)

MCTs have been studied for a variety of health benefits, which primarily stem from the way they're broken down in the body. Basically, MCTs are more quickly converted to energy than LCFAs. Since they're quickly and efficiently converted to fuel, Calories from MCTs are less likely to end up stored as fat. In fact, MCTs are metabolized so efficiently that they result in the body taking in about 10% fewer Calories than when consuming foods containing LCFAs. MCTs have even been shown to help with obesity by reducing both body weight and body fat (Fernando et al., 2015).

In addition, energy from MCTs can cross the blood-brain barrier. The brain prefers to use glucose for energy, but when dogs and people get older, we break down glucose less efficiently, potentially leaving the brain short on fuel. In these situations, ketones produced from MCT metabolism can serve as excellent 'brain food' for individuals with cognitive impairment. Research also shows that MCTs as part of a ketogenic diet help control seizures in children with epilepsy (Chang et al., 2013; Brown & Link, 2020). (See more on the ketogenic diet in Chapter 8.)

Given that MCTs clearly offer some hefty health benefits, what could possibly be the downside of coconut oil? The debate focuses on coconut oil's main fatty acid, lauric acid. It turns out that lauric acid might be an 'imposter' MCT. Consensus is growing that lauric acid behaves more like an LCFA because it is metabolized and absorbed into the body slower than other MCTs. To add to the confusion, there is no one clear definition of an MCT versus an LCFA, as it is often based on comparison. We have seen literature defining LCFAs beginning with 12 carbon atoms, placing lauric acid in that group (Bruss, 2008).

So, while true MCTs show multiple health benefits, lauric acid might not. And almost half the fatty acid content of coconut oil is lauric acid, while caproic, caprylic and capric acid together make up only about 20% (Fernando et al., 2015).

Many studies on the health benefits of coconut oil were conducted using a special man-made formulation of MCTs—not the lauric acid-rich coconut oil found in grocery stores (Malik, 2019; Brown, 2020). A 2015 review article on the benefits of coconut oil for treatment of Alzheimer's disease confirms this:

> *A small number of clinical trials and animal studies using a formulation of MCT have reported significant improvement of cognition in AD patients. At the same time, studies in which the diet has been supplemented with SFA [saturated fatty acids], particularly hydrogenated coconut oil, have reported deleterious effects on hippocampal morphology and behaviour, and increased plasma LDL levels.... It must be emphasised that the use of coconut oil to treat or prevent AD is not supported by any peer-reviewed large cohort clinical data; any positive findings are based on small clinical trials and on anecdotal evidence; however, coconut remains a compound of interest requiring further investigation* (Fernando et al., 2015, pp. 9).

Still, lauric acid shouldn't be dismissed as the 'red-headed stepchild' of fatty acids. Even if it doesn't behave precisely like other MCTs, it's been shown to provide its own health benefits. Perhaps lauric acid's most promising benefit for dogs is its anti-cancer potential. Researchers have found that it mediates gene expression in a way that both reduces proliferation and creates apoptosis of tumor cells (Lappano et al., 2017).

Where do we stand today regarding the use of coconut oil? Given the current state of knowledge, we no longer deem most store-bought coconut oil to be a superfood; however, we agree that it remains a compound of interest requiring further investigation.

We want to point out one more important note about coconut oil: It does not contain essential omega-3 fatty acids (ALA, EPA, DHA) and only a negligible level of essential omega-6s (LA) . Therefore, it cannot be substituted for other dietary oils that are rich in these nutrients, such as seed (LA, ALA) and microalgae (EPA, DHA) oils.

Extra virgin olive oil

There's a good reason why olive oil takes center stage as part of the Mediterranean diet, which is consistently recognized as one of the healthiest diets on the planet. Olive oil is packed with **polyphenols**, phytochemicals that act as antioxidants and may protect against cancer, cardiovascular disease and neurodegenerative disease by:

- Decreasing inflammation
- Fighting free radicals
- Modulating the immune system response
- Inhibiting accumulation of fatty plaque in the arteries
- Protecting cells from transforming into tumors
- Reducing formation of blood clots in blood vessels

  (Gorzynik-Debicka et al., 2018)

Opt for extra virgin olive oil, which uses mechanical pressing rather than chemicals or heat to extract the oil. The higher price tag is well worth the health benefits.

Black currant and evening primrose oils

Black currant and evening primrose oils are rich in gamma-linolenic acid (GLA), a non-essential omega-6 fatty acid. Unlike other omega-6 fatty acids that are pro-inflammatory in high doses, GLA possesses strong *anti-inflammatory* properties. One way that GLA reduces inflammation is by interfering with the body's breakdown of arachidonic acid (AA), an essential omega-6 fatty acid that is pro-inflammatory at high levels. When the body ingests GLA, it quickly converts it into dihomo-GLA, or DGLA. DGLA intervenes with enzymes that break down AA, preventing these enzymes from turning AA into pro-inflammatory signaling molecules. Instead, the enzymes break down DGLA into anti-inflammatory products. GLA also works via other mechanisms in the body to control the inflammatory process.

Some of the conditions GLA is purported to benefit include:

- Autoimmune diseases
- Cancer
- Dry eye
- Eczema and other skin conditions
- Heart disease
- Lung issues

- Obesity
- Rheumatoid arthritis

GLA also helps to restore the skin's moisture barrier, which is why we often recommend it for dogs suffering from dry skin.

Black currant oil contains 15% to 20% GLA and is also rich in ALA. Evening primrose oil is made up of about 13% GLA and about 72% LA.

Note that borage oil, which comes from the seeds of the borage plant, contains more GLA than any other oil, at 20% to 26% of its total fatty acid content. However, we do not recommend it because it might contain pyrrolizidine alkaloids, which are toxic to the liver. Instead, we choose to use caution and opt for either evening primrose or black currant oil.

Be aware that dogs prone to seizures should not consume GLA, as it has been shown to lower the seizure threshold and potentially interact with anti-seizure medications. GLA may also slow blood clotting, so dogs with bleeding disorders or those on medications that slow clotting should not take GLA. If your dog is going to have surgery, including a dental procedure, discontinue use of GLA at least two weeks prior to the procedure.

Oils to avoid
We recommend avoiding the following oils:

Canola
- Highly refined using high heat and chemicals
- Known as an RBD (refined, bleached, deodorized) oil
- A Top 4 GMO oil (93% of U.S. canola crops are GMO)

Corn
- Contains more than 50% omega-6 fatty acids (excessive omega-6 intake is inflammatory)
- Highly refined RBD oil
- Top 4 GMO oil (88% of U.S. corn crops are GMO)

Cottonseed
- Contains more than 50% omega-6 fatty acids
- Highly refined RBD oil
- Top 4 GMO oil (90% of U.S. cotton crops are GMO)

Palm
- Highly refined RBD oil
- High in saturated fat
- Associated with deforestation
- Can increase skin and mouth cancer risk

Soybean (Note that this is different from organic whole-food soy products.)
- Contains more than 50% omega-6 fatty acids
- Highly refined RBD oil
- Top 4 GMO oil (94% of U.S. soy crops are GMO)

Vegetable oil
- Made up of a mixture of different types of oils not listed on the label
- Likely highly refined, RBD and GMO
- Likely high in omega-6 fatty acids

   (Broaddus, 2016; Gunnars, 2018; Kubala, 2019; Pascual et al., 2021)

Pro tips for oils

Avoid heating. Heating dietary oils generates free radicals that cause oxidative damage, which creates cellular and molecular damage (Venkata & Subramanyam, 2016).

Give it a squeeze. Many microalgae-based EPA + DHA supplements contain carrageenan and/or cornstarch as part of their soft gel, which are best avoided. To bypass these ingredients, we recommend pricking the soft gel with a toothpick or cocktail skewer, squeezing the oil into your dog's food and discarding the capsule. Just be careful where you aim, or you might find that you've coated your clothes with oil rather than the food!

Opt for expeller pressed. There are two methods to extract oil from seeds or nuts: mechanically or chemically. Expeller pressing is a chemical-free process that uses a machine to physically squeeze the oil from the nut or seed. If your oil is not expeller pressed, it has likely been extracted using hexane, a petroleum product made from crude oil. (Note that foods carrying the USDA Organic seal cannot use hexane.)

Steer clear of hydrogenated oils (trans fats). Hydrogenated oils are created when oils that are normally liquid at room temperature are converted into a solid by the addition of hydrogen atoms. The result is an abnormal chemical structure that has been directly linked to serious health issues, including cardiovascular diseases, breast cancer, shortening of pregnancy period, risks of preeclampsia, nervous system and vision disorders in infants, colon cancer, diabetes, obesity and allergy. The most common hydrogenated oils are margarine and vegetable shortening (Dhaka et al., 2011).

Store in a cool, dark place. While high levels of unsaturated fat provide health benefits, they also increase the risk of oils turning rancid. Consuming rancid oil doesn't only smell and taste bad; it can also irritate the GI tract and cause nausea, vomiting and diarrhea. But that's not all. When oil spoils, it undergoes a chemical change and can develop harmful free radicals, which when consumed can damage cells and lead to future health issues, including cognitive impairment, diabetes and other conditions (Okparanta et al., 2018). Be sure to store oils in a dark glass container away from heat and light. More delicate oils that go rancid quickly, such as flax and hemp, should be stored in the refrigerator.

Watch out for rosemary. Many vegan omega-3 products contain rosemary extract as a preservative. Avoid these products if your dog suffers from seizures. We have provided a rosemary-free algae omega alternative in the Resources section.

Add-ons

Nutritional yeast

Nutritional yeast is a fungus that comes from the species *Saccharomyces cerevisiae*. The word 'yeast' scares some people because they associate it with bad types of yeast, such as Candida, that contribute to fungal overgrowth in the body. But nutritional yeast has been deactivated through pasteurization. So, while it won't make bread rise, it also won't cause or worsen yeast overgrowth (Tweed, 2017).

Nutritional yeast packs major nutrition into a small quantity. Sixty-three percent of the Calories in nutritional yeast come from protein, with a whopping 10 grams packed into just two tablespoons (MyFoodData., n.d.-c). Nutritional yeast is also a good source of B vitamins, trace minerals, antioxidants and complex carbohydrates.

Note that nutritional yeast is available either fortified or unfortified. Fortified varieties contain higher levels of B vitamins (this will be indicated in the ingredients list). Unfortified nutritional yeast still contains some B vitamins, but at lower levels that form naturally during the yeast growing process. Be aware that unfortified nutritional yeast products do not contain vitamin B12, which is especially important in plant-based diets. We do not recommend relying solely on nutritional yeast to supply your dog's B vitamins, as we find this is not a sufficient source.

Nutritional yeast is sold as flakes, granules or powder, so it's simple to sprinkle onto your dog's meals for a tasty, healthy nutritional boost. (See Resources.)

Many people confuse nutritional yeast with brewer's yeast. While both come from the species *Saccharomyces cerevisiae*, they are not the same product. Brewer's yeast gets its name because it's used in the beer-making process, so it's typically grown on grains, such as malted barley. What's left over can be sold as a nutritional supplement; however, it has a very bitter and unpleasant taste. Nutritional yeast is produced specifically as a food supplement and so is typically grown on molasses from sugar beets or cane sugar (Julson, 2017; Tweed, 2017). It has a cheesy, nutty taste that we love—and so do most dogs. In Chapter 12, we'll talk about an interesting benefit of both types of yeast.

Protein powder

Protein powders made from organic, non-GMO ingredients such as soy, hemp or peas can boost both the total protein and the individual amino acid content of your dog's diet. Review the packaging carefully to ensure the product is free from any animal ingredients, such as whey, casein, egg and collagen. Also be certain that it contains no xylitol or other ingredients that are toxic for dogs. Select unflavored, unsweetened protein powder containing a single dog-friendly ingredient or a combination. (See Resources.)

Spirulina

Spirulina is a type of ancient, microscopic blue-green algae that takes its name from the spiral shape of its strands. Like nutritional yeast, spirulina gets 63% of its Calories from protein (MyFoodData, n.d.-d). Spirulina's beautiful deep green hue comes courtesy of chlorophyll; as we previously discussed, chlorophyll contains powerful anti-cancer properties.

Phycocyanin, another pigment in spirulina that provides an intense blue color, functions as an antioxidant with anti-inflammatory, anti-cancer, neuroprotective and hepatoprotective (liver protective) effects. Phycocyanin is also reported to enhance immune function (Greque de Morais et al., 2018) and is being studied as a promising drug to treat cancer due to its ability to both kill and block the proliferation of cancer cells (Jiang et al., 2017).

Spirulina is considered so nutritious, in fact, that both the National Aeronautics and Space Administration (NASA) and the European Space Agency (ESA) have deemed it worthy of nourishing astronauts on long space missions (Satyaraj et al., 2021)!

If your dog suffers from GI issues, be sure to check out Chapter 12 for the results of an amazing 2021 study demonstrating spirulina's effects on gut immunity and microbiota stability in dogs (Satyaraj et al., 2021).

While spirulina boasts superfood benefits, there are also serious potential dangers. Spirulina grows naturally in both fresh and salt waters. If the waters or surrounding air are contaminated with toxins such as heavy metals (e.g., lead, mercury, arsenic), pesticides, herbicides and/or microcystin, the spirulina will absorb these toxins and become dangerously contaminated. Spirulina grown in sea water can also absorb dangerous levels of iodine. In addition, some types of freshwater blue-green algae form algal blooms that result in the production of cyanotoxins such as microcystins, which the United States Environmental Protection Agency (EPA) classifies as a "potent liver toxin and possible human carcinogen" (EPA, 2021). Be sure to seek out a reputable company that sources their spirulina from pristine waters and provides a recent Certificate of Analysis that includes testing for heavy metals, other environmental pollutants and microcystins. (See Resources.)

Textured vegetable protein (TVP)

Textured vegetable protein (TVP)—also called textured soy protein (TSP)—often gets a bad reputation that is associated with fake meats and other highly processed vegan convenience foods. But does TVP deserve its devilish reputation? Let's see.

What is TVP?

TVP has been around for decades. It was invented in the 1960s by the Archer Daniels Midland company, which still owns the registered trademarked name TVP. TVP is the same as TSP. It's manufactured by separating the protein from the rest of the soybean (fat, fiber, carbs), creating what's known as 'soy protein isolate.' The soy protein flour is mixed with water and then put through an extruder at high temperatures and pressure. As it comes out through holes at the other end, it's cut into small pieces, which expand from the drop in pressure outside the extruder. The pieces are then dried or baked (Kondal, 2019; Sennebogen, 2021).

Is TVP/TSP healthy?

As we've already discussed, soybeans are an excellent source of protein, providing all the essential amino acids that dogs need. TVP is a concentrated source of soy protein, so in that sense it is healthy. It's also fat-free, making it suitable for dogs requiring a low-fat diet. And since TVP basically takes on the flavor of anything you mix it with, it can be a palatable option for picky eaters.

Unfortunately, the story doesn't end there. TVP is highly processed, and we're all about eating as much fresh, whole food as possible. To add another notch against it, non-organic TVP is likely manufactured using the chemical hexane. And even if we and our dogs only get a small amount of hexane from TVP, who needs any extra chemicals?

What's the bottom line on TVP/TSP?

Like many things in life, the case for or against TVP is not black and white. While we don't recommend it as a primary source of protein under normal circumstances, there are times when using it in your dog's diet makes sense. Diana worked with a client whose 95-pound Dogo Argentino dog suffered from colitis, pancreatitis and severe food sensitivities per the NutriScan saliva-based diagnostic test. (See Chapter 10.) However, she was not intolerant to soy. This dog needed a high-Calorie, protein-rich, low-fat, non-antigenic diet to help her gain weight and avoid triggering an attack of colitis or pancreatitis. It was quite a challenge! After trying out many different foods, a balanced diet based on TVP and tapioca pearls did the trick, enabling the dog to gain weight without rousing uncomfortable and concerning gastrointestinal issues.

So, while we prefer using fresh, whole foods whenever possible, there are times when the compromise of a more processed food such as TVP is warranted and even beneficial. As we always say, every dog is an individual. For Diana's client, TVP was literally a lifesaver.

If you do use TVP/TSP in your recipes, always select a non-GMO product. Opting for organic will give even more bang for your buck: you'll get the double benefit of non-GMO soy and a chemical free food, since processing with hexane is not allowed according to USDA organic standards. (See Resources.)

In addition to the tasty, nutritious foods detailed in this chapter, there is an entire plant-based world of functional ingredients, including spices, herbs, seaweed and edible fungi. We'll discuss many of these ingredients in Part 2 under the various health conditions they best support.

Anti-nutrients in plant foods

Anti-nutrients are naturally occurring compounds that protect plants against predators and disease. These compounds can be found in a variety of plant foods, including legumes, grains, nuts and seeds. They are called 'anti' (against) nutrients because they can potentially reduce the bioavailability of certain nutrients, including some minerals. The most common anti-nutrients are goitrogens, lectins, oxalates, phytoestrogens, phytates and tannins (Petroski & Minich, 2020).

An entire industry is built around convincing people to avoid consuming a whole-food plant-based diet due to the presence of anti-nutrients. Interestingly, some of the anti-plant food people (including certain doctors) have built lucrative businesses selling supplements that supposedly counteract the negative effects of anti-nutrients—for a steep cost to the consumer, of course.

Let's look at the different types of anti-nutrients, what science says about them and our recommendations for including them in your dog's diet:

Goitrogens

- **Foods**. Cruciferous vegetables (e.g., broccoli, broccoli sprouts, Chinese cabbage, collard greens, kale), millet, cassava, soy, flaxseeds.

- **Possible anti-nutrient actions**. May impair thyroid function in hypothyroid individuals

- **Health benefits**. Glucosinolates are a type of goitrogen in cruciferous vegetables that break down to sulforaphane, a compound with strong anti-cancer activity. (See Chapter 8.)

- **Reducing**. Steaming and boiling decrease goitrogens, however cooking also reduces beneficial glucosinolates. Steaming broccoli for just five minutes eliminates more than half (51%) of the glucosinolate content (Hwang & Kim, 2013).

Bottom line. Most studies show that goitrogenic foods only negatively impact thyroid function when there is not enough iodine in the diet. For hypothyroid dogs or those at risk of low thyroid function, we recommend lightly steaming these foods to reduce their goitrogenic activity. Also, make sure your dog receives appropriate levels of dietary iodine along with the proper dosage of thyroid hormone replacement medication (Dodds & Laverdure, 2011; Petroski & Minch, 2020). (See also "The scoop on soy" earlier in this chapter.)

Lectins

- **Foods**. Legumes, cereal grains, seeds, nuts, fruits, vegetables (highest levels are found in uncooked legumes and whole grains).

- **Proposed anti-nutrient actions**. Gut inflammation, leaky gut, reduced nutrient absorption, poisoning from phytohemagglutinin (PHA) in raw or undercooked legumes.

- **Health benefits**. Certain lectins possess powerful anti-cancer activity. (See Chapter 8.)

- **Reducing**. Soaking legumes and boiling for at least one hour or cooking in a pressure cooker (such as InstantPot) significantly decreases lectins, including PHA. Microwaving and slow cooking do *not* adequately destroy lectins.

Bottom line. Denature lectins by cooking lectin-containing foods as directed before allowing your dog to enjoy (Petroski & Minch, 2020).

Oxalates

- **Foods**. Certain vegetables (e.g., beets, rhubarb, sorrel, spinach, sweet potato, Swiss chard, taro), amaranth, nuts, raw legumes, whole grains.

- **Proposed anti-nutrient actions**. May bind calcium and decrease absorption; may play a role in the production of calcium oxalate kidney stones.

- **Health benefits**. Oxalate-containing foods are rich in phytochemicals and other compounds that help fight cancer and promote optimum health.

- **Reducing**. Boiling and steaming significantly reduce oxalate levels in legumes and vegetables. In one study, steamed spinach lost 42% of its oxalates and green Swiss chard lost 46% (Chai & Liebman, 2005).

Bottom line: Avoid feeding high-oxalate foods to dogs prone to calcium oxalate stones. Also, avoid giving to dogs suffering from gastrointestinal issues (e.g., IBD, leaky gut), as these conditions may increase oxalate absorption. Healthy dogs can enjoy these foods as a sensible part of a well-rounded whole-food plant-based diet (Petroski & Minch, 2020).

Phytates (phytic acid, IP6)

- **Foods**. Legumes, whole grains, pseudo-grains, nuts, seeds.

- **Proposed anti-nutrient actions**. Bind to certain minerals (iron, zinc, calcium, magnesium, manganese, copper) and protein during digestion and decrease absorption.

- **Health benefits**. IP6 is a powerful antioxidant that boosts immunity, reduces inflammation, lowers the risk of kidney stones (calcium oxalate and calcium phosphate) and diabetes mellitus and contains strong anti-cancer activity. (See Chapter 8.)

- **Reducing**. Soaking, sprouting, fermenting and cooking reduce phytate levels by varying degrees, depending on the food. For legumes, sprouting is most effective. Studies show that chickpeas sprouted for five days lose about 40% of their phytate concentration (Nissar et al., 2017), lentils lose about 50% (Nissar et al., 2017) and black-eyed beans lose about 75% (Lestienne et al., 2005).

Bottom line: Phytate-containing foods provide powerful health benefits, including anti-cancer properties (see Chapter 8) and are an important part of a well-balanced plant-based diet. Consuming ascorbic acid (vitamin C) along with foods containing phytic acid significantly increases non-heme iron absorption (Hallberg et al., 1989). (Remember that non-heme iron is not shown to cause health problems.) Follow our recommendations to reduce phytates. Ensuring your dog gets enough protein and minerals through food and supplementation can also compensate for any inhibitory effects (Petroski & Minich, 2020).

Phytoestrogens

- **Foods**. Soy (isoflavones), flaxseeds (lignans).

- **Proposed anti-nutrient actions**. There is controversy regarding whether phytoestrogens act as endocrine disruptors and increase the risk of estrogen-sensitive breast and uterine cancers.

- **Health benefits**. Phytoestrogens have antioxidant and anti-inflammatory properties (Kładna et al., 2016) and are shown to protect against multiple types of cancers.

- **Reducing**. Preparation methods do not decrease the phytoestrogen content of foods.

Bottom line: Isoflavones and flax lignans provide many health benefits, including anti-cancer activity. Lignans are also used for overactive adrenal gland function (Cushing's disease) in companion animals. Soy is also an excellent source of plant-based protein. Flaxseeds and organic, non-GMO soy are a healthy part of a well-balanced plant-based canine diet (See "The scoop on soy" and "Flaxseeds" earlier in this chapter.)

Tannins

- **Foods.** Tea, berries, apples, stone fruits, nuts, beans, whole grains (particularly high in tea, wine, black grapes and dark chocolate) (Arts et al., 2000; Smeriglio et al., 2017).

- **Proposed anti-nutrient actions**. The anti-nutrient potential of tannins is controversial. Some animal studies have shown that tannins may reduce iron absorption (Lee et al., 2010); however, other studies have found no significant impact (Fiesel et al., 2015).

- **Health benefits**. Tannins are polyphenol phytochemicals with strong antioxidant, anti-cancer, anti-microbial, immune-boosting and cardio-protective properties.

- **Reducing**. Cooking and removing the skins from nuts and fruits can reduce tannin levels; however, this also decreases the nutritional value.

Bottom line. The foods highest in tannins are also those that are toxic for dogs and should be avoided. For dog-friendly foods, no special considerations are warranted when consumed as part of a well-balanced diet (Petroski & Minich, 2020).

As you can see, anti-nutrients are found in basically every type of plant food. If we eliminate them, we also eliminate the foods scientifically proven to defend against chronic diseases, decrease inflammation and promote optimum health.

In addition, many studies that vilify anti-nutrients are conducted on laboratory animals using extracts at doses far higher than normally consumed in a well-rounded whole-food plant-based diet (Petroski & Minich, 2020). When consumed in their whole form, many foods that contain anti-nutrients also contain natural compounds that work together to protect against the very conditions supposedly created by the anti-nutrients. For example, phytates, potassium, calcium and phytochemicals in high-oxalate foods are shown to reduce the formation of kidney stones. Researchers analyzed dietary patterns for more than 240,000 men and women involved in the Health Professionals Follow-up Study (45,821 men), Nurses' Health Study I (94,108 women) and Nurses' Health Study II (101,837) over a combined 50 years of follow-up. The results showed that people consuming a DASH-style diet (Dietary Approaches to Stop Hypertension) were 40% to 50% less likely to suffer from kidney stones. This is interesting because the DASH diet is rich in high-oxalate foods such as fruits, vegetables, nuts, legumes and whole grains, which are the very foods the 'anti-nutrient police' would like us to believe cause kidney stones. Not surprisingly, the DASH diet is also low in red meat and processed meat (Taylor et al., 2009).

The bottom line is that we need to look at the science—not the hype—surrounding so-called anti-nutrients and the powerfully protective plant foods that contain them. In Chapter 8, we'll talk even more about the powerful cancer-fighting effects of certain anti-nutrients.

Dietary toxins

We have just covered *a lot* of amazing plant-based foods to support your dog's optimum health. But before we move on, we want to touch on some foods that you should *never* give your dog. While consuming a whole-food, plant-based diet will nourish your dog with a variety of disease-fighting antioxidants and phytochemicals, some plant-based ingredients are toxic to dogs. To avoid any confusion, we've rounded up our list of toxic plant-based foods in this easy-to-follow-chart.

Toxic Plant-Based Ingredients Chart

Ingredient	Toxic Effects Include
Alcohol	Vomiting, diarrhea, incoordination, breathing problems, tremors, abnormal blood acidity, coma, death
Chocolate, Coffee, Caffeine	Vomiting, diarrhea, excessive thirst and urination, hyperactivity, abnormal heart rhythm, tremors, seizures, death
Grapes/Raisins	Kidney failure
Macadamia Nuts	Vomiting, muscle weakness, elevated body temperature, weakness, tremors
Onions, Leeks, Chives (Note that garlic is safe in appropriate doses; See Chapter 6.)	Anemia, increased heart rate, weakness
Xylitol (artificial sweetener)	Vomiting, lethargy, incoordination, seizures, low blood sugar, liver failure
Raw (unbaked) Yeast Dough	Stomach bloat, torsion, death

(American Kennel Club, 2020; WebMD, 2020; ASPCA, 2022)

Chapter 6
Building Recipes

Welcome to our virtual kitchen! It's time to put on your apron, roll up your sleeves and create delicious, nutrient-dense recipes for your best friend. We hope you're excited to build your dog's diet. It's possible that you're even a little nervous. We understand that preparing home-cooked meals can seem daunting. And it's no wonder. Mass-market commercial pet food companies, social media groups and many veterinary professionals make it seem like feeding companion dogs is a magic act shrouded in mystery and illusion. But we're here to tell you that you can do it—with our expert guidance, of course!

In this chapter, you're going to discover a proprietary recipe-building blueprint, created by Diana, that will empower you to create your own 'almost complete and balanced' recipes for your canine companion. Feeding a variety of meals based on this blueprint will help ensure that, over the long term, your dog will receive all the nutritional components she needs to thrive.

Before we dive into the details, we want to let you know a bit more about this recipe creation method.

It's based on Calories, not cups. Many books about fresh-food dog nutrition provide advice based on the volume (i.e., cups) of food your dog consumes per day. But we find this approach to be vague and confusing because the volume of food will vary depending upon the caloric density. In other words, you can't know how many cups of food to feed your dog unless you know how many Calories are in that cup. Consider this: A cup of dry fava beans contains 512 Calories, while a cup of dry chickpeas has 756 Calories. This means that the chickpeas contain about 1 ½ times the Calories per cup! Using these two ingredients interchangeably by volume would certainly make a big difference in your dog's daily energy intake—and in the potential for her to become overweight.

According to the Association for Pet Obesity Prevention's (APOP) Website:

> *We've got to be specific when it comes to feeding our pets. Don't fall into the trap of inquiring, "How much should I feed?" You'll probably get a generic, inaccurate response. You need to know the precise numbers of calories and nutrients your pet needs. That way, regardless of the type, brand, or formulation of food you feed, you can determine how much to feed. This is a subtle, but incredibly significant difference* (APOP, 2019).

In a few moments, you're going to learn how to build your recipes based on your dog's daily Calorie intake. You might be thinking, "But I don't count Calories for my own meals, so why should I do it for my dog?" Actually, many people do count Calories, which is evident by the growing popularity of Calorie-counting smartphone and computer apps. And, as we pointed out earlier, many people and companion animals are overweight and undernourished. So, the argument could be made that we're not doing a very good job eyeballing portions for ourselves *or* our canine companions! Besides, we're theoretically supposed to stop eating when our body tells us we're full. You can't know when your dog is full, and we're guessing she's not telling.

Building recipes based on Calories accomplishes two major goals that can trip people up when it comes to cooking for their dogs:

- It helps ensure you're feeding a proper amount of food for your dog to reach and maintain a healthy weight.
- It lays the groundwork for providing the correct nutrient density, since nutrient intake is based on Calorie intake.

It uses a 'macro' approach with 'micro' benefits. As we've previously discussed, macronutrients provide energy (Calories). The three macronutrients are proteins, fats and carbohydrates. After you figure out your dog's estimated daily Calorie intake, we'll show you how to determine her RDA for protein and fat (there is no RDA for carbohydrates). However, macronutrients are one piece of the recipe-building process. We also want to be sure that your canine companion receives adequate amounts of micronutrients (e.g., vitamins and minerals). This is where Diana's proprietary Recipe-Builder Pie and Recipe Creation Chart—which we'll introduce soon—come in. Using these tools, along with our recommended supplementation, will enable you to create recipes that are 'almost completely balanced' (i.e., pretty darn close) for both macro and micronutrients. When you add in variety, you've got a winning formula for creating nutrient-dense plant-based recipes that will nurture your dog's optimum health over the short and long term.

Since this formula is more precise than the typical volume/cups method, we want to prepare you that there is some math involved. We know that math makes many people cringe, but we promise the results will be worth the effort. And once you learn the basic calculations, you can apply them over and over to confidently produce an almost endless variety of delicious, whole-food plant-based meals.

Are you ready? Let's begin building recipes!

Make it personal

As we emphasize throughout this book, every dog is an individual, so the first step involves assessing how your dog's health and lifestyle will affect her nutritional needs. As you review the recipe creation formula we'll be sharing shortly, consider how you can personalize it to address your canine companion's unique circumstances. For example, many people think that older dogs require less protein, but it's the opposite. Healthy senior dogs typically require fewer Calories per day because they are less active than their younger adult counterparts, however a greater percentage of these

Calories should come from protein. Here are some factors to consider when designing your dog's diet:

Activity level. Active dogs need more Calories, while less active or sedentary dogs require fewer. High-performance dogs also need higher levels of protein and perhaps fat. (See Chapter 2.)

Age. Senior dogs typically require about 18% fewer Calories per day than adults at maintenance; however, a greater percentage of those Calories should come from protein to help boost the immune system, prevent muscle wasting and support other essential functions affected by aging.

Breed. Naturally active breeds, such as Labrador Retrievers, Border Collies and Jack Russell Terriers will burn more Calories than more sedate breeds of the same size.

Environment. Dogs living in warmer climates typically require fewer Calories than those living in colder areas.

Health conditions. Any medical conditions should be taken into consideration and discussed with your veterinary professional.

Metabolism. Dogs vary in their metabolism, just as people do. In general, spayed and neutered dogs have slower metabolisms than intact dogs and smaller breeds have faster metabolisms than larger breeds.

Season. Calories and ingredients should be adapted according to weather and seasonal food availability. For example, your dog may require fewer Calories in the hot summer months than in the winter.

Weight loss. Always consult with your veterinarian prior to putting your dog on a weight loss diet to rule out a medical reason that your dog is overweight (e.g., hypothyroidism, Cushing's disease). Use the 1x RER multiplier in the following chart and shoot for a safe weight loss of 3% to 5% of body weight per month. If you don't see any weight loss after 90 days, reevaluate your current strategy with your veterinarian (APOP, 2019).

Weight gain. If your dog is underweight, start by increasing Calories by 5% to 10%. (Be sure to visit your veterinarian if your dog is unable to gain weight with adequate caloric intake, as this could signify a medical condition.) (Basko, 2016)

Calculate your dog's daily Calorie requirement

Since you'll be building your dog's recipes based on her daily Calorie intake, you'll want to figure that out first. The following three-step formula provides a starting point to determine your dog's daily Calorie requirement. To illustrate, we'll calculate the daily Calories for Benji, our 22-pound Beagle. You'll recall that Benji is a neutered adult dog at a maintenance stage.

Step 1. Divide the dog's weight in pounds by 2.2 to get the weight in kilograms. Benji weighs 22 pounds.

22 lbs ÷ 2.2 = 10 kg

Step 2. Determine your dog's **Resting Energy Requirement (RER).** RER is the daily Calories needed to support your dog's metabolic functions *at rest.* It is not the final number of daily Calories needed (unless you are using the 1x RER calculation for weight loss). The calculation we'll use to determine RER is:

(30 x dog's body weight in kg) + 70 = RER

For Benji, it looks like this:

(30 x 10 kg) + 70 = 370 Calories daily RER

Step 3. Multiply your dog's RER by the appropriate pre-determined multiplier. (See the Multipliers to Determine Daily Canine MER Chart.). This will give you your dog's **Maintenance Energy Requirement (MER).** MER includes the dog's RER plus the Calories needed to support physical activity. The calculation for MER is:

RER x multiplier = MER

Since Benji is an active neutered adult dog, we will multiply his RER x 1.6 to obtain his MER.

370 Calories x 1.6 = 592 Calories per day MER

To make this a nice even number, let's round it up to 600.

We've just figured out that Benji, our healthy, active 22-lb neutered adult dog should consume about 600 Calories per day.

You can calculate your dog's estimated daily caloric needs in the same manner. First, figure out her RER. Then, use the appropriate multiplier in the Multipliers to Determine Daily Canine MER Chart to determine her MER.

NOTE: We are using this chart because it represents the standard multipliers used to determine MER. However, these multipliers have gained criticism in recent years for potentially overestimating the amount to feed, which can lead to undesired weight gain. For this reason, we recommend using this chart as a starting point, not as a number that is set in stone. Most importantly, *always feed to your dog's ideal body condition.* (More on this in a moment.)

Multipliers to Determine Daily Canine MER Chart

Neutered adult	1.6 x RER
Intact adult	1.8 x RER
Inactive/obese prone	1.2 x 1.4 x RER
Weight loss	1 x RER of ideal weight
Weight gain	1.2 x 1.8 x RER of ideal weight
Light work	2 x RER
Moderate work	3 x RER
Heavy work	6 x RER

(The Ohio State University Veterinary Medical Center, n.d.; Coates, 2017)

To help you figure out your dog's daily caloric needs, we've prepared the following chart on the next page which provides estimated daily Calorie requirements for various size dogs. These calculations use the 1.6 multiplier and so only apply to active, spayed/neutered adult dogs at a maintenance stage. You may need to use another multiplier to determine your dog's MER based on her individual situation. (Note that we have rounded to the nearest Calorie.)

Estimated Daily Calories Chart

Dog's Weight	Calories
5 lbs (2.3 kg)	222
10 lbs (4.5 kg)	328
15 lbs (6.8 kg)	438
20 lbs (9 kg)	544
25 lbs (11.4 kg)	659
30 lbs (13.6 kg)	765
35 lbs (16 kg)	880
40 lbs (18.2 kg)	986
45 lbs (20.5 kg)	1,096
50 lbs (22.7 kg)	1,202
55 lbs (25 kg)	1,312
60 lbs (27.3 kg)	1,422
65 lbs (30 kg)	1,552
70 lbs (31.8 kg)	1,638
75 lbs (34 kg)	1,744
80 lbs (36.4 kg)	1,859
85 lbs (38.6 kg)	1,965
90 lbs (41 kg)	2,080
95 lbs (43 kg)	2,176
100 lbs (45.5)	2,296
105 lbs (47.7 kg)	2,402
110 lbs (50 kg)	2,512
115 lbs (52.3 kg)	2,622
120 lbs (54.5 kg)	2,728

As we previously mentioned, these calculated MER numbers represent a *starting point*. Your dog's daily Calorie needs could vary by as much as 50% from the calculated number (The Ohio State University Veterinary Medical Center, n.d.). You might also come across other Calorie calculation methods that result in different values. According to the NRC's formula, an active 20-pound adult dog consumes about 675 Calories per day (NRC, 2006). However, the Association for Pet Obesity Prevention's website lists the daily Calorie needs for an average lightly active 20-pound spayed or neutered adult indoor dog (one to seven years old) at about 325 to 400 Calories (APOP, 2019). And you can see that our method for the same dog resulted in an estimated daily caloric intake of 544 Calories. These are indeed wide variations!

Also, bear in mind that just because your dog burns a certain amount of energy today doesn't mean that this will be true next week, next month or next year. A dog's energy/Calorie requirements will vary over time and based on certain conditions.

For example, if your dog injures herself or undergoes surgery, she'll require fewer Calories during her sedentary recuperation period.

The bottom line is that no mathematical formula will precisely pinpoint how many Calories your dog needs to consume each day to achieve and maintain an ideal weight. Therefore, the best approach is an individual approach. Start with the calculated value, then closely monitor your dog's weight, body condition, satiety level and overall health, increasing or decreasing the amount fed as necessary.

Once you've determined your dog's approximate daily Calories, please note it down as you'll need this when creating your recipes later in the chapter.

Know your dog's protein needs

In Chapter 2, we busted the myth that dogs can't get enough protein on plant-based diets and even showed that excessive protein can be harmful. However, we find that many plant-based feeders still struggle with understanding how much protein to include in their home-prepared recipes. Well, stress no longer. In this section, we're going to guide you through figuring out your dog's minimum RDA of protein based on her weight and daily Calorie intake.

How to calculate your dog's minimum RDA of protein

We previously mentioned that AAFCO's minimum protein recommendation for adult dogs at maintenance is 45 grams per 1,000 Calories. This is the same as saying that 18% of Calories should come from protein. We know this because proteins, carbohydrates and fats are macronutrients, meaning that they provide energy (Calories). When we're talking about fresh food diets, proteins and carbohydrates each provide four Calories per gram, while fats provide nine Calories per gram.

This means that 45 grams of protein provide 180 Calories (45 grams x 4 Calories/gram = 180 Calories). And 180 is 18% of 1,000 (180 ÷ 1,000 = 0.18 or 18%).

The following formula is used to determine AAFCO's minimum RDA of protein for adult dogs at maintenance based on daily Calorie intake:

(45 g protein x dog's MER) ÷ 1,000 = minimum RDA of protein

Let's try a few calculations for different sized adult dogs, based on our previous Calorie calculation formula. (Note that we round the grams to the nearest whole number.)

Example 1
5 lb (2.3 kg) adult dog consuming 222 Calories/day

(45 g protein x 222 Calories) ÷ 1,000 = 10

Minimum RDA of protein for a 5 lb adult dog = 10 g

Protein per pound (lb) of body weight (BW) = 2 g (10 g protein ÷ 5 lb = 2 g/lb)

Note that we can check this number against our '18% rule' (at least 18% of Calories should come from protein) as follows:

10 g protein x 4 Calories/g = 40 Calories

40 ÷ 222 = 0.18 or 18%

Example 2
10 lb (4.5 kg) adult dog consuming 328 Calories/day

(45 g protein x 328 Calories) ÷ 1,000 = 15

Minimum RDA of protein for a 10 lb adult dog = 15 g

Protein lb/BW = 1.5 g (15 g ÷ 10 lb = 1.5 g/lb)

18% rule:

15 g protein x 4 Calories/g = 60 Calories

60 ÷ 328 = 18%

Example 3
22 lb (10 kg) adult dog consuming 600 Calories/day (Benji)

(45 g protein x 600 Calories) ÷ 1,000 = 27

Minimum RDA of protein for a 22 lb adult dog = 27 g

Protein lb/BW = 1.2 g (27 g ÷ 22 lb = 1.2 g/lb)

18% rule:

27 g protein x 4 Calories/g = 108

108 ÷ 600 = 18%

Example 4
58 lb (26.4 kg) adult dog consuming 1,379 Calories/day

(45 g protein x 1,379 Calories) ÷ 1,000 = 62

Minimum RDA of protein for a 58 lb dog = 62 g

Protein lb/BW = 1 gram (62 g ÷ 58 lb = 1 g/lb)

18% rule:

62 g protein x 4 Calories/g = 248

248 ÷ 1,379 = 18%

Example 5
86 lb (39 kg) adult dog consuming 1,984 Calories/day

(45 g protein x 1,984 Calories) ÷ 1,000 = 89

Minimum RDA of protein for an 86 lb dog = 89 g

Protein lb/BW = 1 gram (89 g ÷ 86 lb = 1 g/lb)

18% rule:

89 g protein x 4 Calories/g = 356

356 ÷ 1,984 = 18%

The following chart reflects the *minimum* daily grams of protein we recommend for active adult dogs at a maintenance stage, based on our previous Calorie calculation method. (Note that in each case we have rounded up to the next highest gram.)

Minimum Protein RDA Chart

Dog's Weight	Calories	Minimum RDA of Protein (grams)
5 lbs (2.3 kg)	222	10 g
10 lbs (4.5 kg)	328	15 g
15 lbs (6.8 kg)	438	20 g
20 lbs (9 kg)	544	25 g
25 lbs (11.4 kg)	659	30 g
30 lbs (13.6 kg)	765	35 g
35 lbs (16 kg)	880	40 g
40 lbs (18.2 kg)	986	45 g
45 lbs (20.5 kg)	1,096	50 g
50 lbs (22.7 kg)	1,202	54 g
55 lbs (25 kg)	1,312	59 g
60 lbs (27.3 kg)	1,422	64 g
65 lbs (30 kg)	1,552	70 g
70 lbs (31.8 kg)	1,638	74 g
75 lbs (34 kg)	1,744	79 g
80 lbs (36.4 kg)	1,859	84 g
85 lbs (38.6 kg)	1,965	89 g
90 lbs (41 kg)	2,080	94 g
95 lbs (43 kg)	2,176	98 g
100 lbs (45.5)	2,296	104 g
105 lbs (47.7 kg)	2,402	108 g
110 lbs (50 kg)	2,512	113 g
115 lbs (52.3 kg)	2,622	118 g
120 lbs (54.5 kg)	2,728	123 g

As you'll see from these calculations, small dogs require more dietary protein per pound of body weight than large dogs. At first glance, this might seem odd. After all, small dogs are small, so shouldn't they require less nutrition? It's just the opposite! Why is this? Small dogs have faster metabolisms than large dogs, meaning that they burn Calories and nutrients much quicker. Because of this, they need to take in more nutrition at each meal. However, they also have small stomachs that can only hold limited amounts of food. To ensure they get everything they need in a quantity of food they can handle, small dogs need to consume more Calories and nutrients per pound of body weight than large dogs (Coates, 2012). For this reason, foods designed for small dogs are more Calorie and nutrient-dense than those made for large dogs.

Please write down your dog's minimum RDA of protein alongside the estimated daily Calories, as you will need it when you create your recipes.

Figuring out fat requirements

The amount of fat your dog needs will vary according to her specific situation. More active dogs and dogs living in colder climates, for example, will require a higher percentage of their Calories to come from fat, while lower-fat diets are recommended for dogs who need to shed weight or who suffer from certain health conditions such as pancreatitis and inflammatory bowel disease (IBD).

A common mistake that people make when their dog needs a reduced-fat diet is to eliminate all fat. Even dogs requiring reduced dietary fat need adequate fat intake. As we've already discussed, fat is necessary for many vital metabolic and physiological functions, from serving as an important source of energy to absorbing fat-soluble vitamins and providing essential fatty acids.

Both the NRC and AAFCO recommend that adult dogs at a maintenance stage consume a minimum of 13.8 grams of fat per 1,000 Calories. In terms of fresh food diets, this works out to about 12.4% of Calories from fat because one gram of fat contains nine Calories:

13.8 g x 9 Calories/gram = 124 Calories

124 ÷ 1,000 = 0.124, or 12.4%

We can figure out a dog's minimum RDA for fat using the following calculation:

(13.8 g fat x dog's MER) ÷ 1,000 = minimum RDA of fat

Example: Benji

Let's use Benji as an example. We know that Benji weighs 22 pounds and consumes about 600 Calories per day.

(13.8 fat x 600 Calories) ÷ 1,000 = 8.3

Based on our calculation, Benji needs at least 8.3 g of fat per day.

We can also see that this equals 12.4% of Calories as follows:

8.3 g x 9 Calories/gram = 74.7

74.7 ÷ 600 = 0.124 or 12.4%

Using the previous sample to guide you, please now calculate your dog's minimum RDA for fat based on her daily Calorie intake. We have also provided a sample chart to help you out. The following chart reflects the minimum RDA of fat for active adult dogs at a maintenance stage, based on our previous Calorie calculation method (MER = 1.6 x RER).

Estimated Minimum Dietary Fat RDA Chart

Dog's Weight	Calories	Minimum RDA of Fat (grams)
5 lbs (2.3 kg)	222	3 g
10 lbs (4.5 kg)	328	4.5 g
15 lbs (6.8 kg)	438	6 g
20 lbs (9 kg)	544	7.5 g
25 lbs (11.4 kg)	659	9 g
30 lbs (13.6 kg)	765	10.5 g
35 lbs (16 kg)	880	12.1 g
40 lbs (18.2 kg)	986	13.6 g
45 lbs (20.5 kg)	1,096	15.1g
50 lbs (22.7 kg)	1,202	16.6 g
55 lbs (25 kg)	1,312	18.1 g
60 lbs (27.3 kg)	1,422	19.6 g
65 lbs (30 kg)	1,552	21.4 g
70 lbs (31.8 kg)	1,638	22.6 g
75 lbs (34 kg)	1,744	24 g
80 lbs (36.4 kg)	1,859	25.6 g
85 lbs (38.6 kg)	1,965	27.1 g
90 lbs (41 kg)	2,080	28.7 g
95 lbs (43 kg)	2,176	30 g
100 lbs (45.5kg)	2,296	31.7 g
105 lbs (47.7 kg)	2,402	33.1 g
110 lbs (50 kg)	2,512	34.7 g
115 lbs (52.3 kg)	2,622	36.1 g
120 lbs (54.5 kg)	2,728	37.6 g

Please write down your dog's minimum RDA of fat alongside the daily Calories and protein that you previously calculated.

Bear in mind that the grams of protein and fat that we have provided are based on levels per 1,000 Calories consumed (per the NRC and AAFCO guidelines). If your dog consumes fewer Calories than normal for her weight, she will also consume fewer nutrients. This means that she may not receive adequate levels of dietary protein, fat and other nutrients. In this situation, you should consider a custom recipe formulation based on your dog's body weight rather than on the amount of nutrients per Calories consumed.

The Four Keys for a new world

In our 2015 *Canine Nutrigenomics* book, we listed three key elements in creating the ideal canine diet, which we called the Three Keys. The Three Keys referred to diets that:

- Provide *variety*
- Comprise *nutrient-dense* ingredients
- Rely on *fresh, whole foods*

The Three Keys are even more applicable to a plant-based way of feeding our canine companions than they are to a diet based on animal ingredients. As we've detailed throughout this book, a diet comprised of a variety of whole plant-based foods is the most nutrient-dense diet on the planet.

Now, we're excited to update the Three Keys with the addition of a fourth key: *Sustainable*. This fourth key reflects a new and changing world—a world that respects the welfare of all living beings, our planet and future generations.

Here's how you can create healthy, delicious recipes for your dog based on the Four Keys:

Variety. Have fun rotating different types of beans, grains, veggies, fruits, seeds and nuts (all dog-safe, of course) into your recipes. This will help ensure that your dog's diet is packed with a wide variety of amino acids, fatty acids, vitamins and minerals.

Nutrient dense. Avoid processed and high-glycemic foods such as white flour and sugar. Opt instead for wholesome ingredients that are packed with antioxidants and phytochemicals as we discuss throughout this book.

Whole food. The rising interest in plant-based feeding has brought with it a host of plant-based junk food—for people and dogs. And while we all need the occasional treat, the bulk of your dog's diet should consist of fresh, unprocessed dog-friendly plant foods.

Sustainable. Plant-based diets are by nature more sustainable because they save animals, land and water and create a far lighter carbon footprint. To further increase sustainability, we recommend purchasing seasonal produce from local farmers whenever possible to reduce greenhouse gas emissions created during food transportation. And consider buying 'ugly' produce to help cut down on food waste, since unpurchased products get tossed by retailers (4Ocean, 2020). The nutritional value is the same, and your dog won't mind a creepy-looking carrot or a bruised banana!

Following the Four Keys will help you create recipes that provide an optimum nutritional profile for your dog while supporting the health of our planet and all its inhabitants. Now, that's what we call an ideal way of eating!

Putting it all together

At this point, you should know three key aspects of your dog's diet:

1. Calories (adjust accordingly)
2. Protein RDA (minimum)
3. Fat RDA (minimum)

If you haven't already determined these values, please do so before continuing. You'll need them when you create your recipes.

We're going to focus our recipe-building process on the following food groups:

Recipe Food Group Chart

Food Group	Ingredient Examples
Protein-rich foods*	Beans, lentils, tofu, tempeh
Starchy vegetables + grains	Amaranth, buckwheat, oats, quinoa, winter squash, sweet potato
Fats	Almond butter, cashew butter, flaxseeds/oil, hemp seeds/oil, olive oil, pumpkin seeds, sunflower seeds
Non-starchy vegetables	Broccoli, Brussels sprouts, carrots, cauliflower, green beans, green leafy vegetables, zucchini
Fruits	Blackberries, blueberries, apples, pears
Add-ons	Herbs, nutritional yeast, spirulina, protein powder, soy sauce (organic/gluten-free), coconut aminos

*Note that we refer to the protein food group as 'protein-rich foods' rather than 'high-protein foods.' This is because in commercial dog food formulation, the term 'high-protein' denotes recipes containing a specific minimum percentage of dietary protein. Our goal is not to compare our recipes to commercial formulations; it's to create nutrient-dense fresh-food meals. Therefore, we use the term 'protein-rich' to describe plant-based foods that contain higher levels of protein relative to other types of plant-based foods—not based on any commercial formulation parameters.

Recipe-Builder Pie

The Recipe-Builder Pie illustrates how much of each food group to include in your recipes, based on a percentage of the recipe's total Calories. The Recipe-Builder Pie provides a range of percentages for each food group. The exact percentage will vary based on your dog's individual needs and by each recipe.

Please note that the Recipe-Builder Pie does *not* refer to the percentages of protein, fat and carbohydrates in the recipe. It indicates the percentages of *types of foods grouped by category.* The Recipe-Builder Pie indicates how much of each food group to include in your recipes, based on a percentage of the recipe's total Calories.

Recipe-Builder Pie

Foods Groups as a Percentage of Total Calories

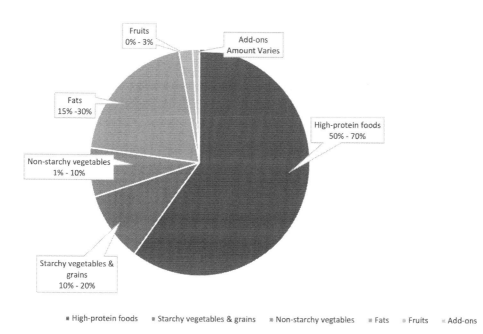

If you've read books that provide feeding advice based on volume (cups) of food, then these percentages might look strange to you. For example, you wouldn't want 20% to 30% of a recipe to be made up of high-fat foods by volume. That would be far too much fat, especially when fats are in such a concentrated form. Imagine if 25%, or one-quarter, of your cup of food were made up of oil! By the same token, 1% to 10% of non-starchy vegetables might not seem like much, but non-starchy vegetables, such as leafy greens, are very low in Calories, so this percentage allows for a good amount. Again, it's important to remember that we are basing our ingredient percentages on the recipe's *Calories*, not cups/volume.

Recipe creation process

The first thing you'll want to do is recreate the following blank Recipe Creation Chart onto a piece of copy paper or your computer. If you're able, we recommend recreating it on your computer, as this will give you the most flexibility to duplicate it and make changes to your recipes during the creation process. Just be sure not to write on the copy in the book, as you'll need this blank chart as a template to create your recipes.

Before we begin building our recipes, we want to mention a few important points:

Cooked vs. uncooked measurements. We base our recipes on uncooked (raw/dry) measurements (and provide them this way in the Ingredients Reference Chart later in this chapter) because we find this method much easier and more accurate. If you begin with cooked amounts, you'll need to backtrack to determine how much of the raw ingredients are needed to obtain the cooked amounts. Legumes and grains can vary in how much they expand during cooking and guessing can be frustrating. In addition, you can either choose to cook your vegetables (e.g., steam or pressure cook) or pulverize/purée and feed them raw. Raw veggies typically provide more nutrition; however, lightly cooking might be the best option if your dog suffers from sensitive digestion.

Number of ingredients per category. Each category of food in the Recipe Creation Chart contains multiple rows in which you can add ingredients. Bear in mind that you do not need to fill up all these rows. You might want to use one type of legume for one recipe and three types for another. The same holds true for the other ingredient categories. The key is that the *total percentage of ingredients in each category* falls within our recommended range (or very close). This is true whether you're using one ingredient in the category or several. We'll show you how to do that in a moment.

Don't stress about exact percentages. You'll notice that the percentage for each food category is given as range. You might even find that you occasionally go a little over or under the range for an ingredient category (as we do in Sample #3 below with starchy veggies/grains). It's okay! Just create a variety of recipes following these guidelines, and you'll have a great formula for creating delicious, nutrient-dense meals.

Total Calories may vary slightly. The final Calories in your recipes might not add up exactly to your target Calories (your dog's daily MER). This is because you'll want to round your ingredient measurements to make them even, which will also affect the total Calories. As long as you are close, you don't need to worry about it. Again, every recipe doesn't have to be exact. This is a guide, not a formulation software tool.

A note on rounding numbers. We used values to the first decimal place in our recipes, but you can feel free to round up or down to the appropriate whole number to keep things 'cleaner' looking. Just be aware that when doing that, your Calories and percentages will become more affected, and your percentages might not add up to 100. Again, don't sweat it. If you come close to 100%, you're good to go. However, if you find that you're far off, you've likely miscalculated somewhere along the way, and you should check your math.

Weight vs. volume measurements. We've included both volume and weight measurements for the ingredients in our recipe samples and in the Ingredients Reference Chart. You can use either, however, weighing the ingredients will provide the greatest accuracy. (See Resources for a recommended food scale.) Note: When we talk about volume measurements in this context, it is *not* the same as our previous discussion regarding building recipes based on cups vs. Calories of food consumed. We are still creating our recipes based on Calories; we're just measuring out the ingredients in each category either by volume or weight.

How to calculate the Calories for each food group in your recipe

If you're creating a recipe based on cups of food, you can simply 'eyeball' the percentages (e.g., one-half cup or one-third cup). This isn't the case when you build your recipes based on the percentage of Calories. For example, you can't eyeball 50% of 600 Calories. However, you probably already know that this would equal 300 Calories because 300 is 50% (half) of 600. By the same token, 25% of 600 Calories equals 150 Calories.

We can calculate the target Calories for each food group in our recipe using the following formula:

(Total Calories in Recipe) x (Calorie % of Food Group) = Calories of Food Group

Based on our Recipe-Builder Pie, we know that we want the following percentages of Calories for each food group:

Food Group	Percentage of Calories
Protein-rich foods	50 to 70
Starchy vegetables/grains	10 to 20
Non-starchy vegetables	1 to 10
Fats	15 to 30
Fruits	0 to 3
Add-ons	Varies by type (See chart on page 140)

Let's see how this works out for a 500-Calorie recipe.

Protein-rich foods
50% to 70% of Calories

(500 Calories) x (0.50) = 250

(500 Calories) x (0.70) = 350

Protein-rich foods = 250 to 350 Calories of a 500-Calorie recipe

Starchy vegetables and grains
10% to 20%

(500) x (0.10) = 50

(500) x (0.20) x = 100

Starchy vegetables/grains = 50 to 100 Calories

Non-starchy vegetables
1% to 10%

(500) x (0.01) = 5

(500) x (0.10) = 50

Non-starchy vegetables = 5 to 50 Calories

Fats

15% to 30%

(500) x (0.15) = 75

(500) x (0.30) = 150

Fats = 75 to 150 Calories

Fruits

0% to 3%

(500) x (0.00) = 0

(500) x (0.03) = 15

Fruits = 0 to 15 Calories

Add-ons

Varies depending on the ingredient(s)

Voila! We now know our desired Calorie range for each food group in a 500-Calorie recipe. We can achieve this in multiple ways. Here is just one of them:

Food Group	Percentage (%)	Calories
Protein-rich foods	60	300
Starchy veggies + grains	10	50
Non-starchy veggies	8	40
Fats	20	100
Fruits	1	5
Add-ons	1	5
Total	100	500

As you create your recipes, you'll of course want to combine Calories for your food groups in a way that adds up to 100% of your recipe's target Calories (or as close to that number as possible). This is precisely what we just did with our 500-Calorie example. If you increase or decrease the percentage (and thus the Calories) for one food group, just be sure to compensate by adjusting the others accordingly. This blueprint gives you the flexibility to vary the amount of each food group in a recipe based on your goals.

You've probably noticed that to calculate your target Calories for each category, you'll first need to convert your desired percentages to a decimal point. In other words, if your goal is for 65% of your recipe's Calories to come from the protein-rich food category, then you need to know that 65% is the same as 0.65. Once you know this, you can use our mathematical formula to figure out the target Calories. In the case of our 500-Calorie example, this would come out to 325 Calories (500 x 0.65 = 325).

If that seems daunting to you, don't sweat it. The following chart gives the percentage-to-decimal conversions for every percentage between 1% and 100%. For example, if you wanted 22% of your Calories to come from fat, you'd simply locate the number 22 under the % column and find the decimal conversion directly to its right. In this case, you'll see that it's 0.22. Then proceed with your calculation. In our 500-Calorie example, this would come out to 110 Calories from fat (500 x 0.22 = 110).

%	Decimal	%	Decimal	%	Decimal	%	Decimal	%	Decimal
1	0.01	21	0.21	41	0.41	61	0.61	81	0.81
2	0.02	22	0.22	42	0.42	62	0.62	82	0.82
3	0.03	23	0.23	43	0.43	63	0.63	83	0.83
4	0.04	24	0.24	44	0.44	64	0.64	84	0.84
5	0.05	25	0.25	45	0.45	65	0.65	85	0.85
6	0.06	26	0.26	46	0.46	66	0.66	86	0.86
7	0.07	27	0.27	47	0.47	67	0.67	87	0.87
8	0.08	28	0.28	48	0.48	68	0.68	88	0.88
9	0.09	29	0.29	49	0.49	69	0.69	89	0.89
10	0.10	30	0.30	50	0.50	70	0.70	90	0.90
11	0.11	31	0.31	51	0.51	71	0.71	91	0.91
12	0.12	32	0.32	52	0.52	72	0.72	92	0.92
13	0.13	33	0.33	53	0.53	73	0.73	93	0.93
14	0.14	34	0.34	54	0.54	74	0.74	94	0.94
15	0.15	35	0.35	55	0.55	75	0.75	95	0.95
16	0.16	36	0.36	56	0.56	76	0.76	96	0.96
17	0.17	37	0.37	57	0.57	77	0.77	97	0.97
18	0.18	38	0.38	58	0.58	78	0.78	98	0.98
19	0.19	39	0.39	59	0.59	79	0.79	99	0.99
20	0.20	40	0.40	60	0.60	80	0.80	100	1.00

You might occasionally want to use less than 1% for fruits or add-ons. The following chart gives the conversions for those values.

%	Decimal	%	Decimal
0	0.000	0.5 (1/2)	0.005
0.1	0.001	0.6	0.006
0.2	0.002	0.7	0.007
0.3	0.003	0.8	0.008
0.4	0.004	0.9	0.009

Building recipes

It's time to create recipes! As we mentioned, the first thing you'll want to do is reproduce the blank Recipe Creation Chart. Next, review the sample recipes on the following pages and use them to guide you in building your own recipes. You'll find examples for small, medium and large-sized dogs. Note that the sample recipes and the ones that you will create provide one day's worth of food based on the dog's calculated daily caloric needs. You can divide the daily recipe into as many servings as you'd like, based on your dog's individual situation.

Preparation guidelines

When it comes to preparing your dog's recipes, there is no one right way, just as there is no one right way to cook for yourself. However, here are some preparation guidelines to help maximize the food's nutritional value and reduce any potential unwanted effects, such as gas or loose stool:

Preparing beans. Soak beans overnight. Boil on the stove top until soft or cook in a pressure cooker/InstantPot. Remember not to cook beans in a slow cooker, as this method will not deactivate the lectin toxins present in raw beans. Mash well before serving. Note that lentils do not need to be pre-soaked.

Preparing grains. Soak grains prior to cooking to reduce their phytic acid content and increase digestibility. (This step is optional but helpful for dogs with sensitive digestive systems.) Note that soaked grains cook faster than unsoaked.

Preparing vegetables. You can serve vegetables raw or cooked, depending on your dog's taste preferences and digestion. When cooking, we recommend steaming or using a pressure cooker/InstantPot to maximize nutrition. Avoid boiling vegetables unless you are also using the boiling water (e.g., vegetable broth). Run raw vegetables through a food processor or blender to increase digestibility. Consider alternating between serving raw and cooked vegetables, as each method provides nutritional benefits.

Cooking methods. To save time and effort, you can combine foods with similar cooking times in a pressure cooker/InstantPot. Or you can cook each ingredient separately (e.g., pressure cook beans, boil grains, steam veggies). It's up to you!

Putting it all together. Combine the prepared ingredients in a bowl. Let cool to room temperature before adding fruits, add-ons and supplements.

Batch cooking. If you batch cook for multiple days (which we highly recommend), be sure not to reheat the food once you have incorporated your supplements, as heat can denature certain nutrients. Instead, remove the food from the refrigerator and let it come naturally to room temperature. You can also mix in a little warm water to help it along. If you prefer to reheat the food, add your supplements daily rather than as part of the batch.

When you become familiar with this formula and gain confidence building your own recipes, you will have a powerful tool at your fingertips. Together, the Recipe-Builder Pie and Recipe Creation Chart offer the best of all worlds: flexibility, creativity and reliability. You will no longer need to follow rigid recipes that are difficult to personalize for your dog or 'wing it,' worrying if you're doing it right. It will take some time and practice to get the hang of it, but that is true of almost everything that is worthwhile learning. And once you master the process, you will have the freedom and confidence to take charge of your dog's nutritional health once and for all. We're excited about that, and we hope you are, too!

Remember: Variety is key!
We recommend that you rotate your recipes at least weekly. We also recommend varying the percentages of your food groups from recipe to recipe (while still staying within the provided ranges). For example, if you use a higher percentage of fat and lower percentage of starchy veggies/ grains in your recipe one week, try switching it around the next time.

The more diversity you provide while following the Recipe Builder Pie, the more your dog will benefit from the nutritional density of a whole-food plant-based diet.

The following chart represents general daily feeding amounts for various add-on ingredients. Be sure to tailor your dog's specific portions to her individual situation and diet plan.

Feeding Guidelines for Add-Ons Chart

Ingredient	Recommended Daily Amount
Brewer's yeast	Small dogs: 1 tsp Medium dogs: 2 tsp Large dogs: 1 TB Mix into the food and divide between a.m. and p.m.
Garlic (fresh, raw)	Small dogs: ½ clove Medium dogs: 1 clove Large dogs: 1 ½ cloves
Ginger (powdered)	Small dogs: 1/8 tsp Medium dogs: 1/4 tsp Large dogs: 1/2 tsp
Herbs (dried) (e.g., basil, cilantro, oregano*, parsley, rosemary*)	Small dogs: 1 tsp Medium dogs: 2 tsp Large dogs: 1 TB Mix into food and divide between a.m. and p.m. * Never give rosemary or oregano to dogs with epilepsy or who are prone to seizures as they can worsen these conditions. Note that fennel and sage are also considered to be neurotoxic herbs.

Ingredient	Recommended Daily Amount
Nutritional yeast	Small dogs: 1 tsp Medium dogs: 2 tsp Large dogs: 1 TB
Turmeric (dried and fresh)	Small dogs: 1/16 tsp or 1/16-inch fresh root Medium dogs: 1/8 tsp or 1/8-inch root Large dogs: 1/4 tsp or 1/4-inch root
Super green foods (spirulina/blue-green algae) See Chapter 5 for cautions	Small dogs: 1/8 tsp Medium dogs: ¼ tsp Large dogs: ½ tsp
Coconut aminos (Provides sodium that is necessary to meet AAFCO and NRC RDAs.)	Small dogs: 1 tsp Medium dogs: 2 tsp Large dogs: 3 tsp
Tamari (wheat-free soy sauce) (Provides sodium that is necessary to meet AAFCO and NRC RDAs.)	Small dogs: 1/4 tsp Medium dogs: 1/2 tsp Large dogs: 1 tsp

Blank Recipe Creation Chart

	Amount	Calories	% of Total Calories	Protein (g)	Fat (g)
Protein-rich foods (e.g., beans, lentils, tofu, protein powder) (50% to 70% of Calories)					
TOTAL CATEGORY %					
Starchy veggies/grains (e.g., sweet potatoes, quinoa) (10% to 20% of Calories)					
TOTAL CATEGORY %					
Non-starchy vegetables (e.g., zucchini, green beans, kale) (1% to 10% of Calories)					
TOTAL CATEGORY %					
Fats (e.g., oil, seeds, nut butter) (15% to 30% of Calories)					
TOTAL CATEGORY %					

	Amount	Calories	% of Total Calories	Protein (g)	Fat (g)
Fruits (e.g., berries, apple, pear) (0% to 3% of Calories)					
TOTAL CATEGORY %					
Add-ons (e.g., nutritional yeast, spirulina, soy sauce) (Varies)					
TOTAL CATEGORY %					
TOTAL					

Sample Recipe Chart #1
10 lb (4.5 kg) adult dog consuming approximately 330 Calories/day

	Amount	Calories	% of Total Calories	Protein (g)	Fat (g)
Protein-rich foods (e.g., beans, lentils, tofu, protein powder) **(50% to 70% of Calories)**					
Lentils (raw)	1/4 cup (48 g)	169.5	50.2	12.4	0.5
TOTAL CATEGORY %			**50.2%**		
Starchy veggies/grains (e.g., sweet potatoes, quinoa) **(10% to 20% of Calories)**					
Butternut squash (raw)	1/8 cup, cubes (17.5 g)	7.9	2.3	0.2	0
Quinoa (uncooked)	1 TB (11 g)	39	11.5	2	0.6
TOTAL CATEGORY %			**13.8%**		
Non-starchy vegetables (e.g., zucchini, green beans, kale) **(1% to 10% of Calories)**					
Carrots (raw)	1/8cup, chopped (16 g)	6.6	2	0.2	0
Kale (raw)	1/8 cup, chopped (8.4 g)	4.2	1.2	0.3	0
Green beans (raw)	2 beans (4" long) (11 g)	3.4	1	0.2	0

	Amount	Calories	% of Total Calories	Protein (g)	Fat (g)
TOTAL CATEGORY %			**4.2%**		
Fats (e.g., oil, seeds, nut butter) **(15% to 30% of Calories)**					
Almond butter (no salt)	1 TB 16 g)	101	30	2.4	9.5
TOTAL CATEGORY %			**30%**		
Fruits (e.g., berries, apple, pear) **(0% to 3% of Calories)**					
Blueberries (raw)	5 berries (5 grams)	5	1.5	0	0
TOTAL CATEGORY %			**1.5%**		
Add-ons (e.g., nutritional yeast, spirulina, soy sauce) **(Varies)**					
Soy sauce (wheat-free tamari)	1/4 tsp (1.5 g)	1	0.3	0.2	0
TOTAL CATEGORY %			**0.3%**		
TOTAL	**134.4 g**	**337.6 Calories***	**100%**	**17.9 g****	**10.6 g**

*Your actual Calories may not add up exactly to your dog's calculated MER.

**17.9 g of protein equals about 1.8 g per lb of BW (17.9 g ÷ 10 lb = 1.79 g/lb).

Given that we've gotten to know Benji very well throughout this book, it seems fitting that we create a recipe for him!

Sample Recipe Chart #2
Benji: 22 lb (10 kg) adult dog consuming approximately 600 Calories/day

	Amount	Calories	% of Total Calories	Protein (g)	Fat (g)
Protein-rich foods (e.g., beans, lentils, tofu, protein powder) **(50% to 70% of Calories)**					
Split peas (raw)	¼ cup (49.3 g)	168	28	12	0.6
Navy beans (raw)	¼ cup 52 g)	175.3	29	11.6	0.8
TOTAL CATEGORY %			**57%**		
Starchy veggies/grains (e.g., sweet potatoes, quinoa) **(10% to 20% of Calories)**					
Sweet potato (raw)	1/4 cup, cubes (33.3 g)	28.5	4.7	0.5	0
Buckwheat groats (roasted, uncooked)	1 TB (10 g)	35	5.8	1	0.3
TOTAL CATEGORY %			**10.5%**		
Non-starchy vegetables (e.g., zucchini, green beans, kale) **(1% to 10% of Calories)**					
Broccoli (raw)	¼ cup, chopped (22.8 g)	7.7	1.3	0.7	0.1
Zucchini (with skin, raw)	5 slices (50 g)	8	1.3	1	0.2
TOTAL CATEGORY %			**2.6%**		

	Amount	Calories	% of Total Calories	Protein (g)	Fat (g)
Fats (e.g., oil, seeds, nut butter) **(15% to 30% of Calories)**					
Pumpkin and squash seed kernels (dried)	1/2 TB (4.5 g)	24	4	1.5	2
Cashew butter (plain, no salt)	1 ½ TB (24 g)	141	23.4	4.2	12
			27.4%		
TOTAL CATEGORY %					
Fruits (e.g., berries, apple, pear) **(0% to 3% of Calories)**					
Raspberries	5 berries (10 g)	5	0.8	0	0
TOTAL CATEGORY %			**0.8%**		
Add-ons (e.g., nutritional yeast, spirulina, soy sauce) **(Varies)**					
Coconut aminos	2 tsp (10 g)	10	1.7	0	0
TOTAL CATEGORY %			**1.7%**		
TOTAL	**266 g**	**602.5 Calories***	**100%**	**32.5 g****	**16 g**

*Your actual Calories may not add up exactly to your dog's calculated MER.

**32.5 g of protein equals about 1.5 grams per lb of body weight (32.5 g ÷ 22 lb = 1.47 g/lb).

Sample Recipe Chart #3
41 lb (18.6 kg) adult dog consuming approximately 1,000 Calories/day

	Amount	Calories	% of Total Calories	Protein (g)	Fat (g)
Protein-rich foods (e.g., beans, lentils, tofu, protein powder) (50% to 70% of Calories)					
Lentils (raw)	½ cup (96 g)	339	33.9	24.8	1
Cranberry beans (raw)	1/3 cup (65 g)	217.6	21.8	15	0.8
TOTAL CATEGORY %			**55.7%**		
Starchy veggies/grains (e.g., sweet potatoes, quinoa) (10% to 20% of Calories)					
Sweet potato (raw)	1/4 cup, cubed (33.25 g)	28.50	2.9	0.5	0
Barley, pearled (raw)	1/4 cup (50 g)	176	17.6	5	0.6
TOTAL CATEGORY %			**20.5%**		
Non-starchy vegetables (e.g., zucchini, green beans, kale) (1% to 10% of Calories)					
Broccoli (raw)	1/3 cup, chopped (30.3 g)	10.3	1	1	0
Kale (raw)	1/2 cup, chopped (33.5 g)	16.8	1.7	1	0.3
TOTAL CATEGORY %			**2.7%**		

	Amount	Calories	% of Total Calories	Protein (g)	Fat (g)
Fats (e.g., oil, seeds, nut butter) (15% to 30% of Calories)					
Cashew butter (plain, no salt)	2 TB (32 g)	187.8	18.8	5.6	15.8
Hemp seeds (shelled or hulled)	½ tsp (1.7 g)	9.2	0.9	0.5	0.8
TOTAL CATEGORY %			**19.7%**		
Fruits (e.g., berries, apple, pear) (0% to 3% of Calories)					
Blueberries	13 berries (13 g)	13	1.3	0	0
TOTAL CATEGORY %			**1.3%**		
Add-ons (e.g., nutritional yeast, spirulina, soy sauce) (Varies)					
Soy sauce (organic, wheat-free)	½ tsp (3 g)	1.8	0.2	0.3	0
TOTAL CATEGORY %			**0.2%**		
TOTAL	357.8 g	1,000 Calories	100.1%	53.7 g*	19.3 g

*53.7 g of protein equals 1.3 grams per lb of body weight (53.7 g ÷ 41 lb = 1.3 g/lb).

Sample Recipe Chart #4
70 lb (31.8 kg) adult dog consuming approximately 1,638 Calories/day

	Amount	Calories	% of Total Calories	Protein (g)	Fat (g)
Protein-rich foods (e.g., beans, lentils, tofu, protein powder) (50% to 70% of Calories)					
Tofu (extra firm), prepared with nigari	4 oz (112 g)	102	6.2	11.2	6.4
Chickpeas (garbanzo beans), raw	1 ¼ cup (250 g)	945	57.6	51.3	15
NorCal Organic Pea Protein	1 scoop (13 g)	50	3	11	0.8
TOTAL CATEGORY %			**66.8%**		
Starchy veggies/grains (e.g., sweet potatoes, quinoa) (10% to 20% of Calories)					
Noodles, Japanese Soba (dry)	2 oz (56.6 g)	190	11.6	8	0.4
Pumpkin, canned (without salt)	¼ cup (61.3 g)	20.8	1.3	0.8	0.2
TOTAL CATEGORY %			**12.9%**		
Non-starchy vegetables (e.g., zucchini, green beans, kale) (1% to 10% of Calories)					
Carrot (raw)	1/2 cup, chopped (64 g)	26.3	1.6	0.6	0.2
Cauliflower (raw)	¼ cup (25 g)	6.3	0.4	0.5	0
Mushrooms, white (raw)	¼ cup, pieces or slices (17.5 g)	4	0.2	0.6	0
TOTAL CATEGORY %			**2.2%**		

	Amount	Calories	% of Total Calories	Protein (g)	Fat (g)
Fats (e.g., oil, seeds, nut butter) (15% to 30% of Calories)					
Almond butter (plain, no salt)	1 ½ TB (24 g)	151.5	9.2	3.6	14.3
Flaxseed	1 tsp, ground (3.5 g)	12.3	0.8	0.3	1
Pumpkin seed kernels (dried)	2 TB (18 g)	96	5.9	6	8.4
TOTAL CATEGORY %			**15.9%**		
Fruits (e.g., berries, apple, pear) (0% to 3% of Calories)					
Apple, with skin (raw)	¼ cup, quartered or chopped (31.3 g)	16.3	1	0	0
TOTAL CATEGORY %			**1%**		
Add-ons (e.g., spirulina, soy sauce) (Varies)					
Nutritional yeast (Bragg's brand)	1 TB (5 g)	20	1.2	2.5	0
TOTAL CATEGORY %			**1.2%**		
TOTAL	681.2 g	1,640.5 Calories*	100%	96.4 g**	46.7 g

*Your actual Calories may not add up exactly to your dog's calculated MER.

**96.4 g of protein equals about 1.4 g per lb of BW (96.4 g ÷ 70 lb = 1.38 g/lb).

Ingredients Reference Chart

The chart below contains a comprehensive list of foods, grouped into the following categories:

- Protein-rich foods
- Starchy vegetables and grains
- Non-starchy vegetables
- Fats
- Fruits
- Add-ons

We have provided two variations of measurements for many ingredients—one that is based on cups and one that is based on a smaller measurement, such as "tablespoon" (TB), "teaspoon" (tsp) or even "berry." If you're feeding a small breed dog, you'll find that the scaled-down measurements will make your life much easier!

Don't worry if you don't see an ingredient in the chart that you'd like to use in your recipes. The Self NutritionData and MyNetDiary websites provide nutrition facts for just about every ingredient imaginable. MyNetDiary also automatically calculates the nutrient information for just about any measurement you'd like to use, which is a huge plus if you're not a math fan. (See Resources.)

Ingredients Reference Chart

Food	Amount	Protein (grams)	Calories	Fat (grams)
Protein-rich foods				
Adzuki beans (raw)	1 cup (197 g)	39.1	648	1
Black beans (raw)	1 cup (194 g)	41.9	662	2.8
Broad beans/fava beans (raw)	1 cup (150 g)	39.2	512	2.3
Chickpeas/garbanzo beans (raw)	1 cup (200 g)	41	756	12.1
Cranberry beans (raw)	1 cup (195 g)	45	653	2.4
Great northern beans (raw)	1 cup (183 g)	40	620	2.1
Kidney beans, red (raw)	1 cup (184 g)	41.5	620	2
Lentils (raw)	1 cup (192 g)	49.5	678	2
Navy beans (raw)	1 cup (208 g)	46.5	701	3.1
NorCal Organic Pea Protein	1 scoop (13 g)	11	50	0.8
Pink beans (raw)	1 cup (210 g)	44	720	2.4
Pinto beans (raw)	1 cup (193 g)	41.3	670	2.4
Small white beans (raw)	1 cup (215 g)	45.4	723	2.5
Split peas (raw)	1 cup (197 g)	48.4	672	2.3
Tempeh (raw)	1 cup (166 g)	30.8	320	17.9

Food	Amount	Protein (grams)	Calories	Fat (grams)
Tofu, extra firm (prepared with nigari)	1 ounce (28 g)	2.8	25.5	1.6
White beans (raw)	1 cup (202 g)	47.2	673	1.7
Vitasoy USA, organic Nasoya extra firm tofu	1 ounce (28 g)	2.8	27.4	1.5
Starchy vegetables and grains				
Beets (raw)	1 cup (136 g)	2.2	58.5	0.2
Amaranth (uncooked)	1 cup (193 g)	26.2	716	13.5
Barley, pearled (uncooked)	1 cup (200 g)	20	704	2.3
Buckwheat groats (roasted, uncooked) (kasha)	1 cup (164 g)	19.2	567	4.4
Buckwheat groats (roasted, uncooked) (kasha)	1 TB (10 g)	1	35	0.3
Butternut squash (raw)	1 cup, cubes (140 g)	1.4	63	0.1
Millet (uncooked)	1 cup (200 g)	22	756	8.4
Noodles, Japanese Soba (dry)	1 oz (28.3 g)	4	95	0.2
Potatoes, white, flesh and skin (raw)	1/2 cup, diced (75 g)	1.5	57.7	0.1
Pumpkin, canned (without salt)	1 cup (245 g)	3	83	0.7
Quinoa (uncooked)	1 cup (170 g)	24	626	10.3
Quinoa (uncooked)	1 TB (11 g)	2	39	0.6
Sorghum (uncooked)	1 cup (192 g)	21.7	651	6.3
Sweet potato (raw, unprepared)	1 cup, cubes (133 g)	2.1	114	0.1
Turnips (raw)	1 cup, cubes (130 g)	1.2	36.4	0.1
Non-starchy vegetables				
Broccoli (raw)	1 cup, chopped (91 g)	2.6	30.9	0.3
Carrots (raw)	1 cup, chopped (128 g)	1.2	52.5	0.3
Cauliflower (raw)	1 cup (100 g)	2	25	0.1
Collards (raw)	1 cup, chopped (36 g)	0.9	10.8	0.2
Green beans (raw)	1 cup (110 g)	2	34.1	0.1
Green beans (raw)	10 beans (4" long) (55 g)	1	17	0.1

Food	Amount	Protein (grams)	Calories	Fat (grams)
Kale (raw)	1 cup, chopped (67 g)	2.2	33.5	0.5
Mushrooms, white (raw)	1 cup, pieces or slices (70g)	2.2	15.4	0.2
Spinach (raw)	1 cup (30 g)	0.9	6.9	0.1
Sweet red pepper (raw)	1 cup, chopped (149 g)	1.5	46.2	0.4
Zucchini, with skin (raw)	1 cup, chopped (124 g)	1.5	19.8	0.2
Zucchini, with skin (raw)	5 slices (50g)	1	8	0.2
Fats (oils, seeds, nut butters)				
Almond butter (plain, no salt)	1 TB (16 g)	2.4	101	9.5
Cashew butter (plain, no salt)	1 TB (16 g)	2.8	93.9	7.9
Coconut oil	1 tsp (4 g)	0	38.8	4.5
Flaxseeds (ground)	1 TB (7 g)	1	37	3
Flaxseeds (whole)	1 TB (10 g)	2	55	4.3
Flaxseed oil	1 TB (14 g)	0	120	13.6
Hemp seeds (shelled or hulled)	1 TB (10 g)	3	55	4.9
Hemp seed oil	1 TB	0	120	13
Olive oil	1 tsp (4 g)	0	39.8	4.5
Pumpkin seed kernels (dried)	1 TB (9 g)	3	48	4.2
Pumpkin seed kernels (dried)	1 tsp (3 g)	1	16	1.4
Pumpkin seed kernels (raw)	1 tsp (3 g)	1	16	1.4
Sunflower seed kernels	1 TB (9 g)	2	53	4.6
Sunflower seed kernels (dried)	1 tsp (3 g)	1	18	1.5
Sunflower seed butter (unsalted)	1 TB (16 g)	3.1	92.7	7.6
Fruits				
Apples, with skin (raw)	1 cup, quartered or chopped (125 g)	0.3	65	0.2
Banana (raw)	1 cup, sliced (150 g)	1.6	133	0.5
Blackberries (raw)	1 cup (144 g)	2	61.9	0.7
Blackberries (raw)	1 TB (9 g)	0	4	0
Blueberries (raw)	1 cup (148 g)	1.1	84.4	0.5
Blueberries (raw)	1 berry (1 g)	0	1	0
Cantaloupe melon (raw)	1 cup, cubes (160 g)	1.3	54.4	0.3

Food	Amount	Protein (grams)	Calories	Fat (grams)
Honeydew melon (raw)	1 cup, balls (177 g)	1	63.7	0.2
Kiwi fruit (raw)	1 cup (177 g)	2	108	0.9
Pear (raw)	1 cup, slices (140 g)	0.5	81.2	0.2
Raspberries (raw)	1 cup (124 g)	1.5	64	0.8
Raspberries (raw)	1 raspberry (2 g)	0	1	0
Strawberries (raw)	1 cup, sliced (166 g)	1.1	53.1	0.5
Strawberries (raw)	1 medium (1-1/4" diameter) (12 g)	0	4	0
Add-ons				
Soy sauce made from soy (tamari)	1 tsp (6 g)	0.6	3.6	0
Coconut aminos	1 tsp (5 g)	0	5	0
Nutritional Yeast (generic)	1 TB (9 g)	5	34	0
Nutritional Yeast (Bragg's)	2 TB (10 g)	5	40	0
Nutritional Yeast flakes (KAL brand)	1.5 TB, rounded (10 g)	5	40	0
Spirulina (dried)	1 TB (7 g)	4	20.3	0.5
Spirulina (raw)	1 ounce (28 g)	1.7	7.3	0.1
Wakame seaweed (raw)	2 TB (1/8 cup) (10 g)	0.3	4.5	0.1

(Sources: Self NutritionData, 2018; MyNetDiary, 2021)

Adding supplementation

Congratulations! You have just discovered the foundation for building nutrient-dense, 'almost complete and balanced' plant-based recipes for your canine companion. But we're not done yet. You'll also need to include key supplements with your recipes to round out their nutritional balance. *Do not skip this step, as if you do, your recipes will not be nutritionally adequate.*

Fortunately, this is easy when you follow our guidelines and include the following:

Plant-based supplement mix

Adding an appropriate supplement mix to your home-made meals is essential. Targeted formulas provide the proper vitamins, minerals, amino acids and other nutrients designed specifically to help balance home-prepared plant-based recipes. (Note: All of the sample recipes in this chapter were created using VegeDog by Compassion Circle, dosed according to the manufacturer's directions.)

The following supplement mixes are appropriately formulated for balancing home-prepared plant-based canine diets:

- Just be Kind (United Kingdom)
- Opal Pets Perfect Powder (United States)
- Shevega (United Kingdom)
- V-Complete (Germany)
- VegDog All-In Veluxe (Germany)
- VegeDog (United States)

  (See Resources.)

When selecting a supplement mix, be sure to check that it contains the full range of essential nutrients. For example, at the time of this writing, not all of the above mixes contain vitamin D. Be sure to communicate with the manufacturer and find out if their mix lacks any nutrients that must be provided separately.

Omega-3 fatty acids (EPA + DHA)

You'll recall that EPA and DHA must come from marine sources. No other type of oil (including flaxseed) provides these essential omega-3 fatty acids. Plant-based dogs get their EPA and DHA from the original source—marine algae.

Dosage: At this time, AAFCO has not determined a minimum recommended level of EPA + DHA for adult dogs at maintenance, however the NRC recommends a combined dosage of EPA + DHA of 30 mg/kgBW0.75 daily. The following chart provides recommended dosages for adult dogs based on the NRC's RDA. (Note that all levels are rounded to the nearest whole number.) Dogs with certain health conditions, such as osteoarthritis, cancer and kidney disease (see Chapter 11) may require a higher dose, so be sure to discuss this with your veterinarian.

EPA + DHA Dosing for Adult Dogs Chart

Dog's Weight	Omega-3 (EPA + DHA) Dose per Day (mg)
5 kg (11 lb)	100
10 kg (22 lb)	169
15 kg (33 lb)	229
20 kg (44 lb)	284
25 kg (55 lb)	335

Dog's Weight	Omega-3 (EPA + DHA) Dose per Day (mg)
30 kg (66 lb)	385
35 kg (77 lb)	432
40 kg (88 lb)	477
45 kg (99 lb)	521
50 kg (110 lb)	564
55 kg (121 lb)	606
60 kg (132 lb)	647
65 kg (143 lb)	687
70 kg (154 lb)	726
75 kg (165 lb)	765
80 kg (176 lb)	802

Taurine

Taurine is an important amino acid for heart health; certain types of DCM in dogs have been correlated with low taurine levels. You will want to check your supplement mix to ensure that it contains taurine. (At the time of this writing, all of the previously listed brands contain taurine.) If you are not able to access a product containing taurine, you will need to add this important supplement to your recipes. Since taurine is not currently considered an essential amino acid for dogs, the NRC and AAFCO have not determined an RDA.

Dosage: The recommended dosage of taurine for dogs ranges from 50 mg to 1,000 mg per day (Wynn & Marsden, 2003; Messonnier, 2012). For healthy adult dogs, we recommend a daily dose of 250 mg for small dogs, 500 mg for medium-sized dogs and 1,000 mg for large dogs, divided between a.m. and p.m. Dogs who suffer from cardiac disease, such as dilated cardiomyopathy (DCM), typically require a higher dose, so be sure to discuss this with your veterinarian. (The suggested dose for Cocker Spaniel cardiomyopathy is 500 mg given every eight hours.) (Wynn & Marsden, 2003; Messonnier, 2012).

L-Carnitine

L-carnitine is considered a non-essential amino acid for dogs; however, it is important for many of the body's functions, including heart health. For this reason, it is an important part of your dog's plant-based nutrition plan. As with taurine, you will want to check your supplement mix to ensure that it contains L-carnitine and supplement separately if it does not.

Dosage: No dosage of L-carnitine for dogs has been established by the NRC or AAFCO; however, 100 mg to 2,000 mg/day in divided doses has been recommended for dogs with heart disease (Messonnier, 2012). Based on this, we think a reasonable dosage for healthy adult dogs is 250 mg/day for small dogs, 500 mg/day for medium-sized dogs and 1,000 mg/day for large dogs, divided between a.m. and p.m. If your dog suffers from hypothyroidism, discuss the addition of L-carnitine with your veterinarian. In humans, L-carnitine may reduce the function of thyroid hormone and could possibly have the same effect in dogs (Wynn & Marsden, 2003; Messonnier, 2012).

Be sure to purchase the L-carnitine form only. Avoid products containing D-carnitine and DL-carnitine. The D form of carnitine is shown to be metabolized as xenobiotic (as an unnatural foreign chemical substance). In fish, D-carnitine triggered inflammation of the liver, oxidative stress and apoptosis as well as negative metabolomic effects (Li et al., 2019).

B-complex

Although the listed supplement mixes provide B vitamins, we find that adding a bit more via a dedicated B-complex product further improves the nutrient profile of home-made plant-based recipes.

Dosage: Using the Thorne Research B-Complex #12 (or a comparable product), we recommend 1/8 capsule daily for small dogs, 1/4 capsule daily for medium dogs and 1/2 capsule daily for large dogs. Note that dogs with certain health conditions, such as CKD or seizures, will benefit from higher levels of B vitamins. In these cases, we recommend discussing dosing with your veterinarian.

Vitamin C (ascorbic acid)

Vitamin C is not considered an essential nutrient for dogs because they can manufacture their own. However, no matter how much we try to reduce toxins in our dog's environment, the reality is that we live in a toxic world. Toxins create stress on the body and send unhealthy epigenetic messages to the cells and microbiome, potentially triggering oxidative damage and dysbiosis. For these reasons, we believe that most modern dogs can benefit from the added antioxidant power of supplemental vitamin C.

Dosage: We prefer the patented Ester C form of vitamin C as it is pH neutral and gentler on the stomach than ascorbic acid. We recommend a daily dose of 250 to 500 mg for small dogs, 500 to 1,000 mg for medium to large dogs and 1,000 to 2,000 mg for large and giant dogs, divided between a.m. and p.m. Begin with the lower dosage and increase according to your dog's GI tolerance. If your dog experiences signs of GI distress, such as loose stool, reduce the dose accordingly.

You can find all the recommended supplements in the Resources section.

Note: Some supplements (and foods) contain rosemary as a preservative. Avoid these if your dog suffers from epilepsy or is prone to seizures. Also avoid products containing oregano, fennel and sage, as these are also considered to be neurotoxic herbs. Many omega-3 softgels contain rosemary, so you will find a rosemary-free omega-3 product in the Resources section.

What about puppies?

If you're disappointed that we haven't provided a recipe creation formula for puppies, hear us out. We've read books that address on a basic level the need for puppies to get more protein or the proper levels and balance of calcium and phosphorus or more Calories. But we can do a great deal of harm to a puppy—especially a large-breed puppy—if we do not provide them with the proper nutrients, especially during the first six months of growth. We understand that we need to walk a fine line here between sounding too regimented and doing what we feel is best for dogs during their crucial developmental stage. After all, what happens during puppyhood sets the tone for a dog's lifelong health.

Studies show that home-prepared puppy diets that are not formulated by a qualified canine nutritionist are often nutritionally imbalanced in a way that can cause serious health issues, such as developmental orthopedic disease (DOD), that can harm a dog for the rest of her life. And we're not just talking about plant-based diets. This is true of all types, including the raw-meat-and-bone diets (RMBDs) that are currently popular.

Puppies have different requirements than adult dogs for many nutrients. We obviously want to start them out right by giving puppies the proper nutrition to maintain optimum health throughout their lives. Otherwise, we run the risk of creating serious long-term damage. Diana formulates puppy diets and tracks the puppy's progress until adulthood, adjusting the recipe at several key growth stages to ensure that proper energy intake and nutritional levels are met and that a desired rate of growth is maintained. Some commercial dog foods are labeled as 'all life stages.' However, 'all life stages' formulas claiming to be appropriate for large-breed puppies must contain the label statement: "[Pet Food Name] is formulated to meet the nutritional levels established by the AAFCO Dog Food Nutrient Profiles for growth/all life stages including growth of large-size dogs (70 lbs or more as an adult)" (Linder, 2017). (See Resources.)

It's also important to note that to date no feeding trials have been conducted on commercial plant-based foods that claim to nutritionally support puppies. As plant-based dog nutrition continues to increase in popularity and companies introduce new plant-based puppy formulations, it's imperative that consumers demand ethical feeding trials to document their safety and adequacy.

Tips for purchasing commercial plant-based products

You want to feed your canine companion a diet rich in fresh, whole foods as often as possible, but as we pointed out in Chapter 3, life happens. Sometimes, you forget to plan ahead. Sometimes, you're so tired or busy that the best you can do is pull something out of the freezer for yourself. During those times, having the option of a high-quality commercial vegan dog food can remove a lot of stress. And after all, feeding your dog a nutritious diet shouldn't create additional stress in your already hectic life.

We're thrilled that plant-based dog nutrition is gaining in popularity, and that new commercial foods are constantly appearing. After all, commercial pet food manufacturers are astute observers of market demand. When they introduce new plant-based foods and treats, it's because they know that consumers want them.

This is great news. But on the flip side, some companies might be tempted to introduce their products to market without the proper expertise or resources to create formulas that truly meet the nutritional needs of our canine companions. Unfortunately, this has resulted in nutritional inaccuracies in several commercial vegan dog foods, with analyzed nutrients not matching those reported in the Guaranteed Analyses on product labels. But this isn't an issue only among vegan pet foods. A study revealed that 16 out of 52 commercial animal ingredient-based dog foods contained ingredients not listed on the label (Okuma & Hellberg, 2015). Obviously, product mislabeling and adulteration with unidentified ingredients could cause potentially serious problems for dogs with food intolerances or other health issues that require specific nutrient parameters. The unfortunate reality is that quality control issues occur all too often across the mass-market commercial pet food industry.

Commercial frozen and freeze-dried pet foods have contained serious pathogens, including *E. coli, Salmonella, Clostridium perfringens, Cl. Difficile* and *Staphylococcus aureus* (Weese et al., 2005), among others. Analyses of commercial raw foods have also shown potentially dangerous nutritional imbalances, including vitamin and mineral deficiencies and toxicities (Davies et al., 2019).

Not even industry giants are immune. On July 30, 2021, a $12.5 million class-action lawsuit against Hill's Pet Nutrition and Colgate-Palmolive was approved for consumers who purchased certain Hill's Prescription Diet or Hill's Science Diet products between September 1, 2018, and May 31, 2019. Sadly, many dogs became sick or died due to excessive levels of vitamin D contained in these products (Kroll Settlement Administration, 2021).

Our point is that no pet (or human) food is immune from quality-control issues. So, you should always do your homework before deciding which products pass your pup's lips. Here are some questions to ask before selecting a commercial plant-based dog food:

Does the food meet AAFCO requirements for 'complete and balanced'?
Part of what makes the study of nutrition so exciting is the more that science advances, the deeper the insight we gain as to how diet affects organisms at the deepest levels—including the genome, microbiome and metabolome. These are terms that just a few decades ago were rare—or unheard of—in nutritional nomenclature. Case in point: look at what we now know about the dangers of animal ingredients, as we've detailed in this book.

Of course, no organization has a monopoly of knowledge on what constitutes ideal nutritional parameters for any organism, including dogs. That includes even the most respected animal nutrition groups such as the NRC and AAFCO. But while the guidelines set by these organizations might not reflect a dog's *ideal* nutrient intake, they do help ensure that dogs on 'complete and balanced' commercial diets won't fall victim to nutritional deficiencies or toxicities.

For this reason, we believe it's important that pet food companies marketing products for daily consumption take the time to understand and meet the AAFCO guidelines for 'complete and balanced.' You can easily determine this by looking for the product's Nutritional Adequacy Statement, which is typically found on the sides or back of a pet food label. (Note that treats do not require this statement.) A nutritional claim of 'complete and balanced' means that the product contains all required nutrients ('complete') at the correct ratios ('balanced') for the intended life stage (AAFCO, 2012).

Nutritional Adequacy Statements can be presented in one of three ways:

1. "__(Product Name)_____ is formulated to meet the nutritional levels established by the AAFCO Dog (or cat) Food Nutrient Profiles for _____(life stage the product is intended for, such as adult, puppy, all-life-stages)_____."

2. "Animal feeding tests using AAFCO procedures substantiate that __(Product Name)_____ provides complete and balanced nutrition for _____ (life stage the product is formulated for)_____."

3. "___(Product Name)_____ provides complete and balanced nutrition for __(life stage)_____ and is comparable to a product which has been substantiated using AAFCO feeding tests."

This last statement is not commonly used. According to AAFCO, "Products justified nutritionally adequate in this way are sometimes referred to as 'family products,' meaning the product is similar, but not identical, to one which has been subjected to animal feeding tests. The differences may include minor formulation changes that do not affect the products' nutritional basis" (AAFCO, 2012).

A nutritional statement of 'complete and balanced' according to AAFCO is important because it means that the manufacturer is serious about compliance with currently known nutritional standards and that it's willing to substantiate its claims.

Does the food contain taurine?

If you purchased a commercial cat food before the late 1980s, chances are likely that it didn't contain taurine. Then, sadly, tens of thousands of feline deaths were connected to taurine-deficient cat foods. It was only when taurine became recognized as an essential amino acid for cats that commercial pet food manufacturers incorporated it into their feline food products. This situation points out that nutritional knowledge is always evolving.

Taurine is not currently recognized as an essential amino acid for dogs because they can metabolize it endogenously (within their bodies). However, we now know that a variety of nutritional and metabolic variables might result in a decreased ability for some dogs to synthesize and metabolize taurine. For this reason, we believe that taurine will one day become recognized as a 'conditionally essential' amino acid for dogs and that manufacturers will add taurine to *all* 'complete and balanced' commercial dog foods.

In the meantime, the presence of taurine in commercial plant-based diets indicates that the manufacturer understands its importance, cares about the health of its canine consumers and practices responsible product formulation. We recommend that you also check for the presence of L-carnitine. Like taurine, L-carnitine is a non-essential amino acid vital for energy production, heart health and many other important bodily functions.

Was digestibility testing conducted?

'Digestibility' is a huge buzzword in the pet food industry, and for good reason. Processed commercial foods are already less digestible than fresh, whole foods. Still, when you purchase commercial dog food, you want assurance that your dog will be able to efficiently digest and absorb its nutrients. Traditionally, when pet food companies conduct digestibility testing, they're showing that they understand its importance and that they are committed to creating products that support optimum nutritional health.

But there is a caveat when it comes to testing. Sadly, manufacturers of commercial animal-based dog foods typically test their products on dogs kept in a laboratory environment. Obviously, this type of animal testing is not in line with an ethos of kindness toward all animals. For this reason, we urge you to ask manufacturers how they test their products, and which tests they conduct, keeping in that mind if a plant-based pet food company does not conduct a certain test, it may be due to an active choice to avoid laboratory testing on animals. Volunteer testing using companion dogs is the preferred standard; it shows that the company takes its science seriously, while also adapting a humane approach to all dogs.

Is it organic and/or non-GMO?

Organic and non-GMO ingredients cost more for the manufacturer, which typically passes that cost along to the consumer. This means that commercial foods containing organic and/or non-GMO ingredients are likely to put a bigger dent in your wallet than conventional products. Manufacturers realize this, which is one reason why producers of plant-based dog foods often use conventional ingredients. They're not trying to skimp; they're just trying to produce quality food that's also affordable. We're aware of several dedicated manufacturers of plant-based dog foods that are both committed to quality and rely on conventional ingredients.

However, we've already pointed out the hazards of GMO ingredients, including their resistance to pesticides and herbicides, such as the weed killer RoundUp (glyphosate), which is labeled as a "probable carcinogen." Due to the possible health hazards, we continue to urge caution regarding GMO ingredients. As we pointed out in Chapter 5, foods that contain toxins are viewed by the body as foreign invaders. Thus, we're not surprised that GMO soy found in mass-market commercial dog foods is a leading cause of food intolerances.

We're not saying to rule out commercial products that contain GMOs. However, we are saying that you might at a minimum want to rotate these products with an organic/non-GMO food. Doing so can help ease any potential strain on your wallet and your dog's health.

Is the company transparent?

Transparency equals trust. If a company isn't transparent about their ingredients, processes and mission, then how can we trust that their motives are in the best interest of our canine companions? Most companies that operate with the highest standards are proud of that fact and happy to shout it from the rooftops, barring revealing any trade secrets. Topics that companies should be transparent about include:

Ingredient function. Why was each ingredient chosen? What does it contribute nutritionally to the recipe?

Ingredient quality. Are the ingredients predominantly organic and/or non-GMO? Is there anything else special about them, such as locally grown, produced from heirloom seeds, etc.?

Sourcing. Where do the ingredients come from? The country of origin is very important, especially in light of deadly recalls that have occurred within the pet food industry over the past several years. For this reason, we advise against purchasing products that contain ingredients originating from China. If a company is not knowledgeable or transparent about its ingredient sourcing, we recommend moving on to another manufacturer. Your dog is part of your family, and her safety is of the utmost importance.

Vitamin D origin. Plant-based vitamin D will usually be listed as vitamin D2, however vegan vitamin D3 from lichen also exists. Traditional D3, however, is made from the lanolin in sheep's wool. Some 'almost vegan' pet food brands contain non-vegan vitamin D. If you can't tell from the ingredients panel, contact the manufacturer for more information.

Third-party testing. All manufacturers should perform regular quality control tests on their products for contaminants such as *E. coli, Salmonella,* mycotoxins and other potential hazards. These tests should be performed after each batch is produced and during a quality control hold, which usually lasts for 24 to 48 hours before the product is released for shipping. Brands should also run regular nutritional testing to ensure their formulas remain consistent. (Remember the excess vitamin D issue in some Hill's products due to a supplier mistake with the vitamin/mineral pre-mix.)

Does the company reflect your values?

Some non-vegan pet food companies are adding plant-based formulations to their line of products due to increased consumer demand. There are many vegans who for ethical reasons won't purchase from these companies, but we'd like to offer a different viewpoint on that stance. Diana remembers attending an event for Farm Sanctuary, the founding farm animal rescue in the United States, based in Watkins Glen, New York. Gene Baur, the sanctuary's co-founder and president, discussed vegans who were boycotting vegan ice cream products made by a popular dairy-based ice cream company. Gene, a staunch vegan for many decades, pointed out that this scenario could backfire. He reasoned that if consumers don't support vegan offerings introduced by non-vegan companies, those companies might simply remove the products due to lack of demand. They will also be unlikely to introduce new vegan offerings in the future. If, however, the vegan products do well in the marketplace, companies will be more inclined to continue producing them and even adding more. Companies are in business to sell their products. As consumers, we have a lot of power in determining which products make it to market—and stay there—by how we choose to spend our money. It's a simple matter of supply and demand economics.

We can also use our purchasing power to change company policies, including letting them know that we are against animal testing of all kinds, including as part of commercial pet food feeding trials. The world is changing, and we can each be a positive part of that change. Of course, we applaud companies that were founded on the principle of kindness to all animals, and we believe in enthusiastically supporting these companies. There's nothing more exciting than helping drive the success of a compassion-based business.

So, as you see, both scenarios offer unique opportunities—one for driving change and one for supporting ethical innovation. And both create value for the world in which we live.

Don't forget to test

Clients often ask us what types of laboratory tests plant-fed dogs should have. Our answer is that *all* dogs need routine wellness testing, regardless of their diet type. After all, you keep on top of your own health with annual doctor visits and screenings, and it's no different for your canine companion. Since clinical symptoms of disease often don't manifest until the situation is advanced, regular checkups and laboratory testing are the best ways to ensure your dog is healthy and to catch any potential issues early.

Adult dogs should have annual wellness check-ups. Seniors are more prone to age-related health problems, so a routine veterinary visit every six months is preferred. We recommend asking your veterinarian for the following at each visit:

Full physical examination. Your veterinarian will perform a thorough check-up, including evaluating your dog's weight and the health of her heart, eyes, teeth, ears, muscles and joints.

Complete Blood Count (CBC) test with differential. This test monitors the health of your dog's red blood cells, white blood cells and platelets, including the different types of white blood cells (neutrophils, lymphocytes, monocytes, basophils, and eosinophils), the amount of hemoglobin (protein molecules in the blood that carry oxygen) and the hematocrit (the total volume of blood that is made up of red blood cells). It can help diagnose and monitor many different conditions, including anemia, autoimmune disorders, heart disease, infection, liver disease, inflammation, allergic responses and certain cancers such as leukemia, lymphoma and cancer of the bone marrow (MedlinePlus, 2020).

Blood Chemistry Profile. The blood chemistry profile measures important substances in the blood, including electrolytes (sodium, potassium, chloride), phosphorus, calcium, magnesium, glucose, protein (total protein, albumin, globulins), bilirubin, liver enzymes (Alkaline phosphatase, GGT, ALT, AST), creatinine kinase, cholesterol, triglycerides, amylase, tCO2 (Bicarb), AGAP (anion gap), blood urea nitrogen (BUN) and creatinine. It helps check the health of the organs, including the adrenals, liver and kidneys, as well as screen for other conditions, such as diabetes mellitus, metabolic acidosis and protein-losing enteropathy (PLE) (Tufts University, 2013; MedlinePlus, 2021).

Fecal exam. This checks for issues such as blood, fats, bilirubin and the presence of parasites.

Urinalysis complete. This test includes urine pH, specific gravity, protein, glucose, ketones, blood and bilirubin. It can help identify conditions such as a urinary tract infection, diabetes, chronic kidney disease (CKD) and liver disease.

Other tests that might be warranted depending upon your dog's situation include:

Plasma and whole blood taurine. This test checks that your dog's taurine levels are within the normal range (performed by UC Davis Amino Acid Laboratory). (See Resources.)

Thyroid Profile Panel. Veterinarians often rely on the standard T4 blood test to diagnose hypothyroidism (low thyroid function) in dogs; however, this test on its own lacks the specificity and reliability for accurate diagnosis (Dodds & Laverdure, 2011). If your dog is lethargic, gaining weight without overeating, suffering from hair loss, itchy skin, dry eye, behavioral issues or other unexplained health issues, we recommend asking your veterinarian to send a sample of your dog's blood to Hemopet for a Thyroid Profile 5, which includes T4, Free T4, T3, Free T3 and Thyroglobulin Autoantibody (TgAA). You can also add a CBC with Differential plus Chemistries to this thyroid panel. (See Resources.)

Vitamin B12/Folate/TLI (trypsin-like immunoreactivity). This test measures deficiency and excess. It can help identify conditions such as acute pancreatitis, renal disease or malnutrition, as well as some malabsorptive disorders of the small intestines, such as exocrine pancreatic insufficiency (EPI) (performed by Cornell University Animal Health Diagnostic Center and others). (See Resources.)

25-Hydroxyvitamin Dx. This test identifies vitamin D deficiency or toxicity (performed by Michigan State University Veterinary Diagnostic Laboratory and others). (See Resources.)

We also recommend monitoring your dog's urine pH every month. All you'll need is a basic urine pH test strip that you can purchase online. Simply collect your dog's first urine of the morning, dip the strip in the urine and compare the color results to the product chart. A normal urine pH for dogs is between 6 to 7.5 (Rizzi, 2014); however, we prefer slightly acidic urine at around 6.5. If your dog's urine pH is too high (alkaline) or contains blood, we recommend that your veterinarian extract a urine sample directly from the bladder by cystocentesis, as free-catch urine can be contaminated by preputial and vaginal secretions. If the alkalinity is diet-related, try incorporating some buffered ascorbic acid or organic cranberry extract, such as Cranimals, to lower the pH. (See Resources.)

We've covered *a lot* of information in this chapter. We don't expect you to digest it all (pun intended) the first time around, or even the second. Like anything worth achieving, mastery will come with practice. Stick with it and you'll soon become an expert at creating delicious, 'almost complete and balanced' plant-based recipes for your canine companion.

But just as with anything worth accomplishing, you might hit some bumps along the road to plant-based bliss. The next chapter provides our time-tested tips to help you navigate them as smoothly as possible. We hope you don't experience any of these issues, but if you do, it's good to know that help is just a few pages away.

Chapter 7
Overcoming Obstacles

Every goal worth achieving has challenges and transitioning your dog to a nutritious plant-based diet is no exception. Hopefully, the action steps from Chapter 3 will help minimize any obstacles, but even with careful planning, you're likely to experience unexpected roadblocks and detours along your journey. So, in this chapter, we've rounded up the five most common questions we receive regarding transitioning dogs to a plant-based lifestyle, compiled them into a "What to do if...." list and offered our time-tested tips on solving them. We hope this chapter on overcoming obstacles solidifies your confidence, reaffirms your enthusiasm and further empowers you to nurture your dog's optimum health with a plant-based lifestyle.

Now, let's talk about "What to do if..."

Your dog experiences gas or loose stool

By now, you likely have a good understanding of the benefits of dietary fiber. From helping manage diabetes mellitus and certain cancers to promoting ideal weight and normal stool formation, fiber can help keep your dog in tip-top shape. You'll recall from our discussion in Chapter 4 that functional fibers, called prebiotics, may just be the most important food to promote a healthy gut microbiome. Since the gut is the largest immune organ in the body, optimizing the microbiome is vital to boosting the immune system, decreasing inflammation, strengthening the intestinal barrier and achieving systemic balance.

Animal ingredients do not contain fiber. A well-balanced plant-based diet provides healthy fiber and ample levels of all macro- and micronutrients. But sometimes, when you first introduce fiber to your dog's (and your own) diet, you might notice some unwanted side effects—namely an increase in gas and possibly loose stool. The chances of these responses occurring increase if your dog currently consumes a high-meat/low-fiber diet. In most cases, they are temporary and will disappear once your dog's gastrointestinal tract adjusts to the new ingredients. In the meantime, there are steps you can take to minimize—or even avoid—these issues.

Go slowly
Just like the children's story of the tortoise and the hare, when transitioning your dog to a plant-based diet, slow and steady wins the race. If your dog isn't used to eating foods such as lentils or beans, begin by offering just a few as a healthy snack for a few

days. If he experiences no adverse effects, slowly increase the amount, incorporating them as a 'topper' to his current food. If gas or loose stool occurs, reduce the amount for several days and slowly build back up.

When your dog has adjusted to the legumes, gradually introduce veggies into his diet. Again, go slowly, monitor and adjust accordingly. Once your dog acclimates to eating a variety of plant-based ingredients, you can begin weaning him off his meat-based diet, but again we urge going slowly. We recommend making a large batch of your plant-based recipe and substituting 20% of the new recipe for 20% of the current recipe *every third day*. On this schedule, your dog should be completely transitioned to the new recipe within 15 days. Adjust the transition time according to your dog's individual response. If he shows no adverse gastrointestinal signs, feel free to decrease the transition time to every other day. On the other hand, if your dog suffers from a gastrointestinal disorder or does not easily tolerate food changes, increase the transition time as needed. Remember that this isn't a sprint, it's a marathon. You are in this for the long haul, and eventually you—and your dog—will triumphantly cross the finish line.

Increase variety gradually

In addition to slowly increasing the *quantity* of your dog's plant-based diet, we also recommend gradually increasing the *variety*. This is because foods vary in their fiber composition and different strains of gut bacteria prefer to munch on and obtain nutrients from different fiber sources (Hewings-Martin, 2019). So, while your dog's GI system may have acclimated to chomping on chickpeas, her microbiome might still need to proliferate additional strains that respond to fermenting other types of dietary fiber. And since every dog's microbiome is unique, so are the best types of fiber to nourish it. By adding one new type of food at a time, you can determine which ingredients will promote optimum stool quality without creating excess gas (Marks, 2017). This is also a great way to determine which foods best tickle your dog's taste buds. Allowing your dog to experience the flavor and texture of each new ingredient separately will enable him to demonstrate his favorite plant-based preferences (perhaps with a vigorous tail wag)!

Keep a food journal

Keeping a journal of your dog's dietary habits is the simplest and most accurate way to associate ingredient intake with adverse reactions such as digestive issues as well as beneficial effects such as improved stool quality. A written record will also help you remember which ingredients your dog prefers. As we mentioned, every dog is an individual and will digest ingredients differently—whether plant-based or not. Journaling will reveal patterns that enable you to create your own custom repertoire of nutritious, satisfying foods that promote the desired health—and happiness—outcomes.

Change up the fiber

As we mentioned in Chapter 4, fiber is typically classified by its ability to dissolve in water (soluble or insoluble) and the rate at which it is fermented by bacteria in the colon. If your dog suffers from large-bowel diarrhea, we advise emphasizing foods rich in soluble fiber and minimizing those that are high in insoluble fiber. Signs of large-bowel diarrhea include rushing to go outside, having accidents in the house or passing loose stool containing mucus or fresh blood. Soluble fiber is shown to help regulate stool quality in individuals with large-bowel diarrhea. As it passes through the GI tract, soluble fiber absorbs water and swells into a gel-like substance that slows the digestive process. Insoluble fiber, on the other hand, speeds up the passage of food through the digestive tract and may help dogs suffering from constipation. Avoid giving insoluble fiber to dogs prone to diarrhea, however, since it can act as a natural laxative. Insoluble fiber has also been shown to worsen symptoms in people suffering from Irritable Bowel Syndrome (IBS.)

Recognize what's normal

Many people worry about the increased volume of stool typically seen in dogs on plant-based diets. However, this is totally normal. Proper elimination and stool volume help maintain healthy anal glands and membranes, but that's not the only benefit. As we discussed earlier, dead bacteria and other undesirable substances make up a large portion of the stool's dry matter. Larger stools that occur when fiber is initially increased can be a sign of detoxification. So, don't be concerned if adding fiber-rich foods increases your dog's stool volume and frequency of defecation. If everything else looks good, this is a natural and healthy change.

Give it time

Remember that many dogs consume high-meat, fiber-deficient diets, so their microbiota need time to adjust to fiber-rich plant-based foods. Follow the steps above and you'll soon find that things are moving along just fine.

What to do if you see undigested food in your dog's poop

Obviously, you want your dog to absorb the nutrients from his food, not pass them out the other end. So, it makes sense that undigested food in your dog's stool is not desirable. But it's also not a reason to panic. You might just need to make some simple dietary adjustments. Here are a few recommendations:

- Be sure to soak beans overnight, then drain and rinse well prior to cooking. Boil or pressure cook until very tender. Mash well before serving.

- Select red or yellow lentils instead of green, brown or black. The red and yellow varieties cook up creamy and are easier to digest.

- Finely dice raw vegetables or puree them in a food processor or blender. When first transitioning your dog, consider steaming the veggies to help break down the cell wall.

- Use a dog-friendly probiotic to help balance the microbiome.

- Add a plant-based digestive enzyme to help break down the food. (See Resources.) While digestive enzymes might be a beneficial short-term solution, we recommend optimizing your dog's own digestive system rather than relying on supplemental enzymes long-term. While generally considered safe, they can cause side effects such as stomach pain, gas, nausea, diarrhea and/or vomiting. Digestive enzymes can also interact with certain medications, such as blood thinners (bromelain), antacids and certain diabetes medications (Brissette, 2019).

If your dog isn't used to digesting plant foods, his GI system might simply need some time to adjust to the new ingredients.

Your dog refuses the new food

Dogs are unique individuals and each one has his own taste preferences. So, while it is of course possible for your canine companion to turn his nose up when introduced to any new diet, in our experience most dogs take quite nicely to their new plant-based offerings. Many people even find that during the transition period, their dog munches on the veggie-based ingredients *before* the meat! And, as we've pointed out earlier, studies show that not only do dogs tolerate plant-based ingredients well; they also find them palatable.

However, some dogs are particularly finicky, resist dietary changes or use mealtimes to exhibit behavioral control. How many of us have hand-fed our dog at one time or another, regardless of the type of diet? This shows that our canine companions have trained us very well!

Here are some tips to help tempt your picky pup:

Try a tasty topper

Some dogs have a sweet tooth, while others prefer salty, savory, fruity, herbal or nutty flavors. Identify your dog's taste preferences and use them to create extra enticement at mealtimes. If your dog swoons for sweets, a dribble or two of maple syrup will likely spark his interest (but don't go overboard). Diana's dog, Moo, goes crazy for the taste of mint. If that sounds like your canine companion, finely chop a little fresh mint and sprinkle it onto his meal.

If your dog's a 'cheese-head,' sprinkle some cheesy-tasting nutritional yeast over his meal (which will also provide a nice dose of amino acids and B vitamins). Other tasty toppers include a dash or two of wheat-free soy sauce (tamari) or coconut aminos, a dribble of dog-friendly nut butter or tahini (be sure it is free of xylitol, added sugars or other problematic ingredients), a dollop of almond, cashew, soy or coconut milk yogurt (again, check the ingredients) and fresh herbs such as parsley, thyme, oregano and rosemary (avoid oregano and rosemary if your dog is prone to seizures). Think outside the bowl and let your dog's taste buds guide you.

Avoid between-meal snacks

If you munched on cookies, cake and potato chips all day, would you be interested in 'real' food at mealtimes? You'd likely come to the table a lot less hungry and wouldn't find your food as enticing. The same holds true for our canine companions. Unless your dog sucks up food like a Hoover vacuum (Labrador Retriever, anyone?), you want him to eagerly approach his bowl when chowtime rolls around. Remember that snacks should only make up a small portion of a dog's diet; they are not a substitute for nutritious, fresh meals.

Become a savvy marketer

How do savvy marketers entice consumers to jump at their products? They employ the age-old tactic of *scarcity*. Marketers understand human nature; tell us that we can't have something, and we want it even more. Have you ever viewed a TV shopping network and panicked as the inventory numbers on the item you were following plummeted toward zero? On the flip side, we are more indifferent towards things that we can have anytime we want (hence the classic dating tactic of playing hard to get).

Dogs also show heightened interest in things they can't have. Try taking away a toy your dog hasn't touched for weeks and watch it transform before your eyes into his most prized possession! The same goes for his food. If you leave your dog's dish out indefinitely, what's the incentive to gobble it up? There's no threat of it disappearing. When presenting a new food to your dog, you need to become a savvy marketer. You need to create scarcity. How do you do that? Place his food down at the regularly appointed mealtimes, but only leave it there for 20 minutes. If he doesn't eat it during that time, pick it up, refrigerate it and *do not put it back down until the next mealtime.* Your dog will soon get the message that if he's hungry, he'd better 'act now' because the item he wants won't be around for long.

If your dog continues to decline his food, consider a trip to the veterinarian. Food refusal could indicate a medical issue.

You are concerned about cost

Since plant-based foods are typically less energy-dense than animal products, it takes a greater volume of food to meet the same Calorie requirements. This is great news for your dog who will reap the benefits of more substantial meals in his bowl. But you might fear that keeping up with your dog's plant-based lifestyle—especially if you have a larger dog or multiple dogs—will eventually take a toll on your wallet. Here's where we have great—and perhaps surprising—news for you; a plant-based diet is typically less expensive than one based on animal ingredients.

The myth that purchasing plant-based foods will leave you broke is based largely on the high cost of vegan convenience foods, such as plant-based burgers and vegan cheeses. At one major health food chain, we found 80/20 pasture-raised ground beef selling for $5.99 per pound, compared to $11.29 per pound for plant-based Beyond Beef—a difference of more than $5 per pound. This enormous price difference reflects the sad reality that slaughtering living, sentient beings for food is often less expensive than growing plants. However, we're optimistic that this scenario will reverse as market demand and production for plant-based products increases.

If you planned to feed your dog pounds and pounds of processed vegan foods, we'd say, "Yes, that's going to get expensive." We'd also say that's not a very healthy nutrition strategy! But, fortunately, that's not your game plan (or ours). Your dog will feast on fresh, whole-food plant-based ingredients, including legumes, whole grains and dog-friendly veggies, fruits, nuts and seeds. These foods are super nutritious and affordable. It doesn't get any better than that!

You may be thinking, "But I want to feed my dog organic produce, and I can't afford that." We've got you covered there, too. By following our simple tips, your canine companion will reap the health benefits of the plant kingdom's most nutritious bounty—and you'll have money left over to buy him (or yourself) a special treat.

Buy from bulk bins

Bulk bins offer everything from lentils, chickpeas and beans to whole grains, nuts, seeds, gluten-free flours and even nutritional yeast—often at a substantial discount from their pre-packaged counterparts. You can even find sizable bulk bin discounts on organic ingredients. Researchers in Portland, Oregon compared prices of organic products in bulk bins and packages at 12 local stores, ranging from co-ops to national grocery chains. They found that buying organic ingredients from bulk bins resulted in a 56% savings. That's like scoring a 'buy one, get one free' deal on all kinds of organic ingredients (Burnham, 2012).

Bear in mind that buying from bulk bins isn't the same as buying in bulk from warehouse stores such as Costco and Sam's Club. Buying in bulk makes sense and can save a lot of money if you have a large dog, multiple dogs or you also consume many of the same foods (which is a likely scenario). Otherwise, you might end up throwing away money on spoiled and outdated items. Buying from bulk bins allows you to control the portions, helping to cut down on food and financial waste.

Be aware, however, that not all bulk bin items offer savings. We recommend conducting your own price comparisons to see which ingredients make sense scooping yourself and which don't.

Go organic wisely

We all want to feed our families—including our four-legged members—the healthiest, most nutritious foods possible. In a perfect world, where price is not an issue, we would all opt to purchase organic ingredients. When we buy organic, we avoid consuming pesticides, herbicides and other toxins that can contaminate conventional produce. We also ensure that our food was not genetically modified (GM), since GMOs are not permitted in organic foods. But the reality is that for many of us, going 100% organic isn't possible. The good news is that there are healthy options.

When deciding which fruits and veggies to purchase organic, we rely on the Environmental Working Group's (EWG) *Shopper's Guide to Pesticides in Produce*. Each year, the EWG publishes its Dirty Dozen and Clean Fifteen lists ranking fruits and vegetables by their level of pesticide residue. We recommend checking the EWG's website for their updated lists, as their rankings change each year. (See Resources.)

By purchasing organic produce wisely, you can enjoy the best of both worlds—feeding your family safely *and* saving money.

Pick frozen produce

Purchasing fruits and veggies in the frozen food aisle is a great way to save money. During our own informal comparison, we discovered some surprising price differences between fresh and frozen produce. For example, Whole Foods 365 brand frozen organic chopped kale cost $2.69 per pound, while their fresh chopped kale cost $5.32 per pound—virtually double. In another comparison, 16 ounces of fresh organic strawberries cost $5.99, compared to $7.49 for a 32 *oz bag* of organic frozen strawberries.

Many of us believe that frozen produce is less nutritious than fresh produce. It's true that frozen vegetables are typically blanched or steamed to kill bacteria prior to freezing, which can decrease the nutrient levels of water-soluble vitamins, such as vitamin C and B vitamins. However, frozen produce is harvested and flash-frozen at the peak of ripeness, which is also the height of its nutritional value. Fresh produce is often picked unripe, stored for months and chemically speed-ripened prior to arriving at your local grocery store. This can reduce the nutritional value (Harvard Medical School, 2014).

Fresh produce that sits too long on your counter or in your refrigerator also loses nutrients. Water-soluble vitamins are especially vulnerable to oxygen, heat and light exposure. Carrots stored for just one week in the fridge can lose up to 80% of their vitamin C content (Harvard Medical School, 2014).

A two-year study published in the *Journal of Food Composition and Analysis* analyzed and compared key nutrient levels in fresh, fresh-stored (refrigerated) and frozen fruits and vegetables (broccoli, cauliflower, corn, green beans, green peas, spinach, blueberries and strawberries). To make the study as realistic as possible, the fresh-stored produce was refrigerated for five days after purchase, mimicking typical consumer practices. In most of the comparisons, the authors found "no significant differences in assessed vitamin contents" between the fresh, fresh-stored and frozen produce. But when there were significant differences, the nutrient levels of the frozen produce surpassed the fresh-stored more often than the other way around. These results led the researchers to conclude that:

> *When considering the refrigerated storage to which consumers may expose their fresh produce prior to consumption, the findings of this study do not support the common belief of consumers that fresh food has significantly greater nutritional value than its frozen counterpart* (Li et al., 2017, pp. 8).

So, there you have it. Purchasing frozen produce can help you avoid storage-related nutrient loss *and* save you money.

We recommend supporting local produce growers whenever possible. But stocking your freezer with frozen fruits and veggies offers a winning combination of value, convenience and nutrition. No matter what life throws at you, with a freezer full of produce, you—and your canine companion—will never miss out on your daily veg.

Choose dry beans over canned

If cutting costs is a priority, then you're literally pouring money down the drain every time you use a can of beans. We found a one-pound bag of Whole Foods 365 organic dry pinto beans for $3.19, compared to $1.29 for a 15 ½-ounce can of the same brand's organic pinto beans. At first glance, the canned beans appear less expensive. However, a one-pound bag of dry beans makes *five to six cups cooked*, while a 15 ½-ounce can (drained) yields about 1 ½ cups cooked (Sweers, 2011). If your recipe calls for one pound of dry beans, you'll need three to four 15 ½ ounce cans to get the same cooked amount. This means that a recipe costing $3.19 using dried organic beans could cost $5.16 using canned organic beans, or more than 1 ½ times the cost.

Dry beans require more prep and cooking time than canned beans, but most of this time is hands off. If you invest in a pressure cooker or InstantPot, you can slash your bean cooking time to under an hour. And since beans freeze well, you can whip up an entire week's worth in practically no time. Plus, just like most dishes made from scratch, dry beans produce a richer, more flavor-packed recipe, which will surely please your canine connoisseur!

Make your own treats

When you purchase commercially produced treats, you're paying for a lot more than the ingredients: You're also helping foot the bill for a slew of other costs, including the manufacturer's production and labor, packaging, transportation, marketing and other expenses. Making your own treats eliminates the 'middleman'—enabling you to enjoy the savings.

Homemade treats also offer other benefits. You can tailor the ingredients to your dog's taste buds and health considerations, such as low fat, gluten free, etc. And since you don't have to worry about nutritionally balancing treats (they should comprise no more than 10% of your dog's daily Calories), you can have fun scouring the Internet for plant-friendly recipes (Diana shares tons of them on her Plant-Powered Dog website. See Resources.) Or get creative experimenting with your own. Dogs are very forgiving customers who will even enjoy eating your 'mistakes'! Plus, what could be more satisfying than the eager look on your dog's face and the excited wag of a tail as you offer him a still-warm treat bursting with fresh-from-the-oven aroma? After all, "Nothing says lovin' like something from the oven!"

Invest in long-term health

When making financial decisions, it's tempting not to see the forest for the trees. In other words, we only look at what's right in front of us, but not the big picture. A diet that decreases inflammation and reduces the chances of chronic diseases down the line is not only good news from a health standpoint, but also from a financial one. Anyone who's raised a dog knows that the price of a chronic illness can add up to thousands of dollars. Even if you feel compelled to purchase everything organic, we strongly believe that you'll more than make up for the investment in a plant-based diet with long-term savings on veterinary bills and medications.

And while we're talking about financial savings, it's important to note another type of savings that's just as important—emotional savings. When a beloved canine companion suffers from illness, we pay a hefty emotional price of stress, anxiety and even guilt. Of course, no diet can guarantee lifelong health. But knowing that you did everything in your power to prevent the condition and that you'll continue to do everything to treat, manage and reverse it will help you remain confident, optimistic and focused when your dog needs you the most.

There's too much time involved

Preparing your dog's meals is, no doubt, more time-consuming than opening a bag or can of commercial food. But home-prepared recipes offer many advantages over packaged, including minimal processing, maximum nutrition and control over the ingredients used. That's why we recommend fresh food as the bulk of your dog's diet. Fortunately, homemade doesn't have to mean homebound. These tips will help you cut your time in the kitchen:

Invest in time-saving tools

A few well-chosen pieces of kitchen equipment can dramatically reduce your meal prep time. Here are a few of our favorites:

- **Food processor.** If your dog fancies raw veggies, you'll want to break down the outer cell wall prior to serving for easier digestion. Chopping, dicing and shredding veggies with a knife, peeler or box grater is difficult and time-consuming labor. We recommend taking the easy and fast route using a food processor. With interchangeable blades to tackle a multitude of tasks, you can chop, shred, grind and even puree veggies in a matter of seconds. You can also mill your own gluten-free flour, grind seeds such as pumpkin and sunflower, shred coconut, whip up fresh almond or peanut butter for treats and perform a multitude of other food prep tasks. Choose a processor with a large bowl (Cuisinart, for example, makes up to 18 cups) and a high-watt motor (at least 625 watts) for bulk processing. Concerned about clean-up? Don't be, since most blades, bowls and lids are top-rack dishwasher safe.

- **High-speed blender.** If you want to create healthy, whole-food plant-based meals, a top-quality high-speed blender is a must. From nutrient-dense smoothies to silky sauces and creamy homemade nut butters, these super-charged machines can power through even the toughest of jobs, leaving regular old blenders in the dust. If your budget allows, we recommend Vita-mix. This brand is an investment, but it will give you many years of reliable food prep service. (We've both had ours for more than 15 years!) You can even chop fresh herbs and vegetables, shred potatoes, grind nuts and seeds and make your own whole-grain flour. Bonus: The Vitamix saves on clean-up time. Simply add a drop of dish soap and warm water to the container, run it at the highest speed for about 60 seconds and you're done.

- **InstantPot (or other multi-use/pressure cooker).** We love these handy electronic multi-use cookers because they can slash hours off your cooking time. According to instructions from the company, you can cook most types of soaked beans in under 10 minutes and unsoaked beans in 30 minutes or less (although we still recommend soaking). Compare this to several hours on the stove top and you've just freed up an entire Sunday afternoon. And since pressure cookers seal in vitamins and minerals, you don't have to sacrifice nutrition for speed.

- **Nut milk maker.** Nut and seed milks are a great way to boost the nutritional content of your dog's meals (see the Appendix for recipes using nut milks). But store-bought nut milks are typically thin and often contain unwanted ingredients, such as thickeners, sweeteners and added flavors. On the other hand, blending and then straining homemade nut milk in a nut milk bag can be time consuming and messy. Fortunately, you can whip up quick and easy nut (and seed) milks without blending or using a nut milk bag. Just get a cow—an Almond Cow, that is! Almond Cow is an ingenious plant-based milk maker that allows you to turn any type of nut or seed into thick, creamy milk with the push of a button. Just add your ingredients of choice into the basket, fill the reservoir with water and in a couple of minutes the Almond Cow produces perfect plant-based milk—no straining required. All you have to do is rinse a couple of parts and you're good to go. Bonus: The leftover pulp makes a delicious addition to your homemade treats. (See Resources.)

Prepare in bulk

Let's face it; sometimes we can barely get our own dinner on the table, let alone muster the energy to whip up a fresh meal for our canine companion (no, that doesn't make you a bad person). Cooking multiple meals at one time can solve that problem. We have clients who set aside a few hours on the weekend and prepare up to a month's worth of their dog's food. Of course, how large a batch you make will depend upon your freezer space and the size of your dog, but most of us can handle storing at least a week's worth of food at a time.

Once you've prepared your batch, let it cool to room temperature and then equally divide it into daily portions. Scoop each portion into a glass food storage container and label each one with the date. Store in the refrigerator for up to four days or in the freezer for up to three months. Defrost frozen meals in the refrigerator the day before you want to use them.

You can mix the appropriate amounts of supplements into the large batch prior to portioning, taking care to evenly distribute them throughout. Avoid reheating the food once the supplements are added, however, as heat can degrade some of the nutrients. If you want to reheat the food, we advise incorporating the supplements into each day's batch after it has been reheated and cooled on the counter to a dog-friendly temperature.

You're feeling pressured to feed your dog animal ingredients

Many people who advocate feeding dogs a plant-based diet know that peer pressure—and even bullying—don't end when we leave school. Food is a deeply engrained part of our culture, and animal-based ingredients often play a key role in significant milestones. Close your eyes and you can likely still conjure images of mom's perfectly stuffed Thanksgiving turkey, grandma's melt-in-your-mouth pot roast and dad grilling up perfectly charred burgers at summer barbecues.

So, it's no surprise that for many people, reframing their position on eating animal products is met with deep internal resistance. If they admit that meat comes from a living, feeling being, what does it mean for their cherished childhood memories? Were their parents and grandparents wrong? These are complex issues that are often uncomfortable to confront.

The same holds true for how we feed our canine companions. The scientific facts prove that dogs are omnivores who can thrive on a well-balanced plant-based diet. Science also shows that animal products, riddled with bioaccumulated toxins, contribute to a host of chronic canine diseases, including cancer. But studies show that when we're faced with facts that contradict our emotional attachments, we typically cling deeper to our beliefs and sometimes even lash out at the messenger.

The situation is compounded when it comes to feeding companion dogs because there is a lot of misinformation floating around online and in books. Some of this misinformation comes from trusted sources who are quite vocal on the topic, which further bolsters the position of meat-based advocates.

How you respond to this judgement or pressure depends on the source. If the situation involves someone you care about, we advise politely but firmly standing your ground, affirming that you have thoroughly researched the topic and are confident in your decision. You can even offer to lend them your copy of this book! If they persist, you might need to set ground rules, letting them know that you're not changing your position and that the discussion is off limits.

If the pressure—or even bullying—takes place on social media, we strongly advise that you do not engage. While social media has advantages, it's also a platform where anyone can anonymously force their opinions—and sometimes direct their anger—toward others with different beliefs. It's unlikely that using facts to counter online harassment will get you anywhere except upset. You have the power to ignore—or better yet, to block—online bullies, and we urge you to do so.

If you ever feel pressured to feed your dog animal products—whether it's by your partner, friend, veterinarian or online—we want to assure you that their opinions are based on outdated science, deeply ingrained cultural norms and decades of misinformation.

Being a leader is not easy. You are 'overturning the apple cart.' You are challenging long-held beliefs that lie at the very core of our culture. You are asking people to refocus their entire perspective of the world. But take heart and keep moving forward, secure in the knowledge that you are doing what's best for your dog as well as for all living beings, our planet and future generations.

Part 2
Plant-Based Diet Solutions For Common Canine Chronic Diseases

Optimum nutrition is the medicine of tomorrow.

- Dr. Linus Pauling

Chapter 8
Plant-Based Diet Solutions For Cancer

If your beloved dog has ever suffered from cancer, then you know that this horrible disease is heartbreaking. It's why we do everything we can to protect the ones we love. Yet, as hard as we try, the statistics of cancer in dogs are shocking and frightening:

- Six million new cases of canine cancer are diagnosed each year.
- Cancer claims the lives of nearly half (47%) of dogs over the age of 10 years.
- More forms of cancer strike dogs than any other companion animal.
- Dogs are affected by nearly 100 types of cancer, including skin, mammary gland (breast), head and neck, lymphoma, abdominal, testicular (prostate) and bone.

(FETCH a Cure, 2021)

Throughout this book, we've talked about the deep bond that has evolved over thousands of years between dogs and people. We share profound genomic similarities. We share many of the same gut bacteria. We share our homes, our hearts and our lifestyles. And, sadly, we share a susceptibility to developing cancer.

Cancer strikes dogs and humans at about the same rate. In fact, canine and human cancers are so similar that research focused on dogs often leads to new therapies for people. For this reason, the National Cancer Institute's Comparative Oncology Program sponsors clinical trials for dogs with naturally occurring cancers to help advance understanding and treatment of cancer in humans (FETCH a Cure, 2021; National Cancer Institute, n.d.).

Yet, with all the research focused on new pharmaceutical treatments (which we commend), one fact is well established; cancer is very much a lifestyle disease. It's estimated that only about 5% to 10% of all cancers have a genetic basis, while 90% to 95% are triggered by environmental factors, with nutrition playing a key role (Donaldson, 2004; Anand et al., 2008).

You might even be astounded to learn that as many as 30% to 35% of all cancer deaths in people are related to diet (Anand et al., 2008). We believe this is likely also true in dogs because:

- Cancer in dogs and people closely mirror each other.
- Dogs and people have shared a parallel genomic evolution over thousands of years.

- We share the same environments and lifestyles, often including similar dietary components.

- Dogs who live with unhealthy people tend to suffer from the same types of chronic conditions.

The good news is that we have more control than we think over whether our companion dogs will suffer from this dreadful disease. It's true that we can't change the genetic cards that our canine companions were dealt. For example, Golden Retrievers and Greyhounds are susceptible to osteosarcoma (a type of bone cancer), while Bernese Mountain Dogs are especially vulnerable to malignant histiocytic sarcoma involving the spleen and liver. But studies in identical twins have shown that epigenetic exposures, such as diet and lifestyle, are the major triggers for most chronic illnesses, including cancer. So, by changing your dog's nutrition, you may be able to affect whether his genes will express for cancer. This means that you can potentially prevent him from ever suffering from cancer in the first place. And if your dog already does have this terrible disease, you can still change his diet and lifestyle to give him the best chance of enjoying a longer, healthier life—and perhaps even entering remission.

In this chapter, we're going to explore two key nutritional aspects of cancer:

- **Dietary triggers**
- **Cancer-fighting foods**

We'll begin with an examination of dietary factors scientifically linked to cancer. This knowledge is critical because the first step in decreasing cancer risk is reducing and eliminating foods that can trigger cancerous epigenetic mutations in cells and DNA. In the second half of the chapter, we'll discuss research-based foods that help protect against the development and proliferation of cancer. Removing cancer-promoting foods from your dog's diet and increasing cancer-fighting foods offers a powerful combination for preventing, managing and even reversing this devastating disease.

Dietary triggers
Bioaccumulated toxins

In Chapter 1, we introduced the concept of bioaccumulation, which is the build-up of toxins in the fatty tissues of animals and people. As you'll recall, the higher up the food chain we eat, the more toxins that bioaccumulate. Bioaccumulation is such an important part of any cancer discussion that we want to take a moment to refresh your memory on how it works.

You can think of bioaccumulation as a ladder. Microorganisms in the soil and water, such as algae, occupy the lowest rung of the ladder. They absorb toxins from the environment, but not from other food sources because they are the lowest on the food chain ladder. People and companion animals occupy the top rung of the ladder because they eat foods all the way up the food chain, from algae to sentient beings such as cows, sheep, pigs, chickens and others. With each rung of the food chain ladder, more chemicals accumulate as the organisms consume and store the chemicals from organisms occupying the lower rungs. This means that when you or your dog eat a food animal, you ingest all the chemicals that have built up (bioaccumulated) in their tissues from all the organisms they have previously consumed, as well as from the environment (Pitcairn & Pitcairn, 2017).

In their book, *Dr. Pitcairn's Guide to Natural Health for Dogs & Cats*, Dr. Richard Pitcairn and Susan Pitcairn, M.S. point out that foods typically associated with protein, such as meat, fish, eggs and dairy, also contain high amounts of fat. And each time we or our dogs consume this fat, we ingest carcinogenic toxins (Pitcairn & Pitcairn, 2017).

Perhaps you don't think you need to worry about toxins in meat because you only feed your dog pasture-raised animals. Did you know that pastures and rangeland can be sprayed with glyphosate (EPA, 2021), the weed killer labeled as a "probable carcinogen"? This means that unless they are raised on certified organic land, pasture-raised animals are likely feasting on—you guessed it—RoundUp. (See Chapter 5 for more information on RoundUp.)

To make the toxic chemical problem even worse, some bioaccumulated toxins are **Persistent Organic Pollutants (POPs)**, which means that they resist breaking down and so remain in the environment for *decades or even centuries* (U.S. Department of State, n.d.; World Health Organization, 2008). Well-known POPs include DDT, PCBs, furans and dioxins, but there are many, *many* more.

According to the World Health Organization and the U.S. Department of State, characteristics of POPs include:

- They are synthetic (man-made) chemicals.
- They are toxic.
- They resist breaking down and can remain in the environment for decades or even centuries.
- They can accumulate to dangerous levels in humans and animals.
- They can travel long distances via the air and oceans.
- They remain in fatty tissues.
- They accumulate up the food chain.
- They cause acute toxicity after high-level exposure.

  (U.S. Department of State, n.d.; World Health Organization, 2008)

There are more than 209 types of PCBs in the environment, and that's just one type of POP. These chemicals were once used in industrial applications, including electrical transformers, hydraulic fluids, lubricants and carbonless paper. PCBs were banned in the United States in 1977, but not before *1.5 billion pounds* were produced. And because they are resistant to breaking down, the effects of these persistent toxins are still felt throughout the environment (Environmental Defense Fund, n.d.).

PCBs can accumulate in bodies of water, such as rivers, lakes, streams and coastal areas. They accumulate in the fatty tissue of fish and then bioaccumulate up the food chain to invertebrates (e.g., insects, crustaceans, mollusks, earthworms, etc.), birds and food animals until they eventually reach the top of the food chain (Environmental Defense Fund, n.d.).

PCBs have been shown to cause cancer in laboratory animals, prompting the Environmental Protection Agency (EPA) to classify them as "probable human carcinogens." They have also been shown to damage the circulatory, nervous, immune, endocrine and digestive systems of animals (EDF, n.d.).

Dioxins are another POP related to PCBs. According to the Environmental Protection Agency (EPA), dioxins:

- Are highly toxic.
- Can cause cancer.
- Can cause other serious health issues, such as reproductive and developmental issues, immune system damage and hormonal interference.
- Bioaccumulate up the food chain.
- They are mainly stored in the fatty tissues of animals.

   (EPA, 2020)

According to the EPA, more than 90% of human exposure to dioxins is through consumption of animal fats, including meat, dairy, fish and shellfish (EPA, 2020).

We can presume a similar scenario for companion dogs, given that the majority are fed an immense amount of these ingredients.

Environmental contamination from POPs is so widespread that many states warn residents against eating fish and shellfish from freshwater or coastal areas (Environmental Defense Fund, n.d.). We discovered a public service pamphlet from the Michigan Department of Community Health warning of persistent bioaccumulated toxins in fish. To illustrate the point, the pamphlet used the example of a factory located at the bank of a body of water. Back in the 1970s, before pollution was strictly regulated, this factory would have released a variety of persistent chemicals through its smokestacks. Where did these chemicals end up? If you guessed the coastal water—and the fish swimming in that water—you're correct. But here's the kicker. Even though that same factory will have since installed devices in its smokestacks to control pollution, the chemicals it released decades ago still exist in the environment (Michigan Department of Community Health, n.d.).

The State of Michigan pamphlet warns:

> *If you eat a lot of fish that have these types of chemicals in them, the chemicals can build up and stay in your body, too. This could someday cause health problems, like cancer or diabetes, in some people* (Michigan Department of Community Health, n.d., pp. 3).

Think about that. Some states warn residents that POPs from fish living in coastal waters can bioaccumulate in their own bodies and lead to serious health issues such as cancer. We and our dogs are, after all, on the top rung of the bioaccumulation ladder, which means that we and they get the full damage caused by these persistent toxins.

But POPs aren't just a problem associated with water and fish. As we mentioned, they are everywhere in the environment. They accumulate in the soil. Some evaporate (volatize) into the air and travel far distances. And the fact that they don't break down means that they are not easily metabolized and eliminated once ingested. According to the organization Safer Chemicals, Healthy Families:

The structural characteristics that enable a chemical to persist in the environment can also help it to resist metabolic breakdown in people or wildlife. For example, synthetic chemicals that contain halogen atoms (particularly fluorine, chlorine, or bromine) are often resistant to degradation in the environment or within organisms (Safer Chemicals, Healthy Families, 2021).

This means that not only are POPs resistant to breaking down in the environment; they also resist the body's efforts to metabolize and eliminate them. This is true in people and animals.

So, what happens to POPs over time? Many are fat-soluble, so they are stored in fat deposits or in the fatty substances in blood. Sadly, these chemicals are often passed from new mothers to their babies through contaminated breast milk. But fat isn't the only place that stores these chemicals. They can also bioaccumulate in other parts of the body, such as bone, muscle and even the brain (Safer Chemicals, Healthy Families, 2021).

As you can imagine, as the body's toxic load increases over time, so do the serious adverse effects, which include:

- Abnormal mutations to DNA
- Cancer
- Damage to the immune system
- Neurological, reproductive and developmental toxicity

   (Safer Chemicals, Healthy Families, 2021; U.S. Department of State, n.d.)

Think about the effects POPs can have (and likely are having) on our canine companions. The average human omnivore is likely to mix up her menu throughout the week with both animal and plant-based foods. She might have oatmeal for breakfast, a salad for lunch and some chicken and vegetables for dinner, for example. Dogs, on the other hand, typically consume enormous amounts of animal ingredients (often in the form of red meat) day in and day out, due to the belief by many people that they need a 'species appropriate' diet.

By the time a dog reaches 10 years old, she'll be lucky if she doesn't succumb to cancer. Our dog's bodies have an incredible ability to achieve balance and heal themselves, but they did not evolve to handle the enormous toxic load of modern-day meat-laden diets. We have no way of knowing for certain if bioaccumulated toxins in animal ingredients are triggering the staggering number of new canine cancer diagnoses seen each year. After all, there is no incentive for the animal agriculture or pet food industries to research this correlation. But common sense tells us that daily consumption of toxins is bound to take its toll on the body over time. And the best way to minimize these toxins is clear: Eat low on the food chain. Eat a plant-based diet.

Diet and cancer-causing viruses

Leukemia, lymphoma and myeloma are three serious types of blood cancers in dogs (and people). Even when treated, dogs who suffer from these cancers survive on average two years or less. Given this, it makes sense that we wouldn't want to feed our canine companions any ingredient that is known to promote blood cancer. Yet, if we give them poultry, we may be doing just that.

In the groundbreaking book, *How Not to Die*, Michael Greger, MD and co-author Gene Stone cite findings from the European Prospective Investigation into Cancer and Nutrition (EPIC) study. The 2011 study found that poultry consumption was associated with an increased risk of non-Hodgkin's lymphoma (NHL) and B-cell lymphomas, including B-cell chronic lymphatic leukemia. According to the study results, the risk of lymphoma and leukemia increased between 56% and 280% for every 50 grams of poultry consumed per day (Greger & Stone, 2015; Rohrmann et al., 2011). That's less than two ounces of poultry per day. Certainly, even a small breed dog can easily eat more than that.

Since the EPIC study showed *correlation*, the authors were cautious about drawing a conclusion of *causation*. In other words, even though poultry consumption was linked with higher rates of blood cancers, they couldn't prove why this occurred. It could have been due to pure chance. Or, it could have been due to antibiotics in the poultry, even though it's unclear whether humans can get cancer from consuming antibiotics in food animals. Or, it could have been due to **oncogenic viruses**, which are *cancer-causing viruses* in poultry (Rohrmann et al., 2011; Greger & Stone, 2015).

In the study authors' own words:

> *Second, poultry may contain oncogenic viruses, especially if the meat is not cooked well* (Rohrmann et al., 2011, pp. 629).

Interestingly, the EPIC study authors discovered that the risk of oncogenic virus transmission increased when consuming rare versus well-cooked poultry. As Dr. Greger notes, cooking the poultry would help to kill the virus(es) (Greger & Stone, 2015). This is certainly not good news for raw feeding advocates, who tend to feed their dogs a lot of raw poultry products.

But it's not only poultry that poses a risk of transmitting cancer-causing viruses. Bovine leukemia virus (BLV) is an oncogenic retrovirus common in cattle (Buehring et al., 2003). BLV infects the cows' lymphoid tissues, causing malignant lymphoma and lymphosarcoma in 1% to 5% of infected animals (USDA, 2008).

And here's the really concerning part. BLV is showing up in people. Greger & Stone point to a 2003 study of 257 people who were tested for antibodies to BLV. *Nearly three-quarters (74%) of them tested positive for BLV antibodies in their blood serum* (Buehring et al., 2003; Greger & Stone, 2015). Antibodies fight off foreign invaders in the body, including viruses. BLV antibodies in a person's blood indicate exposure to the BLV virus. Since an astounding three-quarters of people tested positive, this exposure may be widespread. But it gets even worse. A more recent study using DNA sequencing discovered the presence of BLV DNA in the blood cells of 38% of people tested (Buehring et al., 2019).

The actual DNA of bovine leukemia virus was detected in the blood cells of more than a third of people tested (Buehring et al., 2019).

And guess what? Blood isn't the first place that BLV has shown up in people. It's also been found in human breast and lung cells (Buehring et al., 2019). This is intriguing, given that both dairy and red meat consumption have historically been linked with an increased risk of breast cancer (ChartsBin, 2011; Khazaei et al., 2016; Lipi et al., 2016; Beuhering et al., 2019).

How can a leukemia virus originating in cattle end up in human blood? If you guessed that it's likely via the food chain, you're correct (Beuhering et al., 2019).

In 2007, the United States Department of Agriculture (USDA) tested bulk tank milk from 534 dairy operations with 30 or more cows for BLV antibodies via Enzyme Linked-Immunosorbent Assay (ELISA). The results were 'sickening.' Of the small dairy operations (fewer than 100 cows), 83.2% tested positive for BLV; 82.1% of medium operations (100 – 499 cows) tested positive; and milk from *100% of large dairy operations (500 + cows) tested positive for BLV* (USDA, 2008). On average, 83.9% of U.S. dairy operations tested positive for BLV. In addition, 39% of all beef herds are infected with BLV (Polat et al., 2017).

And here's the kicker. Meat and dairy from BLV-infected cattle are only prohibited from being sold if the infected cow develops leukemia or lymphoma, which occurs about 5% of the time. What happens to the meat and dairy from the other 95% of infected cattle with subclinical symptoms (such as elevated lymphocytes)? They enter the food chain as "a major source of beef and dairy products" sold for human consumption (Olaya-Galán et al., 2017; Buehring et al., 2019).

More research is needed into the link between oncogenic viruses from food animals and cancer in people and dogs. However, we do know several important facts:

- Certain cancer-causing viruses in food animals appear to be **zoonotic**, meaning that they can cross species.
- The viral DNA from an infected animal can infiltrate the DNA of other species via consumption of meat and dairy products.
- "…BLV has the potential to be an important initiator of cancer in human tissues, and the data reported here further strengthen the evidence that BLV-infected cattle pose a likely risk to humans" (Buehring et al., 2019, pp. 9).

More dietary triggers

We could write a book focusing on research linking animal products and cancer, but we know that you are excited to move on to all the amazing *cancer-fighting* foods we'll be covering for the remainder of this chapter. But we encourage you to investigate this topic further because what we've covered is just a fraction of the research. Here are just a few other facts to consider:

- Heme iron in red meat is linked to several types of cancer (Hooda et al., 2014; Czerwonka & Tokarz, 2017). (See Chapter 4.)

- Cooking beef, pork, poultry or fish at high temperatures produces heterocyclic aromatic amines (HCAs or HAAs) and polycyclic aromatic hydrocarbons (PAHs), which are toxic chemicals that cause DNA to mutate in a way that may cause cancer (National Cancer Institute, 2017).

- Animal products used in pet foods pose particular cancer risks, including carcinogenic levels of fluoride in meat and bone meals (EWG, 2009), hormones to suppress estrus (the female heat cycle) in cattle, rendered meat protein from '4D' (dead, dying, diseased, disabled) animals, known carcinogenic preservatives (e.g., BHA) and toxic chemicals, such as heavy metals, dioxins and polychlorinated biphenyls (PCBs) (Sapkota et al., 2007).

We whole-heartedly agree with Dr. T. Colin Campbell, world-renowned nutritional researcher and author of *The China Study*, which is the most comprehensive study of the relationship between nutrition and disease conducted to date. According to Dr. Campbell:

No chemical carcinogen is nearly so important in causing human cancer as animal protein.
- T. Colin Campbell, PhD

Given the strength of comparative oncology between dogs and people, we would adjust Dr. Campbell's quote as follows:

No chemical carcinogen is nearly so important in causing human and canine cancer as animal protein.

Clearly, the first step in any anti-cancer diet is to stop feeding our dogs ingredients that promote cancer.

Meat and canine cancer: The proof is in the fur

If you're still wondering whether your dog should eat meat to prevent or combat cancer, consider this disturbing finding. In 2012, researchers discovered an HCA called 2-Amino-1-methyl-6-phenylimidazo[4,5-b] pyridine (PhIP) in the fur of 14 out of 16 healthy dogs fed various brands of meat-based commercial dog foods (Gu et al., 2012).

HCAs are powerful carcinogens that form when meat is cooked. In people, dietary intake of PhIP is positively associated with increased risk of multiple types of cancer, including breast and pancreatic. Moreover, this correlation is dose dependent. The higher the PhIP exposure, the higher the cancer risk (Zheng & Lee, 2009).

The levels of PhIP found in the dogs' fur were comparable to the amount that exists in the hair of human omnivores. But there are two important differences between human hair and canine fur: the density and amount. As the researchers point out, high-density fur covers most of a dog's body, compared to mainly the scalp and pubic area of people (Gu et al., 2012).

The authors conclude that:

> These findings signify that the exposure and bioavailability of PhIP are high in canines. A potential role for PhIP in the etiology of canine cancer should be considered (Gu et al., 2012, pp. 9371).

Why don't these types of studies gain more public exposure? And why is this information largely (or completely) missing from the mainstream discussion of nutrition and canine cancer? The answer likely relates to financial interests.

Imagine if word spread (which it now will) that dogs who consume meat-based dog foods may be at higher risk of getting cancer. Do you think this would impact the bottom line of the companies who manufacture these foods? We believe they don't want to find out.

Ketogenic diets and cancer

Ketogenic diets are touted as nothing less than a cancer cure-all and have become wildly popular for both people and dogs. We have witnessed the hype surrounding ketogenic diets among our own clients. Panicked after a beloved dog is diagnosed with cancer, many people seek guidance in online canine cancer support groups. What they often find is intense pressure to feed their dogs a high-fat ketogenic diet laden with animal ingredients such as red meat, organ meats and even cottage cheese. This type of misinformation not only moves us in the wrong direction from an animal advocacy and sustainability standpoint; it may also severely harm the very dogs these concerned people are trying so desperately to save.

Here, we'll break down the latest scientific information regarding ketogenic diets and offer our research-based opinions and recommendations.

What are ketogenic diets?

Ketogenic diets are a very high-fat, low carbohydrate, moderate protein type of diet. There isn't one specific macronutrient composition for ketogenic diets, but they typically average 70% to 80% fat, 5% to 10% carbohydrate and 10% to 20% protein. However, some ketogenic diets contain as much as 90% fat (Robbins, 2019; Harvard T.H. Chan School of Public Health, 2021).

Ketogenic diets are based on an observation from the 1920s by Otto Warburg that cancer cells prefer aerobic glycolysis, meaning simply that they preferentially feed on sugar (glucose). This phenomenon is known as the Warburg effect.

The theory is that eating an extremely high-fat, low-carbohydrate diet will force the body into a state of **ketosis** characterized by elevated levels of **ketones** (also called ketone bodies) in the blood. Normally, the body breaks down carbohydrates into glucose, which it uses for energy. However, starving the body of carbohydrates deprives it of glucose, forcing it to switch to emergency mode—burning fat for energy. This process, called ketogenesis, takes place in the liver. The ketones then travel to the bloodstream, where they are used as fuel (Phinney, 2020). The goal of ketogenic diets is to trick the body into a continual state of ketosis (Fuhrman, 2016).

There are three types of ketone bodies produced during ketosis: β-hydroxybutyrate (BHB), acetoacetate (AcAc) and acetone. BHB makes up most of the ketone body pool (78%), while AcAc accounts for about 20% and acetone comprises only about 2% (Sena, 2010). However, AcAc is the parent ketone because it is needed to make both acetone and BHB (Holmer, 2019).

Possible benefits of ketogenic diets

Ketosis brought about by consuming a ketogenic diet may help fight cancer in several ways. The first involves how cells use energy. Healthy cells can burn both glucose from carbohydrates and ketones from fat. Cancerous cells preferentially burn glucose but cannot effectively utilize ketones (Poff et al., 2014). So, switching to a state of ketosis might enable the body to fuel healthy cells with ketones while starving cancerous ones of glucose (Fuhrman, 2016).

Ketosis might also inhibit cancer by reducing insulin and insulin-like growth factor 1 (IGF-1), a hormone similar to insulin. IGF-1 promotes cancer by encouraging cancer cell proliferation and blocking apoptosis. Elevated levels of circulating IGF-1 have been associated with multiple types of cancers, including breast, colorectal and prostate (Shanmugalingam et al., 2016).

BHB (but not AcAc) is also shown to reduce inflammation (Youm et al., 2015), which is beneficial because cancer is an inflammatory disease.

Risks of ketogenic diets

The problem is that ketogenic diets for dogs and people have several serious risks. We'll break them down for you here.

Animal ingredients are linked to cancer. The main risk of ketogenic diets involves the extremely high amount of animal products they contain. Ketogenic refers to the balance of macronutrients (protein, fat, carbohydrates) in the diet, not the specific foods used to achieve that balance. You can meet all the criteria for a ketogenic diet using only plant-based ingredients. (We'll tell you why we don't recommend that in a moment.) However, to date, we are not aware of a commercial plant-based ketogenic dog food. In fact, we've seen articles on certain of these websites warning about the dangers of plant-based diets and cancer (with no legitimate science to back up their claims).

You know what you *won't* find companies that sell ketogenic dog foods discussing? The multitude of studies—such as the ones cited in this chapter and throughout this book—linking meat, poultry, fish, eggs and dairy with cancer.

As we've already stated, six million new cases of canine cancer are diagnosed in the U.S. alone each year. Yet, according to the market research firm Statista, only 1.6% of dogs *worldwide* were fed a strict plant-based diet as of 2019 (Statista, 2021). This means that more than 98% of dogs consume meat-based diets. Science has clearly revealed the link between animal ingredients and cancer. Sadly, our dogs may be living proof.

It is ironic that while the state of ketosis may benefit certain types of cancer, ketogenic diets are packed with animal ingredients that are shown to *promote* cancer.

Ketogenic diets restrict or eliminate cancer-fighting foods. By now, you might have concluded (correctly), that plant-based phytochemicals are perhaps the most health-promoting nutrients on the planet. This is especially true in terms of fighting cancer. Yet, as best-selling medical doctor Joel Fuhrman, MD, points out, ketogenic diets restrict or even eliminate these chemoprotective foods:

> *The very low carbohydrate content of a ketogenic diet restricts important fiber-rich, anti-cancer foods such as beans, berries, and orange vegetables, unnecessarily limiting nutritional variety and phytochemical richness – phytochemicals that have anti-infection, anti-cancer and cardioprotective effects and also build up our immune defenses. The protective phytochemicals and antioxidants in the rainbow of produce have more powerful longevity-promoting effects than simply being in ketosis* (Fuhrman, 2016).

Part of the sales pitch surrounding ketogenic diets is what we call the 'big sugar lie' that vilifies all carbohydrates. Yes—and we will say this as many times as needed—refined and processed high-glycemic carbohydrates are *not* healthy. But lumping nutrient-dense plant-based legumes, vegetables and fruits into this category simply makes no sense. It's like saying you should avoid eating all fats due to the dangers of trans fatty acids.

We simply cannot justify reducing or removing research-based anti-cancer foods from the diet in the name of promoting ketosis.

Ketogenic diets can trigger life-threatening diseases. As we mentioned a moment ago, it's entirely possible to meet the macronutrient criteria for a ketogenic diet by consuming strictly plant-based ingredients. But this would involve feeding your dog *a lot* of high-fat plant foods such as oils, nuts, seeds and coconut. Such a diet would certainly lack proper nutritional balance and would also restrict known cancer-fighting foods.

The problem is that whether based on animal or plant ingredients, the high fat levels in ketogenic diets could trigger acute pancreatitis, or sudden and severe inflammation of the pancreas. An attack of acute pancreatitis can lead to shock and even death if not treated immediately. You've likely read articles warning against feeding your dog fatty table scraps for this very reason. In fact, veterinary clinics routinely treat an increase in acute pancreatitis cases around the holidays, when curious—and hungry—dogs get into the fatty holiday meal.

Pancreatitis isn't the only health risk associated with ketogenic diets. People on therapeutic ketogenic diets have suffered from a variety of serious conditions, including gastrointestinal issues, heart disease and urolithiasis (bladder stones), as well as nutrient-deficiency diseases (McKenzie, 2020). Children on ketogenic diets for epilepsy have experienced severe health consequences, including progressive bone mineral loss (Bergqvist et al., 2008), kidney stones (Choi et al., 2010), scurvy due to lack of vitamin C (Willmott & Bryan, 2008) and even sudden death from heart disease related to selenium deficiency cardiomyopathy (Bank et al., 2008).

There are no bones about it: Dogs are also susceptible to many of these same serious health consequences.

Ketogenic diets may promote certain cancers. Perhaps the most disturbing part of the marketing messages surrounding ketogenic diets is what's *not* revealed: *certain cancers feed on ketones.*

Studies show that dietary fats promote tumor growth and metastasis in several types of cancers, including breast, melanoma and oral (Martinez-Outschoorn et al., 2012; Pascual et al., 2017). In breast cancer, ketone bodies upregulate the expression of genes leading to tumor metastasis in the lungs. A study published in the journal *Cell Cycle* concluded that:

> *Our data provide the necessary genetic evidence that ketone body production and re-utilization drive tumor progression and metastasis. As such, ketone inhibitors should be designed as novel therapeutics to effectively treat advanced cancer patients, with tumor recurrence and metastatic disease* (Martinez-Outschoorn et al., 2012, pp. 3964).

Wondering if you read that correctly? You did. These authors clearly state that:

- Ketone bodies drive both the progression and spread of cancerous tumors.
- Advanced cancer patients should be given therapeutics that inhibit ketones.

We also don't yet know how inducing a chronic state of ketosis will affect the body over time. One concerning side-effect is the possibility of chronic subclinical metabolic acidosis, a condition that may *promote* cancerous epigenetic changes.

Ketogenic diets produce ketone bodies, which are acidic. These ketones are produced by the liver and absorbed into the bloodstream, where they are used as fuel. According to the MD Anderson Cancer Center, excessive ketone production can lead to dehydration and negatively alter the blood's chemical balance (Blackburn, 2018). The body can compensate for short-term dietary 'acid loading' and return to a normal acid-base balance; however, the same may not be true over the long term (Robey, 2012). After just 60 days on a ketogenic diet (86.19% fat / 5.66% carbohydrate), healthy rats suffered from metabolic acidosis, anemia and oxidative stress (Arsyad et al., 2020).

In humans, ongoing consumption of acidic diets characterized by high intake of animal protein can lead to small changes in blood pH that push it to the lower end of the normal range (7.36 to 7.38) rather than the higher end (7.42 to 7.44). This condition goes by several names, including "diet-induced," "low-grade" and "chronic metabolic" acidosis. Note that this chronic sub-clinical type of acidosis is not the same as clinical ketoacidosis that is a complication of diabetes (Robey, 2012).

Researchers haven't yet directly linked chronic subclinical metabolic acidosis to cancer, but the evidence is concerning. For starters, ongoing disequilibrium in the blood's acid-base balance creates systemic stress, which is a known risk factor for cancer. Long-term acidosis also influences multiple molecular pathways that favor carcinogenesis and tumor progression, including increasing the cancer-promoting IGF-1 pathway (Robey, 2012). IGF-1 is the same hormone that ketosis might reduce. It's ironic that this benefit could be negated by the state of chronic subclinical metabolic acidosis produced by ketosis.

Our conclusion

After a thorough evaluation of the research, we whole-heartedly agree with this article published in the journal *Medical Oncology*:

> *This systematic review therefore presents and evaluates the clinical evidence on isocaloric KD dietary regimes and reveals that evidence supporting the effects of isocaloric ketogenic dietary regimes on tumor development and progression as well as reduction in side effects of cancer therapy is missing. Furthermore, an array of potential side effects should be carefully considered before applying KD to cancer patients. In regard to counseling cancer patients considering a KD, more robust and consistent clinical evidence is necessary before the KD can be recommended for any single cancer diagnosis or as an adjunct therapy* (Erickson et al., 2017, pp. 1).

In other words, ketogenic diets:

- Lack strong clinical evidence as to their anti-cancer benefits.
- May cause a variety of negative side effects.
- Are not currently recommended as a treatment or adjunct therapy to a cancer diagnosis.

(Erickson et al., 2017)

No type of diet can cure cancer, and we urge you to steer clear of any individuals, companies or organizations making these types of claims. Be especially wary when the solution involves the ongoing purchase of pricey commercial foods and supplements promising miraculous results.

But guess what type of cancer-fighting diet *is* strongly supported by clinical evidence: a diet brimming with phytochemical-rich whole plant foods. And happily, the only side effects are *healthy* ones: reduced inflammation, decreased oxidative stress, optimum immune function and a greater ability to defend against cancer. For this reason, we encourage you to opt for a whole-food plant-based diet as the nutritional component of your dog's anti-cancer regimen.

Cancer-fighting foods

The plant kingdom is teeming with foods that help prevent and inhibit cancer. Legumes, vegetables, fruits, whole grains, seeds and nuts are packed with antioxidants, fiber and phytochemicals—key anti-cancer nutrients. The more scientists research the pharmacological benefits of plant foods, the more amazing anti-cancer activities they discover.

So far, more than 25,000 different phytochemicals have been discovered in the plant kingdom that may have anti-cancer properties (Anand et al., 2008). Alkaloids, flavonoids, lignans, saponins, terpenes, taxanes and glycosides, just to name a few, play important roles in a multi-level approach to protecting people and dogs from cancer. Sometimes, these plant chemicals inhibit proteins, enzymes and signaling pathways that can lead to cancer, while at other times they activate genes and proteins that protect and repair DNA (Iqbal et al., 2017).

Bioactive plant compounds can prevent cancer from forming and, if it does form, attack it from multiple angles to help stop its progression (Aggarwal and Shishodia, 2006; Anand et al., 2008; Boivin et al., 2009).

Plant compounds fight cancer via multiple key mechanisms:

- **Antioxidant activity:** Defending cells against the oxidative damage caused by free radicals is the first step in protecting the body from developing cancer.
- **Anti-proliferation activity:** Once a tumor has formed, bioactive plant chemicals can nourish the body with ingredients known to inhibit the growth and spread of tumors and even promote tumor cell death (apoptosis).

(Boivin et al., 2009)

'Eating the rainbow' is a vital part of a cancer-protective diet. You'll recall from Chapter 5 that the pigments in plant foods come from different types of phytochemicals that convey important health benefits. Moreover, every part of the plant can contain beneficial phytochemicals, including the fruit, root, flower, leaf, rhizome, sprouts, seeds and even the bark (Iqbal et al., 2017).

While the plant kingdom is chock full of cancer-fighting foods, specific ingredients stand out as cancer-kicking all stars. These ingredients possess especially powerful activities to protect against cancer, and some foods are even able to target specific types of cancers. You'll see examples of these as we move through our top anti-cancer picks.

Throughout the remainder of this chapter, we'll refer to a 2009 study published in the journal *Food Chemistry,* which tested the antioxidant and antiproliferative activity of many commonly consumed vegetables. (Fruits were not tested.) The study analyzed juices extracted from 34 different vegetables to test their chemoprotective activity against eight types of tumor cell lines: stomach, pancreatic, breast, prostate, lung, kidney, medulloblastoma and glioblastoma. The results provide valuable insight into identifying vegetables possessing particularly powerful cancer-fighting benefits (Boivin et al., 2009; Greger & Stone, 2015).

The *Food Chemistry* study also demonstrated that the inhibitory activity of the most protective foods robustly targeted tumor cells while leaving normal cells alone, "strongly suggesting that the antiproliferative properties of these vegetables are specific to cells of tumor origin" (Boivin et al., 2009). This is excellent news, as we of course want to block the growth of tumor cells while encouraging growth of healthy cells.

The following ingredients, listed in alphabetical order, comprise our cancer-fighting all-star team.

Black raspberry
Berries are perhaps the most studied and important group of cancer-fighting foods due to their high levels of antioxidants and phytochemicals. Anthocyanins, the polyphenol pigments that give berries their deep blue, red and purple hues, protect against cancer via a wide variety of biological mechanisms, including:

- Decreasing inflammation
- Defending against cellular oxidation
- Preventing cancerous mutations in DNA
- Inhibiting cancer cell growth and proliferation
- Inducing apoptosis of cancer cells
- Preventing metastasis

  (Lin et al., 2017)

Anthocyanins and other polyphenols also promote a healthy gut environment by boosting beneficial bacteria and suppressing pathogenic bacteria (Cardona et al., 2013). Since the gut is the largest immune organ in the body, a healthy gut is the first line of defense against chronic diseases such as cancer.

Delicious dog-friendly berries include:

- Blackberries
- Blueberries
- Boysenberries
- Chokeberries (Aronia) (not chokecherries, which are toxic)
- Cranberries
- Elderberries
- Goji berries
- Mulberries
- Red raspberries
- Strawberries (be sure your dog is not allergic, and avoid the top white/green core part)

One berry stands out for its potent anti-cancer power—black raspberries. Black raspberries repeatedly beat out other berries for their high levels of anthocyanins and other beneficial compounds (Wang & Lin, 2000; Wada & Ou, 2002) and have been widely studied for their anti-cancer properties (Johnson, 2009; Kresty et al., 2016). Human clinical trials show that black raspberries protect against multiple types of cancers, including colorectal (Johnson et al., 2011; Chen et al., 2018), esophageal (Ohio State University, 2008) and oral (Kresty et al., 2016).

Black raspberries (*Rubus occidentalis* L.) are a special type of raspberry native to eastern North America. Also known as black caps or thimbleberries, black raspberries are often confused with blackberries because they look similar; however, they're not the same. To tell the difference, check out the core, which is located at the end of the fruit that attaches to the stem. Blackberries have a white or green core, but black raspberries have a hollow core, like red raspberries (Danahy, 2020).

Black raspberries are only harvested for a short time in July, but you and your dog can enjoy their health benefits all year long as a freeze-dried powder. In addition to ease and convenience, freeze-drying concentrates the berry's chemoprotective agents by about 10-fold (Ohio State University, 2008).

Dosage: We recommend 1/4 teaspoon for small dogs, 1/2 teaspoon for medium dogs and 1 teaspoon for large dogs per day. Opt for organic black raspberry powder when possible. (See Resources.)

Brussels sprouts

If your mom forced you to finish your Brussels sprouts when you were a kid, she had good reason—even if back then they weren't prepared in the most appetizing manner! That's because cruciferous vegetables are potent cancer-protective veggies, and Brussels sprouts may be the most powerful of them all (Boivin et al., 2009). In the *Food Chemistry* study, Brussels sprouts suppressed the growth of *every type* of cancer cell line tested. They also strongly inhibited the spread of kidney tumor cells, which typically do not respond well to anti-cancer protocols (Boivin et al., 2009).

We recommend feeding your dog a variety of cruciferous vegetables as part of a cancer-preventive diet. Consumption of cruciferous vegetables has been associated with lower rates of cancer in multiple studies, including: 33% lower risk of non-Hodgkin's lymphoma in women (Zhang et al., 2000); 51% decrease in bladder cancer in men (Michaud et al., 1999); 41% (Cohen et al., 2000) and 35% (Kolonel et al., 2000) decrease in prostate cancer; 17 to 22% decrease in lung cancer (Lam et al., 2009); and significant decreases in cancers of the mouth/throat, esophagus, colorectum, breast and kidney (Bosetti et al., 2012).

Cruciferous veggies likely get their powerful anti-cancer activity from glucosinolates. As previously discussed, when glucosinolates are broken down from chopping or chewing, they form isothiocyanates. These phytochemicals can interact with the epigenome to correct harmful epigenetic changes in cancer cells (Novío et al., 2019). Sulforaphane, one of the isothiocyanates produced by consuming cruciferous vegetables, is shown to protect against cancer via multiple pathways and at several stages of cancer development (Anand et al., 2008).

According to the *Food Chemistry* study, the cruciferous vegetables that rated "high" and "very high" in their anti-cancer benefits are (in alphabetic order):

- Broccoli (high)
- Brussels sprouts (very high)
- Cabbage (very high)
- Cauliflower (high)
- Curly cabbage (very high)
- Kale (very high)
- Red cabbage (high)
  (Boivin et al., 2009)

While broccoli sprouts weren't tested as part of the Food Chemistry study, they would logically make an excellent addition to an anti-cancer diet based on their exceptionally high levels of glucosinolates, as previously discussed. Growing your own broccoli sprouts is fun and easy. All it takes is a sprouting bag, some organic seeds and just a couple of minutes a day. In less than a week, you'll have a harvest of fresh broccoli sprouts to boost the nutritional value of your dog's meals—and your own, of course! (See Resources.) Diana is also excited to offer BroccoBoost, a certified organic, non-heat dehydrated whole-food broccoli sprout powder for dogs and people. (See Resources.)

Pro tip: Chop cruciferous veggies raw to increase the sulforaphane content. Chopping releases myrosinase, the enzyme that interacts with glucosinolates to form sulforaphane (Compound Interest, 2017). For more tips on maximizing sulforaphane and other nutrients in your cruciferous vegetables, check out "How to prepare green veggies" in Chapter 5.

If your dog is hypothyroid, limit cruciferous vegetables to moderate amounts because they are goitrogenic, which as we've already discussed means that they can further decrease thyroid function. Cooking decreases some of the goitrogenic properties, but it also decreases the anti-cancer nutrients. (See "Anti-nutrients in plant foods" in Chapter 5 for more information.)

Carrots

If ever a vegetable needed a public relations firm, carrots are it. They're so healthy, yet so easy to take for granted. But carrots have an interesting story to tell—historically and nutritionally. That story includes **falcarinol**, a powerful anti-cancer compound that seems to be one of the health industry's best-kept secrets.

Before we dive into the cancer-fighting activities of falcarinol, let's whet your appetite with some little-known carrot facts:

- Wild carrots were originally purple, not orange (except for some mutated varieties of other colors, including yellow and white).
- Dutch farmers were the first to grow cultivated carrots in the late 16th century.
- Over time, these growers 'bred' the mutated yellow and white varieties into the orange variety that dominates store shelves today.

(Hiskey, 2014)

All carrot colors are rich in cancer-protective phytochemicals, from anthocyanin pigments in purple varieties to carotenoids in orange and yellow types. But scientists now believe that the most powerful anti-cancer activities come courtesy of falcarinol, a natural pesticide found in carrots. Its main job is to protect carrots from fungal diseases, but this pesticide has a happy side-effect; it helps protect against cancer (Graham, 2005). *In vitro* and *in vivo* studies show that falcarinol inhibits multiple types of cancers, including colorectal (Graham, 2005), acute lymphoblastic leukemia (Zidorn et al., 2005) and breast (Tan et al., 2014).

In one study, animals with precancerous tumors were divided into three groups. One group received only regular feed; the second group received the feed along with some raw orange carrots; and the third group received the feed supplemented with an extract of falcarinol equal to the amount found in the raw carrots. After 18 weeks, the animals who consumed either the raw carrots or the falcarinol extract were one-third less likely to develop cancerous tumors than the animals who ate only regular feed (University of Newcastle Upon Tyne, 2005).

Research also shows that even at low doses, falcarinol decreases intestinal inflammation and protects the integrity of the intestinal barrier. This is a huge bonus because as we now know, the gut is a crucial first line of defense in preventing all types of chronic inflammatory diseases, including cancer (Stefanson & Bakovic, 2018).

When it comes to benefiting from falcarinol, how you store and prepare your carrots matters. Long-term storage of raw carrot cubes reduces falcarinol content by almost 35% and steaming results in about the same loss. But boiling is the worst. After 12 minutes, boiled carrots lose almost 70% of their falcarinol (Hansen et al., 2003).

To get the most falcarinol bang for your buck, serve your dog's carrots fresh and raw. If you must boil them, immerse them in boiling water whole and chop them after cooking. Researchers have found that 'boiled-before-cut' carrots contain 25% more falcarinol than carrots that were cut before boiled. This is because cut carrots have a larger surface area exposed to the water, allowing more nutrients to leech out. Whole boiled carrots also retain more of their natural sugars (which are healthfully insulated by fiber), increasing their sweet taste along with their nutrition (Medical Xpress, 2009).

Some cancer-fighting compounds, such as curcumin (more on this soon), are not well-absorbed into the system. But this doesn't appear to be an issue with falcarinol. In one study, 14 young Danish men volunteered to drink either 300 ml (10 oz), 600 ml (20 oz) or 900 ml (30 oz) of carrot juice for breakfast, along with bread and butter. Researchers measured the men's plasma levels of falcarinol 10 times during an eight-hour period, beginning just before their carrot juice breakfast. Even the men drinking the lowest dose of carrot juice experienced a significant increase in plasma falcarinol within just a half hour of drinking the juice. This study illustrates that falcarinol from carrots is biologically available in amounts readily obtained from diet (Hansen-Møller et al., 2002). However, we do not recommend carrot juice for dogs, as juicing removes the healthy fiber that insulates the sugars.

Celery, parsnip and parsley also contain falcarinol. Sounds like the base of a delicious cancer-fighting stew to us!

Garlic

Garlic was the *number one* cancer-fighting food identified in the *Food Chemistry* study. According to the study authors:

> …among all vegetables tested in this study, the extract from garlic was by far the strongest inhibitor of tumor cell proliferation, with complete growth inhibition of all tested cell lines (Boivin et al., 2009, p. 375).

This is amazing. Garlic prevented the growth of every type of tumor cell tested: breast, stomach, prostate, pancreatic, lung, kidney, medulloblastoma and glioblastoma.

Garlic's powerful cancer-fighting activity is thought to come courtesy of allicin, diallyl disulfide, diallyl sulfide and allixin, a group of organosulfur compounds shown to inhibit the growth and proliferation of cancer cells. Garlic exhibits protective benefits against several types of cancers in addition to those tested in the *Food Chemistry* study, including cancers of the skin, colon, and esophagus (Bansal et al., 2018).

This is an excellent reason to include garlic as part of your dog's cancer-fighting diet. At the same time, you want to be aware that garlic is part of the allium family and is a relative of onions, leeks, chives, scallions and shallots—foods that dogs should never have due to toxicity. Fresh garlic, however, is safe for dogs when fed in appropriate amounts. *Do not give garlic powder due to possible excessive levels that can cause toxicity.*

Dosage: We recommend 1/4 clove of *fresh* garlic per 20 pounds of the dog's body weight daily. This works out to 1/4 clove for a 20-pound dog, 1/2 clove for a 40-pound dog, 3/4 clove for a 60-pound dog, 1 clove for an 80-pound dog and 1 1/4 cloves for a 100-pound dog per day.

Green vegetables

Feeding your canine companion an ample variety of green vegetables supercharges her cells with powerful cancer-fighting nutrients, including the potent green pigment chlorophyll. You might recall our earlier discussion of photosynthesis. As we mentioned, chlorophyll is the star of that story. (See Chapter 5.) Without chlorophyll none of us would be alive—literally. Land and sea plants (algae) possess special photosynthetic cells called chloroplasts that capture energy from sunlight. The inner membranes of these cells are rich in chlorophyll, and when the sun interacts with them, a series of events occur that create energy for the plants and oxygen for the rest of us. Talk about the ultimate win-win situation.

Given chlorophyll's key role in supporting life, it's not surprising that this mighty green pigment can help thwart cancer in its tracks. First, chlorophyll acts as an antioxidant, scavenging reactive oxygen species (ROS) and destroying dangerous free radicals. But its powers don't stop there. Chlorophyll can neutralize mutagenic molecules by "capturing" them before they have a chance to enter cells and damage DNA (Pietrzak et al., 2008).

The authors of a 2015 review article published in the journal *Nutrition and Cancer* had this to say about chlorophyllin (CHL), a derivative of chlorophyll used as a food additive:

> CHL has been shown to exhibit potent antigenotoxic, antioxidant, and anticancer effects. Numerous experimental and epidemiological studies have demonstrated that dietary supplementation of CHL lowers the risk of cancer. CHL inhibits cancer initiation and progression by targeting multiple molecules and pathways involved in the metabolism of carcinogens, cell cycle progression, apoptosis evasion, invasion, and angiogenesis (Nagini et al., 2015, pp. 203).

Chlorophyll is so effective at inhibiting cancer that it can significantly block damage caused by orally ingesting a strong carcinogen. In one study, three people were given capsules containing aflatoxin, a powerful carcinogenic mycotoxin. When they also drank chlorophyll equal to what's found in six cups of spinach, the carcinogen in their bodies was reduced by about 40% (Jubert et al., 2009; Greger & Stone, 2015).

When you think of foods rich in chlorophyll, think green. The greener the veggie, the greater the chlorophyll level. Here are some excellent sources for your dog:

- Darky, leafy greens, such as kale, collard greens, green leaf lettuce, spinach, Swiss chard and turnip greens

- Green fruits, such as kiwi *(avoid grapes, which are toxic to dogs.)*

- Green herbs, such as parsley, basil and cilantro

- Non-leafy green vegetables, such as asparagus, beet greens, broccoli, Bok choy, Brussels sprouts, celery, green beans, green bell peppers, green cabbage and green peas

- Green seaweeds and algae, such as nori, spirulina, chlorella and kelp. (See "Commonsense kelp cautions" later in this chapter.)

- Barley grass and wheatgrass (gluten free if harvested prior to growing seeds) (If your dog is gluten intolerant, look for products tested and labeled as gluten free. Avoid if your dog is intolerant to wheat.) (National Celiac Association, 2018)

  (Kahn, 2017)

We recommend getting greens into your dog's diet daily, however even occasional consumption can have a profound cancer-fighting impact. A study published in the *Journal of the American Veterinary Medical Association* found that Scottish Terriers who munched on green-leafy (and yellow/orange) vegetables at least three times per week had a significantly reduced risk of developing transitional cell carcinoma (TCC) of the urinary bladder (Raghavan et al., 2005).

Legumes

In Chapter 5, we discussed phytates and lectins, two anti-nutrients found in legumes. We also promised to reveal how these compounds can help protect cells against cancer. Phytates, lectins and many other bioactive compounds in legumes fight cancer on multiple levels.

Phytate/Phytic acid, also known as inositol hexaphosphate (IP6) and its parent compound myo-inositol hexaphosphate (InsP6), was discovered in 1855 and labeled an anti-nutrient in 1940. But it wasn't until about 1990 that scientists began conducting experiments that led to discovering phytate's health benefits, including the ability to destroy cancer cells in multiple ways, such as:

- Boosting immunity

- Decreasing cancer cell proliferation

- Defending against cellular oxidation

- Increasing host immunity
- Promoting apoptosis
- Starving tumors of nutrients (anti-angiogenesis)
- Reducing inflammation

  (Vucenik & Shamsuddin, 2003; Vucenik et al., 2004; Greger & Stone, 2015; Vucenik et al., 2020)

Phytates have even caused cancer cells to revert into normal cells, effectively stopping cancer in its tracks (Vucenik & Shamsuddin, 2003; Greger & Stone, 2015; Vucenik et al., 2020).

Test tube studies show that phytates inhibit the growth of virtually every type of human cancer cell tested—including blood, colon, liver, mammary, uterine cervix, prostate and soft tissue (Vucenik & Shamsuddin, 2003; Greger and Stone, 2015).

Phytates also demonstrate strong anti-cancer properties when added to the diet or drinking water, including protecting against colon cancer (Vucenik et al., 1992), mammary carcinoma (Vucenik et al., 1993) and skin cancer (Ishikawa et al., 1999), as well as reducing the growth of metastatic fibrosarcoma (Vacenik et al., 1992). IP6 is also shown to block the formation of liver cancer as well as cause existing liver cancer to regress (Vucenik et al., 1998).

Lectins have recently gained attention in cancer research for their therapeutic benefits. Legume lectins, like phytates, can fight cancer on multiple levels, including boosting the immune system, attaching to tumor cell membranes, decreasing cancer cell growth and inducing apoptosis. Studies show that legume lectins are toxic to multiple types of cancer cell lines, including bone, bile duct, breast, liver, lung, oral, ovarian, prostate, nasopharyngeal and skin (Gautam et al., 2020).

The American Institute for Cancer Research includes pulses (edible seeds of legume plants) as part of its Foods that Fight Cancer and points to numerous protective compounds, including:

- Dietary fiber
- Folate
- Lignans
- Resistant starch
- Phytochemicals, including phenolic acids, flavan-3-ols, proanthocyanidins and anthocyanins (in red and black beans)
- Saponins

  (American Institute for Cancer Research, 2021)

Mushrooms

You now know that lectins from legumes possess powerful cancer-preventive properties, but did you know that *mushrooms* also contain beneficial lectins? That's right. Mushroom lectins are just one biologically active compound in these fabulous fungi that help protect against multiple types of cancer. Mushrooms also contain polysaccharides, polysaccharide-protein complex, polysaccharide-peptide complex, terpenoids, steroids, phenols and more—all of which boast anti-cancer properties (Ivanova et al., 2014; Pandya et al., 2019). It seems that humans have been aware of the medicinal powers of mushrooms for thousands of years. An Indian document about the medicinal benefits of mushrooms dates back about 5,000 years (Vetvicka et al., 2021).

Beta-glucans, a type of soluble fiber polysaccharide found in the cell walls of mushrooms, are such powerful anti-cancer compounds that they are currently being studied for their role in cancer immunotherapy. Beta-glucans can cross the gut barrier, enter the circulatory system and interact with the body's immune system to help block tumor metastasis (Ayeka, 2018; Vetvicka et al., 2021). They also prevent normal cells from turning cancerous by protecting against genotoxic carcinogens (agents that damage DNA) and by blocking angiogenesis, among other anti-cancer activities (Akramiene et al., 2007).

Mushroom species contain different levels of cancer-fighting ability. Species where the polysaccharides are attached to proteins (polysaccharide-protein complex) or peptides (polysaccharide-peptide complex) boast greater anti-cancer benefits (Pandya et al., 2019). *Coriolus versicolor* (turkey tail / cloud mushroom / Yun zhi) is one such mushroom. It's not typically consumed as a food, but rather used as a commercial medicinal mushroom supplement for its powerful polysaccharide-protein complexes, most notably polysaccharide Krestin (PSK) and polysaccharide peptide (PSP).

Dozens of studies show that PSP from *Coriolus versicolor* activates lymphocytes and macrophages. These white blood cells increase cancer-fighting cell signaling molecules called cytokines, including TNF-a, IL-1b and IL-6. In human clinical trials, PSP significantly increased both quantity and quality of life of patients with stomach and colon cancer (Vetvicka et al., 2021).

PSP has also been clinically studied in dogs with hemangiosarcoma, a highly invasive and fast-spreading cancer that originates in the cells lining the blood vessels. In one study, 15 dogs with splenic hemangiosarcoma who had their spleens removed but were not receiving follow-up chemotherapy were randomly divided into three treatment groups. Each group received a different level of I'm Yunity (25/mg/kg/day, 50 mg/kg/day or 100 mg/kg/day), a standardized commercial PSP complex extracted from the *Coriolus versicolor* mushroom. (See Resources.) The doses were given orally via capsules from the time of the dogs' assessment until their death. The study was double-blind, meaning that neither the researchers nor the dogs' caretakers knew the dose being given. The dogs receiving the strongest dose (100 mg/kg/day) experienced the longest median survival times ever reported for this type of cancer (199 days)—even longer than reported for dogs receiving doxorubicin-based chemotherapy (141 to 179 days) (Cimino-Brown & Reetz, 2012). The researchers concluded that:

> *Based on this data, one could hypothesize that PSP has the potential to have effects on survival similar to that which is seen with standard of care chemotherapy. Proving, in a biologically aggressive animal model, that PSP delivers antitumor and survival effects*

in a magnitude similar to that which is seen in standard chemotherapy [and] could have significant implications for shifts in standard of care from current cytotoxic therapies to complementary compounds, such as P.SP, that have little to no negative documented effects on normal cells (Cimino-Brown & Reetz, 2012, pp.7).

In other words, dogs may be able to survive as long as—or even longer—on a safe and natural mushroom extract than they would with an expensive, stress-inducing and potentially harmful chemotherapy protocol. Krestin (PSK) isolated from *Coriolus versicolor* also has strong anti-cancer properties. In human patients, it increases immune response by stimulating Natural killer (NK) cell activity. PSK is shown to increase survival time in multiple types of cancers, including lung, breast, stomach, nasopharynx, colon, rectum and esophageal (Standish et al., 2008; Vetvicka et al., 2021).

Coriolus versicolor isn't the only mushroom species with powerful cancer-fighting beta-glucans. Other species are also being studied for their chemoprotective activity, including:

- *Tremella fuciformis* (snow fungus / snow ear / silver ear fungus / white jelly mushroom)
- *Grifola frondosa* (maitake)
- *Lentinus edodes* (shiitake)
- *Agaricus blazei* (native to Brazil, where it's also known as Royal Sun or Hime-matsutake in Japan)
- *Ganoderma lucidum* (reishi / lingzhi)

Even the humble button mushroom offers anti-cancer benefits. Women who consume more white mushrooms have a 64% lower risk of developing breast cancer than non-mushroom eaters (Zhang et al, 2009; Gregor & Stone, 2015).

Never feed your dog (or yourself) wild mushrooms, as they may be poisonous and lead to serious illness or death. Only cultivated, edible mushrooms purchased at the grocery store or medicinal mushrooms purchased from reputable commercial sources should be used. These are safe and packed with cancer-fighting benefits.

Nigella sativa

The name *Nigella sativa* might sound unfamiliar to you, but if you've heard of black cumin, then you're already on to this amazing medicinal herb. *Nigella sativa* goes by many different names. In addition to black cumin, it's referred to as black seed, black caraway, Roman coriander, kalonji, fennel flower and even the "seed of blessing" (Habatul-barakah in Arabic). But regardless of the name, research shows that *N. sativa* provides impressive anti-cancer benefits. In fact, it is among the top evidence-based medicinal plants and has even been called a "miracle herb" (Ahmad et al., 2013; Greger & Stone, 2015; Majdalawieh & Fayyad, 2016; Mollazadeh et al., 2017).

N. sativa is an annual flowering plant native to southwest Asia, parts of the Mediterranean and Africa. It's sometimes grown as an ornamental plant due to its large, beautiful flowers, which are typically pale blue or white with five petals. But it is the black seeds within the fruit that are prized for both their culinary and medicinal properties.

Roasted and ground, black seeds are used to flavor a variety of dishes in India and the Middle East, from curries and rice to sweets (Petruzzello, 2018).

Black seed oil and extracts have been used in medicine for thousands of years and are particularly popular in Eastern modalities like Ayurveda, Siddha and Unani (Majdalawieh & Fayyad, 2016). Ancient Egyptian and Greek physicians, including Hippocrates, used it to treat a variety of illnesses, from nasal congestion to intestinal worms. It is even mentioned in the Bible as "the curative black cumin." but it's just within the last few decades that scientific interest in it has blossomed (Greger & Stone, 2015).

Why is *N. sativa* so special? It contains many active compounds; however, the main therapeutic component is called **thymoquinone**, which comprises close to half of the seed's oil portion. Thymoquinone acts at both a molecular and cellular level to fight cancer, including inhibiting the proliferation and metastasis of cancer cells, fighting free radical damage, preventing cancerous mutations in DNA, reducing inflammation and inducing apoptosis (Majdalawieh & Fayyad, 2016; Mollazadeh et al., 2017).

Studies show that thymoquinone inhibits the growth and spread of multiple types of cancer cell lines, including myeloblastic leukemia, primary effusion lymphoma, multiple myeloma, glioblastoma and neuroblastoma as well as cancer of the blood system, bile duct (cholangiocarcinoma), kidneys, lungs, prostate, colon, cervix, liver and breast (Khader & Eckl, 2014; Mollazadeh et al., 2017).

A 2013 study published in the journal *Oncology Reports* found that thymoquinone can modulate gene expression to create antiangiogenic and antitumor activity in human osteosarcoma (bone cancer) cells by significantly downregulating a transcription factor called the Nuclear Factor-kB pathway (NF-kB) (Peng et al., 2013). The ability to suppress the NF-kB pathway is crucial in preventing and treating cancer, because activated NF-kB is "one of the most important molecules linking chronic inflammation to cancer" (Taniguchi & Karin, 2018).

But can thymoquinone also kill canine *osteosarcoma* cells? This would be a groundbreaking feat, since bone cancer in dogs is a painful and highly malignant type of tumor. Sadly, dogs treated with chemotherapy live an average of just one year (Hardy, 2020). Let's look at a study in *International Journal of Oncology*. Researchers tested the effects of thymoquinone on a canine osteosarcoma cell line as well as on a variant line resistant to treatment by the chemotherapy drug cisplatin. Thymoquinone caused apoptosis (cell death) of both types of canine osteosarcoma cells—including the drug-resistant line. In fact, it had the greatest toxic effect on the drug-resistant cells (Shoieb et al., 2003). This study showed that not only can thymoquinone kill multiple types of cancer cells; it can also decrease the toxic side effects of chemotherapy drugs without interfering with the drug's efficacy (Shoieb et al., 2003). These results indicate that black seed and black seed oil are a powerful ally for both natural and conventional cancer treatment protocols.

Black seed oil is also an excellent source of GLA, the anti-inflammatory omega-6 fatty acid. As we discussed in Chapter 5, GLA offers a host of health benefits, including helping to restore the skin's moisture barrier.

Black seeds are extremely pungent, peppery and bitter and not all dogs will accept the taste. Diana is sensitive to intense spice and finds that black seeds irritate her throat. For this reason, we recommend giving your dog the oil, which we find mellower tasting than the seeds.

Dosage: We recommend 1/4 teaspoon black seed oil for small dogs, 1/2 teaspoon for medium dogs and 1 teaspoon for large dogs per day, divided between morning and evening. Opt for cold pressed oil to provide maximum nutrition. (See Resources.) As always, we recommend introducing black seed oil slowly, starting with half the recommended dose, and monitoring your dog for any negative reactions prior to increasing the amount given.

Caution: Do not give black seed oil to dogs who are pregnant, nursing or who suffer from seizures. Consult with your veterinarian if your dog is taking any medications.

Seaweed

The sea is rich with two types of algae—microalgae and macroalgae. Spirulina and chlorella are microalgae. Microalgae are one-celled organisms that are so small you need a microscope to see them. Macroalgae, on the other hand, are large multi-celled organisms and look like plants that live under water. Like land plants and microalgae, macroalgae are photosynthetic, meaning that they convert the sun's rays to energy in the process of photosynthesis. Microalgae are commonly referred to as phytoplankton, whereas macroalgae are called seaweeds. Seaweeds are grouped by their color—red (Rhodophyta), green (Chlorophyta) and brown (Phaeophyceae) (Udayangani, 2020; Cotas et al, 2021).

If you grew up in a Western society, your childhood meals likely didn't include seaweed. In fact, you probably thought of seaweed as something that stuck to your body at the beach (more on that in a minute) and certainly not something to eat. But if you grew up in Asia—particularly Japan, China and Korea—seaweed would have held a common place at the dinner table. In fact, seaweed has been used as a food source in Asia since ancient times—about 600 BC. Today, there are about 145 different species of edible green, red and brown seaweeds used in cuisines worldwide. Japan, which consumes more seaweed than any other culture, uses about 20 different varieties in their cuisine (Warwicker & Taylor, 2012).

There are many reasons to include edible seaweed in your dog's—and your own—diet. For starters, it provides that delicious umami flavor that has come to be known as the fifth type of taste (along with sweet, sour, salty and bitter). Seaweeds are also packed with an amazing variety of health promoting molecules and minerals, such as sulphated polysaccharides, polyphenolics, terpenoids, flavonoids, pigments, MUFAs (monounsaturated fatty acids), PUFAs (polyunsaturated fatty acids), HUFAs (highly-unsaturated fatty acids), essential amino acids, vitamins (e.g., A, B1, B2, B9, B12, C, D, E, and K) and minerals (e.g., calcium, iron, iodine, magnesium, phosphorus, potassium, zinc, copper, manganese and selenium) (Cotas et al., 2021). Seaweed is also a protein powerhouse. In some species, such as nori (*Porphyra spp*), protein makes up as much as 47% of the dry weight (Warwicker & Taylor, 2012; Thomson, 2017).

Seaweed's bioactive compounds provide a host of health benefits, including anti-fungal, anti-inflammatory, anti-viral, anti-bacterial, anti-allergic, antioxidant, anti-pruritic, neuroprotective, hepatoprotective and immunomodulatory. But it is just recently that scientists began discovering what might be seaweed's greatest attrib-ute—its anti-cancer benefits. Studies have found that seaweeds and their bioactive compounds not only help *prevent* cancer; they can also be used therapeutically to *treat* it (Cotas et al., 2021).

It's not surprising that Japan, with its high rate of seaweed consumption, has a lower cancer rate than Western countries. Westerners aren't exactly known for our taste for seaweed. What are we known for? A love of red meat and dairy. So, what happens when Japanese people follow our lead and increase their intake of red meat and dairy? They, too, suffer from increased incidences of chronic diseases (Cotas et al., 2021).

Studies show that seaweed's anti-cancer benefits might extend beyond preventing cancer in the first place to increasing the rate of survival in cancer patients. Regular seaweed consumption is correlated with lower death rates among Japanese people diagnosed with lung, pancreatic (Iso & Kubota, 2007), colon and rectal cancers (Minami et al., 2020). Bioactive compounds in seaweed fight cancer in multiple ways, including inducing apoptosis, suppressing cancer cell proliferation and increasing the body's immune response against cancer (Alves et al., 2018; Wali et al., 2019; Cotas et al., 2021).

Due to their research-based ability to prevent and treat cancer, seaweeds are consid-ered to convey a **nutraceutical effect**. This means that seaweeds can provide medici-nal anti-cancer benefits in addition to regular health benefits. Their cancer-fighting potential is so exciting (and potentially profitable) that drug companies are develop-ing anti-cancer therapies based on various compounds isolated from seaweeds. Even though this research is still in its infancy, some of these compounds are already pat-ented and undergoing clinical trials (Brown et al., 2014; Cotas et al., 2021).

In a comprehensive 2021 review of seaweed's nutraceutical and biomedical anti-cancer potential, published in the *Journal of Cancer Metastasis and Treatment*, the authors noted that:

> *Even though more work is necessary, the reviewed results reported here can be considered a positive support towards classifying seaweeds as favorable nutraceuticals for humans against cancer incidence* (Cotas et al., 2021, pp. 8).

Since there is a strong correlation regarding cancer in dogs and people, this is also exciting news for our canine companions.

Dried seaweed is convenient and economical, plus it offers the same nutritional value as whole leaf forms. Try mixing some dulse, nori, wakame or other dog-friendly vari-ety into your dog's meals for a flavorful surprise and nutritional boost. (See Resources.)

Caution: You need to be *very* careful of the quality of seaweed products you pur-chase. Seaweed can contain dangerous levels of heavy metals, which are *linked* to cancer. For this reason, we advise only purchasing certified organic seaweed, which must be free of heavy metals and other dangerous contaminants (Ettinger, 2018). (See

Resources.) Avoid Hijiki seaweed altogether, which is shown to contain dangerous levels of inorganic arsenic (Warwicker & Taylor, 2012). And be sure to never let your dog eat seaweed from the beach or any other type of wild seaweed. This is dangerous and can lead to death from poisoning, dangerous sea creatures lurking in the seaweed or intestinal blockage (Rover.com, 2021).

How much seaweed should you give your dog? That depends on various factors because seaweed can contain high levels of iodine, depending upon the species, location of harvest and preparation method (Zava & Zava, 2011). In excessive amounts, iodine can worsen thyroid function in individuals with pre-existing thyroid disorders.

Commonsense kelp cautions

Kelp is a type of brown seaweed. It is also sold as **kombu**, which is the Japanese name for dried kelp. Like other seaweeds, kelp is high in protein, amino acids, vitamins and minerals. But red seaweeds, not brown, are highest in protein. For example, protein makes up about 16% of the Calories in raw kelp (NutritionData, 2018), whereas raw nori (a red seaweed) gets about 44% of its Calories from protein (RawNori, 2021).

What is kelp/kombu especially high in? Iodine. A study published in the *Journal of Food and Drug Analysis* tested 10 samples each of dried nori, wakame and kombu for their iodine content. Kombu contained by far the highest average iodine level at 2,523.5 mg/kg, compared with wakame's average iodine level of 139.7 mg/kg and nori's level of 36.9 mg/kg (Yeh et al., 2014). Obviously, your dog is not going to munch on a kilogram—2.2 pounds—of dried kelp, but this is still a lot of iodine.

Kelp granules are a popular seasoning that many people like to add to their dog's food. Let's compare the iodine content of kelp granules to dulse, another commonly used type of seaweed. We checked the nutritional details from a major organic seaweed company and discovered that one teaspoon of dulse granules contains 284 mcg iodine, while one teaspoon of kelp granules contains 1,638 mcg (Main Coast Sea Vegetables, n.d.). Put into perspective, the NRC's RDA of iodine for our 22-pound dog, Benji, is about 166 mcg per day. This means that feeding Benji just one teaspoon of kelp granules would supply almost *10 times* his RDA of iodine, while one teaspoon of dulse granules provides about 1.7 times the RDA.

Iodine is an essential nutrient and dogs require an adequate dietary intake. But excessive iodine consumption can cause health problems, including iodine-induced hypothyroidism or hyperthyroidism. This is especially true in dogs who already suffer from thyroid dysfunction.

Kombu is popular among plant-based eaters because adding it to a pot of boiling beans reduces the beans' gas-producing qualities, making them easier to digest. This effect is due to the enzyme glutamic acid, which helps to break down the gas-producing raffinose sugars in beans (Seidenberg, 2013). But here's the thing. If you boil kombu for just 15 minutes, it loses up to 99% of its iodine content. That's virtually *all* its iodine (which is a lot). And where do you think that iodine goes? Into the boiling water (Zava & Zava, 2011).

Now, once you're done boiling your beans, you're going to toss out the kombu and pour that iodine-rich water down the drain, so all's cool, right? Well, we don't know. After all, beans absorb water as they cook, which means they also absorb iodine. We don't know how much iodine leeches into the beans, but when it comes to the potential problems related to excessive iodine intake, we'd rather play it safe. Perhaps we're worry-warts, but for this reason we're breaking from the pack and recommending *not* adding kombu when boiling beans for your dog. You can find the gas-blasting tips we *do* recommend in Chapter 7.

What are our favorite seaweeds for dogs? We especially love nori and wakame. They're packed with nutrients and, according to the Japanese iodine study, one gram of dried nori contains just 16 mcg iodine. Wakame comes in second, with 42 mcg/gram (Teas et al., 2004). Add some to your dog's food for a powerful punch of nutrition *and* umami.

Turmeric/curcumin

Turmeric is a spice that comes from the *Curcuma longa* plant, which is related to ginger. Native to Southeast Asia, turmeric is popular in Indian cuisine and has been used for centuries as part of Indian Ayurvedic medicine. Turmeric's rich, vibrant yellow color comes from **curcumin**, a polyphenol pigment that has recently caught the attention of Western medical practitioners and researchers. Over the past 25 years, curcumin has been the subject of extensive human clinical trials to test its safety and efficacy in many types of inflammatory diseases, including cancer (Gupta et al., 2013). In fact, curcumin is currently one of the most widely researched compounds for its cancer-protective role (Anand et al., 2008).

What has all this research shown? It appears that curcumin is one of the 'smarter' natural compounds in outwitting cancer because it's able to modulate not just one or two, but *multiple* cell-signaling pathways (Gupta et al., 2013). This means that curcumin targets and attacks cancer cells in many ways and at various stages of development. And since it's a powerful antioxidant, curcumin helps defend against free radicals that can damage cells and lead to cancerous mutations in DNA. In this way, curcumin may be able to prevent cancer from developing in the first place.

If cancer does take hold, curcumin helps to fight it by changing the behavior of multiple molecular targets, including pro-inflammatory cytokines, apoptotic proteins, cyclooxygenase-2, 5-LOX, STAT3, C-reactive protein, prostaglandin E2, prostate-specific antigen, adhesion molecules, phosphorylase kinase, transforming growth factor-β, triglyceride, ET-1, creatinine, HO-1, AST, and ALT (Gupta et al., 2013). Curcumin even targets the NF-ϰB pathway (Gupta et al., 2013); as we mentioned in our discussion of *Nigella sativa*, this is a transcription factor that plays a key role in all inflammatory responses. In fact, NF-ϰB activation is involved in every known hallmark of cancer (Taniguchi & Karin, 2018).

Curcumin can physically attach to as many as 33 different proteins involved in cancer development and proliferation, including COX 2 and 5-LOX, and block their activity. One study identified more than 40 different biomolecules targeted by curcumin to promote cancer cell death (Aggarwal et al., 2007; Ravindran et al., 2009).

Curcumin can even insert itself into cancer cell membranes and directly or indirectly regulate gene expression in a way that causes the cell to 'commit suicide' (apoptosis). In a one-two-punch against cancer, curcumin can *activate* pathways that cause cancer cells to die while at the same time *blocking* other pathways that enable cancer cells to proliferate. Moreover, this activity is specific to cancer cells, meaning that curcumin leaves healthy cells alone to grow and thrive. And because curcumin attacks cancer via multiple cell-signaling pathways, the chance of developing resistance to its benefits is reduced (Ravindran et al., 2009).

Studies have found that curcumin can block the growth, spread and survival of almost *every* type of tumor cell (Ravindran et al., 2009). Either alone or in combination with other agents, curcumin has demonstrated potential against colorectal cancer, pancreatic cancer, breast cancer, prostate cancer, multiple myeloma, lung cancer, oral cancer and head and neck squamous cell carcinoma (Gupta et al., 2013).

At this point, you may be thinking, "Yes! I am all in on giving my dog curcumin." But you might also wonder about the best way to serve it. Should you give your dog fresh turmeric root, powdered turmeric or even a standardized curcumin supplement?

Mounting clinical evidence indicates that the therapeutic benefits of consuming fresh, whole foods far outweigh those gained from swallowing a pill or capsule. This is likely because nutrients in whole foods work synergistically, and we miss out on these benefits when we ingest an isolated extract. In addition to curcumin, whole turmeric contains many active compounds, including turmerin, turmerone, elemene, furanodiene, curdione, bisacurone, cyclocurcumin, calebin A, and germacrone. Scientists have even created curcumin-free turmeric (CFT) and discovered that it contains powerful anti-cancer, anti-inflammatory and anti-diabetic activity. And in China, elemene is used as an approved therapeutic cancer treatment (Aggarwal et al., 2013).

Why should our canine companions benefit only from curcumin isolated in a supplement, when they can get all the anti-cancer goodness that fresh turmeric has to offer? But how much should you give your dog? Is more turmeric better?

In *How Not to Die*, Dr. Michael Greger points out that turmeric contains potent drug-like activities and so until further studies in people confirm its long-term safety at high doses, he prefers to stick with what he calls "culinary doses" based on the average daily consumption in the Indian diet. And just how much turmeric is that? Likely, a lot less than you think. The average Indian consumes only about one-quarter teaspoon of dried turmeric, or about one-quarter inch of fresh root, per day (Greger & Stone, 2015; Siruguri & Bhat, 2015).

Dosage: Adjusting this amount for dogs, we recommend dried turmeric at 1/16 teaspoon for small dogs, 1/8 teaspoon for medium dogs and 1/4 teaspoon for large dogs per day. This translates into about 1/16-inch fresh root for small dogs, 1/8-inch root for medium dogs and 1/4-inch root for large dogs per day.

Curcumin has low bioavailability when taken orally, which can get in the way of obtaining its full benefits. This is because curcumin goes straight to the liver where it's rapidly metabolized, preventing most of it from entering the bloodstream. Many people combine black pepper with turmeric to increase its absorption. Black pepper contains about 5% of a compound called piperine, which prevents the liver from effectively metabolizing curcumin, enabling more of it to be absorbed into the bloodstream. Piperine is so effective that people who took just one-quarter teaspoon of black pepper along with turmeric had a 2,000% increase in curcumin absorption. Even a pinch—about 1/20 of a teaspoon—given along with turmeric will do the job (Shoba et al., 1998; Greger & Stone, 2015).

However, even though piperine greatly enhances curcumin absorption, we strongly advise using *extreme caution* if adding black pepper to your dog's turmeric and, if you do, using just a couple of grains. We are aware of dogs who have experienced extreme reactions—and tragically even died suddenly—after taking curcumin combined with black pepper. We would rather be 'safe than sorry' and avoid it altogether.

To *safely* increase curcumin's bioavailability, we recommend combining turmeric with dietary fat. Many people mix turmeric with coconut oil; however, we prefer cashew or almond butter as a more nutritious fat source.

Cautions: There are some cautions to be aware of when giving turmeric to your dog:

- Turmeric increases digestive acids, which may cause an upset stomach in dogs with delicate gastrointestinal systems.
- It can act as a blood thinner, increasing the risk of bleeding when given in combination with some medications such as NSAIDs, blood thinners and antiplatelet drugs or when given with certain blood-thinning foods such as botanicals, Gingko biloba, garlic and saw palmetto.
- Turmeric may increase the risk of kidney stones.
- Consult with your veterinarian if your dog is on chemotherapy, as curcumin can decrease the effectiveness of certain chemotherapy medications such as camptothecin (Camptosar), mechlorethamine (Mustargen), doxorubicin (Adriamycin, Rubex) and cyclophosphamide (Cytoxan, Neosar).
- Turmeric may cause contact dermatitis or hives.

  (Ware, 2018; Memorial Sloan Kettering Cancer Center, 2021)

Battling lymphoma, Yogi lived more life with plants

In May 2021, Yogi's 'mom,' Jennifer, began finding lumps on his neck, left shoulder and behind each knee. Jennifer was devastated when Yogi, a seven-year-old Boxer, was diagnosed with lymphoma. Yogi's veterinarian immediately prescribed Prednisone as the sole treatment. Jennifer opted against chemotherapy because she wanted Yogi to enjoy his remaining time, and she knew that chemotherapy could cause unwanted side effects.

Realizing that dogs with lymphoma who aren't treated with chemotherapy only live a short time (two to three months) (Rajewski, 2020), Jennifer immediately reached out to Diana for a plant-based cancer support recipe. Prior to his cancer diagnosis, Yogi received a diet containing a variety of animal ingredients, including wild boar, rabbit, chicken, salmon and Alaskan pollock.

Jennifer had wanted to transition Yogi to a plant-based diet for several years, but she was concerned that she lacked the knowledge to make it properly balanced. But when Yogi was diagnosed with cancer, Jennifer knew that she had to act fast to get him off animal ingredients and onto plant foods. She wanted to do everything nutritionally possible to enhance both the length and quality of his life.

After consulting with Jennifer, Diana formulated a custom plant-based recipe for Yogi packed with foods scientifically shown to help suppress the growth and spread of cancerous tumors. With this recipe and Prednisone as his sole cancer support, Yogi lived six more healthy, happy months. Unfortunately, an existing tumor in his GI tract ruptured, and Yogi passed away on December 18, 2021. However, not only did Jennifer get to share more time with her precious Yogi; she also got to enjoy that time.

According to Jennifer, "He was doing incredible and still running around with puppy energy just the week before."

Yogi's veterinarian even asked Jennifer for Diana's information. She told Jennifer that if she gets another patient with cancer, she's going to recommend that the client investigate a plant-based diet either on its own or in conjunction with chemotherapy.

"My vet and I agree that the diet was incredibly beneficial for Yogi," she says. "Had it not been for a tumor rupturing, he would still be here. He was so full of energy and still playing tug the week before. The food made such a big impact on how he felt and looked, and that's what I'll always remember."

Chapter 9
Plant-Based Diet Solutions For Diabetes

As we mentioned in Chapter 1, cases of canine diabetes are skyrocketing. Between 2006 to 2016, diagnosed cases increased by almost 80% (Banfield Pet Hospital, 2016). And that's just the *diagnosed* cases. Not all dogs are fortunate enough to receive proper veterinary care, so actual cases could be much higher (which is true of all canine chronic illnesses). What is causing this epidemic of canine diabetes? And what can we do about it? Answering these questions is essential, because diabetes dramatically impacts the health and wellbeing of both the canine patient and the human caretaker.

As with all chronic diseases, there is a root cause to diabetes mellitus—and that root cause has an inflammatory basis. In this chapter, we'll distinguish the two primary types of diabetes, explore the primary root cause of diabetes in dogs and recommend nutritional strategies to help manage this condition.

Obesity: a diabetic disaster

In Chapter 1, we introduced an important and enlightening study. This 2017 Spanish study looked at the relationship between obesity and obesity-related metabolic dysfunction (ORMD) in 93 dogs ages two to 14.7 years old and their human families living in an obesity-prone area of Spain. The researchers found that the exact same number of dogs who were obese (40.9%) also suffered from hypertension (high blood pressure). In other words, obesity was directly related to high blood pressure in dogs, just as it is in people. On top of that, 20.4% of all the dogs had fasting hypertriglyceridemia (elevated triglyceride levels), 20.4% had fasting hypercholesterolemia (high cholesterol) and 5.4% had fasting hyperglycemia (high blood sugar) (Montoya-Alonso et al., 2017). These conditions make up metabolic syndrome, the medical term for a collection of risk factors that when they occur together dramatically increase the risk for heart disease, diabetes and other serious health issues.

It's no surprise that more than half of the obese dogs (55.3%) in the study suffered from metabolic syndrome. Moreover, no differences were found based on age and sex, so younger dogs were just as affected as older dogs (Montoya-Alonso et al., 2017). What might surprise you is that *these dogs suffered from the same diet-related metabolic disorders as their human caretakers*. Almost 80% of the overweight or obese people also had an overweight/obese dog and every dog with an obesity-related metabolic disorder lived in an overweight or obese household (Montoya-Alonso et al., 2017).

So, what does all this have to do with diabetes? Think of it as a vicious cycle: Obesity increases the risk of metabolic syndrome and metabolic syndrome increases the risk of

Type 2 diabetes mellitus (as well as other chronic inflammatory conditions). That is, it does in humans. But what about dogs? *Diagnoses by practicing veterinarians also indicate a link between obesity and diabetes mellitus in dogs* (Lund et al., 2006).

Let's look at a study published in the journal *BMC Veterinary Research* which followed 35 obese dogs in the United Kingdom between 2005 and 2011. The dogs were assessed for markers of metabolic syndrome (systolic blood pressure, cholesterol, triglycerides and glucose) at the beginning of the study and again at the study's end, after completing a weight loss regimen. At the beginning of the study, 20% of the obese dogs showed signs of metabolic syndrome. These dogs had levels of plasma adiponectin that were about two-fold less than healthy weight dogs. Adiponectin is a protein hormone with insulin-sensitizing and anti-inflammatory properties. It plays an important role in regulating glucose levels and lipid metabolism (Chandran et al., 2003). Not surprisingly, then, insulin levels in the obese dogs (with the lower adiponectin levels) were also two-fold greater than in the normal weight dogs (Tvarijonaviciute et al., 2012).

But what does this mean, exactly? For starters, the study showed a correlation between obesity, metabolic syndrome and insulin resistance in dogs similar to what occurs in people (Xydakis et al., 2004). And where insulin resistance is present, Type 2 diabetes mellitus isn't far behind. That's because insulin is a hormone responsible for helping glucose enter the cells, where it's used as energy. But when the body is in a state of insulin resistance, the cells don't respond as they should to insulin, and it can't do its job. Instead of entering the cells, glucose builds up in the blood, resulting in diabetes.

This is sobering news, for sure. But the study also offers hope because it shines a light on a solution—weight loss.

To better understand this connection, let's back up for a moment and look at the two main types of diabetes: Type 1 and Type 2. When an individual suffers from Type 1 diabetes, the beta-cells in their pancreas stop producing insulin. This means that they must always take insulin injections or use an insulin pump. With Type 2 diabetes, the body produces insulin, but cannot properly utilize it. Type 2 diabetes is associated with lifestyle factors, such as diet and obesity.

Veterinary professionals used to believe that dogs only suffered from Type 1 diabetes, and perhaps that was once true. But studies such as the one we just mentioned show that's no longer the case. Like people, dogs are susceptible to diet and lifestyle-related metabolic syndrome, insulin resistance and Type 2 diabetes. And the likelihood of that fate playing out increases when the dog lives in a household with obese people (Montoya-Alonso et al., 2017). Clearly, our actions profoundly affect the health of our four-legged family members.

Keeping your dog at an ideal weight is the first line of defense against diabetes. But if the pounds have already crept on, don't despair. A whole-food, plant-based nutrition plan will get your best friend back in tip-top shape and help stabilize his glucose levels.

"But wait," you might be thinking. "Plant-based foods are full of carbohydrates, and aren't carbs bad for Type 2 diabetes?"

Let's find out.

The case for (the right type of) carbohydrates

Here we go again, busting myths. This time, it's the "stay away from carbs if you have diabetes" myth. And, yes, we're going to bust it wide open.

If you read our previous book, *Canine Nutrigenomics*, you might think you've caught us. That's because in that book, we pointed our fingers at the link between high-glycemic carbohydrates and diet-related diabetes. But what we didn't stress was the benefits of the *right types* of carbohydrates. So, we're going to set the record straight here.

Were we wrong in *Canine Nutrigenomics* when we warned people away from high-GI carbs? Not at all. High-GI carbs lead to weight gain and send glucose levels on an up-and-down roller-coaster ride (and not the fun type), triggering metabolic disease and insulin resistance. But as we've already pointed out, high-GI carbohydrates such as sugar, white flour, white rice and processed foods are also largely devoid of nutritional value. It is these types of refined, low-fiber carbohydrates that are associated with an increased risk of Type 2 diabetes. These foods affect the body very differently than *complex carbohydrates*, which offer the best defense against Type 2 diabetes (Venn & Mann, 2004; Aune et al, 2013; Alessa et al., 2015).

In fact, consuming *animal protein* raises the risk of Type 2 diabetes. In Chapter 4, we discussed the dangers of heme iron obtained from red meat and specifically how it increases the risk of cancers, Type 2 diabetes and heart diseases. We also revealed that high levels of heme iron in the body increase the risk of Type 2 diabetes. You might recall that this information came from—of all places—the *Journal of Meat Science* (Czerwonka & Tokarz, 2017). Another large multi-ethnic cohort study we mentioned showed that zinc and heme from red meat were associated with greater risk of cardio-vascular disease and metabolic syndrome (de Oliveira Otto et al., 2012).

The relationship between animal foods and Type 2 diabetes isn't limited to the negative effects of zinc and heme iron from red meat. Multiple large cohort studies show that people who follow a plant-based diet have far less risk of Type 2 diabetes than omnivores or even 'semi-vegetarians.' Even more interesting is that these protective effects are independent of weight and other diabetes risk factors (McMacken & Shah, 2017).

Whole plant foods help fight diabetes on multiple levels because they contain:

Antioxidants
- Fight free radicals (ROS, reactive oxygen species)
- Decrease inflammation
- Decrease glucose output in the liver
- Increase uptake of glucose
- Inhibit absorption of glucose
- Modulate insulin production

Fiber
- Improves glucose response, insulin signaling and insulin sensitivity
- Promotes weight loss, which reduces insulin resistance

- Provides anti-inflammatory benefits
- Shifts the gut microbiome to reduce trimethylamine N-oxide, a compound linked to insulin resistance

(McMacken & Shah, 2017)

Now, let's dive into some of our favorite diabetes-busting plant foods.

Legumes

We place legumes at the top of our diabetes-fighting pedestal because they help protect against obesity and stabilize blood glucose levels. In Chapter 2, we discussed a study published in the *Journal of Obesity & Weight Loss Therapy*, which showed that overweight dogs who consumed a bean-based weight loss diet had improved metabolic biomarkers compared with dogs fed a nutritionally comparable pork and bone-meal-based diet. The bean-fed dogs also trended toward greater weight loss (Forster et al., 2012). Weight control and improved metabolic status are important benefits in protecting against and treating lifestyle-related canine diabetes.

A major study in people found parallel benefits. The Shanghai Women's Health Study (SWHS) was a large population-based cohort study that examined the relationship between consumption of legumes and soy foods on Type 2 diabetes mellitus in Shanghai, China. The study involved 74,942 women aged 40 to 70 from seven urban areas in Shanghai. In-person interviews with each woman were conducted at the time of their recruitment into the study (1997 to 2000), again in 2000 to 2002 and once again at the conclusion of the study (2002 to December 2004). The study found that the women who ate more total legumes and individual types of legumes were less likely to suffer from Type 2 diabetes. Drinking soy milk was also associated with a lower risk of Type 2 diabetes (Villegas et al., 2008). If your dog loves peanut butter—and is non-reactive to peanuts—you'll also be thrilled to discover that consuming peanuts (which are legumes) and peanut butter also lowered the risk of developing Type 2 diabetes.

How did legumes protect against Type 2 diabetes? According to the authors, multiple factors were likely involved, including:

- Higher fiber content, which helps regulate blood sugar
- Polyphenols, such as isoflavones and lignans, which act as antioxidants
- Soy protein and soy isoflavones, which may improve insulin sensitivity
- Soy isoflavones (again), which may exert anti-diabetic effects via peroxisome-proliferator activated receptors (PPAR), nuclear transcription factors that regulate the expression of genes involved in lipid and glucose regulation

(Mezei et al., 2003; Villegas et al., 2008)

This is promising news for dogs, who can also enjoy these legume-based benefits.

Low-GI veggies

Low-glycemic vegetables play an important role in an anti-diabetes diet because they do not spike blood sugar and are loaded with fiber, phytonutrients, antioxidants and important vitamins and minerals. A 2010 review of six studies involving more than 220,000 people found that those who ate an extra one-and-a-half servings of leafy green vegetables per day decreased their risk of developing Type 2 diabetes by 14%. Leafy greens are rich in polyphenols and vitamin C, which act as antioxidants. They also provide magnesium, which is important because low levels of magnesium are associated with insulin resistance. Bonus: They also reduce the risk of bladder cancer in dogs and people (British Medical Journal, 2010; Raghaven et al., 2005).

These low-GI veggies make a tasty and nutritious addition to your dog's diabetic diet:

- Artichokes
- Asparagus
- Beet greens
- Bok choy
- Broccoli
- Broccoli sprouts
- Brussels sprouts
- Cabbage
- Carrots
- Cauliflower
- Celery
- Collard greens
- Cucumbers
- Green beans
- Green peas
- Kale
- Lettuce
- Mushrooms (cultivated, store-bought only)
- Spinach
- Snow peas
- Summer squash
- Sweet pepper (red, green, yellow, orange)
- Swiss chard
- Zucchini

Can diabetic dogs eat starch?

You might have heard that starches are forbidden for diabetes patients because they can cause rapid rises in blood sugar. But starches also offer many health benefits, including fiber, antioxidants, phytochemicals, vitamins and minerals. While some starches are high-GI and best left off your diabetic dog's dish, others are low-GI and can even help stabilize blood sugar. The following starches are considered low-GI because they are listed as 55 or below on the Glycemic Index, making these healthy options for a diabetic diet:

- Barley (avoid if gluten intolerant)
- Buckwheat groats
- Celeriac (celery root)
- Green peas
- Quinoa
- Jerusalem artichoke
- Jicama
- Legumes (See above)
- Taro
- White yam
- Winter squash

We recommend that diabetic dogs avoid these higher GI starches:

- Amaranth
- Brown Rice
- Beetroot
- Cassava
- Gluten-containing grains
- Millet
- Oats
- Parsnip
- Pumpkin
- Rutabaga
- Sorghum
- Sweet corn
- Sweet potato
- Teff
- Turnip
- White potato
- White rice

  (FoodStruct, 2021; The University of Sidney, 2021)

Note that the GI of a particular food can vary depending upon a variety of factors, including the country of harvest, the cooking method and the responses of the individuals tested. To account for these variables, a GI range is often given. If you have questions about a specific ingredient, we recommend looking it up online in The University of Sydney or FoodStruct Glycemic Index databases. (See Resources.)

Cold potatoes

Wait a minute. Didn't we just finish saying to avoid feeding your diabetic dog white potatoes because they are a high-GI carbohydrate? We did indeed! So, how can we in one breath (or, rather, paragraph), claim that white potatoes are not a diabetes-friendly food and then recommend them in the next? Well, let's clear up this potato puzzle right now.

It's true that cooked white potatoes contain a lot of highly digestible starch. This type of starch is absorbed quickly into the bloodstream, which can cause spikes in blood sugar. But this is only true when potatoes are consumed hot or warm. Once potatoes cool, the starch structure transforms into **resistant starch**. Resistant starch is indigestible by enzymes in the upper GI tract (hence the term 'resistant'), so it doesn't raise blood sugar or insulin levels. Like prebiotic fiber, resistant starch reaches the colon intact. Once there, it's fermented by good gut bacteria, promoting a healthy gut microbiome and producing beneficial postbiotics (Zaman & Sarbini, 2015; Edermaniger, 2021). A major benefit of these postbiotics is—drum roll, please—improved glucose response.

In one study, a diet high in resistant starch improved the gut microenvironment, increased SCFA production and decreased the postprandial glucose response in senior dogs (Ribeiro et al., 2019).

The next time your diabetic dog craves carbs, offer her some *cold potatoes*. You can also give some cooked and cooled rice, which undergoes the same transformation!

Fiber-filled fruit

Many people think that fruit is a no-no in diabetic diets due to the natural sugars. But as we pointed out earlier, fresh, whole fruits are packed with fiber that insulates the sugar and delays its release. So, despite their sugar content, many fruits have a low GI. Fruit is also filled with antioxidants and phytochemicals that decrease inflammation. As always, the key is making smart choices.

Analysis of three large cohort studies of U.S. men and women found that certain fruits were associated with a decreased risk of Type 2 diabetes compared with others. Based on these results, we recommend the following dog-friendly fruits as appropriate for diabetic dogs:

- Apple (include the fiber-rich peel) (GI 36)
- Bananas (select under-ripe for a lower GI) (GI 48)
- Blueberry (GI 53)
- Pear (GI 38)

    (Muraki et al., 2013; FoodStruct, 2021)

Avoid cantaloupe, which was associated with an *increased* risk of diabetes (Muraki et al., 2013), as well as higher-GI fruits such as pineapple and watermelon. Also, never feed fruit juice to your diabetic dog (or any dog, for that matter), as it is also linked with higher risk of diabetes. This makes sense, as fruit juice is stripped of its fiber.

Nuts

You might recall that nuts are packed with healthy omega-3 fatty acids, vitamins, minerals, protein, fiber, antioxidants and other bioactive compounds that help fight a variety of chronic inflammatory diseases, including diabetes.

Walnut oil may play a particularly beneficial role in managing blood sugar levels.

In one study, 45 diabetic people of similar age, body composition and health status consumed 15 grams (just over a tablespoon) of walnut oil per day for three months. Another 45 patients (the control group) took nothing. The group taking the walnut oil experienced a significant decrease in fasting blood sugar levels as well as HbA1c, whereas the control group did not (Zibaeenezhad et al., 2016).

More research is needed to confirm these benefits but including some walnut oil in your diabetic dog's diet could offer advantages. We recommend adding walnut oil as part of the overall fat content of your recipes, per your dog's daily RDA. (See Chapter 6.)

When purchasing walnut oil, opt for cold pressed to avoid chemical processing. And be aware that walnut oil may interact with some thyroid medications, so be sure to discuss this with your veterinarian.

Bear dominates diabetes by going plant-based

Bear, a terrier/mini poodle/schnauzer mix, was diagnosed with diabetes mellitus on December 7, 2020, at the age of nine. Bear was overweight and relied upon 5.5 units of Vetsulin insulin given twice daily to manage his condition. But even with the insulin injections, Bear's fasting glucose levels often reached more than 400 mg/dL, with normal reference values between 80 mg/dL and 120 mg/dL.

Bear's 'mom,' Marky, realized the importance of diet in offering her beloved Bear the best chance of many more healthy years. Shortly after his diagnosis, Marky reached out to Diana for a custom, whole-food plant-based diet to help Bear lose weight and control his diabetes, with the goal of lowering his daily insulin dosage.

Diana created a special plant-based recipe for Bear designed to stabilize his blood sugar levels and help him achieve healthy weight loss. Within just a few weeks of starting the recipe, Bear reached his goal weight and his fasting glucose dropped from the 400s to the 100s. As a bonus, Marky noticed that Bear's stool quality became the healthiest it had ever been. And, double bonus, Bear loves his plant-based cuisine!

Marky said, "I am just thrilled with Bear's recipe and his results. I wanted to say thank you so much for everything—and Bear says thank you, too!"

Bear's veterinarian was also thrilled. Rather than increasing Bear's insulin as he had anticipated, he was instead able to reduce the dosage from 5.5 units to 3.5 units given twice daily.

We look forward to following Bear's continued progress as he achieves his own version of optimum wellness with a nutritious whole-food plant-based diabetes diet.

More plant-based foods for diabetes control

The following foods show excellent promise for their natural anti-diabetes properties:

Apple cider vinegar

Apple cider vinegar is credited with a variety of health benefits, including anti-microbial and antioxidant. But did you know that it might also help in the management of Type 2 diabetes?

Here's a sampling of studies indicating its benefits:

- A small study published in the journal *Diabetes Care* revealed that when Type 2 diabetics who were not on insulin took two tablespoons of apple cider vinegar (along with one ounce of cheese) at bedtime, they were able to reduce their waking glucose concentrations by 4%. By contrast, a control group who took water with cheese showed only a 2% reduction (White & Johnston, 2007).

- A meta-analysis of six studies including 317 patients with Type 2 diabetes found that consuming apple cider vinegar resulted in a "significantly better fasting blood glucose and hemoglobin A1c (HbA1c) level" as well as a "remarkable reduction in total cholesterol and low-density lipoprotein" (Cheng et al., 2019).

- In another study, just two teaspoons (10 grams) of apple cider vinegar taken with a meal of complex carbohydrates reduced postprandial blood glucose levels by 20% compared to a placebo (Johnston et al., 2010).

Dosage: We recommend 1 teaspoon for small dogs, 2 teaspoons for medium dogs and 1 tablespoon for large dogs per day, divided between a.m. and p.m. You can mix apple cider vinegar directly into your dog's food or water.

Be sure to purchase raw apple cider vinegar with the 'mother.' You'll recognize the 'mother' because it looks cloudy and stringy from yeast and bacteria, which serves as a probiotic. (See Resources.)

Basil and rosemary

If your dog is diabetic, you might want to dive into your spice cabinet for some basil and rosemary. Not only are these two herbs delicious; they're also shown to significantly impact blood glucose levels in dogs. Remember, however, not to feed rosemary if your dog is prone to seizures.

A 2020 study published in the journal *Veterinary World* examined the effects of feeding rosemary (*Rosmarinus officinalis*) and/or basil (*Ocimum basilicum*) leaf powder on the glycemic status of dogs. The powders were finely ground from fresh basil and/or rosemary leaves that had been harvested, washed and dried. For the study, 45 Rottweiler puppies were divided into five groups based on an experimental diet. Group 1 was fed an unfortified foundation diet; Group 2 was given the foundation diet with an added commercial palatability enhancer; Group 3 was fed the foundation diet fortified with rosemary (0.05%); Group 4 received the foundation diet fortified with basil (0.05%); and Group 5 received the foundation diet fortified with rosemary and basil (0.025% each) (Abdelrahman et al., 2020).

Here's what happened after eight weeks:

- Dogs fed the diets fortified with basil and/or rosemary (Groups 3, 4 and 5) experienced significant decreases in their serum glucose levels compared to the dogs fed the unfortified diets (Groups 1 and 2).

- Dogs fed the basil-fortified diet (Group 4) showed the most notable reduction in blood glucose levels (about 31%).

- Basil leaves inhibited amylase enzyme activity, reducing the rates of carbohydrate metabolism and glucose release.

- Group 5 (rosemary and basil-fortified diet) showed a 16.25% decrease in blood glucose.

- Group 3 (rosemary-fortified diet) had a 14% reduction in blood glucose.

- Group 4 (basil-fortified diet) experienced increased insulin levels and decreased cortisol levels compared to the control dogs.

- Group 3 (rosemary-fortified diet) and Group 4 (basil-fortified diet) also experienced increased levels of:

  o Glutathione: a powerful antioxidant made in the liver

  o Superoxide dismutase (SOD): an antioxidant enzyme that neutralizes harmful free radicals in cells

  o Catalase, an enzyme that protects cells from oxidative damage

- Dogs in Groups 3 and 4 also experienced decreased levels of:

  o Malondialdehyde, a marker of oxidative stress caused by free radicals

  o Lactate dehydrogenase, an enzyme that when found in high levels in the blood can indicate cellular damage

(Abdelrahman et al., 2020)

These are some powerful results. Increased levels of glutathione, SOD and catalase, along with decreased levels of malondialdehyde and lactate dehydrogenase indicate reduced levels of oxidative stress in the body. This is important because oxidative stress leads to inflammation and inflammation leads to chronic inflammatory conditions such as Type 2 diabetes. You can find out the state of your dog's oxidative stress with Hemopet's patented saliva-based CellBIO test. (See Resources.)

Basil and rosemary are rich in polyphenols and flavonoids, which you'll recall are phytochemicals that act as antioxidants and defend against free radicals. The study authors theorized that this antioxidant capability might be responsible for improving glucose levels by preventing tissue damage of pancreatic β-cells that produce insulin (Abdelrahman et al., 2020).

This study echoes results of other studies showing the benefits of basil and rosemary in rats and humans (Hannan et al., 2014; Labban et al., 2014).

Dosage: We recommend 1 teaspoon per day for small dogs, 2 teaspoons per day for medium dogs and 1 tablespoon per day for large dogs, mixed into food and divided between a.m. and p.m.

Again, rosemary should never be given to dogs with epilepsy or who are prone to seizures, as it can worsen these conditions.

Buckwheat

We pointed out in Chapter 5 that buckwheat boasts high levels of bioactive compounds, anti-inflammatory capacity and overall superfood status. You might even have noticed that we included 'anti-diabetic' to our list of buckwheat's many benefits. Specifically, buckwheat is packed with fagopyritols (especially D-chiro-inositol), a type of beneficial soluble carbohydrate. A study in animals showed that a buckwheat concentrate containing D-chiro-inositol lowered blood glucose levels by 12% to 19% at 90 and 120 minutes after ingestion (Kawa et al., 2003).

Please refer to Chapter 5 for our buckwheat preparation suggestions.

Chia seeds

We also mentioned in Chapter 5 that chia seeds curb obesity and help manage obesity-related diabetes. If you care for a diabetic dog, you'll want to take note of these benefits, which were reported by researchers from the University of Toronto.

The study, published in the journal *Nutrition, Metabolism & Cardiovascular Diseases*, divided 77 overweight or obese patients with Type 2 diabetes into two groups. Both groups followed a Calorie-restricted diet. The control group received 36 grams/1,000 Calories per day of oat bran, while the other group received 30 g/1,000 Calories/day of Salba chia. Salba chia is a registered heirloom white chia seed that's even richer in omega-3s and protein than regular chia seeds. (See Resources.)

After six months, the group consuming the Salba chia seeds:

- Lost more weight than the control group

- Lost more visceral fat, a dangerous type of fat associated with insulin resistance

- Significantly reduced their levels of C-reactive protein (a marker of inflammation) compared to the control group

- Increased their levels of plasma adiponectin (see previous discussion of adiponectin), while the control group experienced no change

(Vuksan et al., 2016; Oldfield, 2017)

Dosage: We recommend adding Salba chia seeds to your diabetic dog's diet at a level of 1 teaspoon per day for small dogs, 2 teaspoons per day for medium dogs and 1 tablespoon per day for large dogs, divided between a.m. and p.m. Soak for at least 20 minutes prior to serving, stirring occasionally. (See "Make a puppy pudding" in Chapter 5 for a delicious recipe.)

Cinnamon

Cinnamon is packed with healthful compounds, including antioxidants, polyphenols, manganese, iron and the unique compounds cinnamaldehyde, cinnamic acid and cinnamate. Cinnamon is credited with anti-inflammatory, antimicrobial and anti-cancer effects and has been investigated for its benefits in managing a variety of chronic diseases, including Alzheimer's disease, arthritis, arteriosclerosis, dental and gum disease and diabetes (Hariri & Ghiasvand, 2016).

Cinnamon may help balance blood sugar via several mechanisms, including:

- Improving insulin sensitivity in fat and muscles
- Improving the liver's production of glycogen
- Increasing uptake of glucose
- Slowing the rate at which food moves through the stomach (gastric emptying time)

While the research into cinnamon's benefits on controlling blood glucose levels isn't conclusive, the Cleveland Clinic points to a few small but encouraging studies in people:

- In a 2003 study published in *Diabetes Care*, 60 adult men and women with Type 2 diabetes were randomly split into six groups. Groups 1, 2 and 3 (30 people) consumed one, three and six grams of cinnamon per day, respectively. Groups 4, 5 and 6 (30 people) were given placebos. After 40 days, fasting serum glucose lowered by 18% to 29% in *all three cinnamon groups*. Triglyceride levels in the cinnamon groups were also reduced by 23% to 30%, LDL (bad) cholesterol decreased by 7% to 27% and total cholesterol lowered by 12% to 26%. No benefit was seen in the placebo groups (Khan et al., 2003; Cleveland Clinic, 2020).

- A 2012 study published in the journal *Nutrition Research* divided 69 people with Type 2 diabetes into three groups. Group 1 consumed 120 milligrams (0.12 grams) of cinnamon per day, Group 2 consumed 360 mg (0.36 g) and Group 3 was given a placebo. After three months, Groups 1 and 2 experienced lower A1C levels, while Group 3 (placebo) had no change (Cleveland Clinic, 2020).

- A 2013 meta-analysis published in the *Annals of Family Medicine* reviewed 10 randomized controlled studies involving a total of 543 patients with Type 2 diabetes. The authors concluded that cinnamon had a significant beneficial effect on decreasing levels of fasting plasma glucose. The patients consuming cinnamon also lowered their LDL cholesterol, total cholesterol and triglyceride levels. Doses of cinnamon given ranged from 120 mg/day (0.12 g) to 6 g/day and duration of the studies ranged from four weeks to 18 weeks (Allen et al., 2013; Cleveland Clinic, 2020).

- A 2019 study published in the *International Journal of Food Science* split 41 healthy individuals into three groups. Group 1 consumed one g/day of cinnamon, Group 2 consumed three g/day and Group 3 took six g/day. The participants were monitored prior to the study, after 20 days and at the conclusion of the study at 40 days. All three groups significantly lowered their postprandial (post-meal) blood glucose levels, while the group taking six g/day of cinnamon also experienced significantly lower levels of pre-prandial (pre-meal) blood glucose (Kizilaslan & Erdem, 2019; Cleveland Clinic, 2020).

We advise steering clear of cinnamon supplements and opting instead for the real thing straight from your spice cabinet. But be extremely cautious about which type of cinnamon you choose. There are four kinds of cinnamon commonly found in grocery stores: Cassia (*Cinnamomum cassia*); Ceylon (*Cinnamomum verum*), also called 'true cinnamon,' Saigon and Korintje. If your bottle of cinnamon does not specifically state that it is Ceylon, then it is Cassia. Products labeled as Saigon or Korintje cinnamon are also varieties of Cassia.

It's essential to know which cinnamon variety you're purchasing because Cassia, Saigon and Korintje cinnamons contain coumarin, an anticoagulant compound that causes liver damage at high doses (Canadian Society of Intestinal Research, 2017). Coumarin is so dangerous that the tonka bean, a coumarin-rich legume native to South America and prized for its scents of vanilla, cherry, almond and cinnamon, has been banned in the U.S. since 1954 (Martin, 2017). You should never give Cassia, Saigon or Korintje cinnamon to your dog (or consume it yourself).

Fortunately, Ceylon cinnamon does not contain coumarin, so you don't have to worry about dangerous side effects. For this reason, Ceylon is our go-to cinnamon, for ourselves and our loved ones.

Dosage: We recommend 1/4 teaspoon Ceylon cinnamon per day for small dogs, 1/2 teaspoon per day for medium dogs and 1 teaspoon per day for large dogs, divided between a.m. and p.m.

Final thoughts on diabetes

As we always say, every dog is an individual. This means that how your dog's blood sugar responds to various foods will be unique. We recommend keeping a food journal to track your dog's postprandial (post-meal) glucose levels. Testing your dog's blood sugar two hours after a meal will provide important insights into which foods create spikes and which promote stability. You can use this information to modify your dog's diet for optimum wellness.

Remember to share all dietary information and blood glucose results with your veterinarian so that she can appropriately adjust your dog's insulin dosage. And as we demonstrated earlier in the chapter with our case study of Bear, don't be surprised if a plant-based protocol results in the ability to reduce your dog's insulin dosage!

Chapter 10
Plant-Based Diet Solutions For Food Intolerances

'Novel' and 'exotic' are two current buzzwords in the pet food industry. These terms refer to the ever-increasing array of unusual animal proteins found in commercial pet food products. This has occurred because as dogs (and cats) become progressively intolerant/sensitive to widely consumed animal proteins, desperate consumers search for alternatives to which their canine and feline companions haven't yet been exposed. The hope is that these new (novel) ingredients—which also tend to involve exotic animals—will resolve the food intolerance epidemic rampant in modern companion dogs (and cats).

This rationale doesn't make sense, however. A novel protein is only novel before an animal has ever consumed it. Once that protein becomes a normal part of the diet—regardless of how exotic it is—it's no longer novel and it poses the same risk of creating an adverse reaction as any other ingredient.

There was a time when lamb was considered a novel protein, but now it's so frequently used that it, too, has become a common source of food sensitivities. The same is true for venison, rabbit, pheasant and other animals that at one time held no place in the canine diet. Sadly, the pet food industry has moved on to slaughtering kangaroos, alligators and other outlandish novel protein sources in a seemingly desperate attempt to keep up with consumer demand and skyrocketing incidences of companion animal food intolerances.

As we mentioned in Chapter 5, the top five reactive foods for dogs based on thousands of NutriScan saliva-based food intolerances tests are:

- White-colored fish (or their oils)
- Turkey
- Corn
- Egg
- Soy

As you can see, three of these five ingredients are animal based. Interestingly, the two plant-based foods on the list (corn and soy) are also two of the most common genetically modified (GM) crops. They are also the two most heavily sprayed crops with the toxic herbicide glyphosate, which you'll recall is the key ingredient in Bayer's highly controversial weedkiller RoundUp. We can't know for certain whether it's a coincidence that these two highly sprayed GM crops made the list of top five problematic foods, but we do find it compelling. We also look forward to future research on the possible link between genetically modified organisms (GMOs), chemicals such as glyphosate and food intolerances.

The good news is that we don't need to expand our net of animal suffering, or harm the environment, to eliminate our dogs' food intolerances. There is a far kinder and more sustainable solution right in front of us—plants. To better understand why plants are an excellent choice for food-intolerant dogs, let's take a closer look at what food intolerances are, how we diagnose them and how to address them. Note that we will use the terms 'intolerance' and 'sensitivity' interchangeably throughout our discussion, as they both refer to the same type of adverse food reaction.

What is food intolerance/sensitivity?

Food intolerance refers to a negative reaction to a consumed ingredient. However, many people, including many veterinary professionals, confuse food *intolerances* with food *allergies*, and some even use the two terms interchangeably. This is unfortunate because an improper diagnosis will negatively impact the health and well-being of a food-intolerant dog.

Food allergies involve an acute (immediate) immunologic response to the offending ingredient. This response can be quite severe, such as breaking out in hives, facial swelling or even anaphylaxis (closure of the airwaves, resulting in the inability to breathe). People at risk of experiencing a severe allergic reaction to a food or environmental allergen (e.g., bees, wasps, fire ants, pollen, etc.) carry an EpiPen, which delivers an emergency dose of epinephrin to stop the life-threatening response. Veterinarians also sometimes prescribe EpiPens for severely allergic dogs.

Allergic responses are called Type I hypersensitivity reactions. They show up in the blood as antibodies to two of the body's immune proteins, immunoglobulins E (IgE) and G (IgG) (Foster et al., 2003). The only way to completely avoid an allergic reaction is to avoid the allergen. Some people also take allergy shots, which work by delivering a small dose of the antigen into the system to help the allergic individual build up a tolerance to it. However, parallel studies in companion animals have yielded varying results and this approach is generally not recommended for allergic dogs.

Food intolerances are quite different from food allergies. Food intolerances typically don't provoke an acute, instantaneous response. Rather, they build up over time—perhaps even months or years after initial exposure. During this time, the body tries its best to fight off the antigen. As it does, chronic inflammation develops deep inside the body. At this point, one is typically unaware that a problem is brewing. But if exposure to the antigen continues, the condition worsens. The 'smoldering inflammation' eventually erupts into a full-blown inflammatory fire. As it pushes its way outward in the body, the symptoms become apparent and visible, including:

- GI tract issues like inflammatory bowel disease (IBD)
- Chronic itching
- Chronic burping and gas rumblings (borborygmi)

- Chronic skin, ear and foot infections (especially with the presence of yeast)
- Cognitive dysfunction, including memory loss and confusion

(Dodds, 2017/2018; Dodds, 2018; Dodds, 2019; Dodds, 2019a)

Food intolerances are caused by Types II and III hypersensitivity reactions. These types of reactions involve antibodies to immunoglobulins A (IgA) and M (IgM) (Rinkinen et al., 2003; Lee & Wong, 2009; Miller et al., 2010). While antibodies involved in allergic reactions initially appear in the blood, antibodies involved in food intolerances show up first in feces or saliva (Dodds & Laverdure, 2015; Dodds, 2017/2018; Dodds, 2018; Dodds, 2019; Dodds, 2019a).

Reactions due to food intolerances are typically not life-threatening; however, they can cause great discomfort and distress to those who suffer from them. They can also trigger more serious health problems. Food intolerances are a major cause of systemic inflammation and, as we've seen, chronic systemic inflammation is like a superhighway to chronic illnesses ranging from autoimmune disorders to cancer. Due to the connection between food intolerances, chronic inflammation and chronic diseases, it's essential that the source(s) of the intolerance is identified and removed as soon as possible.

Unlike allergy shots, there is no such thing as a food intolerance shot. The greater the amount of a reactive food that a dog consumes—and the more often she consumes it—the more likely she is to develop an intolerance to it over time. The only 'cure' for food intolerance/sensitivity is to identify the antigenic ingredient and remove it from the diet.

Diagnosing food intolerance/sensitivity

There are several ways that you can diagnose a specific food intolerance. It's important to understand the differences between these methods so that you can make the right decision for your dog. Let's look at the most common diagnostic modalities.

Food elimination trials

If you suspect that your dog suffers from food intolerance, you might have heard that the best way to pinpoint the offending ingredient is to conduct your own food elimination trial. This involves feeding your dog a diet that consists of one protein and one carbohydrate source at a time, typically for a period of eight to 12 weeks, to determine if she shows signs of a reaction. Your veterinarian might even have recommended this, and at first glance it seems like a reasonable strategy. Unfortunately, this rarely works (Dodds, 2018; Dodds, 2019a).

Let's say that you suspect your dog is intolerant to lamb, beef, brown rice or quinoa. You conduct your food elimination trial as your veterinarian instructed—feeding one protein and one carbohydrate at a time. In this case, you begin with lamb and brown rice. You exclusively feed these ingredients and monitor your dog's reaction over the next several weeks. After this time, your dog appears symptom free, so you assume that these ingredients are not the source of the intolerance. You proceed with your test, switching the protein source to beef and the carbohydrate to quinoa. After two weeks on this new diet... bam. Your dog starts scratching. She even experiences some

GI issues, including gurgling and loose stool. Based on this evidence, you conclude that either beef or quinoa (or both) is the culprit.

Not necessarily.

Remember that clinical signs of food intolerance can take months—and even years—to manifest. This means that the source of your dog's skin and GI issues could actually stem from the previously fed lamb or brown rice (or both). It could also be caused by the current beef and/or quinoa. The problem could even originate from a different ingredient your dog consumed prior to starting the food elimination trial. It's impossible to tell!

If this sounds tedious and confusing, you're right. And the scenario we gave assumes you're feeding a home-cooked diet of just one protein and one carbohydrate at a time. Imagine trying to unravel this mystery using a commercial dog food containing combinations of several types of proteins and carbohydrates. Even if you found a 'limited ingredient' product, studies show that commercial pet foods can contain protein and carbohydrate sources that are not listed on the ingredients label (Ricci et al., 2013; Dodds, 2017/2018).

Food elimination trials contain too many variables to provide an accurate result. And while they aren't a recipe for eliminating your dog's food intolerances, they are a recipe for frustration.

Skin prick testing
Skin prick testing has long been considered the gold standard for measuring food reactions in people and companion animals. However, skin prick testing measures *allergic* responses and is not suitable for determining food intolerances. Skin prick testing identifies immune-mediated responses by measuring levels of Immunoglobulin E (IgE) antibodies. After shaving the dog's skin, the veterinarian will place a drop of the allergen onto the surface and prick it into the top layer. The veterinarian will then observe the area to see if a skin reaction such as a bump and redness occurs, indicating the presence of an IgE antibody toward the allergen.

If your dog experiences an acute negative response to a particular ingredient—particularly if that reaction is severe—then she might suffer from an allergy that can be discovered via skin prick testing. However, since food intolerances don't involve IgE antibodies, this test won't show an inflammatory response, and will not provide further information on determining the source(s) of the intolerance (Stukus, 2014).

Skin prick testing also has several drawbacks:

- Must be performed at the veterinarian's office
- Takes approximately two hours
- No food or water four to five hours prior
- Sedation required
- Tested area must be shaved

- Procedure is invasive
- Requires antihistamines afterward
- Might require steroid treatment
- Procedure is expensive (approximately $500 for 20 antigens)

(Dodds & Laverdure, 2015)

A dog should never be put through skin prick testing to determine specific food intolerances. Skin prick testing is stressful, painful, involves risks and simply is an incorrect diagnostic method (Dodds, 2018; Dodds, 2019a).

NutriScan saliva-based food intolerance test

NutriScan is a patented, scientific method of diagnosing food intolerances/sensitivities that was developed by Jean Dodds, DVM. It is currently the only clinically predictive saliva-based food intolerance test for dogs (as well as cats and horses) and has been validated by two double-blinded clinical trials published in peer-reviewed journals (Dodds, 2017/2018; Dodds, 2018; Dodds, 2019a; Hemopet, 2021).

NutriScan measures levels of immunoglobulins A (IgA) and M (IgM) antibodies in an animal's saliva. High antibody levels to a specific food indicate intolerance to that ingredient. NutriScan is far more specific and accurate than simple cheek or gum swabs because these tests offer only positive or negative results. Since cheek and gum swab tests don't provide information about the specificity or sensitivity of the testing assays used, these methods cannot be considered clinically reliable or accurate (Hemopet, 2021).

As of this writing, NutriScan tests for 24 potential food antigens in dogs:

- Barley
- Beef
- Chicken
- Corn
- Cow's milk
- Duck
- Egg (hen)
- Lamb
- Lentil
- Millet
- Oatmeal
- Peanut
- Pork
- Quinoa
- Rabbit

- Rice
- Salmon
- Soy
- Sweet potato
- Turkey
- Venison
- Wheat
- White fish
- White potato

  (Hemopet, 2021)

Saliva vs. blood analysis for food intolerances

You'll recall that the largest immune organ in the body resides on the mucosal layer of the gut. When this lining becomes compromised, leaky gut occurs, providing the perfect gateway for large food particles to escape into the bloodstream. The body recognizes these particles as antigens and tells the immune system to produce protein antibodies to defend itself against the foreign invader. The antibodies produced are IgA, IgM and IgG, which circulate in the bloodstream and other body fluids where they can also travel to tissues and cause damage. For this reason, food intolerances often begin with a compromised gut environment (Hemopet, 2021).

These antibodies also circulate in the bloodstream, so using a blood test to check for food intolerances seems to make sense. However, this is not the best method. One reason is that antibodies produced in saliva and feces (IgA and IgM) are detectable months before significant levels of antibodies (IgA and IgG) appear in the blood. An earlier diagnosis provided by a saliva or fecal test can save your dog immense suffering. It can also save you time, stress and a significant financial investment trying to figure out what's wrong. Saliva and fecal tests are also far more clinically predictive than blood antibody tests. This means that blood testing can provide incorrect information, which again will result in wasted time and money and prolong your dog's suffering.

NutriScan predicts developing food sensitivity long before this is possible via a blood test. Saliva testing also typically identifies food intolerances earlier than a bowel biopsy diagnoses inflammatory bowel disease (IBD) or leaky gut syndrome. This early diagnosis can prolong your dog's life by avoiding a state of full-blown chronic systemic inflammation (Hemopet, 2021). Saliva collection is simple, pain-free and more cost-effective than a blood draw. It also avoids the stress (for you and your dog) of a veterinary visit. (See Resources.)

Addressing food intolerances

As we already mentioned, many people caring for a food-intolerant dog reach for increasingly novel, or exotic, animal proteins in a desperate attempt to resolve the problem. However, this does not work because:

- Once the new protein is no longer novel, it's just as likely to cause an intolerance.
- We are unnecessarily decimating populations of wild animals, such as kangaroos, lions, alligators and other reptiles to feed our dogs unnatural foods.

A plant-based diet is the perfect solution for food-intolerant dogs, as well as for all animals and the environment. Here are some general guidelines that we recommend following.

Plant foods to avoid and foods to opt for
Avoid:
- Corn and soy (best avoided unless a NutriScan test was performed)
- Genetically modified ingredients (GMOs)
- Grains that contain gluten
- High-glycemic carbohydrates (e.g., refined and processed grains)
- Medications, supplements, treats and topicals that contain any potentially reactive ingredients

Opt for:
- A variety of legumes
- Whole, complex carbohydrates, especially ancient grains and pseudo grains
- Root vegetables and winter squash
- Non-starchy vegetables
- Fiber-filled whole fruits
- Dog-friendly nuts and seeds

Remember that no matter how many nutritious ingredients you include in your dog's diet, she can only experience vibrant health if you also *remove* problematic ones. This is because her body will continue struggling to fight off a continuous onslaught of food antigens. Eventually, the simmering chronic inflammation will erupt, and when it does your seemingly healthy dog will 'suddenly' suffer from issues. You might discover her scratching and biting her skin, attempting to quell the terrible itchiness. Or maybe her stool will become soft and wrapped in mucus. We urge you not to ignore these signs.

To help control your dog's inflammation, reactive foods should always be avoided, even if follow-up testing indicates they are non-reactive (because they have not been consumed). If a previously reactive food is consumed, an immune memory recall of the prior reactivity can occur.

Millie gets a second chance with plants
At just five years old, Millie had endured more than her share of health problems in her short life. From the time she was just a few months old, this beautiful Dogo Argentino dog suffered from colitis as well as yeasty, itchy skin. Millie was eventually diagnosed with Irritable Bowel Syndrome (IBS) and pancreatitis. Millie's 'mom,' Anne, did everything she could to help Millie, but no matter what foods she gave her, Millie had a terrible reaction.

She would experience gas and bloating, as well as skin flareups and even occasional diarrhea and vomiting. Millie also began losing a concerning amount of weight because she could not properly absorb nutrients.

Thankfully, Anne did not give up on Millie. A NutriScan test performed in October 2020 showed that Millie was intolerant to almost every tested ingredient. And the couple of foods to which she was not intolerant still created acute gastrointestinal flareups, so those were also out of the question. Anne was very concerned, to say the least, as she watched her beloved Millie suffer and continue to lose weight. Millie's vet prescribed a proton pump inhibitor, which is a medication that reduces stomach acid. Unfortunately, this did not solve the problem, as stomach acid is necessary to digest food and absorb nutrients.

Fortunately, Anne reached out to Diana, who had a few other options up her sleeve. Do you remember the client we mentioned earlier who was intolerant to just about everything except soy? That was Millie! And since organic soy is an excellent protein source for dogs, Diana built a recipe around it that Millie could tolerate and that would provide the nutrition and Calories she needed. She packed the recipe with organic tofu and non-GMO TVP for protein, along with energy-dense tapioca pearls and nutrient-dense veggies and berries that Millie loved *and* that agreed with her.

Many months later, Millie is thriving, and Anne is relieved beyond belief. She said, "Millie is doing amazing. She is literally flourishing on your recipe! You are a lifesaver. We never could have done this without you!"

Now that Millie is consuming only non-antigenic foods, her gut will continue to heal, and her systemic inflammation will subside. And this beautiful girl can look forward to living the long, healthy life she deserves.

Chapter 11
Plant-Based Diet Solutions For Chronic Kidney Disease

Perhaps your dog has had a few uncharacteristic 'accidents' in the house recently. Maybe you've spotted some suspicious yellow puddles on the floor, or even witnessed him urinating. If you live with a senior dog, it's easy to dismiss incontinence as a normal side-effect of aging. If your dog is younger, you might view these episodes as a behavioral issue and be tempted to scold him. But before you decide it's time for a diaper or trainer, please read on because your dog could have **chronic kidney disease (CKD)**, which is a progressive loss of kidney function that occurs over months or years.

Damaged kidneys cannot adequately filter fluids and waste from the body, leading to a host of serious health complications. Increased urination and water consumption are often the first outward signs that your dog's kidneys are failing. But by the time you're aware anything's wrong, he will have already lost about two-thirds of his kidney function (Ward & Weir, n.d.). And, unlike the liver, the kidneys do not regenerate; once the damage is done, it can't be repaired.

CKD is typically considered a disease of aging. And while one out of 10 older dogs will suffer from kidney decline (Brown, 2013), we're also noticing more younger dogs afflicted with this condition. Could environmental and nutritional toxins play a role? Dogs who ingest a toxin such as antifreeze can experience life-threating acute (sudden-onset) kidney failure, but what about the everyday toxins we've discussed throughout the book, such as POPs (Persistent Organic Pollutants), antibiotics and heavy metals? These ingredients can disrupt the gut microbiome, increase inflammation, trigger dangerous DNA mutations and promote cancer. And guess what part of the body plays a crucial role in eliminating them? The kidneys.

Waste removal begins in the liver. Everything we consume passes through the digestive tract to the liver via the hepatic portal vein. The liver acts as a security guard whose job is to keep the 'bad guys' from entering the circulatory system, while letting the 'good guys' pass through. Good guys such as dietary nutrients are sent directly to the circulatory system for immediate use or are stored in the liver for future needs. The liver does what it can to detoxify bad guys such as drugs, chemicals, bacteria, viruses and fungi. It also converts ammonia, a toxic byproduct of protein metabolism, into less toxic urea. When the liver finishes breaking down these toxic products, it filters their byproducts to either the bile or the blood. Waste sent to bile passes through the intestines and is eliminated from the body in feces. Waste passed into blood is sent to the kidneys, which excrete them via urine (Johns Hopkins Medicine, 2021).

The kidneys perform many other functions that keep us and our dogs alive and well, including:

- Releasing essential hormones:
  - Erythropoietin (EPO), which is vital to the production of red blood cells
  - Renin, which regulates blood pressure
  - Calcitriol, the bioactive form of vitamin D
- Helping regulate the blood's pH (acid-base) balance by maintaining proper electrolyte levels (especially sodium and potassium). (Acidosis and alkalosis are serious disorders that require immediate medical attention.)
- Maintaining proper water balance in the body

  (Kidney Research UK, 2006; Lewis, 2020; National Kidney Foundation, 2021)

A person or animal can live with just one kidney, but that kidney must function well enough to fulfill its jobs (American Kidney Fund, 2021). When both kidneys fail, the only options are dialysis or a kidney transplant (see "Dialysis for Dogs?" below). To help avoid a catastrophe, early diagnosis of CKD is essential. Unfortunately, it can also be difficult. This is because dogs often show no clinical signs of illness until late-stage organ deterioration has occurred, when the prognosis is poor.

For this reason, we recommend routine wellness exams and laboratory workups to catch CKD as early as possible. Your veterinarian will recommend tests, which may include:

- Complete Blood Count (CBC) and white blood cell differential to check for red blood cell, white blood cell and platelet counts
- Blood chemistry profile to check for elevated levels of creatinine and BUN (Blood Urea Nitrogen) as well as electrolytes and other important markers of organ health
- SDMA blood test from IDEXX labs (should not be relied upon solely, as it can show false positive results)
- Urinalysis to check for bacteria and protein in the urine, as well as protein:creatinine ratio and urine concentration
- Ultrasound of the kidneys

  (Foster, 2021)

Regular kidney function testing—especially in senior dogs—is an essential part of a comprehensive wellness exam. When kidney damage is caught early and treated appropriately, dogs can live happy, healthy lives for many years (Ward & Weir, n.d.).

But what is 'appropriate treatment'? You'll of course want to discuss prescriptive options with your veterinarian, such as phosphate binders to prevent hyperphosphatemia, blood pressure medications to reduce the effects of hypertension and calcitriol to increase calcium uptake. Your veterinarian will also likely recommend that you feed your dog a commercial prescription kidney diet based on 'highly bioavailable' animal proteins; she might even warn you against plant-based diets.

Here are some common veterinary objections to plant-based diets for dogs with CKD:

- Grains and legumes are too high in phosphorus.
- Your dog needs 'highly digestible' protein (i.e., meat).
- Dogs can't get all the nutrients they need on plant-based diets (that objection conveniently covers *every* situation).

Interestingly, many medical doctors raise these same objections to their human patients with CKD. But the latest research shows that these concerns simply aren't valid. In fact, quite the opposite is true. Studies of more than 26,000 people with CKD show that those who consume a higher proportion of their total protein intake as plant protein have a lower risk of death from all causes than their meat-eating counterparts (Chen et al., 2016; Haring et al., 2017; Moorthi & Moe, 2017; Byrne & Calvo, 2019).

Researchers offer several reasons for the better health outcomes experienced by the plant-eating CKD patients, including:

- The amino acid profile of vegetable proteins is protective against high blood pressure (Elliott et al., 2006; Chen et al., 2016).
- Plant proteins create a net alkalizing effect on the blood, which is kidney protective, while animal ingredients increase acid production that is harmful to the kidneys (Chen et al., 2016).
- Fiber from plants reduces harmful uremic toxins, such as indoxyl sulfate and p-cresyl sulfate that are associated with multiple health complications and increased mortality in patients with CKD (Chen et al., 2016).
- Phytate, the form of phosphorus found in plant proteins, is far less absorbable than animal-based organic phosphate (Chen et al., 2016).

Can dogs benefit from research conducted on human kidney patients? Absolutely. Canine and human kidneys function the same. Dogs with CKD experience the same clinical symptoms, biochemical markers and potential complications as their human counterparts. They are prescribed the same medications and follow the same dietary guidelines. The disease follows a parallel progression.

There is an important difference, however. Dogs suffering from CKD do not yet have ready access to the same advanced treatment options, such as dialysis and kidney transplants, offered to people with renal damage. This means that diet and lifestyle changes, along with necessary prescriptive therapies, offer the best chance at slowing the disease's progression and helping your canine companion enjoy a longer, healthier life.

Dialysis for dogs?

You might know someone with late-stage kidney disease who is on dialysis, which is a manual method of cleaning the blood when the kidneys can no longer perform the job. The patient must visit a dialysis center two to three times per week, where they are connected to a special dialysis machine. The person's blood flows into the machine, which filters out toxins and waste and returns it back to the body (Fresenius Kidney Care, 2020). Unless they receive a kidney transplant, patients must remain on dialysis for life.

While dialysis is common for people, it's still out of reach for most dogs. According to the American Society of Veterinary Nephrology and Urology (ASVNU) website, there are less than 20 canine dialysis centers in the United States, and most are located at university teaching hospitals (ASVNU, n.d.).

You might wonder why dialysis for dogs (and cats) isn't more common. After all, can't the same machines be used? The answer is "no." Since most dogs (and all cats) are much smaller than people, they can't handle even temporarily losing the amount of blood that flows through a human-sized dialysis machine. Because of this, smaller special machines were designed for canine and feline use. As you can imagine, the cost of these machines is prohibitive for a typical veterinary practice (Brooks, 2018).

The high cost of canine dialysis is passed along to clients, adding up to thousands of dollars. In 2016, the estimated cost of dialysis at UC Davis-San Diego dialysis center, not including hospitalization at the Veterinary Specialty Hospital, was $3,500 to $4,000 for the first two to three treatments and $600 to $700 per treatment thereafter (Brooks, 2018).

Hopefully, as pet insurance becomes more widespread and affordable, dialysis for dogs (and cats) will become more common. But for now, at least, lack of availability and a hefty price tag keep it out of reach for most four-legged companions suffering from CKD.

Let's explore key kidney-specific benefits of plant foods to help you stave off the progression of CKD in your canine companion.

Plant foods contain fewer toxins

As we discussed, the kidneys play a vital role in eliminating toxic waste products from the body. This means that the more toxins your dog ingests, the harder his kidneys will have to work. More work means more stress. And, as you likely know from your own life, overwork and stress are not a recipe for optimum health. Fortunately, you can reduce the burden on your dog's kidneys by cutting down on his exposure to chemicals, pesticides, heavy metals, medications, anesthetic agents, POPs and the myriad of other harmful substances that are rampant in the environment and food chain. By now, you probably already know that these poisons bioaccumulate at the highest concentrations in *animal products*.

To keep your dog's toxic load to a minimum, we advise:

- Feeding ingredients low on the food chain (plants)
- Opting for organic products whenever possible
- Steering clear of genetically modified ingredients (GMOs)

Many prescription and non-prescription drugs—including corticosteroids, phenobarbital, carprofen (Rimadyl), flea and tick medications and NSAIDs—can also stress the kidneys. Be sure to discuss this issue with your veterinarian before beginning use. The same goes for vaccinations (Dodds, 2018). If your dog has already completed his puppy vaccines, we recommend opting for serum titer tests instead of automatically revaccinating each year. (Note that the rabies vaccination must be given to healthy dogs as legally required in your community.)

Reducing your dog's exposure to toxins in and around your home is also important. Fortunately, many effective non-toxic household and yard products exist that can do the job without harming your dog or other living beings.

Plant foods reduce the body's acid load

Healthy kidneys maintain tight control over the blood's acid/base balance, which is measured by the pH level. On the pH scale, zero reflects a completely alkaline (basic) state, 14 indicates total acidity and a pH of seven is neutral. The ideal blood pH for dogs falls between 7.31 to 7.42 (Fielder, 2015), which is similar to the desired range of 7.35 to 7.45 for people (Lewis, 2020).

In Chapter 8, we talked about how a long-term state of ketosis might help promote cancer by throwing the body into a chronic, sub-clinical state of acidosis. As we mentioned, sub-clinical acidosis occurs when the body's blood pH dips to the lower end of the normal spectrum (closer to 7.31 for dogs and 7.35 for people). Many researchers believe that sub-clinical acidosis places stress on the body that over time can trigger chronic diseases, such as cancer.

Sub-clinical acidosis may also be present in the early stages of CKD. If not controlled, sub-clinical acidosis can worsen CKD and lead to full-blown **metabolic acidosis**; this is a life-threatening condition that occurs when the blood becomes too acidic, and the pH level drops below the normal range. Metabolic acidosis can lead to a variety of serious health consequences, including bone and muscle loss, high blood sugar and even death.

The kidneys and lungs are the primary organs responsible for maintaining the body's acid-base balance. We'll focus on the kidneys here because respiratory acidosis is a different condition that occurs when the lungs can't efficiently remove carbon dioxide from the body, causing acid to build up in the blood. While respiratory acidosis is also a very serious condition, it involves the lungs rather than the kidneys.

The kidneys control the blood's pH level by excreting acidic compounds via the urine and reabsorbing bicarbonate (a base) into the blood. But when the kidneys stop working properly, they can't efficiently filter out acids or reabsorb bicarbonate. Things might be okay for a while as the kidneys struggle to compensate, but if the damage progresses, eventually the body will enter a state of metabolic acidosis.

This dangerous condition is more common in dogs than you might realize. According to one study, six out of every 38 dogs with CKD have metabolic acidosis severe enough to require treatment (Jacob et al., 2002).

Acidosis and CKD have a very toxic (literally) relationship. CKD leads to acidosis and acidosis worsens CKD. This happens because an acidic state further decreases kidney function and poor kidney function causes more acid to build up (National Kidney Foundation, 2019). Unless this vicious cycle is stopped, it will lead to irreparable kidney damage and eventual death.

If your dog is at risk of metabolic acidosis, you should of course discuss prescription treatment options, such as sodium bicarbonate therapy, with your veterinarian. But you don't have to stop there. Feeding a plant-based diet can reduce stress on your dog's kidneys by helping maintain an optimum state of blood alkalization.

According to the National Kidney Foundation:

> *A diet that includes more plant-based proteins than animal-based proteins, along with a high intake of fruits and vegetables, can also help keep acid levels from rising in the blood* (National Kidney Foundation, 2019).

Let's unravel how plant foods help prevent acidosis in CKD patients.

Every ingredient your dog consumes must be metabolized, or broken down, by the body. This process creates chemical by-products that are either acid, base (alkaline) or neutral. Acids generated during digestion must be excreted by the kidneys. This means that the more acid-producing the diet, the harder the kidneys must work to maintain the body's acid-base balance (Scialla & Anderson, 2013; Passey, 2017; Cordain, 2018).

It makes sense that when the kidneys are struggling with CKD, we want to do everything we can to reduce their workload. The best way to accomplish this is by eating low-acid foods. The less acid generated by the diet, the less stress that's put on the kidneys.

But what is an 'acidic' food?

If your mind is conjuring up images of sour-tasting foods such as lemons, cranberries and vinegar, we understand. These foods do indeed contain acids, such as citric acid, malic acid, L-ascorbic acid and acetic acid. But while they may make your mouth pucker when you eat them, they do not produce acid in the body. In fact, all of these foods are *alkalizing*. There is no correlation between how acidic a food tastes and how much of an acidic load it produces in the body.

A scoring system called the Potential Renal Acid Load (PRAL) is used to determine the true acidic effect of a food or diet. The higher the PRAL score, the more acid the food or diet produces in the blood. Foods with a negative PRAL score have an alkaline (basic) effect on the body (Hernandez, 2021).

But how do we determine a food's PRAL? Fortunately, scientists have already done this for us, using a mathematical formula based on five key nutrients that produce either a net acid or net alkaline effect in the body when digested. These are:

- Protein (acid)
- Phosphorus (acid)
- Potassium (base/alkaline)
- Magnesium (base/alkaline)
- Calcium (base/alkaline)

(Cordain, 2018; Betz, 2021)

We can calculate the PRAL value of any food using the following equation:

PRAL (mEq/day) =

0.49 x protein (g/day)

+ 0.037 x phosphorus (mg/d)

- 0.021 x potassium (mg/day)

- 0.026 magnesium (mg/day)

- 0.013 x calcium (mg/day)

(Hernandez, 2021; Nutritiontable.com, 2021)

Based on this equation, food groups are broadly categorized based on their net acid load (PRAL score) as follows:

Acid-producing foods
- Cheese
- Eggs
- Grains
- Meat

Alkalizing foods
- Vegetables
- Fruits

Neutral-acid foods
- Legumes
- Nuts

(Scialla & Anderson, 2013)

(See the Resources for information on where you can find the PRAL value of just about every common food or enter your own custom nutrient levels to instantly calculate the PRAL value of an ingredient.)

Except for certain grains, foods that produce the most acid in the body as a by-product of metabolism are *animal ingredients*.

This might sound shocking, because you've likely heard that dogs with CKD must eat 'high biological value' proteins such as meat, fish and poultry. But the net acid load created by these animal proteins can further damage the kidneys and increase the risk of metabolic acidosis.

Research shows that reducing the net dietary acid load using alkaline-forming plant proteins, fruits and vegetables can be as effective as sodium bicarbonate therapy in decreasing kidney damage (Goraya et al., 2012; Goraya et al., 2013; Goroya et al., 2014) and improving metabolic parameters, including serum bicarbonate levels (Scialla et al., 2012).

While some forms of CKD (such as proteinuria) warrant moderate protein restriction, slashing your dog's protein level isn't a desired option. This is because feeding too little protein can result in malnutrition, muscle wasting and other negative health issues such as a decreased ability to fight infection and maintain a healthy microbiome and balanced immune system. These concerns are especially relevant in older dogs with CKD, who are already more at risk of these conditions than their younger counterparts.

Fortunately, you don't have to sacrifice protein on an alkalizing, kidney-sparing diet. Simply fill your dog's bowl with lower-PRAL plant-based proteins. And don't forget to include lots of alkalizing dog-friendly fruits and veggies.

Plant foods provide a better form of phosphorus for CKD

People and dogs need phosphorus to stay alive and healthy. Next to calcium, phosphorus is the second most abundant mineral in the body. Most phosphorus is found in the teeth and bones, but it's also needed by every cell and plays a role in just about every metabolic process, including making protein to repair cells and tissues, serving as a component of DNA and RNA, regulating heartbeat, promoting healthy muscle contractions and nerve signaling, filtering waste in the kidneys and working with vitamins B and D. Phosphorus even helps maintain the body's acid-base balance by serving as an important buffering agent (Madell & Kubala, 2020; MedlinePlus, n.d.).

But when it comes to CKD and phosphorus, your dog can get too much of a good thing. The kidneys play a crucial role in regulating phosphorus levels in the body by excreting excess dietary phosphate. But damaged kidneys can't effectively eliminate phosphate, so instead of being urinated out, it accumulates in the blood. This dangerous condition is called **hyperphosphatemia**.

The kidneys also control the balance of phosphate and calcium by turning vitamin D into the hormone calcitriol, which regulates how much phosphate and calcium are absorbed from food. Damaged kidneys are unable to activate vitamin D, which 'tricks' the parathyroid gland into thinking there isn't enough calcium in the blood. To compensate, the parathyroid gland produces extra parathyroid hormone (PTH), which draws calcium from the bones into the bloodstream, causing the bones to weaken (Dorough & Solman, 2021; National Kidney Foundation, 2021b). High blood levels of phosphorus and calcium can lead to calcification of the heart, lungs, joints and blood vessels. This in turn creates serious health complications, including bone diseases, reduced blood flow, difficulty breathing, secondary hyperparathyroidism, heart diseases and increased risk of death (Shaman & Kowalski, 2016; Dorough & Solman, 2021; National Kidney Foundation, 2021b).

Hyperphosphatemia further damages the kidneys and reduces kidney function, which can speed the progression to end-stage renal disease (Cases et al., 2019). In fact, hyperphosphatemia is such a "strong predictor of mortality in advanced CKD" (Kalantar-Zadeh, 2013) that it's referred to as a 'silent killer' (Bacchetta et al., 2021).

Controlling your dog's dietary phosphorus intake might be the most important thing you can do to slow his progression of CKD and reduce the risk of serious health complications. Given this, your veterinary professional will likely recommend that you switch your dog to a commercial low-phosphorus kidney diet (based on animal proteins, of course).

But here's something you might not have been told…

Not all dietary phosphorus is created equal.

There are three forms of phosphorus found in food, and each has a different level of bioavailability, meaning how much is absorbed in the intestines (González-Parra et al., 2012; Kalantar-Zadeh, 2013; Greger & Stone, 2015; Cases et al., 2019). The three types are:

- Inorganic phosphorus, a synthetic form of phosphorus added to many processed foods, is 100% bioavailable (see Beware of Hidden Phosphorus below).

- Phosphate, organic phosphorus found in animal-based proteins, is up to 80% percent absorbable by the intestines.

- Phytate, organic phosphorus derived from plants, is the least bioavailable at 30% to 40%.

  (González-Parra et al., 2012; Kalantar-Zadeh, 2013; Greger & Stone, 2015; Cases et al., 2019)

Phytate is the least absorbable form of phosphorus because mammals lack the enzyme phytase to break it down (see Chapter 5.) Phosphate from animal ingredients, on the other hand, is quickly absorbed via the intestines (Greger & Stone, 2015; Cases et al., 2019). In this instance, high bioavailability is definitely not better. If your dog has CKD, the more phosphorus that's sent into the bloodstream, the greater the risk of hyperphosphatemia—and even death.

The good news is that you can help your dog achieve desired phosphorus balance—without sacrificing protein—by switching him from a meat-based to a plant-based diet. In fact, after just one week on a plant-based diet, people with IRIS stage 3 to 4 CKD showed a significant decrease in blood phosphorus levels and FGF-23 levels (a marker of decreased kidney function), as well as a decrease in 24-hour urinary phosphorus excretion compared to those on a nutritionally comparable meat-based diet.

The authors stated that:

> *We show that equivalent total protein and phosphorus from grain-based vegetarian sources has a significant effect on serum phosphorus and on the homeostatic response to dietary phosphate intake* (Moe et al., 2011, pp. 257).

Thanks to phytate, dogs with CKD can benefit from more protein and lower blood phosphorus levels. As you see, we have yet another benefit provided by this so-called anti-nutrient.

Beware of 'hidden' phosphorus

Typically, phosphorus is associated with protein intake, which is one reason why many clinicians recommend low-protein diets for patients with CKD. But a more dangerous type of phosphorus may be hiding in your dog's diet—and it has nothing to do with protein. We're talking about synthetic inorganic phosphorus additives used in processed foods. This type of phosphorus is *100% absorbable* and can spell disaster for individuals suffering from CKD.

Synthetic phosphorus additives serve a variety of functions in processed foods, including acting as emulsifiers, stabilizers and thickeners, controlling pH, enhancing flavor and providing added supplementation (Kalantar-Zadeh, 2013).

Inorganic phosphorus hides under the following names:

- Dicalcium phosphate
- Disodium phosphate
- Monosodium phosphate
- Phosphoric acid
- Sodium hexametaphosphate
- Sodium tripolyphosphate
- Tetrasodium pyrophosphate
- Trisodium phosphate
- (Kalantar-Zadeh, 2013)

If your dog has CKD, be sure to read food labels carefully and steer clear of this dangerous form of phosphate.

There is one industry that isn't required to list added phosphate on nutrition labels: the meat industry. If you purchase fresh meat for your dog, you could be feeding him a product called 'enhanced' meat. Enhanced meats are injected with a solution containing water and additional ingredients, such as phosphate salts, sodium salts and flavorings, among others (Murphy-Guekunst & Uribarri, 2005).

The meat industry enhances meat for many reasons, including to retain the product's moisture, prevent oxidation caused by metals in the meat (yes, you read that right), increase shelf life, improve color and make the meat more attractive (Murphy-Guekunst & Uribarri, 2005).

You can't identify an enhanced meat product by looking at it, but the nutritional difference can be astounding. For example, while unenhanced meat might contain 50 to 75 mg sodium per three-ounce serving, that number shoots up to over 300 mg for the same serving size of enhanced meat (Murphy-Guekunst & Uribarri, 2005).

According to an article in *The Journal of Renal Nutrition:*

> Currently, there is no practical way to know how much additional phosphate enhanced meats have. The nutrition label no longer requires the inclusion of phosphorus, and specifics about how much phosphate salt is used is considered proprietary information by the food manufacturers (Murphy-Guekunst & Uribarri, 2005, pp. e2).

If your dog suffers from CKD, the only sure way to avoid the dangers of added phosphate in enhanced meat is to bypass the meat aisle.

Plant-based superfoods strengthen the kidneys

Imagine you're on the game show Jeopardy. You've waited years for this chance, and now you're here. You're standing at the center podium, and the man and woman to your right and left are tough competition. You've managed to hold your own, though, and now the three of you are virtually tied heading into Final Jeopardy. You sure hope you know the answer to this one! Then, the host reads the card. "What are the healthiest foods for the kidneys?" You freeze. Where on Earth did the writers come up with that one? The clock ticks in time with your heartbeat, reverberating like bongo drums in your ears. Everything is riding on this....

Okay, chances are you'll never be on Jeopardy and, if you are, this question will likely not come up! But that's okay because your dog's health is your own personal grand prize. So, let's get back to that question.... "What are the healthiest foods for the kidneys?"

Before reading this book, you may have jumped to the typical response: animal ingredients. But now you know better. So, what do professionals who specialize in kidney health recommend? Not surprisingly, they opt for phytochemical-rich plant foods. These beneficial plant chemicals defend cells against oxidative damage caused by free radicals, decrease systemic inflammation and boost the immune system. Sounds like good stuff for the kidneys, don't you think? The National Kidney Foundation thinks so. They recommend these seven nutrient-rich superfoods as part of a kidney-friendly diet:

- Apples
- Blueberries
- Omega-3 fatty acids (While they list high-omega fish, we know that microalgae are the original source of marine-based EPA and DHA.)
- Kale*
- Strawberries (be sure your dog is not allergic, and avoid the top white /green core part)
- Spinach*
- Sweet potatoes*

   *These foods are a rich source of potassium, so limit if your dog requires a low-potassium diet.

(National Kidney Foundation, 2021a)

Plant fiber reduces uremic toxins

According to the Oxford Languages dictionaries, putrefaction is "the process of decay or rotting in a body or other organic matter" (Oxford Languages, 2021). Obviously, this is something we want to avoid for ourselves and our dogs. So, what does putrefaction have to do with the kidneys? It turns out, a lot.

You'll recall that carbohydrates, proteins and fats that remain undigested in the small intestine pass to the colon (large intestine), where they serve as food for the colonic microbiota. Many different species of bacterial microbiota reside in the colon. Some species produce enzymes that can break down multiple types of undigested matter, while other species specialize in digesting just one type. For example, saccharolytic species of bacteria produce enzymes that only ferment carbohydrates. As we've previously discussed, when colonic bacteria ferment undigested matter, they produce metabolic byproducts called postbiotics. Postbiotics are bioactive compounds, meaning that they affect the health of the microbes and the host. You might recall from Chapter 4 that when colonic bacteria ferment fiber, they produce beneficial postbiotics, such as short chain fatty acids (SCFAs). But not all postbiotics are good. In fact, some are harmful (Kaur et al., 2017; Schafer-Evans, 2019).

This leads us back to putrefaction. **Putrefaction** is the fermentation of undigested protein in the colon by **proteolytic bacteria**, a species that specializes in breaking down protein into amino acids. But unlike beneficial postbiotics created when saccharolytic bacteria break down carbohydrates, putrefaction by proteolytic species creates toxic waste by-products that can disrupt the microbiome and damage the health of the host (Kaur et al., 2017).

One of the jobs of healthy kidneys is to filter out these toxic waste products, called uremic toxins, from the body via the urine. But when kidney function declines, uremic toxins build up in the blood, creating a serious condition called uremia, or uremic syndrome. In addition to further damaging the kidneys, these poisonous substances wreak havoc on other organs and disrupt a variety of biochemical and physiological functions. Uremic toxins can lead to serious complications, including cardiovascular disease, mineral bone disorders and increased risk of death (Webb, 2021).

If your dog has kidney disease, you may have heard of blood urea nitrogen (BUN), creatinine and symmetric dimethylarginine (SDMA); these are uremic toxins commonly used to diagnose and track the progression of CKD. Phosphate, as we just discussed, is also a uremic toxin (Burke, 2008). Other uremic toxins include 3-methyl catechol sulfate, 4-ethylphenyl sulfate, 3- methoxycatechol sulfate, 4- vinylphenol sulfate, indoxyl sulfate and p-Cresol sulfate (Ephraim et al., 2020).

Indoxyl sulfate, which is created when proteolytic bacteria metabolize the amino acid tryptophan, has recently gained attention among researchers. Indoxyl sulfate is shown to cause free radical production, atherosclerosis (buildup of plaque in the arteries) and toxicity of the kidneys, heart and osteoblasts (bone cells). It is also an important biomarker of renal impairment in people, dogs and cats; as renal function declines, plasma levels of indoxyl sulfate rise (Cheng et al., 2015; Chen et al., 2018).

Recent research in dogs and cats shows that indoxyl sulfate is more than a biomarker of current kidney function; it can also predict future kidney decline more accurately than creatinine. A three-month study of 36 dogs and 58 cats with CKD showed that dogs with IRIS Stages 2 and 3 progressive CKD had higher concentrations of indoxyl sulfate than dogs with non-progressive CKD of the same stages. Similar results were found in the feline group. Since indoxyl sulfate levels differed between animals with progressive and non-progressive CKD, the authors determined that:

> *In agreement with a previous study in humans (Wu et al., 2011), our study demonstrated that indoxyl sulfate not only serves as a renal function biomarker but is also an independent predictor for CKD progression in both dogs and cats with stages 2 and 3 CKD. Moreover, our results also suggested that similar to another previous study (Chakrabarti et al., 2012), the loss of renal function as determined by serum creatinine concentrations alone, cannot predict renal progression in dogs or cats with CKD* (Chen et al., 2018, pp. 36).

Indoxyl sulfate and p-Cresol sulfate are particularly challenging uremic toxins because they bind to the protein albumin in the blood. This means that the best way to deal with these poisonous waste products may be to target them right at the source—the colon microbiome (Lekawanvijit et al., 2016; Persaud, 2021; Yang et al., 2021).

One of the main reasons that protein restriction is recommended for individuals with CKD is to reduce putrefaction and the production of toxic waste products. But, as we just discussed, restricting protein can also result in health problems. So, then, why not reduce putrefaction by feeding your dog more 'highly-digestible' proteins from animal ingredients? That certainly is the prevailing opinion among the pet food industry and veterinary professionals. But as we've revealed throughout this chapter, animal products worsen kidney damage for several reasons, including that they:

- Contain phosphate, a far more absorbable form of organic phosphorus than plant-based phytate
- Increase the net acid load in the body, which worsens kidney decline
- Lack phytochemicals that fight cellular oxidation and reduce inflammation
- Store bioaccumulated toxins that stress the kidneys

Fortunately, there's a simple way to reduce uremic toxins in dogs and people without reducing protein: increase dietary fiber. The microbiome affects every part of the body, including the kidneys. Fiber-rich foods improve the diversity of the gut microbiome. Fiber increases beneficial saccharolytic postbiotics, while at the same time decreasing harmful putrefaction by proteolytic bacteria. SCFAs produced during carbohydrate fermentation also decrease colon pH. A lower colon pH in turn reduces the activity of proteolytic bacteria, which favor a more neutral or alkaline gut environment (Jackson & Jewell, 2019; Schafer-Evans, 2019). (Note that a lower pH in the colon is beneficial, unlike dangerous acidosis of the blood that we discussed earlier.)

When healthy senior dogs (age seven and above) consumed a test food with added soluble fiber from fruit and vegetables (citrus, carrot, tomato and spinach), they experienced significant decreases in several uremic toxins compared to dogs eating a low-fiber control diet. One uremic toxin, 3-methyl catechol sulfate, declined by a whopping 175% while another, 4-ethylphenyl sulfate, decreased by 73%. Circulating

SDMA also declined in dogs consuming the test food. This is significant because elevated SDMA detects reduced glomerular filtration rate (GFR), a key sign of kidney decline, much sooner than creatine. A drop in SDMA levels means the dogs eating the high-fiber diet may have experienced an increase in GFR and improvement in kidney function (Ephraim et al., 2020).

In another study, dogs with IRIS Stage 1 CKD were given either test foods supplemented with betaine and fiber from oat beta-glucans and scFOS (short-chain fructooligosaccharides) or an unfortified control food. The dogs consuming the betaine and fiber-fortified food experienced a decrease in several uremic toxins compared to the dogs who received the unfortified control food (Ephraim & Jewell, 2020).

Research in people echoes these results. A meta-analysis of 10 randomized controlled trials involving 292 CKD patients showed that taking a daily fiber supplement significantly reduced levels of the uremic toxins indoxyl sulfate, p-cresyl sulfate, uric acid and BUN. Even patients who consumed lower doses (less than 20 g/day) achieved the same health benefits as those who took more. The types of fiber supplements studied also varied and included brans, lignin, cellulose, arabinoxylan, inulin, beta-glucans, guar gum, gum acacia, pectin, psyllium, fructooligosaccharides (FOS) and resistant starch (Alvi, 2021; Persaud, 2021; Yang et al., 2021). These results indicate that various types of fiber provide kidney health benefits.

In addition to decreasing uremic toxins, studies show that increasing daily fiber intake reduces pro-inflammatory markers, cholesterol and risk of CKD-related heart disease (Meijers et al., 2009; Salmean et al., 2015; Lu et al., 2017; Yang et al., 2021). Even children with CKD have good reason to eat more fiber; it seems the more fiber in kids' diets, the lower their concentration of protein-bound uremic toxins, including indoxyl sulfate (El Amouri et al., 2021).

Ryder goes plant-based for kidney health

In April 2021, Ryder's lab work showed some surprising results. The Labrador/American pit bull mix had increased creatinine and BUN levels, along with a high result on his IDEXX SDMA test. At just four years old, Ryder suffered from Stage 2 CKD. Prior to his diagnosis, Ryder had been eating a high-quality human-grade diet commercially prepared by a fresh-food dog food company.

Ryder's 'mom,' Kenzie, acted quickly when she heard the diagnosis. Kenzie knew the importance of diet to stave off the progression of CKD, so in May 2021 she contacted Diana for a custom-formulated CKD recipe. Diana created a plant-based recipe with the appropriate nutritional levels to address Ryder's individual situation. She packed the recipe with whole plant foods to support healthy kidney function, along with increased levels of algae-based omega-3 fatty acids for additional anti-inflammatory effects.

Ryder has now been on his plant-based CKD recipe for several months, and Kenzie reports that his condition remains stable, with no progression or further decline in kidney function. She says that Ryder has maintained a very healthy weight and has more energy than before. In addition, Ryder's partially torn ACL has healed while he remains active. And this picky dog loves his food!

"We're thrilled with Ryder's results on his custom plant based CKD diet," Kenzie says. "Ryder is a young boy, and we're confident that we're doing everything possible to support his kidney health so that he can live a long and happy life."

Omega-3 fatty acids and CKD

Supplementation with omega-3 fatty acids, especially marine-based EPA and DHA, are routinely recommended for dogs and people with CKD; however, the research on their benefits remains controversial. Two meta-analyses of studies conducted on human CKD patients and published just over a year apart show dramatically different results. One review of 12 randomized control trials involving a total of 487 patients with CKD found "insufficient evidence to conclude the benefit of omega-3 fatty acids oral supplementation…." (Hu et al., 2017). A second review of nine randomized control trials involving a total of 444 patients with CKD concluded that "omega-3 supplementation is associated with a significantly reduced risk of end-stage renal disease and delays the progression of this disease" (Hu et al., 2018). (Note that while both lead authors share the same name, they are different people.)

Studies in dogs indicate that while supplementation of omega-6 fatty acids speeds kidney decline, supplementation with omega-3 fatty acids (EPA + DHA) has a variety of protective effects, including:

- Lowering BUN and triglyceride levels
- Increasing blood flow to the kidneys
- Increasing serum albumin levels
- Maintaining kidney structure
- Reducing glomerular capillary hypertension
- Reducing kidney inflammation
- Slowing progression of CKD

  (Brown et al., 1998; Asif, 2015; Kaur et al., 2020)

Dogs given omega-3 fatty acids in combination with antioxidants also experienced an increase in GFR and decreased proteinuria (Valle et al., 2015). Given these positive outcomes, we recommend supplementation of EPA + DHA for dogs with CKD.

The therapeutic dose of EPA + DHA for dogs with CKD is 140 mg/kgBW$^{0.75}$ per day (Bauer, 2011; Raditic & Gaylord, 2020). Based on this recommendation, the following chart contains the daily dose of omega-3 fatty acids (combined EPA + DHA) for dogs of various body weights. (Note that all doses have been rounded up or down to the nearest whole number.) Always be sure to discuss your dog's individual situation with your veterinarian prior to adding supplementation.

Therapeutic Daily Dose of EPA + DHA for Dogs with CKD Chart

Dog's Weight	Omega-3 (EPA + DHA) Dose per Day (mg)
5 kg (11 lb)	468
10 kg (22 lb)	787
15 kg (33 lb)	1,067
20 kg (44 lb)	1,324
25 kg (55 lb)	1,565
30 kg (66 lb)	1,795
35 kg (77 lb)	2,015
40 kg (88 lb)	2,227
45 kg (99 lb)	2,432
50 kg (110 lb)	2,632
55 kg (121 lb)	2,828
60 kg (132 lb)	3,018
65 kg (143 lb)	3,205
70 kg (154 lb)	3,388
75 kg (165 lb)	3,568
80 kg (176 lb)	3,745

If you feed your dog a commercial therapeutic kidney diet, share this information with your veterinarian before supplementing with additional omega-3 fatty acids. A commercial renal diet may already contain omega-3 fatty acids (EPA + DHA) at levels that meet or exceed your dog's daily requirement and adding extra could push the amount over the NRC's safe upper limit (Raditic & Gaylord, 2020).

If you want to feed a fresh-food plant-based CKD diet to your dog, we highly recommend investing in a professionally formulated recipe. Kidney-sparing diets must meet precise nutritional criteria, which require specialized expertise and experience, along with the appropriate scientific tools to achieve the desired results. Diana has formulated custom-balanced CKD recipes for more than a dozen years and has focused solely on plant-based CKD recipes for many years. (See Resources.)

Chapter 12
Plant-Based Diet Solutions For Gastrointestinal Disorders

Without a doubt, gastrointestinal (GI) disorders are the most common canine chronic conditions we address in our respective veterinary and nutrition practices. From Irritable Bowel Syndrome (IBS), Inflammatory Bowel Disease (IBD) and food intolerances to chronic idiopathic diarrhea and Gastroesophageal Reflux Disease (GERD), an alarming number of companion dogs suffer from some type of chronic intestinal inflammation. This shouldn't come as a surprise, however, considering the astounding number of humans who also suffer from GI disorders.

If your dog suffers from chronic GI disease, you've likely tried just about everything to help her heal, from bland chicken and rice diets to commercial hydrolyzed formulas. But these 'solutions' have their own issues. A hydrolyzed diet might work in the short term because these products consist of proteins that are broken down into such small molecules that they are touted to be no longer recognized by the dog's digestive system. Although these diets are 'complete and balanced,' we don't believe that hydrolyzed ingredients are an ideal long-term feeding solution because they don't provide nutrients from fresh, whole foods that the body needs to thrive. And while eating a bland diet might solve an acute bout of diarrhea, it doesn't address the underlying dysbiosis, or imbalance in gut bacteria, that's seen in cases of chronic GI disorders such as canine idiopathic IBD (Dodds, 2018; Dodds, 2018a).

'Idiopathic IBD,' which indicates that the root cause is unknown, is a common chronic autoimmune GI disorder in dogs (Jergens & Simpson, 2012; Vázquez-Baeza et al., 2016). This is a frustrating diagnosis because it can stem from a wide range of underlying issues, from chronic infection and food sensitivities to lymphoma and other types of cancers. In addition, a true diagnosis of IBD can only be made via a biopsy, and many people understandably don't want to put their dog through an invasive, costly, stressful and potentially risky procedure.

But even though we can't always determine the underlying cause of a dog's IBD, we do know that development of the disease stems from an important interaction between genetics and the gut microbiota. This genetic/microbial link explains the predisposition of certain dog breeds toward **chronic enteropathies** (inflammatory intestinal diseases) such as protein-losing enteropathy (PLE) in soft-coated wheaten terriers, immunoproliferative enteropathy in basenjis, granulomatous colitis in boxers and chronic enteropathy in German shepherd dogs (Jergens & Simpson, 2012).

The intersection of genetics and the gut microbiome illustrates the epigenetic link to disease that we've discussed a great deal throughout this book. Even though your dog might be genetically predisposed to a chronic inflammatory GI disorder, you can help prevent the disorder from manifesting by sending the proper epigenetic signals to her gut microbiome. But how do you do this? Fortunately, we can draw upon research in both dogs and people to discover what works—and what doesn't. This is possible because the pathogenesis (underlying cause) of intestinal inflammation in dogs and people is very similar. In fact, as with cancer, researchers have recommended that results of clinical trials in dogs with IBD be applied to benefit human trials (Jergens & Simpson, 2012). As one study points out:

> *Research on the canine gut microbiota and GI diseases may predict results in humans* (Huang et al., 2020, pp. 648).

This comparative medicine approach makes sense. After all, living in close quarters and sharing the same food resources for thousands (and perhaps tens of thousands) of years has resulted in a parallel genomic and microbial evolution among people and dogs, especially in the areas of digestion and metabolism (Wang et al., 2013; Coelho et al., 2018). Why not use these similarities to help both species?

A comparative medicine approach to GI disorders in dogs (and cats) occurs every day in veterinary practices. Veterinary professionals routinely prescribe medications for their patients with IBD and other chronic enteropathies that medical doctors prescribe for people with similar conditions. As a result, countless modern companion dogs (and cats) now depend upon pharmaceutical interventions such as antibiotics, corticosteroids and immunosuppressive drugs to manage their damaged guts. While these medications are sometimes necessary for extreme cases, we believe that they are doled out more often than necessary, especially considering that long-term use can cause serious side effects. When the authors of an article published in *Frontiers in Bioscience* looked at the data on pharmaceutical therapy in companion animals, they commented that, "It is clear that there are many aspects of IBD drug therapy in companion animals for which the data are lacking or inadequate, similar to human IBD" (Jergens & Simpson, 2012).

One example is metronidazole (Flagyl), a common antibiotic used to treat certain types of bacterial and parasitic infections in people. Although it is not FDA-approved for use in dogs, veterinarians commonly prescribe it 'off-label' to treat infections that can cause diarrhea. The problem is that metronidazole offers only short-term relief in treating chronic inflammatory bowel disorders such as IBD. It's also associated with potentially serious side effects, including:

- Ataxia
- Fever
- Gagging
- Inappetence
- Lethargy
- Nausea and vomiting

- Rapid heartbeat
- Seizures
- Trouble breathing
- Worsening of kidney and liver problems

Metronidazole is also unsafe for pregnant and lactating females, as it can cause birth defects to fetuses and harm to nursing puppies.

And here's the real irony. Metronidazole can destroy the good bacteria in the gut, thereby causing or worsening diarrhea (Sarwar, 2021). A 2020 study published in the *Journal of Veterinary Internal Medicine* found that taking metronidazole for 14 days significantly disrupted the microbiome of healthy dogs, including decreasing beneficial bacteria. These effects lasted for at least four weeks after the medication was stopped (Pilla et al., 2020).

For dogs with IBD who do require long-term pharmaceutical treatment, the antibiotic tylosin (Tylan) is a safer alternative. However, Tylan is also shown to affect the composition and diversity of canine intestinal microbiota (Suchodolski et al., 2009).

Given the seriousness of long-term prescription medication use, it makes sense to seek out safe, natural therapies to manage your dog's chronic GI issues. The ideal remedy would create positive epigenetic changes to the gut microbiome, harbor no negative side-effects and prove safe for long-term use. Not surprisingly, such a remedy can be found in plants. In this chapter, we'll take a deep dive into the many GI benefits of plant foods, with a focus on:

- **Prebiotic foods (detailing psyllium, spirulina and nutritional and brewer's yeasts)**
- **Low-FODMAP diet**
- **Fermented foods**

Prebiotic foods and gastrointestinal health: An overview

As we discussed in Chapter 4, fibers are carbohydrates (plus lignan, a non-carbohydrate dietary fiber) that resist digestion by enzymes in the stomach and small intestine and so pass intact to the colon. Fibers possess varying chemical structures that affect how they behave when consumed. Some fibers are soluble (e.g., psyllium, pectin, beta-glucans), meaning that they dissolve in water, while others (e.g., cellulose, wheat bran, lignan) are insoluble. In addition, some fibers are rapidly fermented (e.g., beta-glucans, inulin, oligosaccharides), while others ferment slowly or are resistant to fermentation (e.g., psyllium, wheat bran, cellulose, lignan) (Linus Pauling Institute, 2021).

Researchers have recently focused on a special type of fiber, called prebiotics or functional fibers, for their potential health benefits. You might recall that prebiotics serve as food for probiotics, the good bacteria in the gut. Prebiotics are especially important for the health of both the gut microbiota and the host because fermentation creates beneficial postbiotics, such as short chain fatty acids (SCFAs) (butyrate, acetate, propionate) (Jackson & Jewell, 2019; Tizard & Jones, 2018). SCFAs are vital to GI health for many reasons, which we'll discuss in a moment.

It's important to recognize that not all dietary fibers are functional fibers. You can't just put any type of fiber in a bottle or capsule and call it a prebiotic or functional supplement. Research-based evidence must exist linking consumption of the product with health benefits (McRorie Jr, 2015). This is where supplement companies can get into trouble with making false or misleading marketing claims. You've probably seen fiber supplements advertised on TV and the Internet that promise all kinds of health benefits. But supplements aren't regulated by the FDA, and they often lack concrete data to back up their promises. According to the Academy of Nutrition and Dietetics:

> *Few fiber supplements have been studied for physiological effectiveness, so the best advice is to consume fiber in foods* (Slavin, 2008, pp. 1716).

We agree with this recommendation to opt for food-based fiber over fiber supplements whenever possible. Why pop a fiber pill (or give one to your dog) when the plant world offers a cornucopia of whole, fresh foods that contain known prebiotic fibers? As we previously mentioned, prebiotic fibers include beta-glucans, fructooligosaccharides (FOS), oligofructose, inulin, mannan oligosaccharides (MOS), pectin, guar gum, xanthan gum, gum arabic and lactulose, among others (Carlson et al., 2018; Suchodolski, 2020).

When we talk about prebiotics, we also want to include resistant starch, which we introduced in Chapter 9 for its glucose-balancing benefits. Remember those cold potatoes? Resistant starch isn't fiber; it's starch that escapes digestion in the upper GI tract and travels to the large intestine. Once there, it conveys the same effect on the microbiome as prebiotic fiber (Zaman & Sarbini, 2015; Edermaniger, 2021). The good bacteria in the colon gobble it up, creating beneficial postbiotics such as SCFAs. Resistant starch is important for all dogs but might especially benefit senior dogs with poor gut health. Senior dogs who consume diets high in resistant starch have higher butyrate and total SCFAs and lower ammonia in their feces than dogs consuming a diet low in resistant starch (Ribeiro et al., 2019).

Prebiotics improve gut microbial function

When it comes to linking the gut microbiome with host health, a lot of research focuses on taxonomy—in other words, naming and classifying the types of bacteria that are present. Which bacteria are 'good,' and which are 'bad'? This is of course important and something that we've talked a lot about throughout this book. But this type of approach also has limitations. For starters, knowledge of the microbiome is still in its infancy. Researchers involved with the Human Microbiome Project note that "Many key properties of the human microbiome remain to be characterized even in healthy cohorts, in addition to microbiome contributions to disease" (Lloyd-Price et al., 2017). In other words, there's still a lot we don't know about those tiny 'bugs' that call our bodies home and how the composition of the microbial environment affects the health and disease of the host. This is true of dogs and people.

There is another important aspect of the gut microbiome that we can focus on to help determine its health: how well it functions (Lloyd-Price et al., 2017; Wernimont et al.,

2020). One important determiner of healthy microbial function is how efficiently the colonic bacteria produce beneficial postbiotics, such as SCFAs. This is vital because SCFAs perform many important jobs, including:

- Balancing electrolyte and fluid levels in the colon
- Encouraging a healthy colonic bacterial environment by promoting growth of good bacteria and inhibiting growth of pathogenic bacteria
- Improving the structure of the colon
- Helping intestinal inflammation
- Providing 70% of the energy for colonocytes (colon epithelial lining cells)
- Regulating intestinal motility

  (Sanderson, 2008)

In addition, SCFAs help control intestinal inflammation in numerous ways, including:

- Increasing the production of anti-inflammatory cytokines, such as IL-10 and TGF-β
- Decreasing proinflammatory cytokines, such as IL-6, IL-8, and TNF-α
- Decreasing intestinal pH, which helps to block the growth of pathogenic microbes such as *Enterobacteriaceae* and *Clostridia*, which favor a more alkaline environment
- Suppressing macrophages (cells that can initiate inflammation by releasing cytokines) (Saldana, n.d.) and promoting production of anti-inflammatory Treg cells

(O'Keefe et al., 2009; Kim et al., 2013; Smith et al., 2013; Tizard & Jones, 2018; Minamoto et al., 2019)

As pointed out in the journal *Veterinary Clinics of North America: Small Animal Practice,* "As a result [of producing SCFAs] high-fiber diets play a key role in regulating intestinal inflammation" (Tizard & Jones, 2018). And guess what? Dogs who suffer from chronic enteropathies have lower fecal concentrations of SCFAs compared to healthy dogs. A 2019 study published in the *Journal of Veterinary Internal Medicine* found that the concentration of propionate, a SCFA known to decrease intestinal inflammation via several pathways, was especially low in these dogs. The decrease in SCFAs was also correlated to unhealthy changes in the fecal microbiome (Minamoto et al., 2019).

Based on their discoveries, the researchers concluded:

> *These findings mandate further clinical studies to determine whether fecal SCFAs can be manipulated by various interventions and whether manipulating SCFAs concentrations and patterns in the GI tract could be beneficial in these patients, leading to the restoration of a proper immune response and remission of clinical signs* (Minamoto et al., pp. 1616).

It makes sense that to promote a healthy gut microbiome, we want to increase production of SCFAs. This involves encouraging beneficial saccharolytic processes (carbohydrate fermentation) and decreasing detrimental proteolytic catabolism (breakdown of proteins into amino acids). And how do we do this? We 'feed' the saccharolytic species of microbes (e.g., Lachnospiraceae) (Jackson & Jewell, 2019). Those are the colonic bacteria that love to munch on non-digestible carbohydrates, particularly prebiotic fibers. Studies show that adding prebiotic fibers to the diet beneficially alters the saccharolytic/proteolytic bacteria. This in turn improves clinical signs as well as metabolic markers associated with canine chronic inflammatory GI diseases. In fact, the addition of functional fibers improves GI health in dogs regardless of the type of diet consumed or gut health status (Jackson & Jewell, 2019).

It turns out the proof is in the poop—literally.

A study published in the journal *Gut Microbes* looked at the effects of added fiber on the gastrointestinal health of dogs fed a high-meat/low-grain hydrolyzed food (HM) and a grain-rich (GR) food. Sixteen healthy beagles and 16 beagles with chronic enteritis/gastroenteritis participated in two separate dietary intervention trials. Study #1 looked at the impact of adding fiber to an HM food, while Study #2 assessed the impact of adding fiber to a GR food. For each study, the dogs were randomized into two groups. In Study #1, one group consumed the HM food alone, while the other group consumed the HM food plus fiber. After four weeks, feces and blood samples were collected and the groups were switched to consuming the opposite diet for another four weeks. Study #2 applied the same methodology using the GR food with and without fiber. Each dog's stool quality was examined, along with changes in the fecal microbiome and metabolome. So, what were the results? All the dogs experienced an improvement in stool quality with the added fiber bundle, regardless of their initial health status or the type of diet (HM or GR) consumed. In addition, microbiome diversity of the dogs with chronic enteritis/gastroenteritis became more similar to healthy dogs (Jackson & Jewell, 2019).

According to the study's designers:

> *In conclusion, several beneficial effects were seen upon the addition of the fiber bundle to the HM and GR foods in canines. The improved canine stool quality; microbiome composition and shift in the alpha diversity of dogs with chronic enteritis/gastroenteritis toward that of healthy dogs; and microbiome metabolism of postbiotics such as SCFAs, polyamines, tryptophan metabolites, bile acids, and endocannabinoids indicate that the fiber bundle positively contributed to gastrointestinal health* (Jackson & Jewell, 2019, pp. 313).

Other researchers wanted to see what would happen when they inoculated Toy Poodle poop with soybean husk in a test tube. It turns out that the microbes in the poop fermented the soybean husk, which increased the levels of fecal SCFAs and beneficial *Bifidobacterium*. When the same researchers directly fed young (seven- to 48-months-old) Shiba Inu dogs a commercial diet supplemented with 5.6% soybean husk, the dogs experienced *increased* concentrations of SCFAs and lactate (a beneficial organic acid), along with a *decrease* in two harmful metabolites, indole and skatole. The soybean husk supplement also promoted the growth of beneficial bacteria and inhibited the growth of bad bacteria. These results indicate that soybean husk qualifies as a functional fiber for dogs due to its ability to improve GI health both by increasing beneficial byproducts of fermentation, such as SCFAs, and by promoting the growth of good bacteria (Myint et al., 2017).

In another study, 39 healthy adult dogs were fed a lower-fiber control food for four weeks. They were then switched to a test food higher in soluble and insoluble sources such as flaxseed, dried citrus pulp, pressed cranberries, dried pumpkin, psyllium seed husks and ginger root. After four weeks on the test food, the dogs experienced increased fecal concentrations of the SCFA acetic acid and decreased putrefactive byproducts. *Bacteroides* and *Faecalibacterium*, beneficial bacterial species that produce acetate and lactate, were also significantly increased on the test food, while the unhealthy species *Streptococus* and *Enterococcus* were significantly decreased. These results illustrate that increasing total dietary fiber intake positively shifted both the composition and function of the dogs' gut microbiomes in a manner that promoted GI health (Fritsch et al., 2019).

While we often think of diarrhea in relation to chronic GI issues, constipation can also pose a problem, particularly in senior dogs. A decrease in beneficial bacteria and an increase in pathogenic bacteria can lead to age-related constipation and malabsorption of nutrients. In Chapter 11, we mentioned a study showing that senior dogs who consumed a test food enhanced with omega-3 fatty acids and fiber from citrus, carrot, spinach and tomato had decreased levels of uremic toxins. But that wasn't the only benefit. The food also shifted the dogs' gut microbiomes in favor of beneficial bacteria and decreased pathogenic bacteria. Glycerol, an organic compound, was also increased in the dogs' feces. This is significant because glycerol increases water in the gut, which acts as a laxative and is used to help treat constipation (Ephraim et al., 2020).

Prebiotics may provide even greater benefits when paired with probiotics in a combination known as **synbiotics**. In a double-blind, randomized study, 44 healthy companion dogs aged one to 12 years received either a daily synbiotic supplement containing 20 billion total CFUs of probiotics and 50 mg inulin (a prebiotic) or a placebo for four weeks. Dogs in the synbiotic group experienced "small but significant" beneficial shifts in their gut microbiomes not seen in the placebo group, including an increase in the good bacterial strains contained in the synbiotic and a decrease in pathogenic bacteria. In addition, 16% of the dogs in the placebo group experienced diarrhea during the four-week period, while no instances of diarrhea occurred among the dogs in the synbiotic group. This is particularly interesting because dogs who had low fecal levels of beneficial lactic acid-producing bacteria (*Lactobacillales*) and high levels of pathogenic bacteria at the start of the study showed the best response to the synbiotic supplement. Since those dogs did not yet suffer from diarrhea, the researchers suggested that synbiotic supplementation could serve as a preventive therapy by correcting microbial dysbiosis before it manifests into clinical signs (Tanprasertsuk et al., 2021).

Psyllium prebiotic manages GERD and chronic colitis

Our dogs shower us with love and loyalty, but all too often we repay them by sharing our chronic lifestyle diseases. It seems that gastroesophageal reflux disease (GERD) is no exception. GERD shows up in dogs and people at the same rate, affecting about 20% of the human and canine populations (Meineri et al., 2008).

A study published in the *Journal of Animal and Veterinary Advances* used a questionnaire to evaluate the relationship between GERD symptoms and diet in dogs and their human caretakers. Based on the answers, the authors discovered that dogs and people suffered from the *same* symptoms and consumed the *same* types of foods. Was this a coincidence? We don't think so, and neither did the study authors. They concluded that, "As in man, it [GERD] is strictly related to the type of diet. A dietary relationship between the owners and dogs suffering from the same symptoms further confirms this hypothesis" (Meineri et al., 2008).

Unlike GI diseases of the lower intestines, GERD originates in the epigastric region, or the upper part of the stomach. GERD refers to a disorder in which gastric juices in the stomach reflux, or escape, into the esophagus. The esophagus serves as the 'tunnel' connecting the mouth and the stomach. When dogs and people chew and swallow food, automatic muscle contractions called peristalsis push it down the esophageal tunnel and into the stomach, which begins the digestion process by breaking down the food with acid and digestive enzymes. The esophagus contains a layer of smooth, circular muscle at the bottom where it meets the stomach, called the lower esophageal sphincter (LES). When functioning properly, the LES contracts to allow food to pass and then closes to block stomach contents from regurgitating back into the esophagus. GERD occurs when the LES improperly relaxes, enabling gastric juices from the stomach to re-enter the esophagus (Rosen & Winters, 2021).

GERD causes distressing symptoms, including acid reflux, indigestion and cough (Hosseini et al., 2018). Many dogs with GERD vomit up bile, especially on an empty stomach. Left uncontrolled, GERD can cause serious complications, including Barrett's esophagus, which are precancerous lesions that can lead to esophageal cancer (Meineri et al., 2008).

Proton Pump Inhibitors (PPIs), such as omeprazole (Prilosec, Prilosec OTC, Zegerid), esomeprazole (Nexium) and lansoprazole (Prevacid), among others, are designed to ease discomfort associated with GERD by blocking the production of acid produced in the stomach. But acid production is not an accident of nature. It serves important functions in the digestion and absorption of nutrients. Blocking the production of acid can have serious adverse consequences. A 2019 analysis published in the *International Journal of Molecular Sciences* reported on decades of epidemiological studies in people showing side-effects of PPIs including gastric cancer, increased risk of chronic kidney disease (CKD), fractures resulting from osteoporosis, dementia and Alzheimer's disease, liver cirrhosis and liver cancer and micronutrient deficiencies (Fossmark et al., 2019).

The goal in treating GERD shouldn't be to abolish stomach acid; it should be to strengthen the LES. A study of 30 people diagnosed with non-erosive GERD (NERD) showed that adding 15 g/day of psyllium fiber (5 g TID) to the diet for just 10 days significantly increased resting LES pressure and decreased the number of gastroesophageal refluxes and frequency of heartburn per week. In addition, 60% of the patients reported no heartburn for the entire final seven days of the study (Morozov et al., 2018).

GERD is often accompanied by lower-GI symptoms like IBS and chronic constipation. About one-third of people with GERD also suffer from constipation (Dickman et al., 2006). In a two-month study, 132 patients with GERD-related constipation were randomly split into two groups. One group took omeprazole capsules twice per day (20 mg, a half hour before breakfast and dinner), while the second group took 5 mg of psyllium seed dissolved in warm water an hour before breakfast and dinner. After two months, the response rate to the treatments was nearly the same in the two groups (89.2% in the psyllium seed group compared to 94% in the omeprazole group, which is not considered statistically significant). And here's the really interesting part. While the omeprazole acted more quickly (which makes sense as it eradicates stomach acid), patients taking the psyllium eventually reported a greater "feeling of well-being without GERD symptoms" (Hosseini et al., 2018).

But that's not all. The psyllium husk performed far better at stopping the recurrence of GERD compared to the PPI. In fact, 69.8% of patients taking the omeprazole experienced recurrences, compared to 24.2% in the psyllium group. People taking the PPI were about three times as likely to have their GERD symptoms return than those taking the psyllium, and the omeprazole relapses happened much sooner (Hosseini et al., 2018).

The results led the study authors to conclude that:

> *The use of psyllium seed in the treatment of functional constipation in patients with GERD is very safe, effective, cheap, and easily available, and this treatment also minimizes the chance of recurrence of GERD compared to omeprazole* (Hosseini et al., 2018, pp. 5).

Supplementation with psyllium husk also helps alleviate symptoms in dogs with chronic idiopathic large bowel diarrhea (Leib, 2000; Alves et al., 2021). When police working dogs suffering from colitis were given four tablespoons of psyllium husk per day for a month, 90% showed either a very good (50%) or good (40%) response to the treatment without any pharmaceutical intervention. The dogs defecated less frequently, their stool quality improved and they gained weight. Moreover, these positive effects continued during a second month of monitoring, even after supplementation was stopped (Alves et al., 2021).

If your dog suffers from GERD or large bowel diarrhea, why not give psyllium husk powder a try? It just might do the trick and doesn't have the potential negative side effects associated with prescription medications such as PPIs or metronidazole.

Dosage: We recommend 1/2 tablespoon for small dogs, 1 tablespoon for medium dogs and 2 tablespoons for large dogs daily, divided between a.m. and p.m. When purchasing psyllium, be sure to select the powder rather than the whole husk. The powder is smoother and contains about twice the fiber (Dannie, 2018). (See Resources.)

Introduce psyllium slowly to give your dog's colonic bacteria time to adjust. We recommend starting with half the recommended dosage for your dog's size and slowly increasing to the full amount over the course of a week.

Never give your dog dry psyllium, as it can swell in the throat and block the airway. *Always mix psyllium powder with ample water before adding it into your dog's food.* Do not give psyllium to young puppies or dogs with swallowing problems. Consult with your veterinarian if you plan to give your dog psyllium, as it can affect other medications.

Spirulina prebiotic boosts gut health and immune response

Spirulina, as previously discussed, is a microalgae that is packed with antioxidants and phycocyanin, so it's no surprise that this micro-alga boasts impressive benefits for both the immune and GI systems. But thanks to a 2021 study published in *Frontiers in Nutrition*, we know that supplementation with spirulina also increases gut mucosal immunity and microbiota stability in dogs—and that's great news for GI-impaired pups.

The 42-week trial measured the effect of spirulina supplementation on the immune response in dogs after two challenging events: receiving a Rabies vaccination and undergoing strenuous exercise. 30 adult husky-mix dogs participated in the study. During an eight-week pre-test period, all dogs were fed the same commercial 'complete and balanced' food manufactured by Nestlé Purina. At the start of the test, the dogs received a three-year rabies vaccine (IMRAB 3 by Merial) and then were randomly divided into two groups of 15 dogs each. The control group continued to consume the pre-vaccination diet, while the test group was switched to the same pre-vaccination diet supplemented with 0.2% spray-dried spirulina. (See Resources for the brand used in the study.) All dogs consumed their assigned diet for the duration of the trial. At the end of the 42 weeks, the dogs rested for two days and then ran for 10 miles in a harness pulling an unladen sled. Blood and fecal samples were collected and tested every four weeks from week 0 to week 42 (Satyaraj et al., 2021).

The following tests were performed:

- Rabies virus neutralizing antibodies were measured in the dogs' serum to indicate how effectively the immune system could fight off a potential rabies virus infection.
- Fecal secretory IgA (sIgA) levels were measured to evaluate activity of the gut-associated lymphoid tissue (GALT). IgA is an important marker of GALT activity because it is the most abundant immunoglobulin produced by the GALT. Low levels of fecal sIgA have previously been associated with certain types of chronic enteropathies in dogs (Littler et al., 2006; Maeda et al., 2013).
- C-Reactive protein (CRP) was measured toward the end of the trial as a general marker of inflammation.
- Fecal swabs taken 24 hours before and 24 hours after the 10-mile sled run were used to assess exercise-induced changes in the gut microbiota.

  (Satyaraj et al., 2021)

Here's what the researchers found:

- Dogs who received the spirulina supplement exhibited a faster and stronger immune response to the rabies vaccine than the control group.

- Fecal sIgA levels increased after just nine weeks in dogs on the spirulina supplement and continued throughout the trial.

- The gut microbiota of the spirulina-supplemented dogs remained significantly more stable in response to exercise than the control group.

(Satyaraj et al., 2021)

The study's message is clear. Supplementing with spirulina checks off three important canine health boxes:

- Better overall immune function

- Better intestinal immune function

- More stable gut microbiota

Summed up in the researchers' own words:

> … *diets supplemented with Spirulina significantly enhanced immune response and gut health in dogs* (Satyaraj et al., 2021, pp. 1).

The authors also 'tease' us with the prospect that spirulina may help prevent food intolerances:

> *The production of antigen specific sIgA from IgA-secreting cells in Peyer's patches, and accompanying higher fecal sIgA levels, has been suggested to be a mechanism for the development of food tolerance (Frossard et al., 2004). Therefore, by supporting intestinal immune function, Spirulina may not only help reduce opportunistic infections but may also help prevent food intolerance. In our current study, fecal sIgA levels were increased after just 2 months of feeding Spirulina and the positive enhancement was maintained to the end of the 42-week study (Satyaraj et al., 2021, pp. 5).*

This sounds like exciting news. Wouldn't it be great if you could simply feed your food-intolerant dog some spirulina and—*voilà*—he was magically able to eat anything with no negative effects? If only it were that simple. In fact, you'll notice that we didn't include this study in Chapter 10 on food intolerances. The reason is that the study was not designed to test whether spirulina benefited dogs with food intolerances. So, while we welcome more research in this area, currently the only sure way to eliminate food intolerance is to eliminate the food(s) causing the intolerance. We wouldn't want anyone to think that giving their dog spirulina can counteract the effects of feeding antigenic foods because this could backfire and worsen intestinal inflammation, leaky gut and dysbiosis.

But as this study and others mentioned throughout the book illustrate, there are plenty of other reasons to include spirulina as part of your dog's nutritious plant-based diet. Just be sure to heed the purchasing cautions discussed in Chapter 5 to ensure your dog receives the purest product possible.

Nutritional and brewer's yeasts contain a special type of prebiotic

In Chapter 5, we mentioned that nutritional and brewer's yeasts are made from a species of yeast called *Saccharomyces cerevisiae*. This is important because the cell walls of *Saccharomyces cerevisiae* contain mannan oligosaccharides (MOS), a type of prebiotic fiber offering unique gut health benefits.

MOS works differently than other prebiotic fibers. Pathogenic bacteria have finger-like projections, called fimbriae, that enable them to attach to cells on the intestinal wall and colonize the gut. Certain pathogenic bacteria, such as *E. coli* and *Salmonella*, have fimbriae that attach to mannose, the main sugar molecule in MOS. By binding these bad bacteria, MOS prevents them from adhering to the intestinal cells. MOS then ushers the bad bacteria out of the body via the feces (Sanderson, 2008; Pinna & Biagi, 2014).

A meta-analysis published in the *World Journal of Gastroenterology* reviewed two clinical trials involving 579 people with IBS. The patients taking *Saccharomyces cerevisiae* experienced significant decreases in abdominal pain, discomfort and bloating compared to those who took a placebo (Cayzeele-Decherf et al., 2017; Murray, 2021).

Multiple studies have found that supplementation with MOS/*Saccharomyces cerevisiae* beneficially alters gut microbiota, improves GI health, boosts immune function and reduces inflammation in dogs (Swanson et al., 2002; Swanson et al., 2002a; Royal Canin, 2012; Pawar et al., 2017; Lin et al., 2019; Strompfová et al, 2021). *Saccharomyces cerevisiae* might also benefit dogs undergoing a rapid diet change (although we advise a slow transition whenever possible). While the results weren't dramatic, supplementation modestly improved the intestinal health of dogs in this situation (Lin et al., 2020).

MOS given in combination with fructooligosaccharides (FOS) may offer an additional health boost. One study found that healthy dogs who were fed a capsule supplement containing 2 grams FOS plus a separate capsule containing 1 gram MOS with their kibble twice daily had improved immune function and microbial populations compared to dogs who received a placebo. FOS plus MOS supplementation increased concentrations of fecal bifidobacteria and fecal and ileal lactobacilli. It also resulted in a beneficial shift in the dogs' plasma neutrophils and lymphocytes, two types of white blood cells (Swanson et al., 2002a). This research expanded upon a previous study showing that supplementation with FOS plus MOS positively affected markers associated with improved gut health and immune status in dogs. However, the earlier study did not examine the dogs' small intestinal microbial populations as did the later study (Swanson et al., 2002; Swanson et al., 2002a). The MOS supplement used in both studies was Bio-MOS by Alltech. (See Resources.)

MOS is often given to German shepherd dogs and other breeds with weak digestive systems to help eliminate pathogenic bacteria and improve assimilation of foods (Royal Canin, 2012).

Dosage: We recommend 1 teaspoon of nutritional or brewer's yeast for small dogs, 2 teaspoons for medium-sized dogs and 1 tablespoon for large dogs per day, mixed into the food and divided between a.m. and p.m. (See Resources.) Be aware that the MOS content of food yeasts will vary and that dogs might not accept brewer's yeast due to the bitter flavor.

Always introduce nutritional and brewer's yeasts slowly and avoid giving too much, which can cause gastrointestinal upset. Do not feed them to dogs who are allergic to yeast. And while these yeasts are inactive, it's best to play it safe and avoid giving them to dogs who suffer from frequent yeast infections. Also avoid if your dog suffers from IBD, as this could potentially worsen symptoms. Yeasts are high in the compound tyramine, which can cause dangerous interactions with certain medications, including anti-anxiety medications, anti-depressants such as MAOIs, anti-fungal drugs and narcotic pain medications. Always consult with your veterinarian in these instances. Also consult with your veterinarian if your dog is taking diabetes medication, since nutritional and brewer's yeasts can further decrease blood sugar levels (Murray, 2021; Mount Sinai, 2022).

Benefits of MOS Plus Saccharomyces boulardii

For acute cases of GI disruption, such as those related to antibiotics or stress, we recommend a product by Jarrow Formulas that combines the yeast-based probiotic *Saccharomyces boulardii* plus MOS from *Saccharomyces cerevisiae*. (See Resources.) Studies show that S. Boulardii helps prevent antibiotic-related diarrhea (Surawicz, 1989), while MOS sweeps away pathogenic bacteria.

Dosage: For this formula, our recommended dosage is 1/4 capsule per day for small dogs, 1/2 capsule per day for medium-sized dogs and 1 capsule per day for large dogs. Use the same cautions when giving this product as apply to nutritional and brewer's yeasts.

Dog-friendly prebiotic foods

Adding prebiotics to your canine companion's diet is easy. Simply select from the following list of prebiotic foods to help feed your dog's gut microbiome. Be sure to note which ones work best for your dog—and which ones receive the biggest tail wag!

- Apples: pectin
- Asparagus: inulin, fructooligosaccharides (FOS)
- Bananas (ripe): inulin, FOS
- Bananas (green/unripe): resistant starch
- Barley: beta-glucans (avoid if your dog is gluten intolerant)
- Chicory root: inulin, FOS
- Dandelion greens: inulin
- Garlic (see Chapter 8 for dosing): inulin, FOS
- Grains (cooked and cooled): resistant starch
- Jerusalem artichoke (sunchoke): inulin, FOS
- Jicama: inulin
- Legumes: pectin, resistant starch
- Macroalgae (e.g., seaweeds such as arame, hijiki, nori, sea lettuce, sea spaghetti, wakame): alginate, agar, fucoidan, mannitol, laminaran, ulvan
- Microalgae (e.g., chlorella, spirulina): beta-glucans, oligosaccharides
- Nuts/seeds (avoid toxic macadamia and black walnuts): pectin

- Oats (cooked): beta-glucans (use certified gluten-free oats)
- Oats (uncooked): resistant starch (use certified gluten-free oats)
- Potato, white (cooked and cooled): resistant starch
- Psyllium: oligosaccharides
- Root vegetables: pectin
- Yacon root: inulin, FOS
- Yeasts (nutritional and brewer's): beta-glucans, mannan oligosaccharides (MOS)

  (Lahaye, 1991; de Jesus Raposo, 2016; Jalanka et al., 2019; Monash University, 2019; Tarantino, 2019; Gotteland et al., 2020; Semeco & Kelly, 2021)

Always introduce prebiotic foods slowly. Since prebiotic fibers are highly fermentable by colonic bacteria, introducing them too quickly can cause gas, cramping and other unpleasant GI side effects.

A plant-based diet puts Archie on the path to GI health

Archie, a 10 1/2-year-old pug, had suffered from GI issues since he was a puppy. Per his veterinarian's recommendation, he had been eating Royal Canin's Hydrolyzed Protein diet since he was three years old. But in April 2020, Archie's symptoms worsened and his 'mom,' Chaza, began noticing blood and mucus in his stool. After multiple veterinary visits, a biopsy confirmed that Archie suffered from idiopathic IBD.

Archie's veterinarian prescribed the steroid Prednisone along with Azathioprine, an immunosuppressant drug, to manage his symptoms. But after a year, Archie still showed signs of intestinal inflammation. By June 2021, Chaza had discontinued both prescriptions because she was concerned about their potential long-term side effects. She decided to seek out a safer, natural approach to manage Archie's condition.

Since Chaza was aware of the gut benefits of plant-based foods, she began home cooking meals for Archie. Encouraged by the improvement, she decided to take the plant-based approach to the next level. In July 2021, Chaza contacted Diana for a custom-formulated plant-based recipe that would help decrease Archie's intestinal inflammation, mend his leaky gut and rebalance his microbiome.

Diana created a low-fat recipe for Archie using legumes and vegetables rich in antioxidants, phytochemicals and prebiotic fiber. She also recommended that Archie take a glutamine supplement, as glutamine is shown to promote intestinal healing.

After just a few weeks on Diana's GI-support recipe, Chaza reported that the blood and mucus in Archie's stool had "reduced significantly" and that the irritation now appears "minimal." She has also reported that his coat is much softer on a plant-based diet and that his energy level is excellent for his age.

She says, "I am relieved to know we are on a good path for Archie and that with time we'll see even more gut healing with the power of a whole-food, plant-based diet."

Low-FODMAP diet and gut health

As you now know, prebiotic fibers feed the good bacteria in the gut, which in turn creates beneficial postbiotics that help to address a whole host of GI problems. But there can be a downside to this healthy fermentation process. Namely, it produces gas. And the more fermentable the fiber, the more gas that's produced. This can create bloating and increase pain and discomfort in individuals with certain GI conditions, which is obviously the opposite to the healing effect we want to create.

To address this issue, researchers at Monash University in Australia created the low-FODMAP diet. **FODMAP** is an acronym that refers to Fermentable Oligosaccharides, Disaccharides, Monosaccharides and Polyols, a group of non-digestible carbohydrates that are highly fermentable in the colon. The low-FODMAP diet has gained traction in recent years for treating symptoms associated with IBS, such as intestinal gas, bloating, pain, distension, diarrhea and/or constipation (Monash University, 2019a).

But there's a dilemma with the low-FODMAP diet. When you remove ingredients that feed the good bacteria in the colon, you lose the benefits of all those healthy metabolic byproducts, such as SCFAs, that are created as a result of microbial fermentation.

So, which is better for easing symptoms of chronic intestinal inflammation? Prebiotics or low-FODMAP?

The two protocols went head-to-head (or, we should say, gut-to-gut) in a randomized, parallel, double-blinded study in patients with functional gut disorders and flatulence. For four weeks, the patients followed one of two dietary protocols: 1) a prebiotic supplement (1.37 g/day beta-galactooligosaccharide) along with a Mediterranean-type diet or 2) a low-FODMAP diet along with a placebo (Huaman et al., 2018; Scientific Wellness, 2018).

The interventions produced opposite effects on the patients' fecal microbiota. *Bifidobacteria*, an important beneficial bacterial species, increased in the prebiotic group and decreased in the low-FODMAP group. At the same time, *Bilophila wadsworthia* increased in the low-FODMAP group and decreased in the prebiotic group (Huaman et al., 2018; Scientific Wellness, 2018). *Bilophila wadsoworthia* is a pathogenic bacterium in the Proteobacteria phylum. While small numbers *Bilophila wadsworthia* are a normal part of the gut microbiome, overgrowth can lead to leaky gut and worsen IBD (Mansfield, 2019).

Based on these results, prebiotic therapy beat the low-FODMAP diet in the 'battle of the bacteria.' But what about reducing clinical symptoms?

Both patient groups experienced significant decreases in digestive issues, such as bloating, distension and abdominal pain. The only difference was that the prebiotic group did not experience a significant decline in flatulence and borborygmi (gurgling). However, patients on the prebiotic protocol continued to experience a decrease in symptoms even when tested two-weeks *after* supplementation was discontinued, while the low-FODMAP group relapsed immediately upon stopping the diet (Huaman et al., 2018; Scientific Wellness, 2018).

Based on this study, if your dog has intestinal inflammation accompanied by severe symptoms of flatulence or borborygmi, a low-FODMAP diet could temporarily make sense. Otherwise, prebiotics appear to come out on top, especially in treating intestinal inflammation at the source—the gut microbiome.

A low-FODMAP diet also poses some real-world obstacles. Namely, it's restrictive and impractical over the long term. It's also nutritionally tricky since it eliminates many healthy foods. Even the Monash University website states that the low-FODMAP diet "is best followed under the supervision of a qualified dietician or healthcare professional who is experienced in this specialized area" (Monash University, 2019a). And, as the study we just mentioned shows, the low-FODMAP diet is not a cure, since stopping the diet results in an immediate return of symptoms. The Monash University website also states that "Of course, the diet does not cure IBS symptoms, it just helps people to live more comfortably with their condition" (Monash University, 2019a).

If your dog suffers from GERD, temporarily reducing or eliminating FODMAPs could be an important step in the healing process. A small study of nine people with GERD showed that adding 6.6 g/day of FOS increased the number of transient LES relaxations, esophageal acid exposure and reflux episodes (Piche et al., 2003). So, FODMAPs can clearly interfere with normal LES functioning, allowing acid to escape back into the esophagus and worsening symptoms of GERD.

If your canine companion suffers from GERD, IBS or other intolerance to FODMAPs, we recommend contacting Diana for a custom-formulated recipe to ensure that all your dog's nutritional needs are met. After a period of FODMAP restriction, we also recommend—as do the researchers at Monash University—slowly reintroducing certain FODMAP foods until an ideal balance of variety and symptom reduction has been achieved.

Even if you must temporarily restrict FODMAPs, your dog can still benefit from prebiotic fibers. Moderately fermentable fiber sources can create beneficial postbiotics without producing the negative side effects associated with FODMAPs.

Moderately fermentable fibers for dogs include:

- Gum arabic (acacia gum)
- Rice bran
- Xanthan gum

(Sanderson, 2008)

If you suspect your dog suffers from GERD or an intolerance to FODMAPs, here are some low-FODMAP substitutes you can try. If you notice an improvement in your dog's symptoms after making these switches, a low-FODMAP diet—at least temporarily—might be the way to go.

FODMAP Foods Swaps Chart

Food Group*	High FODMAP	Low FODMAP
Vegetables	Artichoke, asparagus, cauliflower, garlic, green peas, mushrooms, sugar snap peas	Green beans, bell pepper, Bok choy, carrot, cucumber, lettuce, potato, zucchini
Fruits	Apples, mango, pears, watermelon	Cantaloupe, kiwi, strawberries**
Dairy alternatives	Soy milk (made from whole soybeans)	Almond milk, soy milk (made from soy protein)
Protein	Most legumes	Tofu (firm), tempeh
Grains	Wheat, rye, barley	Corn, oats***, quinoa, rice
Nuts & seeds	Cashews, pistachios	Peanuts, pumpkin seeds/pepitas

(Adapted from Monash University, 2019a)

*Purchase organic/non-GMO ingredients as recommended throughout the book.

**Ensure that your dog is not allergic to strawberries.

***Opt for certified gluten-free oats.

If you're interested in learning more about the FODMAP level in foods, Monash University offers the Monash University FODMAP Diet App for mobile phones and certain other devices. (See Resources.)

Fermented foods foster a healthy gut microbiome

If you've noticed a lot more kombucha and kefir on your grocery store shelves recently, it's no accident. Savvy food manufacturers and marketers are taking advantage of the fermented foods frenzy that's sprouted up over recent years. Whole cookbooks are now even devoted to fermenting your own ingredients. (We own a couple of them ourselves!)

So, what's the big deal about fermented foods and beverages? Aside from creating some varied and unique flavor profiles, fermentation enables the growth of beneficial probiotics that already exist on certain foods, such as fruit and vegetable skins. When we consume fermented foods, good bacteria help to promote a healthy gut microbiome, which, as we've discussed leads to improved digestion and a whole host of health benefits.

The process of fermentation has been around for more than 9,000 years, dating as far back as the Neolithic period about 7,000 BCE. Fermentation began as a way for our ancient ancestors to preserve food, but they soon figured out that it also made a mighty fine alcoholic beverage. Around 7,000 BCE, an ancient Chinese civilization used fermentation to create kui, a beer-like beverage made from rice, honey, grapes and the fruit of hawthorn plants. Even pickles have been around since about 2,000 BCE, when they were first documented in the Middle East (Garbarino, 2020).

While ancient folks knew how to ferment a wide variety of foods and beverages, we can thank Louis Pasteur for identifying the metabolic process behind the fermentative magic. Through his experiments, Pasteur showed that live microorganisms, such as yeast and bacteria, create fermentation when they feed on sugar and starch. He described this process as "la vie sans l'air," meaning "life without air" because fermentation takes place in the absence of oxygen (Garbarino, 2020).

According to one study, fermented foods even beat out prebiotics for their beneficial effects on the microbiome. Researchers at the Stanford School of Medicine randomly divided 36 healthy adults into two groups. One group ate a high-fiber diet, while the other group consumed a diet high in fermented foods for a period of 10 weeks. The group eating the fermented foods experienced increased microbiota diversity accompanied by decreases in markers of inflammation, while microbiota diversity did not increase in the high-fiber group. However, the high-fiber group did experience an increase in the percentage of microbial proteins in the stool, which indicated that the high-fiber diet was shifting the microbiome. One explanation the authors gave was that the study duration might not have been long enough for the fiber to increase the total bacterial species. In the end, they decided that:

> *Given the distinct responses of participants to these two diets, whether a diet composed of both high-fiber and fermented foods could synergize to influence the host microbiota and immune system is an exciting possibility that remains to be determined* (Wastyk et al., 2021, pp. 12).

In other words, why not benefit from the best of both worlds by consuming a diet rich in fiber and fermented foods? Given the research, this seems like a common-sense approach to 'fermenting' a healthy gut microbiome.

Dog-friendly fermented foods

There are a wide variety of dog-friendly fermented foods on the market. We recommend experimenting to see which ones tickle your dog's taste buds. Here are a few to try:

- Apple cider vinegar
- Fermented vegetables (Avoid vegetables in the allium family, including onions, chives, leeks, scallions and shallots. Use garlic per the recommended dosages in Chapter 8.)
- Kefir (dairy-free, such as coconut)
- Sauerkraut
- Tempeh
- Yogurt (e.g., organic almond, cashew, coconut and soy)

Never give your dog kombucha. While it is a tasty—and healthy—beverage for humans, kombucha can be harmful for dogs because it contains both caffeine from tea and a small amount of alcohol as a byproduct of the fermentation process.

Be sure to read labels carefully when selecting fermented foods for your canine companion. Avoid high-sodium foods, such as miso, as well as any ingredients that are unsafe for dogs, such as those previously listed. Also be aware that "pickled" does not mean "fermented." To ensure you select a product containing probiotics, look for mention of specific terms such as "live bacteria," "fermented" or "probiotics" on the label (Villines & Marengo, 2019).

Dosage: We recommend approximately 1 teaspoon of fermented foods or beverages daily for every 20 pounds of your dog's body weight.

Always introduce fermented foods slowly so that your dog's gut bacteria have time to adjust. As with prebiotics, adding too much fermented ingredients at one time can cause digestive upset, including diarrhea.

There are times when pharmaceutical intervention for acute GI flare-ups may be warranted. But this approach will not address the root cause of the disease and comes with potentially serious side effects. Fortunately, there is a safe and effective long-term solution for chronic GI and other lifestyle-related chronic inflammatory diseases: nutritional modification. A low-toxin, anti-inflammatory and phytochemical-rich diet that sends healthy epigenetic messages to the genome and microbiome can help your dog live longer and healthier without the negative side effects associated with medications.

And as you now know, this diet is a *whole-food plant-based diet*.

Final Thoughts

We hope you have enjoyed traveling on this amazing journey of discovery with us. Along the way, we've busted myths, revealed amazing scientific facts about the nutritional needs of modern dogs and provided a step-by-step action plan to help your canine companion live a longer and healthier life. We realize that we've given you a lot to chew on; so, we'd like to offer some recommendations on where to go from here:

- **Use this book as your personal guide.** Refer to it whenever you have a question or feel a bit unsure along your journey. We're confident that with every read, you'll find new answers and inspiration.

- **Go at your own pace.** There is no correct speed at which to implement the action steps and recipe formulas. As long as you keep moving forward, you—and your dog—will reach your destination.

- **Trust the science.** Many people cling to outdated beliefs, even when presented with research-based facts. Don't stress trying to change others who aren't ready. Just breathe easy in the knowledge that you have science on your side.

- **Stay the course.** Some people might feel threatened by your decision to feed your dog a plant-based diet and try to persuade you against it. Refer back to the 'why' section in Chapter 3 for motivation to keep going in the face of adversity.

We are honored that you have chosen to participate in this exciting movement. Each time someone feeds their canine companion a nutritious plant-based diet, we move closer to a kinder, more sustainable future for our beautiful planet and everyone who calls it home.

As Maya Angelou so eloquently stated:

Do the best you can until you know better. Then when you know better, do better.

We hope that this book has helped you to know better. And we thank you for doing better.

Appendix:
Supplemental Recipes to
Support Your Dog's Health

In Chapter 6, you discovered how to use the Recipe Builder Pie and Recipe Creation Chart to design your own 'almost complete-and-balanced' recipes for your canine companion. And while these are excellent tools, you don't need to create *all* your dog's meals with such precise detail. As you become more familiar with the method, we hope it leads you to a deeper understanding of how to best combine ingredients to optimally support your dog's plant-based lifestyle. This is true even when making what we call 'supplemental' recipes, such as the ones in this section. These refer to recipes that are meant to be fed in addition to your dog's regular meals (e.g., snacks, sides or toppers) or offered occasionally as a meal. Even supplemental recipes can—and should—be created with an eye for optimal nutritional density. This is exactly what we've done with the following recipes. We hope your dog loves them, and that they inspire you to get creative in the kitchen. And of course, all our recipes are human-safe (and tested), so feel free to share them with your canine companion—if he'll let you!

Before we dive into the delicious recipes, we want to mention a few important notes:

- The recommended feeding amounts after each recipe represent what we believe is a reasonable portion for various size dogs when fed in *addition* to regular meals. The exception is the Sweet Potato and Hemp 'Cheese' Enchiladas, which we allotted as a day's meal. To be sure you don't overfeed, you'll want to monitor your dog's weight, body condition, satiety and general health regularly and adjust the amount offered accordingly.

- These recipes are meant to be served as snacks, sides or toppers (with the exception of the enchiladas), so no supplementation is necessary. When feeding any of them as an interim meal, we recommend that you add VegeDog (or an equivalent product as listed in the Resources) per the manufacturer's instructions to help round out the nutritional profile.

- We have noted within each recipe our recommendation to purchase organic for specific ingredients containing high levels of pesticides/herbicides or that are commonly genetically modified.

- For your convenience, we have provided Calorie, fat and protein information for each recipe. These values are calculated via a sophisticated diet and recipe analysis tool created by the nutritional software company ESHA Research. Bear in mind, however, that everyone cooks differently, so your yields (the amount your recipe makes) and nutrient levels may differ from ours. Even different brands of the same ingredient can vary nutritionally. So, please use this information as a general guide, recognizing that based on certain variables, your recipe's nutrient levels will likely fluctuate from our calculated values.

- We have provided recipe preparation times as a guide, however your times may differ. We all prep at our own speed, and oven cooking times can vary widely.

- We recommend using home-made nut and seed milks whenever possible. Store-bought plant milks tend to be quite thin, which can change the consistency of the recipe. They can also contain sweeteners, thickeners, flavors, oils and other undesirable additives. We used either home-made nut milk (made with the Almond Cow) or store-bought soy milk containing just two ingredients (organic soybeans and water) in all of the recipes calling for these ingredients. (See Resources.)

- By human standards, these recipes might taste a bit bland because they don't contain added salt or pepper. If you want to share them (and why wouldn't you?), we recommend setting aside your dog's portion and then adding seasoning to taste for your serving. (Note, however, that this isn't possible with every recipe.)

- We have used the following abbreviations to designate the amounts of ingredients to be used:
    - TB = tablespoon
    - tsp = teaspoon
    - g = gram
    - oz = ounce

We hope that you and your dog love these recipes and that they enhance not only your taste buds, but also your relationship!

Protein Superfood Smoothie

This smoothie makes a nutritious snack and can also serve as an occasional meal replacement for dogs suffering from sensitive stomachs due to illness or chemotherapy. It even contains a surprise ingredient (chickpeas!) to kick up the protein level. Try pouring this smoothie into an ice cube tray and offering a cube as a frozen treat on a hot summer's day!

If you plan to use this recipe as a meal replacement for a dog with inappetence due to cancer/chemotherapy, we recommend adding one-half to one scoop of NorCal unflavored pea protein powder and VegeDog per the package directions.

Prep time: 10 min

Yield: About 8 ounces (We recommend doubling the recipe to share!)

Ingredients

½ cup Almond milk (or substitute cashew, oat or soy milk)*

¼ cup Blueberries (fresh or frozen)*

1 ounce-weight Banana

1/3 cup Baby kale*

3 TB Chickpeas (from fresh boiled or canned)

1 tsp Black raspberry powder*

*Purchase organic. Be sure your plant milk is free of sweeteners, thickeners, oils, fillers or other additives.

Instructions

1. If using canned chickpeas, drain and rinse.
2. Place all ingredients in a blender and blend on high until smooth.
3. Pour the mixture into a bowl and serve.

Nutrition Facts (per full batch)
   Calories: 120
   Protein: 4 g
   Fat: 2.5 g

Recommended Daily Feeding Amount

Tiny Dog (Less than 10 lbs)	Small Dog (10 to 30 lbs)	Medium Dog (31 to 54 lbs)	Large Dog (55 to 99 lbs)	Giant Dog (100 lbs +)
1/8 cup	1/4 cup	1/2 cup	3/4 cup	1 cup

Spirulina Energy Balls

Who doesn't love a midday pick-me-up? Instead of reaching for junk food packed with refined sugar and empty Calories, it's so much better to reach for a healthy snack to rev up your energy and flood your body with nutrients. This is true for people and dogs! These Spirulina Energy Balls fit the bill perfectly. The ingredients provide an excellent combination of unrefined carbohydrates and healthy fats to fuel your dog's afternoon activities, and the spirulina offers an extra nutritional boost. We think you'll love them, too!

Prep Time: 20 minutes (plus 30 minutes to soak dates)

Yield: 24 balls (30 g each) (The exact yield and nutritional content will vary based on the amount and type of plant milk used and the creaminess of the nut butter.)

Ingredients

3 cups Rolled oats (certified gluten free)*

12 Medjool dates, pitted and soaked in warm water for 30 minutes to soften

12 TB Cashew butter, plain, unsweetened (or substitute almond butter)*

12 tsp Hemp seeds, plus extra to coat the balls

6 tsp Spirulina powder

A few drops of Almond, soy, cashew or oat milk to moisten (if needed)*

*Purchase organic. Be sure your plant milk is free of sweeteners, thickeners, oils, fillers or other additives.

Instructions

1. Add rolled oats, spirulina and hemp seeds to a food processor. Process until well combined.

2. Add the cashew butter and pre-soaked dates and process again until a dough forms.

3. If the mixture feels too crumbly, add a few drops of the plant-based milk. Process again. Continue to add additional milk a few drops at a time until the mixture is moist enough to form into balls.

4. Scoop the mixture into a bowl. Using your hands, roll into 24 balls (about 30 g each). Roll each of the balls in the extra hemp seeds to coat.

5. Place the balls on a plate and refrigerate for 30 minutes to set prior to serving.

Store the balls in a sealed container in the refrigerator for up to four days or in the freezer for up to two months. If storing in the freezer, let thaw prior to serving.

This recipe makes a large batch because we know that you'll also want to indulge in these delicious Spirulina Energy Balls, so we wanted to make sure there were plenty to go around!

Nutrition Facts (per 30-gram ball)

   Calories: 130

   Protein: 4 g

   Fat: 6 g

Recommended Daily Feeding Amount

Tiny Dog (Less than 10 lbs)	Small Dog (10 to 30 lbs)	Medium Dog (31 to 54 lbs)	Large Dog (55 to 99 lbs)	Giant Dog (100 lbs +)
1/8 ball	1/3 ball	3/4 ball	1 ball	1 1/2 balls

Cancer-Kicking Broth

If your dog has a sensitive stomach due to cancer or chemotherapy, he might not be able to tolerate eating whole veggies. But don't despair. He can still benefit from the most potent cancer-fighting foods with this nutrient-rich broth. It's easy for you to prepare and for your dog to digest, which is a winning combination. As with all the recipes in this section, this broth is meant for incremental or supplemental feeding. (You can even mix it with your dog's regular food to kick up the nutrient content and create a cancer-kicking stew). However, if you find you must give it alone for a few days due to your dog's nausea, we recommend adding VegeDog (if tolerated) to each serving per the manufacturer's instructions.

Prep time: 1 ½ hours

Yield: About 6 Cups

Ingredients

2 cups mixed Broccoli, cauliflower and Brussels sprouts, chopped

1 Carrot (medium/large), chopped*

1 cup Kale (stalk removed), chopped and tightly packed*

¼ cup fresh Italian parsley*

6 cups Water, filtered or spring

*Purchase organic.

Instructions

1. In a large pot, add the water and all the veggie ingredients.
2. Bring to a boil.
3. Once it reaches a boil, reduce the heat to medium-low, cover and simmer for at least 1 hour. The longer you cook this broth, the deeper the flavor and more imbued with nutrients it will become.
4. Let the broth cool for 10-15 minutes.
5. Strain into another pot.
6. Divide the strained broth into heat-safe glass containers/jars and let cool completely.

Seal and store in the refrigerator for up to four days or freeze in freezer-safe containers for up to three months.

Nutritional Facts (per 1 cup)

Calories: 15

Total fat: 0 g

Protein: 1 g

Recommended Daily Feeding Amount

Tiny Dog (Less than 10 lbs)	Small Dog (10 to 30 lbs)	Medium Dog (31 to 54 lbs)	Large Dog (55 to 99 lbs)	Giant Dog (100 lbs +)
1/8 cup	1/3 cup	¾ cup	1 cup	1 1/2 cups

Mushroom Medley Gravy

This mushroom gravy is packed with umami *and* cancer-fighting compounds. You can fully blend it to create a delicious silken texture (especially good if your dog has an upset stomach) or leave some mushroom pieces for added chewiness. It works great as a delicious topper for your dog's regular meals, or as a nutrient-dense snack. Whichever way you choose to serve this Mushroom Medley Gravy, your dog is sure to love it—and he'll never even know it's healthy for him!

Prep time: 35 minutes

Yield: About 2 ½ cups (once reduced and thickened)

Ingredients*

350 g (12 1/3 oz) mixed White, shiitake and cremini mushrooms, sliced (117 g or 4 1/8 ounces of each or any desired combination) (or substitute with any cultivated dog-friendly mushroom or blend)

2 cups Water, filtered or spring (substitute with Cancer-Kicking Broth for added nutrition and flavor)

1 cup Soy milk (Soy milk makes the thickest and creamiest sauce.)**

2 TB Arrowroot powder

*Feel free to include some nutritious dog-friendly mix-ins to this gravy, such as coconut aminos, nutritional yeast or fresh parsley.

**Purchase organic. Be sure your plant milk is free of sweeteners, thickeners, oils, fillers or other additives.

Instructions
1. Add the mushrooms and water (or Cancer-Kicking Broth) to a medium-sized pot. Bring to a gentle boil.
2. Reduce the heat and simmer, uncovered, for 15 minutes.
3. In a cup or small bowl, mix 1/4 cup of the cold soy milk with the arrowroot powder until well combined. Add the mixture along with the other 3/4 cup soy milk to the pot.
4. Simmer uncovered until the sauce has thickened, stirring frequently to prevent burning.
5. Once the sauce has thickened, use an immersion blender to blend the mixture to the desired consistency. If you don't have an immersion blender, you can puree the mixture in a countertop blender. However, let the gravy cool first as otherwise the heat can cause it to expand, blowing the top off the blender and creating both a mess and a burn hazard.
6. Let cool to room temperature prior to serving to your canine companion.

Store in a sealed container in the fridge for up to four days.

Nutritional Facts (per full recipe)

    Calories: 250

    Total fat: 6 g

    Protein: 17 g

Recommended Daily Feeding Amount

Tiny Dog (Less than 10 lbs)	Small Dog (10 to 30 lbs)	Medium Dog (31 to 54 lbs)	Large Dog (55 to 99 lbs)	Giant Dog (100 lbs +)
1/8 cup	1/3 cup	3/4 cup	1 cup	1 1/2 cups

Super Seaweed Salad

We've sung the praises of seaweeds, especially wakame and nori, throughout the book, so what more is there to say? Well, maybe a bit more! As a reminder, these magnificent macroalgae boast a wide variety of health benefits, including anti-fungal, anti-inflammatory, anti-viral, anti-bacterial, anti-allergic, antioxidant, anti-pruritic, neuroprotective, hepatoprotective and immunomodulatory. They're also packed with protein and offer prebiotics to feed the good bacteria in your dog's gut. And research continues to reveal that seaweeds possess amazing anti-cancer benefits. Oh, and did we mention that seaweeds also offer that elusive umami flavor? So, what are you waiting for? Treat your dog (and yourself) to this tasty and nutrient-packed Super Seaweed Salad today.

Prep time: 20 mins

Yield: 2 ½ Cups

Ingredients

> 1/4 cup dried Wakame seaweed, rehydrated (equal to 1 cup fresh), chopped*
>
> 2 sheets toasted Nori seaweed, cut into small pieces*
>
> 1 medium Carrot, diced*
>
> 1/3 English cucumber, with skin, diced*
>
> 2 tsp Sesame oil
>
> 1 tsp Apple cider vinegar (we like Bragg)
>
> 1/8 tsp powdered Ginger

*Purchase organic. See Chapter 8 for our seaweed purchasing tips.

Instructions

1. Place dried wakame in a bowl and pour in enough water to cover the wakame by at least 1/2 inch. Let soak for 10 minutes to reconstitute. While the wakame is soaking, prepare the rest of the recipe.

2. Using kitchen shears, cut the nori into thin strips. Stack the strips and cut them again into small pieces (about 3/4-inch square or smaller for small dogs).

3. Dice the cucumber into small pieces. If you have a smaller dog, create smaller sized pieces.

4. Peel the carrot and dice it into small pieces. Again, adjust the size of your dice based on your dog.

5. When the wakame is rehydrated, drain and squeeze out as much water as possible. Then, chop it into bite-sized pieces.

6. Combine the wakame, nori, cucumber and carrot in a medium-sized bowl. Set aside.

7. Whisk together the sesame oil, apple cider vinegar and ginger powder. Pour the mixture into the bowl with the wakame, nori, carrot and cucumber.

8. Gently stir the ingredients until they are well combined and everything is coated with the liquid.

9. Place in the refrigerator for at least one hour to allow the flavors to meld together.

Store for up to four days in a covered container in the refrigerator.

Important Note

The seaweed makes this recipe chewy, so we don't recommend feeding it to dogs with missing teeth, weak teeth or other dental issues. For small dogs, we recommend processing the completed recipe in a food processor to further break down the pieces and create more of a 'seaweed stew.'

Nutritional Facts (per full 2 ½ cup recipe)

Calories: 130

Total fat: 9 g

Protein: 4 g

Recommended Daily Feeding Amount

Tiny Dog (Less than 10 lbs)	Small Dog (10 to 30 lbs)	Medium Dog (31 to 54 lbs)	Large Dog (55 to 99 lbs)	Giant Dog (100 lbs +)
1/8 cup	1/4 cup	1/2 cup	3/4 cup	1 cup

Prebiotic Potato Salad

Potato salad for dogs? You bet! But this isn't just any potato salad. This potato salad is packed with gut-friendly cold potatoes which, as you'll recall, serve as prebiotics for the good bacteria in the colon. What you won't find: oily, fattening, unhealthy mayonnaise. This potato salad gets its rich taste and creamy texture courtesy of protein-rich, low-fat white beans. Add in some cashew milk, nutritional yeast and chopped herbs, and you've got a winning combination your dog and his gut will love. This potato salad makes a great topper or side along with your dog's main meal, or as a light midday snack.

Prep time: 30 minutes (plus extra time to cool the potatoes before adding the 'mayonnaise')

Yield: About 3 Cups

Ingredients

370 g / 13 oz Yellow potatoes (about 3 medium)*

2/3 cup cooked Great Northern beans (use boiled or low/no-sodium canned, drained and rinsed)*

2 TB Cashew milk (or substitute soy, oat or almond milk), plus additional to achieve desired consistency (if needed)*

2 tsp Nutritional yeast

1 TB Dill, chopped*

1 TB fresh Italian parsley, chopped*

*Purchase organic. Be sure your plant milk is free of sweeteners, thickeners, oils, fillers or other additives.

Instructions

1. Wash the potatoes, then add them to a large pot and cover with water by about 1 1/2 inches. Bring the water to a boil, then reduce and simmer for about 20 minutes or until the potatoes are fork tender. Be careful not to overcook or you will get "mashed potato salad"!

2. When the potatoes are almost done cooking, prepare an ice water bath by adding cold water and ice to a medium-sized bowl.

3. Once the potatoes are fork-tender, immediately drain and transfer them to the ice water bath to prevent them from overcooking.

4. When the potatoes have cooled in the ice water bath, drain them and pat dry. Dice into dog bite-sized cubes. The size of the cubes will depend upon your dog's mouth size. (Note that you don't need to peel the potatoes, since the skin of yellow potatoes is very thin.)

5. Put the potato cubes in a medium bowl and place in the refrigerator to cool completely.

6. While the potatoes are cooling, make your white bean "mayonnaise." In a food processor or high-speed blender, add the beans, nutritional yeast and cashew milk. Process until smooth and creamy. Add a few additional drops of the plant-based milk if necessary to achieve the desired consistency.

7. Pour the white bean mixture into the bowl with the potatoes. Make sure the potatoes are completely cooled before adding the sauce (at least 30 minutes in the refrigerator).

8. Add chopped dill and parsley and stir gently until well combined.

9. Return the potato salad to the refrigerator for at least one hour to allow the flavors to meld.

Store in a covered bowl in the fridge for up to three days.

Nutrition Facts (per 1 cup)
 Calories: 160
 Fat: 0 g
 Protein: 6 g

Recommended Daily Feeding Amount

Tiny Dog (Less than 10 lbs)	Small Dog (10 to 30 lbs)	Medium Dog (31 to 54 lbs)	Large Dog (55 to 99 lbs)	Giant Dog (100 lbs +)
1/8 cup	1/4 cup	1/2 cup	3/4 cup	1 cup

Carob Protein Pancakes

Who doesn't love pancakes as an indulgent breakfast? But, let's face it, as delicious as they are, pancakes aren't typically considered healthy—until now, that is! We've taken the famous flapjack and reimagined it as a healthy breakfast or anytime snack for your canine (and human) companions. And if you're into Paleo, you'll love the use of cassava and almond flours in place of wheat flour. The pea protein gives these pancakes an extra protein boost, while the carob powder provides a dog-friendly stand-in for chocolate, adding to the delicious richness. Feel free to incorporate healthy mix-ins as well, such as blueberries or sliced banana. Then cook up a batch of these Carob Protein Pancakes and get ready for some major tail wagging!

Prep time: 45 to 50 minutes (includes 15 minutes batter resting time)

Yield: 10 to 12 pancakes (depending on how generous you are with your measurements)

Ingredients*

1 cup Cassava flour

1/4 cup Almond flour

1/4 cup Carob powder

2 scoops Pea protein, unflavored (See Resources for NorCal brand used.)

2 TB Flaxseeds (ground)

1 TB Coconut sugar

2 tsp Baking powder (non-aluminum)

1 1/2 cups Almond milk, plain, unsweetened (or substitute soy, oat or cashew milk)*

2 TB Cashew or almond butter, plain, unsweetened*

*All ingredients are best purchased organic. Be sure your plant milk and nut butter are free of sweeteners, thickeners, oils, fillers or other additives.

Instructions

1. In a medium-sized bowl, mix together the dry ingredients (cassava flour, almond flour, carob powder, pea protein, flaxseed, coconut sugar and baking powder).

2. Add the almond milk and cashew butter to the same bowl. Mix just until combined and no lumps remain.

3. Set aside for 15 minutes to allow the flaxseed to gel. Stir again before using.

4. Preheat a non-stick pan over medium heat. If you don't have a good non-stick pan, you can add a drop of neutral dog-friendly oil, such as coconut oil. Just bear in mind that this will increase the fat and Calories per pancake.

5. Pour 2 TB portions of batter into the pan, arranging them so that they don't blend together as they spread.

6. Cook until bubbles appear on the surface of the batter and the edges are cooked. Flip and cook for another 1-2 minutes on the other side.

7. Repeat the process with the rest of the pancake batter.

8. Let cool to a dog-friendly temperature prior to serving.

Store extra batter in a sealed container in the refrigerator for up to two days.

Nutrition Facts (Per pancake, based on 10 pancakes)
  Calories: 120
  Fat: 4.5 g
  Protein: 4 g

Recommended Daily Feeding Amount

Tiny Dog (Less than 10 lbs)	Small Dog (10 to 30 lbs)	Medium Dog (31 to 54 lbs)	Large Dog (55 to 99 lbs)	Giant Dog (100 lbs +)
1/8 pancake	1/3 pancake	1/2 pancake	1 pancake	1 ½ pancakes

Sweet Potato and Hemp 'Cheese' Enchiladas

This is the most time-consuming recipe of the bunch, so we recommend making a 'date' to share them with your dog! We love enchiladas, especially when they're plant-based, gluten-free and dog-approved. For this version, we combined antioxidant-packed sweet potatoes, black beans, spinach and red bell peppers all rolled up inside a gluten-free tortilla and topped with a creamy hemp cheese and sweet red pepper enchilada sauce. These enchiladas are so decadent that we recommend serving them as a meal. Add VegeDog to your dog's portion (after cooling) to boost the nutrient profile and watch your dog have a fiesta!

Note: To reduce the fat in this recipe, eliminate the hemp cheese topping. We're sure your dog will still love it! For your convenience, we've provided the Nutrition Facts both with and without the hemp cheese.

Total time: 1 hour, 20 mins

Yield: 12 enchiladas (See note below under Other.)

Ingredients for the filling

460 g / 1 lb (2 medium) Sweet potatoes, peeled and diced*

142 g / 5 oz Spinach, fresh, chopped*

1 can Black beans (425 g / 15 oz), low sodium or no sodium, drained and rinsed*

1 medium Red bell pepper, seeded and diced*

1/4 cup Water (or substitute with Cancer-Kicking Broth for added nutrition and flavor)

Ingredients for the sweet red pepper sauce

4 medium Red bell peppers, roasted*

1/3 cup Water (or Cancer-Kicking Broth)

1 tsp Nutritional yeast

1 tsp Apple cider vinegar

Ingredients for the hemp cheese

½ cup Hemp hearts

1 cup Water

4 TB Tapioca flour*

1 TB Nutritional yeast

1 tsp Apple cider vinegar

*Purchase organic.

Other

12 Gluten-free tortillas (We used Siete cassava flour tortillas, 25 g each.)
VegeDog or comparable product (amount per the manufacturer's instructions)

Instructions

1. First, roast the red bell peppers. Line a rimmed baking sheet with foil. Slice the peppers in half lengthwise and remove the stems, seeds and membranes. (Note: Removing the seeds *before* roasting the peppers is much easier than doing it afterwards, when those little guys like to cling on!) Place the peppers cut side down on the lined baking sheet.

2. Turn your oven's broiler to the high setting. Place the baking sheet on a rack in the upper third of the oven and roast until the skin is scorched, black and blistered all around. Be careful not to put the rack too close to the broiler, or the peppers will scorch before they have time to fully cook and soften.

3. Once the peppers are done, remove them from the oven and let cool until you can safely handle them. Rub the skins off with your fingers. (They should come off easily.) We like to run the peppers under cold water while we remove the skins to help wash away the debris. This also enables us to handle them with less cooling time. Once all the skin is removed, lightly blot the peppers with a clean paper towel to remove excess water.

4. Dice three of the peppers and set aside in a small bowl. Dice the fourth pepper and set aside in a separate small bowl.

5. Next, make the enchilada filling. In a medium pan, add water (or broth), diced sweet potatoes and diced red pepper. Cover and cook for about 10 minutes, stirring occasionally. Monitor the water level throughout and add a little extra if needed to prevent the veggies from sticking to the pan and burning. When the potatoes are soft, add the black beans and spinach and cook until the spinach has wilted, about three minutes. Remove pan from heat and set aside.

6. Now, make the red pepper sauce. In a high-powered blender, add the three diced roasted peppers, nutritional yeast, water (or broth) and apple cider vinegar. Blend until well combined and creamy. Add the fourth diced roasted red pepper pieces to the sauce and mix to combine.

7. Assemble and bake the enchiladas. Preheat the oven to 350 F / 177 C. Set up a prep area where you can lay out the tortillas and fill each one with the prepared filling mixture. Place a 9-inch by 13-inch baking dish next to your prep area. Spread half of the roasted red pepper sauce into the bottom of the baking dish. One-by-one, lay out a tortilla and spread 1/12 (one-twelfth) of the enchilada filling in a line down the center. Roll up and place into your baking dish. Once all 12 enchiladas are placed into the baking dish, spread the remaining roasted red pepper sauce over the enchiladas. Bake, uncovered, for 10 minutes or until the edges of the tortillas are golden.

8. While the enchiladas are baking, prepare the hemp cheese. Add the hemp hearts, tapioca flour, nutritional yeast, apple cider vinegar and water into a blender and process until well combined. Transfer the mixture to a medium pot and cook for about five minutes over medium-high heat, stirring constantly. The cheese will start forming clumps. Keep stirring vigorously until the clumps become smooth and the mixture turns into a thick and melty cheese sauce.

9. Remove the enchiladas from the oven, spread the hemp cheese sauce over them and return them to the oven, uncovered, for another five to 10 minutes.

10. Allow the enchiladas to cool to a dog-friendly temperature. Sprinkle the Vege-Dog (or comparable product) on top of the hemp cheese prior to serving.

Nutrition Facts (per enchilada *with* hemp cheese)

Calories: 190

Fat: 4.5 g

Protein: 6 g

Nutrition Facts (per enchilada without hemp cheese)

Calories: 150

Fat: 2 g

Protein: 4 g

Recommended Daily Feeding Amount*

Tiny Dog (Less than 10 lbs)	Small Dog (10 to 30 lbs)	Medium Dog (31 to 54 lbs)	Large Dog (55 to 99 lbs)	Giant Dog (100 lbs +)
1 1/8 to 1 ½ enchiladas	1 ¾ to 3 ¾ enchiladas	4 to 6 ½ enchiladas	6 ¾ to 11 ½ enchiladas	12 enchiladas

*When fed as the day's meal *with* the hemp cheese.

Crustless Canine Mini Quiches

When your dog bites into one of these light and fluffy Crustless Canine Mini Quiches, he'll think he's dining in a Parisian bistro! Best of all, these delicious quiches are quick and easy to prepare. All you need are six ingredients and a blender to make the batter. We used broccoli florets in ours, but feel free to mix it up with your (and your dog's) favorite dog-friendly veggies, such as cremini mushrooms, cauliflower or spinach. Serve them to your canine companion, and don't be surprised if he says, "More, *s'il vous plait!*"

Prep time: 45 mins

Yield: 12 mini quiches (prepared in a 24-cavity mini-muffin pan)

Ingredients

300 g (10 ½ oz) Silken tofu, drained and patted as dry as possible*

2 TB Nutritional yeast

2 TB Tapioca flour*

2 TB Cashew butter, plain, unsweetened (or substitute almond butter)*

4 TB Cashew milk (or substitute soy, oat or almond milk)*

145 g (5 oz) fresh Broccoli florets, chopped very small

*Purchase organic. Be sure your plant milk is free of sweeteners, thickeners, oils, fillers or other additives.

Instructions

1. Preheat oven to 375 F / 190 C. Spray 12 cavities of a 24-cavity mini-muffin pan with olive oil and set aside.

2. In a food processor, add the silken tofu, nutritional yeast, tapioca flour, cashew butter and cashew milk. Blend until well combined and creamy.

3. Transfer the mixture to a medium-sized bowl and add the chopped broccoli florets. Combine the ingredients until the broccoli is well covered with the tofu mixture.

4. Divide the mixture evenly between 12 mini-muffin cavities (note that you'll only be using half of the cavities in the pan), filling each cavity to the top.

5. Bake for 25 to 35 minutes** or until a toothpick inserted in the middle comes out clean and the tops of the quiches are golden. Be sure the quiches are completely set inside (not jiggly) before removing them from the oven.

6. Place the muffin pan on a wire rack to allow the quiches to cool and further set before removing from pan.

7. Cool to room temperature prior to serving to your canine companion.

Store the quiches in a sealed container in the refrigerator for up to four days.

**The cooking time for these mini quiches can vary significantly based on hydration factors of the ingredients (e.g., wetness of the tofu, creaminess of the nut butter and thickness of the plant milk). We recommend checking for doneness at 25 minutes, then continuing cooking and checking frequently until they are well set (via the 'toothpick test') and golden brown in color.

Nutrition Facts (per quiche)

    Calories: 40

    Total fat: 2 g

    Protein: 3 g

Recommended Daily Feeding Amount

Tiny Dog (Less than 10 lbs)	Small Dog (10 to 30 lbs)	Medium Dog (31 to 54 lbs)	Large Dog (55 to 99 lbs)	Giant Dog (100 lbs +)
1/2 quiche	1 quiche	1 ½ quiches	2 ½ quiches	4 quiches

PB & Chickpea Blondies

A scrumptious treat made from healthy, protein-rich chickpeas? Now, that's something to wag your tail about! We went all out with the addition of peanut butter to these treats, but feel free to substitute cashew, almond or even pumpkin seed butter. These blondies taste extravagant, but because they're made with a chickpea and oat base, they're also healthy. And while they do contain wholesome maple syrup and coconut sugar, you'll notice that these PB & Chickpea Blondies are not as sweet as the 'made for humans' versions. We'd rather let the natural peanut butter flavor shine through, and we think your dog will agree. You might even find that your own tastebuds prefer the subtlety. Share this satisfying snack with your canine companion and you'll both be licking your chops!

Prep Time: 30 to 35 mins

Yield: 16 Pieces (2" x 2")

Ingredients

480 g cooked Chickpeas (equal to about two 439 g / 15.5 oz cans, drained and rinsed)*

1/2 cup Rolled oats (certified gluten-free)*

1/2 cup Maple syrup

1/4 cup creamy Peanut butter, plain, unsweetened (or sub almond, cashew or pumpkin seed butter)*

2 TB Coconut sugar*

1 tsp Baking powder (non-aluminum)

*Purchase organic. Be sure your nut butter is free of sweeteners, thickeners, oils, fillers or other additives.

Instructions

1. Preheat oven to 350 F / 177 C. Line a square 8" x 8" brownie pan with parchment paper and set aside.

2. In a food processor, add the oats, coconut sugar and baking powder and process until well combined and the mixture turns into flour.

3. Add the remaining ingredients and process until a smooth batter forms.

4. Transfer the batter into the lined baking pan. Smooth the batter evenly into the pan with the back of a large spoon.

5. Bake for 20 to 25 minutes, or until a toothpick inserted into the center comes out clean.

6. Allow them to cool completely (at least one hour) before slicing to prevent them from falling apart.

Store in the refrigerator to promote a firmer texture.

Nutrition Facts (per 2" square)

Calories: 120

Total fat: 3 g

Protein: 4 g

Recommended Daily Feeding Amount

Tiny Dog (Less than 10 lbs)	Small Dog (10 to 30 lbs)	Medium Dog (31 to 54 lbs)	Large Dog (55 to 99 lbs)	Giant Dog (100 lbs +)
1/8 blondie	1/3 blondie	1/2 blondie	3/4 blondie	1 blondie

Resources

We hope that you find the following Resources helpful. We have done our best to compile a comprehensive guide for you; however, this list certainly is not exhaustive. If we missed a business or product that you are aware of, we apologize. Please note that while we have used many of the items listed, we have not tried them all. Also, be aware that manufacturers may change product formulations, so always stay up-to-date regarding the ingredient compositions and levels in any products you purchase, understanding that you may need to discontinue the use of a product in some cases (such as the addition of an extract or essential oil that is not suitable for dogs). When introducing a new food or supplement, always start off slowly and monitor your dog for any potential adverse reactions before increasing the amount given.

For those of you reading this book on a digital device, your results when clicking on the links provided to the cited article may vary due to the computer and software you use and how well the website is maintained and updated. For these reasons, some links may not take you to the desired destination. Going directly to the website and using the search function provided to find the article in question may be an effective alternative.

Films & Documentaries

73 Cows: https://vimeo.com/293352305

A Prayer for Compassion: https://aprayerforcompassion.com/

Blackfish: https://itunes.apple.com/us/movie/blackfish/id727472242

Called to Rescue: https://www.youtube.com/watch?v=wGT8ott4dTo

Cowspiracy: https://www.netflix.com/title/80033772

Deadly Dairy: https://animalequality.in/india-deadly-dairy/

Dominion: https://www.dominionmovement.com/watch

Earthlings: https://www.filmsforaction.org/watch/earthlings/

Eating Animals: https://www.amazon.com/Eating-Animals-Natalie-Portman/dp/B07JKCSJ3K

Empathy: https://vimeo.com/ondemand/empathy

Food, Inc.:
https://www.amazon.com/Food-Inc-Michael-Pollan/dp/B002UZ5CHO

Forks Over Knives: https://www.forksoverknives.com/the-film/

H.O.P.E. What You Eat Matters: https://www.hope-theproject.com/the-film/the-film/

Lucent: https://www.farmtransparency.org/videos?id=7Teq4Icbec

Maximum Tolerated Dose: https://maximumtolerateddose.vhx.tv/

Meet Your Meat: https://www.peta.org/videos/meet-your-meat/

Racing Extinction:
ttps://www.amazon.com/Racing-Extinction-Louie-Psihoyos/dp/B0184RE1TG

Test Subjects: https://vimeo.com/359497969

The Animals Film: http://www.theanimalsfilm.com/

The Cove: https://www.opsociety.org/our-work/films/the-cove/

The End of Meat:
https://www.amazon.com/End-Meat-Steve-Jenkins/dp/B07G4S78T3

The Game Changers: https://gamechangersmovie.com/the-film/where-to-watch/

The Ghosts in Our Machine:
https://itunes.apple.com/us/movie/the-ghosts-in-our-machine/id1563821316

The Last Pig: https://www.thelastpig.com/

Watson: https://www.fubo.tv/welcome/series/119976934/watson

What the Health:
https://www.netflix.com/title/80174177?trkid=13747225&s=i&vlang=en&clip=81030320

Vegan Dog Nutritionist
Diana Laverdure-Dunetz, MS: https://www.plantpowereddog.com/

Commercial Vegan Dog Food + Treats
Ami: https://vecado.ca/collections/ami

Because Animals (organic treats): https://becauseanimals.com/

Benevo (organic options; puppy food): http://www.benevo.com/

Bond Pet Foods (treat bar): https://www.bondpets.com/

Bramble (partially organic): https://bramblepets.com/

Canidae Sustain: https://canidae.com/sustain-dry-dog-food-planet-friendly-plant-based-brewers-yeast-recipe/

Front Porch Pets (treats; only certain types are plant-based, including Sam's Yams): https://www.frontporchpets.com/all-products

Evolution (organic options; 'all life stages' food): https://petfoodshop.com/

Fruitables (treats; only certain types are plant-based): https://www.feedpetaluma.com/

Halo Holistic Garden of Vegan: https://halopets.com/search?q=vegan

Just Be Kind: https://vegan-dogfood.co.uk/

K9 Granola Factory (treats; only certain types are plant-based): https://www.k9granolafactory.com/

Natural Balance Vegetarian: https://www.naturalbalanceinc.com/dog-formulas/vegetarian

Omni: https://omni.pet/

Petaluma (50% organic): https://www.feedpetaluma.com/

Petcurean Gather Endless Valley (organic): https://www.petcurean.com/product/endless-valley-recipe-adult-dogs/

PetGuard (organic option): https://www.ecodogsandcats.com/organic-vegetarian-entree-vegan-2/

V-Dog: https://v-dog.com/

Vegan4Dogs: https://vegan4dogs.com/

VegDog: https://www.vegdog.de/

VGRRR: https://vgrrr.com/

Wild Earth: https://wildearth.com/

Wysong Vegan: https://www.wysong.net/vegan

Vegan Dog Food & Supplement Retailers Online

Aistra (Mumbai): https://myaistra.com/

Compassion Circle (US): https://compassioncircle.com/

Eco Dogs and Cats (US): https://www.ecodogsandcats.com/

Ethical Pets (UK): https://www.ethicalpets.co.uk/

Fabulous (Switzerland): https://www.fabulous.ch/veganshop/

Just be Kind (UK): https://vegan-dogfood.co.uk/product/just-be-kind-supplement/

Opal Pets Perfect Powder for Dogs (US): https://opalpets.com/

PlantX (Canada): https://plantx.ca/

Shevega (UK): https://www.shevega.com/

Taffy & Lilly (Slovenia): https://taffylilly.com/

The Vegan Kind Supermarket (Scotland): https://www.thevegankindsupermarket.com/

Vantastic Foods (Bavaria): https://www.vantastic-foods.com/

Vecado (Canada): https://vecado.ca/

Vegan4Dogs (Germany): https://vegan4dogs.com/

Vegan Essentials (US): https://veganessentials.com/

Veganpets (Netherlands): https://www.veganpets.nl/

VegaVriend (Netherlands): https://vegavriend.nl/en/

VegDog (Germany): https://www.vegdog.de/

VeggiePets (UK): https://www.veggiepets.com/

VFoods (South Africa): https://vfoods.co.za/

VGRRR (Canada): https://vgrrr.com/

VPets (Australia): https://www.vpets.com.au/

'Human' Foods for Dogs

Apple Cider Vinegar
Bragg: https://www.bragg.com/

Black Raspberry Powder
BerriHealth: https://www.berrihealth.com/

Sunset Valley Organics: https://www.sunsetvalleyorganics.com/

Broccoli Sprout Powder
BroccoBoost (Diana's product):
https://plantpowereddog.thrivecart.com/broccoboost/

Edible Seaweed
Eden Foods: https://store.edenfoods.com/

Main Coast: https://seaveg.com/

Heirloom Bean Purveyors

Native Seeds/SEARCH (Southwestern Endangered Aridlands Resource Clearing House) : https://www.nativeseeds.org/

Purcell Mountain Farms: https://purcellmountainfarms.com/

Rancho Gordo: https://www.ranchogordo.com/

Seed Savers Exchange: https://www.seedsavers.org/

Nutritional Yeast

Bob's Red Mill: https://www.bobsredmill.com/nutritional-yeast.html

Bragg: https://www.bragg.com/products/nutritional-yeast

KAL: https://www.kalvitamins.com/products/nutritional-yeast-flakes-1

Red Star: https://redstarnutritionalyeast.com/

Protein Powder

NorCal Organic Hemp Protein (Canada sourced): https://norcal-organic.com/

NorCal Organic Pea Protein (Canada sourced): https://norcal-organic.com/

Psyllium Husk Powder

Anthony's (organic): https://anthonysgoods.com/

NOW Foods (organic): https://www.nowfoods.com/products/supplements/psyllium-husk-powder-organic

Salba Chia Seeds

https://salbasmart.com/

Soy Milk

EdenSoy (organic unsweetened plain): https://store.edenfoods.com/unsweetened-edensoy-organic/

WestSoy (organic unsweetened plain): https://www.westsoymilk.com/products/%20organic-unsweetened/organic-unsweetened-plain

Spirulina

Nutrex Hawaii, Pure Hawaiian Spirulina Powder: https://www.nutrex-hawaii.com/

Sprouting Seeds and Kits

Sproutman: https://sproutman.com/

Textured Vegetable Protein (TVP)/Textured Soy Protein

Bob's Red Mill TVP: https://www.bobsredmill.com/

Now Foods, Organic Textured Soy Protein, Granules:
https://www.nowfoods.com/products/natural-foods/textured-vegetable-protein-crumbles-organic

Anthony's Organic Textured Vegetable Protein:
https://anthonysgoods.com/products/organic-tvp-gluten-free-vegan

Canine Supplements

Brewer's Yeast
VegeYeast (Compassion Circle): https://compassioncircle.com/product/vegeyeast-1-lb/

Buffered Vitamin C
Rx Vitamins for Pets Bio-C (buffered Vitamin C as sodium ascorbate) (Not recommended for dogs on a low-sodium diet):
https://www.rxvitamins.com/rxvitaminsforpet/product-category/urinary-tract-health-products/

Cranberry Extract (organic)
Cranimals:
https://compassioncircle.com/product/cranimals-original-urinary-tract-supplement/

Digestive Support
Animal Essentials Plant Enzyme & Probiotics:
https://animalessentials.com/plant-enzyme-w-probiotics-3-5-oz-100-gm/

Wild Earth Immunity & Digestion Dog Supplements:
https://wildearth.com/products/immunity-and-digestion-dog-supplements

Mannan oligosaccharides (MOS)
Bio-MOS by Alltech: https://www.alltech.com/bio-mos

Multi-Vitamin/Mineral Products
Just be Kind (UK): https://vegan-dogfood.co.uk/product/just-be-kind-supplement/

Opal Pets Perfect Powder for Dogs (US): https://opalpets.com/

Shevega (UK): https://www.shevega.com/

V-Complete (Germany): https://vegan4dogs.com/

VegDog All-In Veluxe (Germany):
https://taffylilly.com/vegdog-all-in-veluxe-mineral-powder

VegeDog by Compassion Circle (US): https://compassioncircle.com/

Nigella Sativa (Black Seed Oil)
Doggysupps (Nigella Sativa/black seed oil):
https://doggysupps.com/products/black-cumin-oil

Polysaccharopeptide (PSP) Complex
I'm Yunity: http://www.imyunityfordogs.com/

'Human' Dog-Safe Supplements

B-Complex
Thorne Research B-Complex #12:
https://www.thorne.com/products/dp/b-complex-12

Buffered Vitamin C
Klaire Labs Ester-C:
https://www.pureformulas.com/ester-c-100-vegetarian-capsules-by-klaire-labs.html

L-Carnitine
Now Foods, L-Carnitine (500 mg/capsule):
https://www.nowfoods.com/products/supplements/l-carnitine-500-mg-veg-capsules

Now Foods, L-Carnitine, Pure Powder (1/4 level tsp = 635 mg L-carnitine):
https://www.nowfoods.com/products/supplements/l-carnitine-pure-powder

Nigella Sativa (Black Seed Oil)
Maju Superfoods (Nigella Sativa/black seed oil):
https://majusuperfoods.com/collections/black-seed-oil/products/black-seed-oil-cold-pressed-maju

The Blessed Seed (Nigella Sativa/black seed oil):
https://theblessedseed.com/shop/%20mild-black-seed-oil-100ml-bottle/

Omega-3 Fatty Acids (EPA + DHA)
Cytoplan Vegan Omega-3 Liquid (UK):
https://www.cytoplan.co.uk/shop-by-range/vegan-supplement-support/vegan-omega-3-liquid

Nordic Naturals Algae Omega:
https://www.nordic.com/products/algae-omega/?variant=39472182919352

Sports Research Vegan Omega-3:
https://sportsresearch.com/products/vegan-omega

Zenwise Health Marine-Algae Derived Vegan Omega-3 (rosemary free):
https://zenwise.com/products/vegan-omega-3?variant=32962599485533

Saccharomyces boulardii + MOS
Jarrow Formulas, Saccharomyces Boulardii Plus MOS:
https://jarrow.com/products/saccharomyces-boulardii-mos-5-billion-cfu-delayed-release-veggie-caps

Taurine
Cytoplan Taurine (UK) (500 mg/capsule): https://www.cytoplan.co.uk/l-taurine

NOW Foods Taurine, Pure Powder (1/4 level tsp = 1,000 mg taurine):
https://www.nowfoods.com/products/supplements/taurine-pure-powder

Thorne Research, Taurine (500 mg/capsule):
https://www.thorne.com/products/dp/taurine

Kitchen Tools

Food Processor
Cuisinart® All-In-One Food Processors:
https://www.cuisinart.com/shopping/appliances/food_processors/

Food Scale
Nicewell 22-lb Digital Kitchen Scale:
https://www.amazon.com/Nicewell-Digital-Graduation-Stainless-Tempered/dp/B07S6F6LHQ?th=1

High-Speed Blender
Vitamix®: https://www.vitamix.com/us/en_us/

Multi-Use Pressure Cooker
InstantPot: https://www.instanthome.com/

Plant-Based Milk Maker
Almond Cow: https://almondcow.co/

Laboratory Testing

Cornell University Animal Health Diagnostic Center
Vitamin B12/Folate/TLI:
https://www.vet.cornell.edu/animal-health-diagnostic-center/testing/protocols/metabolic-function

Hemopet
CellBio oxidative stress marker test: https://hemopet.org/cellbio

NutriScan saliva-based food intolerance test: https://hemopet.org/nutriscan

Thyroid panels, CBC, Differential, full Chemistries, titer testing, von Willebrand test:
https://hemopet.org/hemolife/

Michigan State University Veterinary Diagnostic Laboratory
25-Hydroxyvitamin Dx: https://vdl.msu.edu/Bin/Catalog/Catalog.exe

UC Davis Amino Acid Laboratory
Plasma and whole blood taurine:
https://www.vetmed.ucdavis.edu/labs/amino-acid-laboratory

General Resources

Chemicals in Foods, Water and Products Information
Environmental Working Group (EWG): https://www.ewg.org/

FODMAP Information
Monash University: https://www.monashfodmap.com/get-app-help/

Glycemic Index (GI) Information
FoodStruct: https://foodstruct.com/

The University of Sydney: https://www.glycemicindex.com/foodSearch.php

Nutrition Data
MyNetDiary: https://www.mynetdiary.com/foodSearch.do

Self NutritionData: https://nutritiondata.self.com/

PRAL (Potential Renal Acid Load) Information
Comprehensive PRAL Value List:
https://www.clinicaleducation.org/documents/revised-summary-pral-list.pdf

Custom PRAL Calculation Website:
http://www.maxmcarter.com/pral/pral_calc_form.php

State Water Quality Reports
EWG's National Drinking Water Database:
https://www.ewg.org/tapwater/

Veterinary Resources

American Holistic Veterinary Medical Association (AHVMA):
Email: office@ahvma.org or phone 410-569-0795

AHVMA VetFinder: https://www.ahvma.org/find-a-holistic-veterinarian/

Veterinary Association for the Protection of Animals (VAPA):
https://vapavets.org/

Website of Andrew Knight, Veterinary Professor of Animal Welfare, University of Winchester Centre for Animal Welfare, UK: https://sustainablepetfood.info/

Cited Works

For those of you reading this book on a digital device, your results when clicking on the links provided to the cited article may vary due to the computer and software you use and how well the website is maintained and updated. For these reasons, some links may not take you to the desired destination. Going directly to the website and using the search function provided to find the article in question may be an effective alternative.

Part 1: Steps to Raising a Thriving Plant-Based Dog

Introduction

Dodd, S.A.S., Cave, N.J., Adolphe, J.L., Shoveller, A.K. & Verbrugghe, A. (2019). Plant-based (vegan) diets for pets: a survey of pet owner attitudes and feeding practices. *PLoS ONE, 14*(1). https://doi.org/10.1371/journal.pone.0210806

Dodd, S., Khosa, D., Dewey, C. & Verbrugghe, A. (2022). Owner perception of health of North American dogs fed meat- or plant-based diets. *Research in Veterinary Science, 149*, 36–46, https://www.sciencedirect.com/science/article/pii/S0034528822001345

Knight, A. & Satchell, L. (2021). Vegan versus meat-based pet foods: owner-reported palatability behaviours and implications for canine and feline welfare. *PLoS ONE, 16*(6). https://doi.org/10.1371/journal.pone.0253292

Research and Markets. (2021). North America vegan pet food market to 2028 - COVID-19 impact and regional analysis and forecast by product type, pet type, and distribution channel. *Research and Markets.* https://www.researchandmarkets.com/reports/5416152/north-america-vegan-pet-food-market-forecast-to?utm_source=BW&utm_medium=PressRelease&utm_code=qgzgpq&utm_campaign=1637010+-+North+America+Vegan+Pet+Food+Market+2021-2028+%7C+Projected+to+Reach+%246.48+Billion+by+2028+%7C+Product+Innovations+%26+Developments+are+Key+in+this+Highly+Competitive+Space&utm_exec=joca220prd

The Good Food Institute. (2019). 2019 U.S. State of the Industry Report: plant-based meat, eggs, and dairy. *The Good Food Institute.* https://www.gfi.org/files/soti/INN-PBMED-SOTIR-2020-0507.pdf?utm_source=form&utm_medium=email&utm_campaign=SOTIR2019

Chapter 1: A Review of Nutritional Science

Abdulkhaleq, L.A., Assi, M.A., Abdullah, R., Zamri-Saad, M., Taufiq-Yap, Y.H. & Hezmee, M. (2018). The crucial roles of inflammatory mediators in inflammation: a review. *Veterinary World, 11*(5), 627–635. https://doi.org/10.14202/vetworld.2018.627-635

Alessandri, G., Milani, C., Mancabelli, L., Mangifesta, M., Lugli, G.A., Viappiani, A., Duranti, S., Turroni, F., Ossiprandi, M.C., van Sinderen, D. & Ventura, M. (2019). Metagenomic dissection of the canine gut microbiota: insights into taxonomic, metabolic and nutritional features. *Environmental Biology, 21*(4). https://doi.org/10.1111/1462-2920.14540

Animal Equality. (2020). Help us ban wet markets. *Animal Equality.* https://animalequality.org/action/markets

Association for Pet Obesity Prevention. (APOP). (2019). https://petobesityprevention.org/

Banfield Pet Hospital. (2016). State of Pet Health 2016 Report. https://www.banfield.com/banfield/media/pdf/downloads/soph/banfield-state-of-pet-health-report-2016.pdf

Banfield Pet Hospital. (2019). Banfield Pet Hospital's Ninth Annual State of Pet Health Report tackles weighty issue of osteoarthritis [Press release]. https://www.prnewswire.com/news-releases/banfield-pet-hospitals-ninth-annual-state-of-pet-health-report-tackles-weighty-issue-of-osteoarthritis-300871954.html

Bresciani, F., Minamoto, Y., Suchodolski, J.S., Galiazzo, G., Vecchiato, C.G., Pinna, C., Biagi, G. & Pietra, M. (2018). Effect of an extruded animal protein-free diet on fecal microbiota of dogs with food-responsive enteropathy. *Journal of Veterinary Internal Medicine, 32*(36). https://www.ncbi.nlm.nih.gov/pmc/articles/PMC6271313/

Bulsiewicz, W. (2020). *Fiber Fueled: The Plant-Based Gut Health Program for Losing Weight, Restoring Your Health, and Optimizing Your Microbiome.* New York, NY, USA: Avery Publishing

Carrington, D. (2018). Humans just 0.01% of all life but have destroyed 83% of wild mammals – study. *The Guardian.* https://www.theguardian.com/environment/2018/may/21/human-race-just-001-of-all-life-but-has-destroyed-over-80-of-wild-mammals-study

Carrington, D. (2018a). Avoiding meat and dairy is 'single best way' to reduce your impact on Earth. *The Guardian.* https://www.theguardian.com/environment/2018/may/31/avoiding-meat-and-dairy-is-single-biggest-way-to-reduce-your-impact-on-earth

Ceballos, G., Ehrlich, P.R. & Raven, P.H. (2020). Vertebrates on the brink as indicators of biological annihilation and the sixth mass extinction. *Proceedings of the National Academy of Sciences of the United States of America.* https://www.pnas.org/content/117/24/13596.short

Centers for Disease Control and Prevention (CDC). (2018). Facts about cyanobacterial HABs for poison professionals. *Centers for Disease Control and Prevention.* https://www.cdc.gov/habs/materials/factsheet-cyanobacterial-habs.html

Centers for Disease Control and Prevention (CDC). (2020). Chronic diseases in America. *National Center for Chronic Disease Prevention and Health Promotion (NCCDPHP)*. https://www.cdc.gov/chronicdisease/resources/infographic/chronic-diseases.htm

Centers for Disease Control and Prevention (CDC). (2022). What is epigenetics? *Centers for Disease Control and Prevention*. https://www.cdc.gov/genomics/disease/epigenetics.htm#:~:text=Epigenetics%20is%20the%20study%20of,body%20reads%20a%20DNA%20sequence

Dodds, W.J. (2016). Cellular oxidative stress and chronic inflammatory disease results in obesity, infections and cancers, Parts 1 and 2. *Proceedings of the American Holistic Veterinary Medical Association*, 53–57, 58–63

Dodds, W.J. (2017/2018). Diagnosis of canine food sensitivity and intolerance using saliva: report of outcomes. *Journal of the American Holistic Veterinary Medical Association*, 49, 32–43

Dodds, W.J. (2019). Food sensitivity and intolerances associated with diet type in Golden Retrievers: a retrospective study. *Journal of the American Holistic Veterinary Medical Association*, 56(Fall), 52–57

Dodds, W.J. (2019a). Salivary Diagnostics for Managing Cellular Oxidative Stress. *Biomedical Journal of Scientific & Technical Research*, 18(1), 13250-13252

Dodds, W.J. (2020). The microbiome in health & disease [Lecture presentation]

Dodds, W.J. & Callewaert, D.M. (2016). Novel biomarkers of oxidative stress for veterinary medicine, Parts 1 and 2. *Proceedings of the American Holistic Veterinary Medical Association*, 64–70; 71–73

Dodds, W.J. & Laverdure, D.R. (2011). *The Canine Thyroid Epidemic: Answers You Need for Your Dog*. Wenatchee, WA, US: Dogwise Publishing

Dodds, W.J. & Laverdure, D.R. (2015). *Canine Nutrigenomics: The New Science of Feeding Your Dog for Optimum Health*. Wenatchee, WA, US: Dogwise Publishing

FETCH a Cure. (2020). Facts. *FETCH a Cure*. https://fetchacure.org/resource-library/facts/#:~:text=Living%20longer%20lives%20exposes%20our,diagnosed%20with%20cancer%20this%20year

Ferrão-Filho, A.S. & Kozlowsky-Suzuki, B. (2011). Cyanotoxins: bioaccumulation and effects on aquatic animals. *Marine Drugs*. https://doi.org/10.3390/md9122729

Halo, J.V., Pendleton, A.L., Shen, F., Doucet, A.J., Derrien, T., Hitte, C., Kirby, L.E., Myers, B., Sliwerska, E., Emery, S., Moran, J.V., Boyko, A.R. & Kidd, J.M. (2021). Long-read assembly of a Great Dane genome highlights the contribution of GC-rich sequence and mobile elements to canine genomes. *PNAS*, 118(11) e2016274118. https://www.pnas.org/doi/full/10.1073/pnas.2016274118

Harvard Medical School. (2020). Fighting inflammation: how to stop the damage before it compromises your health. *Harvard Health Publishing*. https://www.health. harvard.edu/staying-healthy/understanding-inflammation

InformedHealth.org. (2018). What is an inflammation? *Institute for Quality and Efficiency in Health Care (IQWiG)*. https://www.ncbi.nlm.nih.gov/books/NBK279298/

Kavli Foundation. (2020). About the microbiome. *The Kavli Foundation*. https://www. kavlifoundation.org/about-microbiome

Kim, J., An, J.U., Kim, W., Lee, S. & Cho, S. (2017). Differences in the gut microbiota of dogs *(Canis lupus familiaris)* fed a natural diet or a commercial feed revealed by the Illumina MiSeq platform. Gut pathogens, *9*(68). https://doi.org/10.1186/s13099-017-0218-5

Knight, A., Huang, E., Rai, N. & Brown, H. (2022). Vegan versus meat-based dog food: guardian-reported indicators of health. *PloS ONE, 17*(4), e0265662. https://doi.org/10.1371/journal.pone.0265662

Li, R., Jia, Z. & Trush, M.A. (2016). Defining ROS in Biology and Medicine. *Reactive Oxygen Species* (Apex, N.C.), *1*(1), 9–21. https://doi.org/10.20455/ros.2016.803

Maron, D.F. (2020). 'Wet markets' likely launched the coronavirus. Here's what you need to know. *National Geographic*. https://www.nationalgeographic.com/ animals/2020/04/coronavirus-linked-to-chinese-wet-markets/

McDougall, J. (2010). Parkinson's disease and other diet-induced tremors. *McDougall Newsletter*. https://www.drmcdougall.com/misc/2010nl/nov/parkinsons.htm

Mondo, E., Marliani, G., Accorsi, P.A., Cocchi, M. & Di Leone, A. (2019). Role of gut microbiota in dog and cat's health and diseases. *Open Veterinary Journal, 9*(3), 253–258. https://doi.org/10.4314/ovj.v9i3.10

Montoya-Alonso J.A., Bautista-Castaño, I., Peña, C., Suárez, L., Juste M.C. & Tvarijonaviciute, A. (2017). Prevalence of canine obesity, obesity-related metabolic dysfunction, and relationship with owner obesity in an obesogenic region of Spain. *Frontiers in Veterinary Science*, 4. https://www.frontiersin.org/article/10.3389/ fvets.2017.00059

Mullis, E., van Heel, D., Balkwill, F. & Islam, K. (2022). Genes made easy. *Genes & Health*. http://www.genesandhealth.org/genes-your-health/genes-made-easy

National Human Genome Research Institute (NHGRI). (2012). Epigenomics. *National Institutes of Health (NIH)*. http://www.genome.gov/27532724

National Human Genome Research Institute (NHGRI). (2019). *Introduction to genomics*. *National Institutes of Health (NIH)*. https://www.genome.gov/About-Genomics/ Introduction-to-Genomics

National Research Council (US) Committee on Drug Use in Food Animals. (1999). *The Use of Drugs in Food Animals: Benefits and Risks. Food-Animal Production Practices and Drug Use.* Washington (DC): National Academies Press. https://www.ncbi.nlm.nih.gov/books/NBK232573/

O'Hara, A.M. & Shanahan, F. (2006). The gut flora as a forgotten organ. *EMBO Reports, 7*(7), 688–693. https://www.embopress.org/doi/full/10.1038/sj.embor.7400731

Pahwa, R., Goyal, A. & Jialal, I. (2020). Chronic inflammation. *StatPearls.* https://www.ncbi.nlm.nih.gov/books/NBK493173/

Pilla, R. & Schodolski, J.S. (2020). The role of the canine gut microbiome and metabolome in health and gastrointestinal disease. *Frontiers in Veterinary Science, 6,* 498. https://doi.org/10.3389/fvets.2019.00498

Pitcairn, R.H. & Pitcairn, S.H. (2017). *Dr. Pitcairn's Complete Guide to Natural Health for Dogs & Cats (4th ed.).* Emmaus, PA: Rodale

Poore, J. & Nemecek, T. (2018). Reducing food's environmental impacts through producers and consumers. *Science, 360,* 987–992. https://josephpoore.com/Science%20360%206392%20987%20-%20Accepted%20Manuscript.pdf

Qin, Y. & Wade, P.A. (2018). Crosstalk between the microbiome and epigenome: messages from bugs. *Journal of Biochemistry, 163*(2), 105–112. https://academic.oup.com/jb/article/163/2/105/4638433

Rappaport, S.M. (2016). Genetic factors are not the major causes of chronic diseases. *PLoS ONE, 11*(4), e0154387. https://doi.org/10.1371/journal.pone.0154387

Sanders, B. (2018). Global animal slaughter statistics and charts. *Faunalytics.* https://faunalytics.org/global-animal-slaughter-statistics-and-charts/#:~:text=Worldwide%2C%20more%20than%2070%20billion,EXCLUSIVE&text=Every%20year%2C%20billions%20of%20animals,by%20the%20animal%20agriculture%20industry

Sandri, M., Dal Monego, S., Conte, G., Sgorlon, S. & Stefanon, B. (2017). Raw meat based diet influences faecal microbiome and end products of fermentation in healthy dogs. *BMC Veterinary Research, 13*(1), 65. https://doi.org/10.1186/s12917-017-0981-z

Schmidt, M., Unterer, S., Suchodolski, J.S., Honneffer, J. B., Guard, B. C., Lidbury, J.A., Steiner, J.M., Fritz, J. & Kölle, P. (2018). The fecal microbiome and metabolome differs between dogs fed Bones and Raw Food (BARF) diets and dogs fed commercial diets. *PLoS ONE,* 13(8), e0201279. https://doi.org/10.1371/journal.pone.0201279

Science Learning Hub. (2014). Proteins—what they are and how they're made. *New Zealand Government.* https://www.sciencelearn.org.nz/resources/1901-proteins-what-they-are-and-how-they-re-made

Shryock, T.R. (1999). Relationship between usage of antibiotics in food-producing animals and the appearance of antibiotic resistant bacteria. *International Journal of Antimicrobial Agents, 12*(4), 275–278. https://doi.org/10.1016/s0924-8579(99)00089-8

Simpson, J.M., Martineau, B., Jones, W.E., Ballam, J.M. & Mackie, R.I. (2002). Characterization of fecal bacterial populations in canines: effects of age, breed and dietary fiber. *Microbial Ecology, 44*(2), 186–197

Slow Food. (2020). Covid-19 outbreaks in slaughterhouses reveal dreadful conditions for humans and animals in food production. *Slow Food.* https://www.slowfood.com/covid-19-outbreaks-in-slaughterhouses-reveal-dreadful-conditions-for-humans-and-animals-in-food-production/

The Guardian. (2018). Avoiding meat and dairy is 'single biggest way' to reduce your impact on Earth. *The Guardian.* https://www.theguardian.com/environment/2018/may/31/avoiding-meat-and-dairy-is-single-biggest-way-to-reduce-your-impact-on-earth

Vegan Calculator. (2018). https://vegancalculator.com/

Wernimont, S.M., Radosevich, J., Jackson, M.I., Ephraim, E., Badri, D.V., MacLeay, J.M., Jewell, D.E. & Suchodolski, J.S. (2020). The effects of nutrition on the gastrointestinal microbiome of cats and dogs: impact on health and disease. *Frontiers in Microbiology,* 11, 1266. https://doi.org/10.3389/fmicb.2020.01266

World Health Organization (WHO). (2020). Nutrition health topics. *World Health Organization.* https://www.who.int/teams/nutrition-and-food-safety

Worldometer. (2022). Coronavirus death toll. https://www.worldometers.info/coronavirus/coronavirus-death-toll/

Zampa, M. (2018). How many animals are killed for food every day? *Sentient Media.* https://sentientmedia.org/how-many-animals-are-killed-for-food-every-day/#:~:text=Anywhere%20between%2037%20and%20120,and%20killed%20in%20the%20wild

Zimmer, C. (2021). Scientists finish the human genome at last. *The New York Times.* https://www.nytimes.com/2021/07/23/science/human-genome-complete.html

Chapter 2: The Facts About Plant-Based Diets

Alessandri, G., Milani, C., Mancabelli, L., Mangifesta, M., Lugli, G.A., Viappiani, A., Duranti, S., Turroni, F., Ossiprandi, M.C., van Sindeen, D. & Ventura, M. (2019). Metagenomic dissection of the canine gut microbiota: insights into taxonomic, metabolic and nutritional features. *Environmental Biology, 21*(4). https://doi.org/10.1111/1462-2920.14540

American Veterinary Medical Association (AVMA). (2019). U.S. pet ownership statistics. *American Veterinary Medical Association.* https://www.avma.org/resources-tools/reports-statistics/us-pet-ownership-statistics

Anderson, J.W. & Major, A.W. (2002). Pulses and lipaemia, short- and long-term effect: potential in the prevention of cardiovascular disease. *British Journal of Nutrition,* 88(Suppl 3). https://pubmed.ncbi.nlm.nih.gov/12498626/

Arendt, M., Fall, T., Lindblad-Toh, K. & Axelsson, E. (2014). Amylase activity is associated with AMY2B copy numbers in dog: implications for dog domestication, diet and diabetes. *Animal Genetics*. https://onlinelibrary.wiley.com/doi/pdf/10.1111/age.12179

Aune, D., De Stefani, E., Ronco, A., Boffetta, P., Deneo-Pellegrini, H., Acosta, G. & Mendilaharsu, M. (2009). Legume intake and the risk of cancer: a multisite case-control study in Uruguay. *Cancer Causes Control, 20*(9). https://link.springer.com/article/10.1007/s10552-009-9406-z

Axelsson, E., Ratnakumar, A., Arendt, M.L., Maqbool, K., Webster, M.T., Perloski, M., Liberg, O., Arnemo, J.M., Hedhammar, A. & Lindblad-Toh, K. (2013). The genomic signature of dog domestication reveals adaptation to a starch-rich diet. *Nature*, 495, 360–364. https://doi.org/10.1038/nature11837

Backus, R.C, Cohen, G., Pion, P.D., Good, K.L., Rogers, Q.R. & Fascetti, A.J. (2003). Taurine deficiency in Newfoundlands fed commercially available complete and balanced diets. *Journal of the American Veterinary Medical Association, 223*(8). https://doi.org/10.2460/javma.2003.223.1130

Backus, R.C., Ko, K.S., Fascetti, A.J., Kittleson, M.D., MacDonald, K.A., Maggs, D.J., Berg, J.R. & Rogers, Q.R. (2006). Low plasma taurine concentration in Newfoundland dogs is associated with low plasma methionine and cyst(e)ine concentrations and low taurine synthesis. *The Journal of Nutrition, 136*(10). https://doi.org/10.1093/jn/136.10.2525

Ball, R.O., Urschel, K.L. & Pencharz, P.B. (2007). Nutritional consequences of interspecies differences in arginine and lysine metabolism. *The Journal of Nutrition*, 137(6). https://doi.org/10.1093/jn/137.6.1626S

Bélanger, M.C., Ouellet, M., Queney, G. & Moreau, M. (2005). Taurine-deficient dilated cardiomyopathy in a family of Golden Retrievers. *Journal of the American Animal Hospital Association, 41*(5). https://doi.org/10.5326/0410284

Bergström, A., Laurent, F., Schmidt, R., Ersmark, E., Lebrasseur, O., Girdland-Flink, L., Lin, A.T., Stora, J. Sjogren, K-L., Anthony, D., Antipina, E., Amiri, S., Bar-Oz, G., Bazaliiskii, V., Bulatovic, J., Brown, D., Carmagnini, A., Davy, T., Fedorov, S., Fiore, I., Fulton, D., Germonpre, M., Haile, J., Irving-Pease, E.K., Jamieson, A., Janssens, L., Kirillova, I., Horwitz, L.K., Kuzmanovic-Cvetkovic, J., Kuzmin, Y., Losey, R.J., Dizdar, D.L., Mashkour, J., Novak, M., Onar, V., Orton, D., Pasaric, M., Radivojevic, M., Rajkovic, D., Roberts, B., Ryan, H., Sablin, M., Shidlovskiy, F., Stojanovic, I., Tagliacozzo, A., Trantalidou, K., Ullen, I., Villaluenga, A., Wapnish, P., Dobney, K., Gotherstrom, A., Linderholm, A., Dalen, L., Pinhasi, R., Larson, G. & Skoglund, P. (2020). Origins and genetic legacy of prehistoric dogs. *Science, 370*(6516), 557–564. https://science.sciencemag.org/content/370/6516/557

Biology Dictionary. (2020). Omnivore definition. *Biology Dictionary*. https://biologydictionary.net/omnivore/

Brooks, D. (2020). Pet food makers' perspective: the need for a comprehensive approach to understanding and communicating about dilated cardiomyopathy in dogs. [Presentation: Kansas State Veterinary Diagnostic Laboratory—Scientific Forum Exploring Causes of Dilated Cardiomyopathy in Dogs]. https://www.ksvdl.org/resources/documents/dcm-forum/20200928-KSU-symposium-DanaBrooks-PFI.pdf

Brown, W.Y., Vanselow, B.A., Redman, A.J. & Pluske, J.R. (2009). An experimental meat-free diet maintained haematological characteristics in sprint-racing sled dogs. *British Journal of Nutrition*, 102, 1318–1323. https://doi.org/10.1017/S0007114509389254

Calvert, C.A., Jacobs, G.J., Smith, D.D., Rathbun, S.L. & Pickus, C.W. (2000). Association between results of ambulatory electrocardiography and development of cardiomyopathy during long-term follow-up of Doberman pinschers. *Journal of the American Veterinary Medical Association*, *216*(1), 34–39. https://doi.org/10.2460/javma.2000.216.34

Case, L.P. (2021). Protein—Are we feeding too much? *The Science Dog*. https://thesciencedog.com/2021/03/23/protein-are-we-feeding-too-much/

Case, L.P., Daristotle, L., Hayek, M.G. & Raasch, M.F. (2011). *Canine and Feline Nutrition [3rd ed.]*. Maryland Heights, MI. US: Mosby Elsevier

Cedars Sinai. (2021). Dilated cardiomyopathy. *Cedars Sinai Health Library*. https://www.cedars-sinai.org/health-library/diseases-and-conditions/d/dilated-cardiomyopathy.html#:~:text=Dilated%20cardiomyopathy%20(DCM)%20is%20when,the%20upper%20chambers%20(atria)

Center for Responsive Politics. (2020). Dairy: lobbying 2020. *Center for Responsive Politics*. https://www.opensecrets.org/industries/lobbying.php?ind=A04

Center for Responsive Politics. (2020a). Meat processing and products: lobbying 2020. *Center for Responsive Politics*. https://www.opensecrets.org/industries/lobbying.php?ind=G2300

Coelho, L.P., Kultima, J.R., Costea, P.I., Fournier, C., Pan, Y., Czarnecki-Maulden, G., Hayward, M.R., Forslund, S.K., Benedikt Schmidt, T.S., Descombes, P., Jackson, J.R., Li, Q. & Bork, P. (2018). Similarity of the dog and human gut microbiomes in gene content and response to diet. *Microbiome*, *6*(72). https://doi.org/10.1186/s40168-018-0450-3

Colledge, S. & Conolly J. (eds.). (2007). *The Origin and Spread of Domestic Plants in Southwest Asia and Europe*. Walnut Creek, CA: Left Coast Press

Clapper, G.M., Grieshop, C.M., Merchen, N.R., Russett, J.C., Brent, Jr, J.L. & Fahey Jr, G.C. (2001). Ileal and total tract nutrient digestibilities and fecal characteristics of dogs as affected by soybean protein inclusion in dry, extruded diets. *Journal of Animal Science*, 79. http://jas.fass.org/content/79/6/1523

Darmadi-Blackberry, I., Wahlqvist, M.L., Kouris-Blazos, A., Steen, B., Lukito, W., Horie, Y. & Horie, K. (2004). Legumes: the most important dietary predictor of survival in older people of different ethnicities. *Asia Pacific Journal of Clinical Nutrition,* *13*(2). https://pubmed.ncbi.nlm.nih.gov/15228991/

Deng, P. & Swanson, K. (2015). Gut microbiota of humans, dogs and cats: current knowledge and future opportunities and challenges. *British Journal of Nutrition, 113*(S1), S6-S17. doi:10.1017/S0007114514002943

Dodds, W.J. (2021). Dilated cardiomyopathy in the news again. *Hemopet.* https:// hemopet.org/dilated-cardiomyopathy-in-the-news-again

Dodds, W.J. & Laverdure, D.R. (2015). Canine Nutrigenomics: The New Science of Feeding Your Dog for Optimum Health. Wenatchee, WA, US: Dogwise Publishing

Dukes-McEwan, J., Borgarelli, M., Tidholm, A., Vollmar, A.C. & Häggström, J. (2003). Proposed guidelines for the diagnosis of canine idiopathic dilated cardiomyopathy. Journal of Veterinary Cardiology, 5(2). https://www.sciencedirect.com/science/ article/abs/pii/S1760273406700479?via%3Dihub

Ephraim, E., Cochrane, C.Y. & Jewell, D.E. (2020). Varying protein levels influence metabolomics and the gut microbiome in healthy adult dogs. *Toxins, 12*(8), 517. https://doi.org/10.3390/toxins12080517

Forster, G.M., Ollila, C.A., Burton, J.H., Hill, D., Bauer, J.E., Hess, A.M. & Ryan, E.P. (2012). Nutritional weight loss therapy with cooked bean powders regulates serum lipids and biochemical analytes in overweight and obese dogs. *Journal of Obesity & Weight Loss Therapy*, 2(149). https://www.omicsonline.org/open-access/nutritional-weight- loss-therapy-with-cooked-bean-powders-regulates-serum-lipids-and-biochemical- analytes-in-overweight-and-obese-dogs-2165-7904.1000149.php?aid=8920

Forster, G.M., Hill, D., Gregory, G., Weishaar, K.M., Lana, S., Bauer, J.E. & Ryan, E.P. (2012a). Effects of cooked navy bean powder on apparent total tract nutrient digestibility and safety in healthy adult dogs. *Journal of Animal Science*, 90(8). https:// pubmed.ncbi.nlm.nih.gov/22367072/

Gaynor, L. (2017). Metabolomics: Personalized healthcare throughout measuring metabolites? *University of Cambridge.* https://www.phgfoundation.org/blog/what-is- metabolomics

Gillette, R.L. (1999). Feeding the canine athlete for optimal performance. *Sportsvet.com.* http://www.sportsvet.com/Art3.html

Gowda, G.A., Zhang, S., Gu, H., Asiago, V., Shanaiah, N. & Raftery, D. (2008). Metabolomics-based methods for early disease diagnostics. *Expert Review of Molecular Diagnostics*, 8(5), 617–633. https://doi.org/10.1586/14737159.8.5.617

Gupta, S.C., Kim, J.H., Prasad, S. & Aggarwal, B.B. (2010). Regulation of survival, proliferation, invasion, angiogenesis, and metastasis of tumor cells through modulation of inflammatory pathways by nutraceuticals. *Cancer Metastasis Reviews*, *29*(3), 405–434. https://doi.org/10.1007/s10555-010-9235-2

Hangen, L. & Bennink, M.R. (2002). Consumption of black beans and navy beans (Phaseolus vulgaris) reduced azoxymethane-induced colon cancer in rats. *Nutrition and Cancer*, 44(1). https://pubmed.ncbi.nlm.nih.gov/12672642/

Harvard Medical School. (2020). The lowdown on glycemic index and glycemic load. *Harvard Health Publishing*. https://www.health.harvard.edu/diseases-and-conditions/the-lowdown-on-glycemic-index-and-glycemic-load

Hasler, C.M. (2002). Functional foods: benefits, concerns and challenges—a position paper from the American Council on Science and Health. *The Journal of Nutrition*, 132(12), 3772–3781. https://doi.org/10.1093/jn/132.12.3772

Heffernan, A. (2012). All about your metabolic energy systems. *Experience Life*. https://experiencelife.com/article/all-about-your-metabolic-energy-systems/

Helmstädter, A. (2010). *Phaseolus vulgaris* preparations as antihyperglycemic agents. *Journal of Medicinal Food*, 13(2). https://pubmed.ncbi.nlm.nih.gov/20132042/

Hermsdorff, H.H., Zulet, M.Á., Abete, I. & Martínez, J.A. (2011). A legume-based hypocaloric diet reduces proinflammatory status and improves metabolic features in overweight/obese subjects. *European Journal of Nutrition*, 50(1). https://pubmed.ncbi.nlm.nih.gov/20499072/

Hill, R.C. (1998). The nutritional requirements of exercising dogs. *The Journal of Nutrition*, 128(12), 2686S-2690S. https://doi.org/10.1093/jn/128.12.2686S

Hill, R.C., Bloomberg, M.S., Legrand-Defretin, V., Burger, I.H., Hillock, S.M., Sundstrom, D.A. & Jones, G.L. (2000). Maintenance energy requirements and the effect of diet on performance of racing Greyhounds. *American Journal of Veterinary Research*, 61(12), 1566–1573. https://doi.org/10.2460/ajvr.2000.61.1566

Hill, R.C., Lewis, D.D., Scott, K.C., Omori, M., Jackson, M., Sundstrom, D.A., Jones, G.L., Speakman, J.R., Doyle, C.A. & Butterwick, R.F. (2001). Effect of increased dietary protein and decreased dietary carbohydrate on performance and body composition in racing Greyhounds. *American Journal of Veterinary Research*, 62(3), 440–447. https://doi.org/10.2460/ajvr.2001.62.440

Hughes, J.S., Ganthavorn, C. & Wilson-Sanders, S. (1997). Dry beans inhibit azoxymethane-induced colon carcinogenesis in F344 rats. *Journal of Nutrition*, 127(12). https://doi.org/10.1093/jn/127.12.2328

Jiménez-Cruz, A., Manuel Loustaunau-López, V. & Bacardi-Gascón, M. (2006). The use of low glycemic and high satiety index food dishes in Mexico: a low cost approach to prevent and control obesity and diabetes. *Nutricion Hospitalaria*, 21(3). https://pubmed.ncbi.nlm.nih.gov/16771117/

Johnston, J. (2020). Implication of grain-free foods in the development of dilated cardiomyopathy is an inappropriate over-generalization; rather, DCM is scientifically complex and subject to a combination of multiple factors. [Presentation: Kansas State Veterinary Diagnostic Laboratory—Scientific Forum Exploring Causes of Dilated

Cardiomyopathy in Dogs]. https://www.ksvdl.org/resources/documents/dcm-forum/Confidential-Privileged-Colloquium-Slides-for-Release-October-14-2020.pdf

Kerr, K.R., Forster, G., Dowd, S.E., Ryan, E.P. & Swanson, K.S. (2013). Effects of dietary cooked navy bean on the fecal microbiome of healthy companion dogs. *PloS ONE*, *8*(9), e74998. https://doi.org/10.1371/journal.pone.0074998

Key, T.J., Silcocks, P.B., Davey, G.K., Appleby, P.N. & Bishop, D.T. (1997). A case-control study of diet and prostate cancer. *British Journal of Cancer*, *76*(5). https://www.ncbi.nlm.nih.gov/pmc/articles/PMC2228001/

Lewis, L., Morris, M. & Hand, M. (2000). *Small Animal Clinical Nutrition*, (Ed. 4). Topeka, KS. US: Mark Morris Institute

Luntz, S. (2020). Genomes from ancient dogs reveal their evolution, and ours. *IFLScience*, *18*(21). https://www.iflscience.com/plants-and-animals/genomes-from-ancient-dogs-reveal-their-evolution-and-ours/

Martin, M.W., Stafford Johnson, M.J. & Celona, B. (2009). Canine dilated cardiomyopathy: a retrospective study of signalment, presentation and clinical findings in 369 cases. *The Journal of Small Animal Practice*, *50*(1), 23–29. https://doi.org/10.1111/j.1748-5827.2008.00659.x

Martín, R., Miquel, S., Benevides, L., Bridonneau, C., Robert, V., Hudault, S., Chain, F., Berteau, O., Azevedo, V., Chatel, J.M., Sokol, H., Bermúdez-Humarán, L.G., Thomas, M. & Langella, P. (2017). Functional characterization of nove *Faecalibacterium prausnitzii* strains isolated from healthy volunteers: a step forward in the use of *F. prausnitzii* as a next-generation probiotic. *Frontiers in Microbiology*, *8*, 1226. https://doi.org/10.3389/fmicb.2017.01226

McCauley, S.R., Clark, S.D., Quest, B.W., Streeter, R.M. & Oxford, E.M. (2020). Review of canine dilated cardiomyopathy in the wake of diet-associated concerns. *Journal of Animal Science*, *98*(6), skaa155. https://doi.org/10.1093/jas/skaa155

McDonald, P., Edwards, R.A., Greenhalgh, J.F.D., Morgan, C.A., Sinclair, L.A. & Wilkinson, R.G. (2011). *Animal Nutrition [7th ed.]*. Harlow, Essex. England: Pearson Education Limited.

McGee, S. (2020). Quotes of plant-based athletes. *Tennis Fitness & Plant-Based Performance*. https://www.tennisfitnesslove.com/books/quotes-of-plant-based-athletes/

Meurs, K.M. (2010). Genetics of cardiac disease in the small animal patient. *Veterinary Clinics of North America: Small Animal Practice*, *40*(4). https://doi.org/10.1016/j.cvsm.2010.03.006

Mocharla, H., Mocharla, R. & Hodes, M. E. (1990). Alpha-amylase gene transcription in tissues of normal dog. *Nucleic Acids Research*, *18*(4), 1031–1036. https://doi.org/10.1093/nar/18.4.1031

Morgane, O., Tresset, A., Frantz, L.A.F., Brehard, S., Bălăşescu, A., Mashkour, M., Boroneant, A., Pionnier-Capitan, M., Lebrasseur, O., Arbogast, R.M., Bartosiewicz, L., Debue, K., Rabinovich, R., Sablin, M.V., Larson, G., Hänni, C., Hitte, C. & Vigne, J.D. (2018). Dogs accompanied humans during the Neolithic expansion into Europe. *Dryad, Dataset.*

NutritionData. (2020). https://nutritiondata.self.com/

Oxford Learner's Dictionaries. (2020). Herbivore. *Oxford University Press.* https://www.oxfordlearnersdictionaries.com/us/definition/english/herbivore#:~:text=herbivore-,noun,carnivore%2C%20insectivore%2C%20omnivore%2C%20vegetarian

Plantastic Life. (2020). Quotes from plant-based athletes. *Plant Based Greatness.* http://www.wholefoodplantbasedrd.com/2015/09/quotes-from-plant-based-athletes/

Pointing, C. (2022). Breaking: Burger King launches vegan nuggets. *LiveKindly.* https://www.livekindly.co/burger-king-vegan-nuggets/

Quest, B.W., Leach, S.B., Garimella, S., Konie, A. & Clark, S.D. (2022). Incidence of canine dilated cardiomyopathy diagnosed at referral institutes and grain-free pet food store sales: a retrospective survey. *Frontiers in Animal Science, 3.* https://www.frontiersin.org/article/10.3389/fanim.2022.846227

Quilliam, C., Ren, Y., Morris, T., Ai., Y. & Weber, L.P. (2021). The effects of 7 days of feeding pulse-based diets on digestibility, glycemic response and taurine levels in domestic dogs. *Frontiers in Veterinary Science, 8.* https://doi.org/10.3389/fvets.2021.654223

Rajilić-Stojanović, M., Biagi, E., Heilig, H.G., Kajander, K., Kekkonen, R.A., Tims, S. & de Vos, W.M. (2011). Global and deep molecular analysis of microbiota signatures in fecal samples from patients with irritable bowel syndrome. *Gastroenterology, 141*(5), 1792–1801. https://doi.org/10.1053/j.gastro.2011.07.043

Reilly, L.M., He, F., Rodriguez-Zas, S.L., Southey, B.R., Hoke, J.M., Davenport, G.M. & de Godoy, M.R.C. (2021). Use of legumes and yeast as novel dietary protein sources in extruded canine diets. *Frontiers in Veterinary Science, 8,* 586. https://doi.org/10.3389/fvets.2021.667642

ScienceDaily. (2019). Overweight dogs may live shorter lives. *ScienceDaily.* https://www.sciencedaily.com/releases/2019/01/190103110747.htm

Shi, J., Arunasalam, K., Yeung, D., Kakuda, Y., Mittal, G. & Jiang, Y. (2004). Saponins from edible legumes: chemistry, processing, and health benefits. *Journal of Medicinal Food, 7*(1), 67–78. https://doi.org/10.1089/109662004322984734

Smith, C.E., Parnell, L.D., Lai, C.Q., Rush, J.E. & Freeman, L.M. (2021). Investigation of diets associated with dilated cardiomyopathy in dogs using foodomics analysis. *Scientific Reports, 11.* https://doi.org/10.1038/s41598-021-94464-2

Sokol, H., Pigneur, B., Watterlot, L., Lakhdari, O., Bermúdez-Humarán, L.G., Gratadoux, J.J., Blugeon, S., Bridonneau, C., Furet, J.P., Corthier, G., Grangette, C., Vasquez, N., Pochart, P., Trugnan, G., Thomas, G., Blottière, H.M., Doré, J., Marteau, P., Seksik, P. & Langella, P. (2008). Faecalibacterium prausnitzii is an anti-inflammatory commensal bacterium identified by gut microbiota analysis of Crohn disease patients. *Proceedings of the National Academy of Sciences of the United States of America,* 105(43), 16731–16736. https://doi.org/10.1073/pnas.0804812105

Solomon, S.M. (2020). Scientific forum exploring causes of dilated cardiomyopathy in dogs [Opening Remarks: Kansas State Veterinary Diagnostic Laboratory—Scientific Forum Exploring Causes of Dilated Cardiomyopathy in Dogs]. https://www.ksvdl. org/resources/documents/dcm-forum/DCM-Forum-SolomonOpening-Remarks.pdf

Sriskantharajah, S. (2018). Ever feel in your gut that you and your dog have more in common than you realized? *BioMed Central.* https://blogs.biomedcentral.com/ on-biology/2018/04/19/ever-feel-gut-dog-common-realized/

Suchodolski, J.S., Markel, M.E., Garcia-Mazcorro, J.F., Unterer, S., Heilmann, R.M., Dowd, S.E., Kachroo, P., Ivanov, I., Minamoto, Y., Dillman, E.M., Steiner, J.M., Cook, A.K. & Toresson, L. (2012). The fecal microbiome in dogs with acute diarrhea and idiopathic inflammatory bowel disease. PloS ONE, 7(12), e51907. https://doi. org/10.1371/journal.pone.0051907

The Ohio State University Veterinary Medical Center. (n.d.). Basic Calorie calculator. The Ohio State University Veterinary Medical Center. https://vet.osu.edu/vmc/ companion/our-services/nutrition-support-service/basic-calorie-calculator

Thompson, M.D., Thompson, H.J., Brick, M.A., McGinley, J.N., Jiang, W., Zhu, Z. & Wolfe, P. (2008). Mechanisms associated with dose-dependent inhibition of rat mammary carcinogenesis by dry bean (Phaseolus vulgaris, L.). Journal of Nutrition, *138*(11), 2091–7. https://academic.oup.com/jn/article/138/11/2091/4670019

U.S. Food & Drug Administration (FDA). (2019). Questions & answers: FDA Center for Veterinary Medicine's investigation into a possible connection between diet and canine heart disease (Updated June 27, 2019). U.S. Food & Drug Administration. https://www.fda.gov/animal-veterinary/animal-health-literacy/questions-answers-fda-center-veterinary-medicines-investigation-possible-connection-between-diet-and

U.S. Food & Drug Administration (FDA). (2021). Questions & Answers: FDA's work on potential causes of non-hereditary DCM in dogs. U.S. Food & Drug Administration. https://www.fda.gov/animal-veterinary/animal-health-literacy/questions-answers-fdas-work-potential-causes-non-hereditary-dcm-dogs

U.S. Food & Drug Administration (FDA). (2022). FDA investigation into potential link between certain diets and canine dilated cardiomyopathy. U.S. Food & Drug Administration. https://www.fda.gov/animal-veterinary/outbreaks-and-advisories/ fda-investigation-potential-link-between-certain-diets-and-canine-dilated-cardiomyopathy

Venn, B.J. & Mann, J.I. (2004). Cereal grains, legumes and diabetes. European Journal of Clinical Nutrition, *58*(11), 1443–1461. https://doi.org/10.1038/sj.ejcn.1601995

Villegas, R., Gao, Y.T., Yang, G., Li, H.L., Elasy, T.A., Zheng, W. & Shu, X.O. (2008). Legume and soy food intake and the incidence of type 2 diabetes in the Shanghai Women's Health Study. The American journal of clinical nutrition, *87*(1), 162–167. https://doi.org/10.1093/ajcn/87.1.162

Vollmar, A., Fox, P.R., Ing, E.S. & Biourge, V. (2013). Determination of the prevalence of whole blood taurine in Irish wolfhound dogs with and without echocardiographic evidence of dilated cardiomyopathy. Journal of Veterinary Cardiology, *15*(3). https://doi.org/10.1016/j.jvc.2013.03.005

Wall, T. (2022). FDA ends DCM updates; No causality data with dog foods. PetFoodIndustry.com. https://www.petfoodindustry.com/articles/11862-fda-ends-dcm-updates-no-causality-data-with-dog-foods?utm_source=Omeda&utm_medium=Email&utm_content=NL-Trending+Topics+Weekly+Pet&utm_campaign=NL-Trending+Topics+Weekly+Pet_20221231_0800&oly_enc_id=6355F4926923F7Z

Webber, J. (2022). Burger King's flagship London restaurant is going fully vegan for a 1-month trial. *Plant Based News*. https://plantbasednews.org/lifestyle/food/burger-king-vegan-london/

Wells, S. (2020). New analysis shows ancient dogs and humans shared a surprising bond. *Inverse*. https://www.inverse.com/science/ancient-dog-dna-reveal

Wess, G., Schulze, A., Butz, V., Simak, J., Killich, M., Keller, L.J., Maeurer, J. & Hartmann, K. (2010). Prevalence of dilated cardiomyopathy in Doberman Pinschers in various age groups. *Journal of Veterinary Internal Medicine*, *24*(3), 533–538. https://doi.org/10.1111/j.1939-1676.2010.0479.x

Yamka, R. (2021). DCM and grain-free pet foods: 3 strikes and you're out! *PetFoodIndustry.com*. https://www.petfoodindustry.com/blogs/10-debunking-pet-food-myths-and-misconceptions/post/10554-dcm-and-grain-free-pet-foods-3-strikes-and-youre-out

Zhou, Z., Topping, D.L., Morell, M.K. & Bird, A.R. (2010). Changes in starch physical characteristics following digestion of foods in the human small intestine. *British Journal of Nutrition*, *104*(4), 573–81. https://doi.org/10.1017/S0007114510000875

Chapter 3: Setting Yourself Up for Success

Brown, S. (2019). How livestock farming affects the environment. *DownToEarth*. https://www.downtoearth.org.in/factsheet/how-livestock-farming-affects-the-environment-64218

Hewitt, A. (2017). The truth about cats' and dogs' environmental impact. *UCLA Newsroom*. https://newsroom.ucla.edu/releases/the-truth-about-cats-and-dogs-environmental-impact

Patience, S. (2016). Religion and dietary choices. *Independent Nurse.* https://www.independentnurse.co.uk/clinical-article/religion-and-dietary-choices/145719/#:~:text=Vegetarian%20and%20vegan%20diets,observe%20vegetarian%20or%20vegan%20diets

Mind Tools. (n.d.). SMART goals: How to make your goals achievable. *Mind Tools.* https://www.mindtools.com/pages/article/smart-goals.htm

Chapter 4: Essential Nutritional Components

Ackland, L. (2018). Don't waste your dog's poo—compost it. *The Conversation.* https://theconversation.com/dont-waste-your-dogs-poo-compost-it-107603

American Animal Hospital Association (AAHA). (2020). Is my dog at risk for cancer? *American Animal Hospital Association.* https://www.aaha.org/your-pet/pet-owner-education/ask-aaha/canine-cancer/#:~: text= Yes%2C%20dogs%20are%20susceptible%20to,made%20in%20dogs%20each%20year.

Aminoacid-studies.com. (2020). What amino acids can be used for. *Aminoacid-studies.com.* https://www.aminoacid-studies.com/areas-of-use/

Association of American Feed Control Officials (AAFCO). (2021). *2021 Official Publication.* Champaign, IL, US: AAFCO

Bauer, J. (2017). What is BPA, and what are the concerns about BPA? *Mayo Clinic.* http://www.mayoclinic.org/healthy-lifestyle/nutrition-and-healthy-eating/expert-answers/bpa/faq-20058331

Boesler, M. (2013). Bottled water costs 2,000 times as much as tap water. *Business Insider.* http://www.businessinsider.com/bottled-water-costs-2000x-more-than-tap-2013-7

Cargo-Froom, C.L., Fan, M.Z., Pfeuti, G., Pendlebury, C. & Shoveller, A.K. (2019). Apparent and true digestibility of macro and micro nutrients in adult maintenance dog foods containing either a majority of animal or vegetable proteins. *Journal of Animal Science, 97*(3), 1010–1019. https://doi.org/10.1093/jas/skz001

Carlson, J., Erickson, J.M., Lloyd, B.B. & Slavin, J.L. (2018). Health effects and sources of prebiotic dietary fiber. *Current Developments in Nutrition.* https://doi.org/10.1093/cdn/nzy005

Case, L.P., Daristotle, L., Hayek, M.G. & Raasch, M.F. (2011). *Canine and Feline Nutrition* [3rd ed.]. Maryland Heights, MI. US: Mosby Elsevier

Centers for Disease Control and Prevention (CDC). (2014). Water-related diseases and contaminants in public water systems. *Centers for Disease Control and Prevention.* https://www.cdc.gov/healthywater/drinking/public/water_diseases.html

Chandler, M.L. (2015). Top 5 therapeutic uses of omega-3 fatty acids. *Clinician's Brief.* https://www.cliniciansbrief.com/article/top-5-therapeutic-uses-omega-3-fatty-acids

Collins, K. (2015). Difference between antioxidants and phytochemicals? *American Institute for Cancer Research.* https://www.aicr.org/resources/blog/healthtalkwhats-the-difference-between-an-antioxidant-and-a-phytochemical/#:~:text= Phytochemicals%20are%20naturally%20occurring%20compounds,their%20 power%20to%20create%20damage

Czerwonka, M. & Tokarz, A. (2017). Iron in red meat–friend or foe. *Journal of Meat Science*. 123, 157–165. https://doi.org/10.1016/j.meatsci.2016.09.012

Danks, L. (2014). The importance of vegetable protein. *Veterinary Practice*. https:// veterinary-practice.com/article/the-importance-of-vegetable-protein

Deckelbaum, R.J., Worgall, T.S. & Teo, S. (2006). N-3 fatty acids and gene expression. *American Journal of Clinical Nutrition*, *83*(6), S1520-S1525. https://doi.org/10.1093/ ajcn/83.6.1520S

de Oliveira Otto, M.C., Alonso, A., Lee, D.H., Delclos, G.L., Bertoni, A.G., Jiang, R., Lima, J.A., Symanski, E., Jacobs Jr, D.R. & Nettleton, J.A. (2012). Dietary intakes of zinc and heme iron from red meat, but not from other sources, are associated with greater risk of metabolic syndrome and cardiovascular disease. *The Journal of Nutrition,* 142(3), 526–533. https://doi.org/10.3945/jn.111.149781

Dillitzer, N., Becker, N. & Kienzle, E. (2011). Intake of minerals, trace elements and vitamins in bone and raw food rations in adult dogs. *British Journal of Nutrition,* *106*(Suppl 1), S53–S56. https://doi.org/10.1017/S0007114511002765

Dodds, W.J. (2016). Cellular oxidative stress and chronic inflammatory disease results in obesity, infections and cancers, Parts 1 and 2. *Proceedings of the American Holistic Veterinary Medical Association*, 53–57, 58–63

Dodds, W.J. & Callewaert, D.M. (2016). Novel biomarkers of oxidative stress for veterinary medicine, Parts 1 and 2. *Proceedings of the American Holistic Veterinary Medical Association*, 64-70; 71-73

Donadelli, R.A., Titgemeyer, E.C. & Aldrich, C.G. (2019). Organic matter disappearance and production of short- and branched-chain fatty acids from selected fiber sources used in pet foods by a canine in vitro fermentation model. Journal of Animal Science, *97*(11), 4532–4539. https://doi.org/10.1093/jas/skz302

Dunbar, B.L., Bigley, K.E. & Bauer, J.E. (2010). Early and sustained enrichment of serum n-3 long chain polyunsaturated fatty acids in dogs fed a flaxseed supplemented diet. Lipids, 45(1), 1–10. https://doi.org/10.1007/s11745-009-3364-9

Egan, S. (2013). Making the case for eating fruit. The New York Times. https:// well.blogs.nytimes.com/2013/07/31/making-the-case-for-eating-fruit/#:~:text= Experts%20agree%20that%20we%20are,wars%2C%20many%20nutrition%20 experts%20say

Environmental Protection Agency (EPA). (2016). Types of drinking water contaminants. Environmental Protection Agency. https://www.epa.gov/ccl/types-drinking-water-contaminants

Environmental Working Group (EWG). (2008). Harmful chemicals found in bottled water. Environmental Working Group. http://www.ewg.org/news/news-releases/2008/10/15/harmful-chemicals-found-bottled-water

Environmental Working Group. (2009). What's in your water? National Drinking Water Database. http://www.ewg.org/tap-water/whats-in-yourwater.php

Eswaran, S., Muir, J. & Chey, W.D. (2013). Fiber and functional gastrointestinal disorders. The American Journal of Gastroenterology, *108*(5), 718–727

European Food Information Council (EUFIC). (2012). Carbohydrates. European Food Information Council. http://www.eufic.org/article/en/expid/basics-carbohydrates/

Florence, T.M. (1995). The role of free radicals in disease. Australian and New Zealand Journal of Ophthalmology, *23*(1), 3–7. https://doi.org/10.1111/j.1442-9071.1995.tb01638.x

Fuhrman, J. (2017). ANDI food scores: rating the nutrient density of foods. DrFuhrman.com. https://www.drfuhrman.com/elearning/blog/128/andi-food-scores-rating-the-nutrient-density-of-foods

Gerster H. (1998). Can adults adequately convert alpha-linolenic acid (18:3n-3) to eicosapentaenoic acid (20:5n-3) and docosahexaenoic acid (22:6n-3)? International Journal for Vitamin and Nutrition Research, *68*(3), 159–173. https://pubmed.ncbi.nlm.nih.gov/9637947/

Gibson, G.R., Willis, C.L. & Van Loo, J. (1994). Non digestible oligosaccharides and bifidobacteria – implications for health. International Sugar Journal, 96, 381–387

Gibson, G.R., Scott, K.P., Rastall, R.A., Tuhoy, K.M., Hotchkiss, A., Dubert-Ferrandon, A., Gareau, M., Murphy, E.F., Saulnier, D., Loh, G., Macfarlane, S., Delzenne, N., Ringel, Y., Kozianowski, G., Dickmann, R., Lenoir-Wijnkoop, I., Walker, C. & Buddington, R. (2010). Dietary prebiotics: current status and new definition. Food Science & Technology Bulletin: Functional Foods, 7(1), 1–19. https://isappscience.org/publications/dietary-prebiotics-current-status-and-new-definition/

Hand, M.S., Thatcher, C.D., Remillard R.L., Roudebush P. & Novotny B.J. (2010). Small Animal Clinical Nutrition (5th ed.). Topeka, KS: Mark Morris Institute

Harvard Medical School. (2019). Fill up on phytochemicals. Harvard Health Publishing. https://www.health.harvard.edu/staying-healthy/fill-up-on-phytochemicals

Hooda, J., Shah, A. & Zhang, L. (2014). Heme, an essential nutrient from dietary proteins, critically impacts diverse physiological and pathological processes. Nutrients, *6*(3), 1080–1102. https://doi.org/10.3390/nu6031080

Kozisek, F. (n.d.). Health risks from drinking demineralised water. World Health Organization (WHO). http://www.who.int/water_sanitation_health/dwq/nutrientschap12.pdf?ua=1

Lawson S. (2016). Minerals: functions and food sources. Study.com. https://study.com/academy/lesson/minerals-functions-food-sources.html

Mandal, A. (2012). Lipid biological functions. NewsMedical. https://www.news-medical.net/life-sciences/Lipid-Biological-Functions.aspx

Marsden, S. (2020). Dermatological dilemmas: the potential for diet, herbs, and the microbiome to resolve skin inflammation in small animals. Journal of Integrative Veterinary Therapy, *8*(1), 4–16.

McDonald, P., Edwards, R.A., Greenhalgh, J.F.D., Morgan, C.A., Sinclair, L.A. & Wilkinson, R.G. (2011). Animal Nutrition [7th ed.]. Harlow, Essex. England: Pearson Education Limited

Medical News Today (MNT). (2019). How long can you live without water? Healthline Media UK, Ltd. https://www.medicalnewstoday.com/articles/325174

MedlinePlus. (2020). What are proteins and what do they do? U.S. National Library of Medicine. https://medlineplus.gov/genetics/understanding/howgeneswork/protein/

MedlinePlus. (2020a). Vitamins. U.S. National Library of Medicine. https://medlineplus.gov/ency/article/002399.htm

Mineralogical Society of America. (2020). Frequently asked questions minerology – general. Mineralogical Society of America. http://www.minsocam.org/msa/collectors_corner/faq/faqmingen.htm#:~:text=in%20extraterrestrial%20bodies.-, How%20many%20minerals%20are%20there%3F,minerals%20are%20discredited%20each%20year

Moinard, A., Payen, C., Ouguerram, K., André, A., Hernandez, J., Drut, A., Biourge, V.C., Suchodolski, J.S., Flanagan, J., Nguyen, P. & Leray, V. (2020). Effects of high-fat diet at two energetic levels on fecal microbiota, colonic barrier, and metabolic parameters in dogs. Frontiers in Veterinary Science, 7, 566282. https://doi.org/10.3389/fvets.2020.566282

Morris, J.G. (1985). Nutritional and metabolic responses to arginine deficiency in omnivores. The Journal of Nutrition, *115*(4), 524–531. https://doi.org/10.1093/jn/115.4.524

MyFoodData. (n.d.). Nutrient ranking tool. MyFoodData. https://tools.myfooddata.com/nutrient-ranking-tool/Calcium/All/Highest/Household/Common/No

National Cancer Institute. (n.d.). What is comparative oncology? National Cancer Institute. https://ccr.cancer.gov/Comparative-Oncology-Program/pet-owners/what-is-comp-onc

National Research Council of the National Academy of Sciences (NRC). (2006). Nutrient Requirements of Dogs and Cats. Washington, DC, US: NRC Press

NutritionData. (2020). Conde Nast. https://nutritiondata.self.com/

Oxford University Museum of Natural History. (2006). What is a mineral? The Learning Zone. https://www.oum.ox.ac.uk/thezone/minerals/define/index.htm

Pascual, G., Domínguez, D., Elosúa-Bayes, M., Beckedorff, F., Laudanna, C., Bigas, C., Douillet, D., Greco, C., Symeonidi, A., Hernández, I., Gil, S.R., Prats, N., Bescós, C., Shiekhattar, R., Amit, M., Heyn, H., Shilatifard, A. & Benitah, S.A. (2021). Dietary palmitic acid promotes a prometastatic memory via Schwann cells. Nature, 599(7885), 485–490. https://doi.org/10.1038/s41586-021-04075-0

Pedrinelli, V., Gomes, M. & Carciofi, A.C. (2017). Analysis of recipes of home-prepared diets for dogs and cats published in Portuguese. *Journal of Nutritional Science*, 6, e33. https://doi.org/10.1017/jns.2017.31

Pedrinelli, V., Zafalon, R., Rodrigues, R., Perini, M.P., Conti, R., Vendramini, T., de Carvalho Balieiro, J.C. & Brunetto, M.A. (2019). Concentrations of macronutrients, minerals and heavy metals in home-prepared diets for adult dogs and cats. Scientific Reports, 9(1), 13058. https://doi.org/10.1038/s41598-019-49087-z

Pitcairn, R.H. & Pitcairn, S.H. (2017). Dr. Pitcairn's Complete Guide to Natural Health for Dogs & Cats (4th ed.). Emmaus, PA: Rodale

Schauf, S., de la Fuente, G., Newbold, C.J., Salas-Main, A., Torre, C., Abecia, L. & Castrillo, C. (2018). Effect of dietary fat to starch content on fecal microbiota composition and activity in dogs. Journal of Animal Science, 96(9), 3684–3698. https://europepmc.org/article/PMC/6127775#free-full-text

Scheer, R. & Moss, D. (2011). Dirt poor: have fruits and vegetables become less nutritious? Scientific American. https://www.scientificamerican.com/article/soil-depletion-and-nutrition-loss/

Shen, W., Gaskins, H.R. & McIntosh, M.K. (2014). Influence of dietary fat on intestinal microbes, inflammation, barrier function and metabolic outcomes. Journal of Nutritional Biochemistry, *25*(3), 270-80. https://doi.org/10.1016/j.jnutbio.2013.09.009

Silk, D.B., Davis, A., Vulevic, J., Tzortzis, G. & Gibson, G.R. (2009). Clinical trial: the effects of a trans-galactooligosaccharide prebiotic on faecal microbiota and symptoms in irritable bowel syndrome. Alimentary Pharmacology & Therapeutics, *29*(5), 508–518. https://doi.org/10.1111/j.1365-2036.2008.03911.x

Slavin, J. (2013). Fiber and prebiotics: Mechanisms and health benefits. *Nutrients, 5*(4), 1417–1435. https://doi.org/10.3390/nu5041417

Stoeckel, K., Nielsen, L.H., Fuhrmann, H. & Bachmann, L. (2011). Fatty acid patterns of dog erythrocyte membranes after feeding of a fish-oil based DHA-rich supplement with a base diet low in n-3 fatty acids versus a diet containing added n-3 fatty acids. Acta Veterinaria Scandinavica, *53*(1), 57. https://doi.org/10.1186/1751-0147-53-57

Suchodolski, J. (2020). Probiotics, prebiotics, synbiotics, and intestinal health of dogs and cats. Today's Veterinary Practice. https://todaysveterinarypractice.com/probiotics-prebiotics-synbiotics-dogs-cats/

Tan, J., McKenzi, C., Potamitis, M., Thorburn, A.N., Mackay, C.R. & Macia, L. (2014). The role of short chain fatty acids in health and disease. *Advanced Immunology*, 121, 91–119

The 5 Gyres Institute. (2017). Take action: plastic bottles. The 5 Gyres Institute. https://www.5gyres.org/plastic-bottles/

The Editors of Encyclopedia Britannica. (2015). Feces. Encyclopedia Britannica. https://www.britannica.com/science/feces

Turner, H. (2022). Comparing algae-based EPA + DHA supplements. Today's Dietician. https://www.todaysdietitian.com/enewsletter/enews_0917_01.shtml

University of Arizona. (2003). The chemistry of amino acids. Department of Biochemistry and Molecular Biophysics. http://www.biology.arizona.edu/biochemistry/problem_sets/aa/aa.html

U.S. Geological Survey (USGS). (n.d.). Facts about water. U.S. Geological Survey. https://www.usgs.gov/special-topic/water-science-school/science/facts-about-water?qt-science_center_objects=0#qt-science_center_objects

Uttara, B., Singh, A.V., Zamboni, P. & Mahajan, R.T. (2009). Oxidative stress and neurodegenerative diseases: a review of upstream and downstream antioxidant therapeutic options. Current neuropharmacology, 7(1), 65–74. https://doi.org/10.2174/157015909787602823

Veterinary Cancer Society. (2020). Frequently asked questions. Veterinary Cancer Society. http://vetcancersociety.org/pet-owners/faqs/

WebMD. (2020). Types of dietary fats. Nourish by WebMD. https://www.webmd.com/diet/guide/types-fat-in-foods#1

Wernimont, S.M., Radosevich, J., Jackson, M.I., Ephraim, E., Badri, D.V., MacLeay, J.M., Jewell, D.E. & Suchodolski, J.S. (2020). The effects of nutrition on the gastrointestinal microbiome of cats and dogs: impact on health and disease. Frontiers in Microbiology, 11, 1266. https://doi.org/10.3389/fmicb.2020.01266

Whitbread, D. (2020). 10 foods highest in zinc. MyFoodData. https://www.myfooddata.com/articles/high-zinc-foods.php

Whitbread, D. (2020a). 17 vegetables highest in water. MyFoodData. https://www.myfooddata.com/articles/vegetables-high-in-water.php#:~:text=Of%20all%20foods%2C%

Woodford, K. (2009). The Devil in the Milk. White River Junction, VT: Chelsea Green Publishing

Yamada, M., Takahashi, N., Matsuda, Y., Sato, K., Yokoji, M., Sulijaya, B., Maekawa, T., Ushiki, T., Mikami, Y., Hayatsu, M., Mizutani, Y., Kishino, S., Ogawa, J., Arita, M., Tabeta, K., Maeda, T. & Yamazaki, K. (2018). A bacterial metabolite ameliorates periodontal pathogen-induced gingival epithelial barrier disruption via GPR40 signaling. Scientific Reports, 8(9008). https://doi.org/10.1038/s41598-018-27408-y

Chapter 5: Comprehensive Ingredients Guide

Adams, C. (2019). Chlorophyll helps prevent cancer. *The Journal of Plant Medicines.* https://plantmedicines.org/chlorophyll-helps-prevent-cancer/

Association of American Feed Control Officials (AAFCO). (2021). Hemp and hemp byproducts in animal food: AAFCO position and call to action. *AAFCO*. https://www.aafco.org/Portals/0/SiteContent/Announcements/AAFCO_HempUpdate-9-21.pdf

American Institute for Cancer Research (AICR). (2020). Walnuts: support a cancer-preventive diet. *American Institute for Cancer Research*. https://www.aicr.org/cancer-prevention/food-facts/walnuts/

American Kennel Club (AKC). (2020). Human foods dogs can and can't eat. *AKC*. https://www.akc.org/expert-advice/nutrition/human-foods-dogs-can-and-cant-eat/

American Society for the Prevention of Cruelty to Animals (ASPCA). (2022). People foods to avoid feeding your pets. *ASPCA*. https://www.aspca.org/pet-care/animal-poison-control/people-foods-avoid-feeding-your-pets

Arterburn, L.M., Oken, H.A., Bailey Hall, E., Hamersley, J., Kuratko, C.N. & Hoffman, J.P. (2008). Algal-oil capsules and cooked salmon: nutritionally equivalent sources of docosahexaenoic acid. *Journal of the American Dietetic Association, 108*(7), 1204–1209. https://pubmed.ncbi.nlm.nih.gov/18589030/

Arts, I.C., van de Putte, B. & Hollman, P.C. (2000). Catechin contents of foods commonly consumed in The Netherlands. 1. Fruits, vegetables, staple foods, and processed foods. *Journal of Agricultural and Food Chemistry, 48*(5), 1746–1751. https://doi.org/10.1021/jf000025h

Borowitzka, M.A. (1997). Microalgae for aquaculture: opportunities and constraints. *Journal of Applied Phycology, 9*, 393. https://doi.org/10.1023/A:1007921728300

Broaddus, H. (2016). Which oils are naturally non-GMO? *Centra Foods*. http://www.centrafoods.com/blog/which-oils-are-naturally-non-gmo#:~:text=Commonly%20GMO%20Oils,as%20the%20%E2%80%9Cbig%20five%E2%80%9D%3A&text=Corn%20(Corn%20Oil),Sugar%20Beets

Brown, G.D. & Gordon, S. (2003). Fungal beta-glucans and mammalian immunity, *Immunity. 19*(3), 311–315. https://doi.org/10.1016/s1074-7613(03)00233-4

Brown, M.J. (2020). Sweet potatoes vs. yams: what's the difference? *Healthline*. https://www.healthline.com/nutrition/sweet-potatoes-vs-yams

Brown, M.J. & Link, R. (2020). MCT oil 101: a review of medium-chain triglycerides. *Healthline*. https://www.healthline.com/nutrition/mct-oil-101

Brufau, G., Boatella, J. & Rafecas, M. (2006). Nuts: source of energy and macronutrients. *British Journal of Nutrition, 96*(Suppl. 2), S24–S28. https://www.cambridge.org/core/services/aop-cambridge-core/content/view/AAAEDDA038B08C0A00C802F00A7F4171/S0007114506003

Bruss, M.L. (2008). Chapter 4—Lipids and Ketones. In *Clinical Biochemistry of Domestic Animals* [6th ed]. [Kaneko, J.J., Harvey, W.J. & Bruss, M.L. (Editors)]. 81–115. Academic Press. https://doi.org/10.1016/B978-0-12-370491-7.00004-0

Caselato-Sousa, V.M. & Amaya- Farfán, J. (2012). State of knowledge on amaranth grain: a comprehensive review. *Journal of Food Science*. https://doi.org/10.1111/j.1750-3841.2012.02645.x

Castle, S. (2019). A guide to the different types of field peas. *Southern Living*. https://www.southernliving.com/food/field-peas?

Chai, W. & Liebman, M. (2005). Effect of different cooking methods on vegetable oxalate content. *Journal of Agricultural and Food Chemistry*, *53*(8), 3027–3030. https://doi.org/10.1021/jf048128d

Chandrasekara, A. & Shahidi, F. (2010). Content of insoluble bound phenolics in millets and their contribution to antioxidant capacity. *Journal of Agriculture and Food Chemistry*, *58*(11), 6706–14. https://doi: 10.1021/jf100868b

Chang, P., Terbach, N., Plant, N., Chen, P.E., Walker, M.C. & Williams, R.S. (2013). Seizure control by ketogenic diet-associated medium chain fatty acids. *Neuropharmacology*, *69*, 105–114. https://doi.org/10.1016/j.neuropharm.2012.11.004

Chiorando, M. (2020). 41% of US households now buy vegan milk, says data. *PlantBased News*. https://plantbasednews.org/news/41-us-households-buy-vegan-milk/

Ciftci, O.N., Przybylski, R. & Rudzinska, M. (2012). Lipid components of flax, perilla, and chia seeds. *European Journal of Lipid Science and Technology*, *114*(7), 794–800. https://doi.org/10.1002/ejlt.201100207

Cleveland Clinic. (2020). The health benefits of beets: why you should fall in love with this ruby-red root. *Cleveland Clinic: Health Essentials*. https://health.clevelandclinic.org/the-health-benefits-of-beets/

Compound Interest. (2017). Broccoli color changes and cancer-fighting compounds. *Compound Interest*. https://www.compoundchem.com/2017/10/19/broccoli/

Collins, K. (2019). Soy and cancer: myths and misconceptions. *American Institute for Cancer Research*. https://www.aicr.org/resources/blog/soy-and-cancer-myths-and-misconceptions/

Conchillo, A., Valencia, I., Puente, A., Ansorena, D. & Astiasarán, I. (2006). Functional components in fish and algae oils. *Nutricion Hospitalaria*, *21*(3), 369–373. https://europepmc.org/article/med/16771120

Consumer Reports. (2014). How much arsenic is in your rice? Consumer Reports. https://www.consumerreports.org/cro/magazine/2015/01/how-much-arsenic-is-in-your-rice/index.htm

Cook's Country. (2008). Getting to know: fresh beans and peas. *Cook's Country*. https://www.cookscountry.com/how_tos/6557-getting-to-know-fresh-beans-and-peas

Cooperstone, J.L. & Schwartz, S.J. (2016). 20 – Recent insights into health benefits of carotenoids. *Handbook on Natural Pigments in Food and Beverages* [Editor(s): Reinhold Carle, Ralf M. Schweiggert]. Woodhouse Publishing Series in Food Science, Technology and Nutrition, 473–497. https://doi.org/10.1016/B978-0-08-100371-8.00020-8

Danby, S.G., AlEnezi, T., Sultan, A., Lavender, T., Chittock, J., Brown, K. & Cork, M.J. (2013). Effect of olive and sunflower seed oil on the adult skin barrier: implications for neonatal skin care. *Pediatric Dermatology, 30*(1), 42–50. https://pubmed.ncbi.nlm.nih.gov/22995032/

Delany, A. (2018). All the types of lentils (and what the hell to do with them). *Basically.* https://www.bonappetit.com/story/types-of-lentils

Del Coro, K. (2020). Jerusalem artichoke nutrition facts and health benefits. *VeryWell Fit.* https://www.verywellfit.com/jerusalem-artichoke-nutrition-facts-and-health-benefits-5076353

Dhaka, V., Gulia, N., Ahlawat, K.S. & Khatkar, B.S. (2011). Trans fats—sources, health risks and alternative approach - A review. *Journal of Food Science and Technology, 48*(5), 534–541. https://doi.org/10.1007/s13197-010-0225-8

Dodds, W.J. & Laverdure, D.R. (2011). *The Canine Thyroid Epidemic: Answers You Need for Your Dog.* Wenatchee, WA, US: Dogwise Publishing

Dolson, L. (2020). Celery root nutrition facts and health benefits. *VeryWell Fit.* https://www.verywellfit.com/carbs-in-celeriac-celery-root-2241778

Donsky, A., Boyer, R. & Naturally Savvy.com. (2013). Seeds of life: chia, flax, hemp and pumpkin. *Chicago Tribune.* https://www.chicagotribune.com/lifestyles/sns-green-seeds-of-life-story.html

Dolan, S. (2021). Februdairy: a desperate attempt to promote the declining dairy industry. *PlantBased News.* https://plantbasednews.org/opinion/opinion-piece/februdairy-desperate-attempt-promote-declining-dairy/#:~:text=Februdairy%20is%20a%20social%20media,a%20direct%20response%20to%20Veganuary

El Khoury, D., Cuda, C., Luhovyy, B.L. & Anderson, G.H. (2012). Beta glucan: health benefits in obesity and metabolic syndrome. *Journal of Nutrition and Metabolism, 2012,* 851362. https://doi.org/10.1155/2012/851362

Environmental Protection Agency (EPA). (2019). Glyphosate: response to comments, usage, and benefits (PC Codes: 103601 103604, 103605, 103607, 103608, 103613, 417300) [Memorandum from Caleb Hawkins, Charmaine Hanson & Dexter Sells]. *United States Environmental Protection Agency.* https://www.epa.gov/sites/production/files/2019-04/documents/glyphosate-response-comments-usage-benefits-final.pdf

Environmental Protection Agency (EPA). (2021). Indicators: algal toxins (microcystin). *United States Environmental Protection Agency.* https://www.epa.gov/national-aquatic-resource-surveys/indicators-algal-toxins-microcystin

Fahim, A.T., Abd-el Fattah, A.A., Agha, A.M. & Gad, M.Z. (1995). Effect of pumpkin-seed oil on the level of free radical scavengers induced during adjuvant-arthritis in rats. *Pharmacological Research, 31*(1), 73–79. https://pubmed.ncbi.nlm.nih.gov/7784309/

Fernando, W.M.A.D.B., Martins, I.J., Goozee, K.G., Breannan, C.S., Jayasena, V. & Martins, R.N. (2015). The role of dietary coconut for the prevention and treatment of Alzehimer's disease: potential mechanisms of action. *British Journal of Nutrition, 114*(1), 1–14. https://doi.org/10.1017/S0007114515001452

Fiesel, A., Ehrmann, M., Geßner, D.K., Most, E. & Eder, K. (2015). Effects of polyphenol-rich plant products from grape or hop as feed supplements on iron, zinc and copper status in piglets. *Archives of Animal Nutrition, 69*(4), 276–284. https://doi.org/10.1080/1745039X.2015.1057065

Fincher, M. (2020). How to cook lentils perfectly every time. *AllRecipes.* https://www.allrecipes.com/article/how-to-cook-lentils/

Geertsema, C. (2020). 5 different types of lentils + a recipe for each one. *Wide Open Eats.* https://www.wideopeneats.com/5-different-types-of-lentils/

Giménez-Bastida, J.A. & Zieliński, H. (2015). Buckwheat as a functional food and its effects on health. *Journal of Agricultural and Food Chemistry, 63*(36), 7896–7913. https://doi.org/10.1021/acs.jafc.5b02498

Glass, D. (2007). Color changing veggies. *Moment of Science.* https://indianapublicmedia.org/amomentofscience/color-changing-veggies.php

Gorzynik-Debicka, M., Przychodzen, P., Cappello, F., Kuban-Jankowska, A., Marino Gammazza, A., Knap, N., Wozniak, M. & Gorska-Ponikowska, M. (2018). Potential health benefits of olive oil and plant polyphenols. *International Journal of Molecular Sciences, 19*(3), 686. https://doi.org/10.3390/ijms19030686

Greque de Morais, M., da Fontoura Prates, D., Botelho Moreira, J., Hartwig Duarte, J. & Vieira Costa, J.A. (2018). Phycocyanin from microalgae: properties, extraction and purification, with some recent applications. *Industrial Biotechnology, 14*(1), 30–37. https://doi.org/10.1089/ind.2017.0009

Gross, T. (2018). The science—and environmental hazards—behind fish oil supplements. [Interview with Paul Greenberg, author of *The Omega Principle: Seafood and the Quest for a Long Life and a Healthier Planet*]. *Fresh Air* [NPR]. https://www.npr.org/2018/07/09/627229213/the-science-and-environmental-hazards-behind-fish-oil-supplements

Gunnars, K. (2018). How to optimize your omega-6 to omega-3 ratio. *Healthline.* https://www.healthline.com/nutrition/optimize-omega-6-omega-3-ratio

Haddad, E.H., Gaban-Chong, N., Oda, K. & Sabaté, J. (2014). Effect of a walnut meal on postprandial oxidative stress and antioxidants in healthy individuals. *Nutrition Journal, 13*(4). https://doi.org/10.1186/1475-2891-13-4

Hallberg, L., Brune, M. & Rossander, L. (1989). Iron absorption in man: ascorbic acid and dose-dependent inhibition by phytate. *The American Journal of Clinical Nutrition, 49*(1), 140–144. https://doi.org/10.1093/ajcn/49.1.140

Han, E. (2020). The difference between types of fresh tofu. *Kitchn.* https://www. thekitchn.com/tofu-varieties-whats-the-difference-201345

Hanneman, A. & Colgrove, K. (n.d.). How to cook dry beans from scratch. *University of Nebraska, Lincoln, Institute of Agriculture and Natural Resources—UNL Food.* https://food.unl.edu/article/how-cook-dry-beans-scratch#:~:text=Stovetop%20 Instructions,hours%20depending%20on%20the%20variety

Hardy, T.M. & Tollefsbol, T.O. (2011). Epigenetic diet: impact on the epigenome and cancer. *Epigenomics, 3*(4), 503–518. https://www.ncbi.nlm.nih.gov/pmc/articles/ PMC3197720/

Harris, C. (2012). Thyroid disease and diet – nutrition plays a part in maintaining thyroid health. *Today's Dietician, 14*(7), 40. https://www.todaysdietitian.com/ newarchives/070112p40.shtml#:~:text=The%20potential%20exception%20is%20 millet,they%20choose%20a%20different%20grain

Harvard Medical School. (2017). Why nutritionists are crazy about nuts. *Harvard Health Publishing.* https://www.health.harvard.edu/nutrition/why-nutritionists-are-crazy-about-nuts

Harvard School of Public Health. (2021). Winter squash. *The Nutrition Source.* https:// www.hsph.harvard.edu/nutritionsource/food-features/winter-squash/

Harvard School of Public Health. (2021a). Oats. *The Nutrition Source.* https://www. hsph.harvard.edu/nutritionsource/food-features/oats/

Harvard School of Public Health. (2021b). Quinoa. *The Nutrition Source.* https://www. hsph.harvard.edu/nutritionsource/food-features/quinoa/

Helpots. (2013). Confused by different types of lentils? *The Everyday Vegetarian UK.* https://theeverydayvegetarianuk.wordpress.com/2013/11/22/confused-by-different-types-of-lentils/

Henne, B. (2013). Parsnips: packing a nutritional punch. *Michigan State University: MSU Extension.* https://www.canr.msu.edu/news/parsnips_packing_a_nutritional_punch

Hudthagosol, C., Haddad, E. & Jongsuwat, R. (2012). Antioxidant activity comparison of walnuts and fatty fish. *Journal of the Medical Association of Thailand, 95*(Suppl 6), S179–188. https://pubmed.ncbi.nlm.nih.gov/23130505/

Huffstetler, E. (2020). How to store dried beans. *The Spruce Eats.* https://www. thespruceeats.com/how-to-store-dried-beans-1389336

Hwang, E.S. & Kim, G.H. (2013). Effects of various heating methods on glucosinolate, carotenoid and tocopherol concentrations in broccoli. *International Journal of Food Sciences and Nutrition, 64*(1), 103–111. https://doi.org/10.3109/09637486.2012.704904

Jalali-Khanabadi, B.A., Mozaffari-Khosravi, H. & Parsaeyan, N. (2010). Effects of almond dietary supplementation on coronary heart disease lipid risk factors and serum lipid oxidation parameters in men with mild hyperlipidemia. *Journal of Alternative and Complementary Medicine, 16*(12), 1279–1283. https://doi: 10.1089/acm.2009.0693

Jiang, L., Wang, Y., Yin, Q., Liu, G., Liu, H., Huang, Y. & Li, B. (2017). Phycocyanin: a potential drug for cancer treatment. *Journal of Cancer, 8*(17), 3416–3429. https://doi.org/10.7150/jca.21058

Julson, E. (2017). Why is nutritional yeast good for you? *Healthline.* https://www.healthline.com/nutrition/nutritional-yeast

Kang J.X. (2011). Omega-3: a link between global climate change and human health. *Biotechnology Advances, 29*(4), 388–390. https://doi.org/10.1016/j.biotechadv.2011.02.003

King, J.C. & Slavin, J.L. (2013). White potatoes, human health, and dietary guidance. *Advances in Nutrition, 4*(3), 393S–401S. https://doi.org/10.3945/an.112.003525

Kite-Powell, J. (2018). See how algae could change our world. *Forbes.* https://www.forbes.com/sites/jenniferhicks/2018/06/15/see-how-algae-could-change-our-world/?sh=729939503e46

Kładna, A., Berczyński, P., Kruk, I., Piechowska, T. & Aboul-Enein, H.Y. (2016). Studies on the antioxidant properties of some phytoestrogens. *Luminescence: The Journal of Biological and Chemical Luminescence, 31*(6), 1201–1206. https://doi.org/10.1002/bio.3091

Kondal, A. (2019). What is textured vegetable protein (TVP)? Everything you need to know about TVP. *Totally Vegan Buzz.* https://www.totallyveganbuzz.com/trending/what-is-textured-vegetable-protein-tvp-everything-you-need-to-know-about-tvp/

Kopustinskiene, D.M., Jakstas, V., Savickas, A. & Bernatoniene, J. (2020). Flavonoids as anticancer agents. *Nutrients, 12*(2), 457. https://doi.org/10.3390/nu12020457

Krill Facts. (n.d.). Krill facts. *Krill Facts.* http://www.krillfacts.org/krill-facts.html

Kubala, J. (2019). Is canola oil healthy? All you need to know. *Healthline.* https://www.healthline.com/nutrition/is-canola-oil-healthy

Kumari, S., Gray, A.R., Webster, K., Bailey, K., Reid, M., Kelvin, K., Tey, S.L., Chisholm, A. & Brown, R.C. (2020). Does 'activating' nuts affect nutrient bioavailability? *Food Chemistry, 319,* 126529. https://doi.org/10.1016/j.foodchem.2020.126529

Lappano, R., Sebastiani, A., Cirillo, F., Rigiracciolo, D.C., Galli, G.R., Curcio, R., Malaguarnera, R., Belfiore, A., Cappello, A.R. & Maggiolini, M. (2017). The lauric acid-activated signaling prompts apoptosis in cancer cells. *Cell Death Discovery, 3,* 17063. https://doi.org/10.1038/cddiscovery.2017.63

Lee, S.H., Shinde, P.L., Choi, J.Y., Kwon, I.K., Lee, J.K., Pak, S.I., Cho, W.T. & Chae, B.J. (2010). Effects of tannic acid supplementation on growth performance, blood hematology, iron status and faecal microflora in weanling pigs. *Livestock Science, 131*(2–3), 281–286. https://doi.org/10.1016/j.livsci.2010.04.013

Lelley, T., Loy, B. & Murkovic, M. (2009). Hull-less oil seed pumpkin. In *Oil Crops, Handbook of Plant Breeding*. Vollmann, J. & Rajcan, I. (eds.). https://www.researchgate.net/publication/227184866_Hull-Less_Oil_Seed_Pumpkin

Lestari, B. & Meiyanto, E. (2018). A review: the emerging nutraceutical potential of pumpkin seeds. *Indonesian Journal of Cancer Chemoprevention, 9*(2), 92–101. https://ijcc.chemoprev.org/index.php/ijcc/article/view/225

Lestienne, I., Caporiccio, B., Besançon, P., Rochette, I. & Trèche, S. (2005). Relative contribution of phytates, fibers, and tannins to low iron and zinc in vitro solubility in pearl millet (Pennisetum glaucum) flour and grain fractions. *Journal of Agricultural and Food Chemistry, 53*(21), 8342–8348. https://doi.org/10.1021/jf050741p

Li, D., Wang, P., Luo, Y., Zhao, M. & Chen, F. (2017). Health benefits of anthocyanins and molecular mechanisms: update from recent decade. *Critical Reviews in Food Science and Nutrition, 57*(8), 1729–1741. https://www.tandfonline.com/doi/full/10.1080/10408398.2015.1030064

Magee, E. (2007). The super-veggies: cruciferous vegetables. *WebMD*. https://www.webmd.com/food-recipes/features/super-veggies-cruciferous-vegetables

Malik, V. (2019). Is there a place for coconut oil in a healthy diet? *Harvard Health Publishing*. https://www.health.harvard.edu/blog/is-there-a-place-for-coconut-oil-in-a-healthy-diet-2019011415764

Mayo Clinic. (2018). Cash in on the health benefits of corn. *Mayo Clinic Health System*. https://www.mayoclinichealthsystem.org/hometown-health/speaking-of-health/cash-in-on-the-health-benefits-of-corn#:~:text=Corn%20has%20several%20health%20benefits,%2C%20copper%2C%20iron%20and%20manganese.

Mayo Clinic. (2019). Nuts and your heart: eating nuts for heart health. *Mayo Clinic*. https://www.mayoclinic.org/diseases-conditions/heart-disease/in-depth/nuts/art-20046635

McClees, H. (2015). 5 reasons wild rice rocks on a gluten-free or grain-free diet. *One Green Planet*. https://www.onegreenplanet.org/vegan-food/reasons-wild-rice-rocks-on-a-gluten-free-or-grain-free-diet/#:~:text= Wild%20rice%20is%20the%20easiest,a%20vegetable%2C%20not%20a%20grain

Melgar, D. (2020). The real cost of Bayer's RoundUp settlement. *U.S. PIRG*. https://uspirg.org/blogs/blog/usp/real-cost-bayer%E2%80%99s-roundup-settlement#:~:text=Bayer%20will%20pay%20its%20%2410,children's%20cereal%20to%20our%20bodies

Mendel, M. (2013). Anticarcinogenic, cardioprotective, and other health benefits of tomato compounds lycopene, α-tomatine, and tomatidine in pure form and in fresh and processed tomatoes. *Journal of Agricultural and Food Chemistry, 61*(40), 9534–9550. https://pubs.acs.org/action/showCitFormats?doi=10.1021%2Fjf402654e&href=/doi/10.1021%2Fjf402654e

Mohan, S. & Nandhakumar, L. (2014). Role of various flavonoids: hypotheses on novel approach to treat diabetes. *Iranian Journal of Medical Hypotheses and Ideas, 8*(1), 1–6. https://www.sciencedirect.com/science/article/pii/S2251729413000153

Mori-Nu. (2021). Products. *Mor-Nu.* https://www.morinu.com/products/

Murugkar, D.A. (2014). Effect of sprouting of soybean on the chemical composition and quality of soymilk and tofu. *Journal of Food Science and Technology, 51*(5), 915–921. https://doi.org/10.1007/s13197-011-0576-9

MyFoodData. (n.d.). Nutrition facts comparison tool. *MyFoodData.com.* https://tools.myfooddata.com/nutrition-comparison/169414-580382-170148/wt9-oz-wt9/1-1-1

MyFoodData. (n.d.-a). Recipe nutrition calculator. *MyFoodData.com.* https://tools.myfooddata.com/recipe-nutrition-calculator/740206/wt1/1

MyFoodData. (n.d.-b). Recipe nutrition calculator. *MyFoodData.com.* https://tools.myfooddata.com/recipe-nutrition-calculator/170148/wt9/1

MyFoodData. (n.d.-c). Bragg—Nutritional Yeast Seasoning. *MyFoodData.com.* https://tools.myfooddata.com/nutrition-facts/623470/wt1/2

MyFoodData. (n.d.-d). Spirulina. *MyFoodData.com.* https://tools.myfooddata.com/nutrition-facts/170091/oz/1

MyNetDiary. (2021). *MyNetDiary.* https://www.mynetdiary.com/

Nandha, R., Singh, H., Garg, K. & Rani, S. (2014). Therapeutic potential of sunflower seeds: an overview. *International Journal of Research and Development in Pharmacy and Life Sciences, 3*(3), 967–972. https://ijrdpl.com/index.php/ijrdpl/article/view/335/332

National Institutes of Health (NIH). (2021). Vitamin A: fact sheet for consumers. *NIH Office of Dietary Supplements.* https://ods.od.nih.gov/factsheets/VitaminA-Consumer/

Nesaretnam, K., Gomez, P.A., Selvaduray, K.R. & Razak, G.A. (2007). Tocotrienol levels in adipose tissue of benign and malignant breast lumps in patients in Malaysia. *Asia Pacific Journal of Clinical Nutrition, 16*(3), 498–504. https://pubmed.ncbi.nlm.nih.gov/17704032/

Nissar, J., Tehmeena, A., Naik, H.R. & Hussain, S.Z. (2017). A review phytic acid: as antinutrient or nutraceutical. *Journal of Pharmacognosy and Phytochemistry, 6*(6), 1554–1560. https://www.phytojournal.com/archives/2017/vol6issue6/PartV/6-6-208-319.pdf

Nugent, A.P. (2005). Health properties of resistant starch. *Nutrition Bulletin, 30*(1), 27–54. https://doi.org/10.1111/j.1467-3010.2005.00481.x

NutritionData.com. (2018). Nuts, almonds, blanched, nutrition facts & calories. *NutritionData*. https://nutritiondata.self.com/facts/nut-and-seed-products/3086/2

Oceana. (n.d.). Cephalopods, crustaceans & other shellfish: Antarctic krill. *Oceana*. https://oceana.org/marine-life/cephalopods-crustaceans-other-shellfish/antarctic-krill#:~:text=Blue%20whales%20and%20other%20large,huge%20numbers%20of%20Antarctic%20krill

Okparanta, S., Daminabo, V. & Solomon, L. (2018). Assessment of rancidity and other physicochemical properties of edible oils (mustard and corn oils) stored at room temperature, *Journal of Food and Nutrition Sciences, 6*(3), 70–75. https://www.sciencepublishinggroup.com/journal/paperinfo?journalid=154&doi=10.11648/j.jfns.20180603.11

Oldfield, J. (2017). Chia seeds promote weight loss in people with diabetes: study. *University of Toronto*. https://medicine.utoronto.ca/news/chia-seeds-promote-weight-loss-people-diabetes-study#:~:text=Chia%20Seeds%20Promote%20Weight%20Loss%20in%20People%20with%20Diabetes%3A%20Study,-Pinterest&text=University%20of%20Toronto%20researchers%20have,maintaining%20good%20blood%20sugar%20control

Oliver, J. (2022). Butternut squashed. *Jamie Oliver Enterprises Limited*. https://www.jamieoliver.com/recipes/vegetables-recipes/butternut-squashed/

Pascual, G., Domínguez, D., Elosúa-Bayes, M., Beckedorff, F., Laudanna, C., Bigas, C., Douillet, D., Greco, C., Symeonidi, A., Hernández, I., Gil, S.R., Prats, N., Bescós, C., Shiekhattar, R., Amit, M., Heyn, H., Shilatifard, A. & Benitah, S.A. (2021). Dietary palmitic acid promotes a prometastatic memory via Schwann cells. *Nature, 599*(7885), 485–490. https://doi.org/10.1038/s41586-021-04075-0

Pate, K.M., Rogers., M., Reed, J.W., van der Munnik, N., Vance, S.Z. & Moss, M.A. (2018). Anthoxanthin polyphenols attenuate Aβ *oligomer-induced neuronal responses associated with Alzheimer's disease. CNS Neuroscience & Therapeutics*. https://www.ncbi.nlm.nih.gov/pmc/articles/PMC5239747/

Patel, A. (2016). Teff benefits: 8 healthy reasons to add teff to your diet. *Huffington Post*. https://www.huffingtonpost.ca/2014/02/06/teff-benefits-_n_4740219.html

PetFoodIndustry.com. (2009). Soy may aid in canine cancer therapy. *PetFoodIndustry.com*. https://www.petfoodindustry.com/articles/1229-soy-may-aid-in-canine-cancer-therapy

Petroski, W. & Minich, D.M. (2020). Is there such a thing as "anti-nutrients"? A narrative review of perceived problematic plant compounds. *Nutrients, 12*(10), 2929. https://doi.org/10.3390/nu12102929

Phillips, K.M., Ruggio, D.M. & Ashraf-Khorassani, M. (2005). Phytosterol composition of nuts and seeds commonly consumed in the United States. *Journal of Agriculture and Food Chemistry, 53*(24), 9436–9445. https://pubmed.ncbi.nlm.nih.gov/16302759/

Ramprasath, V.R. & Awad, A.B. (2015). Role of phytosterols in cancer prevention and treatment. *Journal of AOAC International, 98*(3), 735–738. https://academic.oup.com/jaoac/article/98/3/735/5654475

Randall, D., Liana, B. & Agradi, E. (1990). Fish in human nutrition research and the implications for aquaculture. *Ambio, 19*(5), 272–275. https://www.jstor.org/stable/4313710?seq=1

Reese, C.A., Bauer, J.E., Burkholder, W.J., Kennis, R.A., Dunbar, B.L. & Bigley, K.E. (2001). Effects of dietary flax seed and sunflower seed supplementation on normal canine serum polyunsaturated fatty acids and skin and hair coat condition scores. *Veterinary Dermatology, 12*(2), 111–117. https://pubmed.ncbi.nlm.nih.gov/11360337/

Robbins, J. (2010). What about soy? *John Robbins.* https://www.johnrobbins.info/what-about-soy/

Robbins, O. (2019). 5 health benefits of jicama and how you can add it to your diet. *Food Revolution Network.* https://foodrevolution.org/blog/jicama-health-benefits/

Robb-Nicholson, C. (2006). By the way, doctor: do soy products cause thyroid problems? *Harvard Women's Health Watch.* https://www.health.harvard.edu/newsletter_article/By_the_way_doctor_Do_soy_products_cause_thyroid_problems

Rogers, K. (2020). Tofu. *Encyclopedia Britannica.* https://www.britannica.com/topic/tofu

Sarita & Singh, E. (2016). Potential of millets: nutrients composition and health benefits. *Journal of Scientific and Innovative Research, 5*(2), 46–50. http://www.jsirjournal.com/Vol5_Issue2_04.pdf

Satyaraj, E., Reynolds, A., Engler, R., Labuda, J. & Sun, P. (2021). Supplementation of diets with *spirulina* **influences immune and gut function in dogs.** *Frontiers in Nutrition, 8*, 667072. https://doi.org/10.3389/fnut.2021.667072

Sennebogen, E. (2021). What is textured vegetable protein? *How Stuff Works.* https://recipes.howstuffworks.com/textured-vegetable-protein.htm

Silva-Sánchez, C., Barba de la Rosa, A.P., León-Galván, M.F., de Lumen, B.O., de León-Rodríguez, A. & de Mejía, E.G. (2008). Bioactive peptides in amaranth (*Amaranthus hypochondriacus*) seed. *Journal of Agricultural and Food Chemistry, 56*(4), 1233–40. https://pubs.acs.org/doi/full/10.1021/jf072911z

SimplyHealthy. (2020). What do lentils taste like? Why should you eat more lentils? *SimplyHealthy.* https://www.simplyhealthyfamily.org/lentils-taste/#:~:text= The%20brown%20lentils%2C%20for%20example,rich%20and%20deep%20earthy%20notes

Slagle, A. (2019). The difference between pepitas & pumpkin seeds. *Food52*. https://food52.com/blog/14456-the-difference-between-pepitas-and-the-seeds-from-your-halloween-pumpkin

Smeriglio, A., Barreca, D., Bellocco, E. & Trombetta, D. (2017). Proanthocyanidins and hydrolysable tannins: occurrence, dietary intake and pharmacological effects. *British Journal of Pharmacology, 174*(11), 1244–1262. https://doi.org/10.1111/bph.13630

Smith, J. (2019). Split peas: are they peas or lentils? *Illinois Extension*. https://extension.illinois.edu/blogs/simply-nutritious-quick-and-delicious/2019-09-27-split-peas-are-they-peas-or-lentils#:~: text=Split%20peas%20are%20a%20member,field%20pea%20that%20is%20dried.&text=Green%20split%20peas%20are%20sweeter,used%20in%20split%20pea%20soup

Sorrells, A. (2019). Are lentils healthy, and can you eat them raw? *Cooking Light*. https://www.cookinglight.com/eating-smart/nutrition-101/what-are-lentils-healthy

Staughton, J. (2020). 9 interesting benefits of rutabaga. *Organic Facts*. https://www.organicfacts.net/health-benefits/vegetable/rutabaga.html

Stevenson, D.G., Eller, F.J., Wang, L., Jane, J.L., Wang, T. & Inglett, G.E. (2007). Oil and tocopherol content and composition of pumpkin seed oil in 12 cultivars. *Journal of Agriculture and Food Chemistry, 55*, 4005–4013. https://pubs.acs.org/doi/10.1021/jf0706979

Taylor, E.N., Fung, T.T. & Curhan, G.C. (2009). DASH-style diet associates with reduced risk for kidney stones. *Journal of the American Society of Nephrology: JASN, 20*(10), 2253–2259. https://doi.org/10.1681/ASN.2009030276

Taylor, H., Webster, K., Gray, A.R., Tey, S.L., Chisholm, A., Bailey, K, Kumari, S. & Brown, R.C. (2018). The effects of 'activating' almonds on consumer acceptance and gastrointestinal tolerance. *European Journal of Nutrition, 57*, 2771–2783. https://doi.org/10.1007/s00394-017-1543-7

The Bean Institute. (2020). Beans, beans, the magical "fruit": the more you eat, the less you toot! *Northarvest Bean Growers Association*. https://beaninstitute.com/beans-beans-the-magical-fruit/

Tweed, V. (2017). Brewer's yeast versus nutritional yeast. *Betternutrition*. https://www.betternutrition.com/supplements/brewers-yeast-versus-nutritional-yeast/

University Of Newcastle Upon Tyne. (2005). Carrot component reduces cancer risk. *ScienceDaily*. www.sciencedaily.com/releases/2005/02/050212184702.htm

Venkata, R.P. & Subramanyam, R. (2016). Evaluation of the deleterious health effects of consumption of repeatedly heated vegetable oil. *Toxicology Reports, 3*, 636–643. https://doi.org/10.1016/j.toxrep.2016.08.003

Vuksan, V., Jenkins, A.L., Brissette, C., Choleva, L., Jovanovski, E., Gibbs, A.L., Bazinet, R.P., Au-Yeung, F., Zurbau, A., Ho, H.V.T., Duvnjak, L., Sievenpiper, J.L., Josse, R.G. & Hanna, A. (2016). Salba-chia (*Salvia hispanica* L.) in the treatment of overweight and obese patients with type 2 diabetes: a double-blind randomized controlled trial. *Nutrition, Metabolism & Cardiovascular Diseases.* https://doi.org/10.1016/j.numecd.2016.11.124

Wang, Q. & Xiong, Y.L. (2019). Processing, nutrition, and functionality of hempseed protein: a review. *Comprehensive Reviews in Food Science and Food Safety, 18*(4), 936–952. https://doi.org/10.1111/1541-4337.12450

Watson, M. (2020). Quick-soak method for dried beans. *The Spruce Eats.* https://www.thespruceeats.com/quick-soak-method-for-dried-beans-2215821

WebMD. (2019). Health benefits of sweet potatoes. *WebMD.* https://www.webmd.com/food-recipes/benefits-sweet-potatoes#1

WebMD. (2020). Slideshow: foods your dog should never eat. *WebMD.* https://pets.webmd.com/dogs/ss/slideshow-foods-your-dog-should-never-eat.

Weg, A. (2017). Not all lentils are created equal—which variety is right for you? *Cooking Light.* https://www.cookinglight.com/cooking-101/different-types-lentils

Westcott, P. (2018). Health benefits of root vegetables. *Saga.* https://www.saga.co.uk/magazine/health-wellbeing/diet-nutrition/nutrition/root-vegetable-health-benefits#:~:text=Root%20vegetables%20are%20especially%20rich,heart%20disease%20and%20bowel%20cancer

Willett, W.C. (2018). Ask the doctor: coconut oil and health. *Harvard Health Publishing.* https://www.health.harvard.edu/staying-healthy/coconut-oil#:~:text=Coconut%20oil%20is%20about%2090,the%20risk%20of%20heart%20disease

Winwood, R.J. (2013). Recent developments in the commercial production of DHA and EPA rich oils from micro-algae. *OCL (Oilseeds and Fats Crops and Lipids), 20*(6), D604. https://doi.org/10.1051/ocl/2013030

Xanthopoulou, M.N., Nomikos, T., Fragopoulou, E. & Antonopoulou, S. (2009). Antioxidant and lipoxygenase inhibitory activities of pumpkin seed extracts. *Food Research International, 42*(5–6), 641–646. https://doi.org/10.1016/j.foodres.2009.02.003

Xiong, Y., Zhang, P., Warner, R.D. & Fang, Z. (2019). Sorghum grain: from genotype, nutrition and phenolic profile to its health benefits and food applications. *Comprehensive Reviews in Food Science and Food Safety, 18*(6). https://doi.org/10.1111/1541-4337.12506

Xu, W., Han, F., Piao, W., Sun, J., Bi, Y. & Huo, J. (2015). Study of DHA algal oil compound preparation on improving memory in mice. *Wei Sheng Yan Jiu* (Journal of Hygiene Research), *44*(1), 86–90. https://pubmed.ncbi.nlm.nih.gov/25958644/

Yan, L. (2016). Dark green leafy vegetables. *USDA Agricultural Research Service.* https://www.ars.usda.gov/plains-area/gfnd/gfhnrc/docs/news-2013/dark-green-leafy-vegetables/

Zeratsky, K. (2020). I know lentils are supposed to be good for me. But how do I prepare them? *Mayo Clinic.* https://www.mayoclinic.org/healthy-lifestyle/nutrition-and-healthy-eating/expert-answers/lentils/faq-20058072

Zeratsky, K. (2020a). Will eating soy increase my risk of breast cancer? *Mayo Clinic.* https://www.mayoclinic.org/healthy-lifestyle/nutrition-and-healthy-eating/expert-answers/soy-breast-cancer-risk/faq-20120377

Chapter 6: Building Recipes

4Ocean. (2020). 11 sustainable grocery shopping tips. *4Ocean.* https://www.4ocean.com/blogs/blog/11-sustainable-grocery-shopping-tips

Association of American Feed Control Officials (AAFCO). (2012). Reading labels. *Association of American Feed Control Officials.* https://talkspetfood.aafco.org/readinglabels#Adequacy

Association for Pet Obesity Prevention (APOP). (2019). https://petobesityprevention.org/

Basko, I.J. (2013). *Fresh Food & Ancient Wisdom* [2nd ed.]. Kapaa, HI: Makana Kai Publishing

Coates, J. (2012). Nutritional differences for small, toy and large-breed dogs. *PetMD.* https://www.petmd.com/blogs/nutritionnuggets/jcoates/2012/feb/nutrition_differences_for_small_toy_large_breeds-12459

Coates, J. (2017). How many Calories does a dog need? *PetMD.* https://www.petmd.com/blogs/nutritionnuggets/jcoates/2013/aug/how-many-calories-does-dog-need-30849#math

Davies, R.H., Lawes, J.R. & Wales, A.D. (2019). Raw diets for dogs and cats: a review, with particular reference to microbiological hazards. *Journal of Small Animal Practice, 60,* 329–339. https://doi.org/10.1111/jsap.13000

Dodds, W.J. & Laverdure, D.R. (2011). *The Canine Thyroid Epidemic: Answers You Need for Your Dog.* Wenatchee, WA, US: Dogwise Publishing

Kroll Settlement Administration, LLC. (2021). Hill's Pet Food settlement. *Kroll Settlement Administration, LLC.* https://www.petfoodsettlement.com/

Li, J.M., Li, L., Zhang, Y., Jiang, Z.Y., Limbu, S., Qiao, F., Degrace, P., Zhang, M.L. & Du, Z.Y. (2019). Functional differences between L-and D-carnitine in metabolic regulation evaluated using a low-carnitine Nile tilapiamodel. *British Journal of Nutrition, 122*(6), 625–638. https://www.cambridge.org/core/journals/british-journal-of-nutrition/article/functional-differences-between-l-and-dcarnitine-in-metabolic-regulation-evaluated-using-a-lowcarnitine-nile-tilapia-model/56B8BD809DB53EC2CBB1AB5-0966697DA

Linder, D.E. (2017). Confused about what to feed your large-breed puppy? New rules may help! *Petfoodology.* https://vetnutrition.tufts.edu/2017/02/confused-about-what-to-feed-your-large-breed-puppy-new-rules-may-help/

Maugh II, T.H. (1987). Thousands of cat deaths traced to pet food deficiency. *Los Angeles Times.* https://www.latimes.com/archives/la-xpm-1987-08-14-mn-805-story.html.

MedlinePlus. (2020). Complete Blood Count (CBC). *MedlinePlus.* https://medlineplus.gov/lab-tests/complete-blood-count-cbc/

MedlinePlus. (2021). Comprehensive Metabolic Panel (CMP). *MedlinePlus.* https://medlineplus.gov/lab-tests/comprehensive-metabolic-panel-cmp/

Messonnier, S. (2012). *Nutritional Supplements for the Veterinary Practice: A Pocket Guide.* Lakewood, CO: American Animal Hospital Association Press.

National Research Council of the National Academy of Sciences (NRC). (2006). *Nutrient Requirements of Dogs and Cats.* Washington, DC, US: NRC Press

Okuma, T.A & Hellberg, R.S. (2015). Identification of meat species in pet foods using a real-time polymerase chain reaction (PCR) assay. *Food Control, 50,* 9–17, https://pubag.nal.usda.gov/catalog/5430781

Rizzi, T.E. (2014). Urinalysis in companion animals, Part 2: evaluation of urine chemistry & sediment. *Today's Veterinary Practice,* May/June. https://todaysveterinarypractice.com/wp-content/uploads/sites/4/2016/06/T1405C09.pdf

Self NutritionData. (2018). NutritionData. *Self Nutrition Data.* https://nutritiondata.self.com/

The Ohio State University Veterinary Medical Center. (n.d.). Basic Calorie calculator. *The Ohio State University Veterinary Medical Center.* https://vet.osu.edu/vmc/companion/our-services/nutrition-support-service/basic-calorie-calculator

Toresson, L. (2012). The fecal microbiome in dogs with acute diarrhea and idiopathic inflammatory bowel disease. *PLoS ONE, 7*(12), e51907. https://doi.org/10.1371/journal.pone.0051907

Tufts University. (2013). Interpreting your dog's blood chemistry profile. *Your Dog.* https://www.tuftsyourdog.com/doghealthandmedicine/interpreting-your-dogs-blood-chemistry-profile/

Weese, J.S., Rousseau, J. & Arroyo, L. (2005). Bacteriological evaluation of commercial canine and feline raw diets. *The Canadian Veterinary Journal (La Revue Veterinaire Canadienne), 46*(6), 513–516. https://www.ncbi.nlm.nih.gov/pmc/articles/PMC1140397/

Wynn, S. & Marsden, S. (2003). *Manual of Natural Veterinary Medicine: Science and Tradition.* St. Louis, MO: Mosby

Chapter 7: Overcoming Obstacles

Brissette, C. (2019). Why you should be wary of some digestive enzyme supplements. *The Washington Post.* https://www.washingtonpost.com/lifestyle/wellness/why-you-should-be-wary-of-some-digestive-enzyme-supplements/2019/02/18/4531ef3e-2fdc-11e9-8ad3-9a5b113ecd3c_story.html

Burnham, T. (2012). What's the scoop on bulk foods? *The Salt.* https://www.npr.org/sections/thesalt/2012/04/12/149931279/whats-the-scoop-on-bulk-foods

Environmental Working Group (EWG). (2021). EWG's shopper's guide to pesticides in produce. *Environmental Working Group.* https://www.ewg.org/foodnews/full-list.php

Harvard Medical School. (2014). Fresh or frozen produce? The health benefit is all in the mix. *Harvard Health Publishing.* https://www.health.harvard.edu/staying-healthy/fresh-or-frozen-produce-the-health-benefit-is-all-in-the-mix#:~:text=The%20good%20news%20is%20that,fresh%20anymore%2C%22%20says%20Dr

Hewings-Martin, Y. (2019). How different kinds of fiber affect the microbiome. *Medical News Today.* https://www.medicalnewstoday.com/articles/326402

Li, L., Pegg, R.B., Eitenmiller, R.R., Ji-Yeon Chun, J.-Y. & Kerrihard, A.L. (2017). Selected nutrient analyses of fresh, fresh-stored, and frozen fruits and vegetables. *Journal of Food Composition and Analysis, 59,* 8–17. https://www.sciencedirect.com/science/article/pii/S0889157517300418

Marks, J.W. (2017). How can I reduce stomach gas when I eat fiber? *MedicineNet.* https://www.medicinenet.com/can_i_reduce_stomach_gas_when_i_eat_fiber/ask.htm

Sweers, R. (2011). Dried beans, peas and lentils can help you save $$$. *Iowa State University, Extension and Outreach.* https://www.extension.iastate.edu/dallas/sites/www.extension.iastate.edu/files/dallas/N3515.pdf

Part 2: Plant-Based Diet Solutions for Common Canine Chronic Diseases

Chapter 8: Plant-Based Diet Solutions for Cancer

Aggarwal, B.B. & Shishodia, S. (2006). Molecular targets of dietary agents for prevention and therapy of cancer. *Biochemical Pharmacology, 71*(10), 1397–1421. https://doi.org/10.1016/j.bcp.2006.02.009

Aggarwal, B.B., Sethi, G., Baladandayuthapani, V., Krishnan, S. & Shishodia, S. (2007). Targeting cell signaling pathways for drug discovery: an old lock needs a new key. *Journal of Cellular Biochemistry, 102*(3), 580-592. https://pubmed.ncbi.nlm.nih.gov/17668425/

Aggarwal, B.B., Yuan, W., Li, S. & Gupta, S.C. (2013). Curcumin-free turmeric exhibits anti-inflammatory and anticancer activities: identification of novel components of turmeric. *Molecular Nutrition & Food Research, 57*(9),1529–1542. https://pubmed.ncbi.

nlm.nih.gov/23847105/

Ahmad, A., Husain, A., Mujeeb, M., Khan, S.A., Najmi, A.K., Siddique, N.A., Damanhouri, Z. A. & Anwar, F. (2013). A review on therapeutic potential of Nigella sativa: a miracle herb. *Asian Pacific Journal of Tropical Biomedicine, 3*(5), 337–352. https://doi.org/10.1016/S2221-1691(13)60075-1

Akramiene, D., Kondrotas, A., Didziapetriene, J. & Kevelaitis E. (2007). Effects of beta-glucans on the immune system. *Medicina (Kaunas), 43*(8), 597–606. https://pubmed.ncbi.nlm.nih.gov/17895634/

Alves, C., Silva, J., Pinteus, S., Gaspar, H., Alpoim, M.C., Botana, L.M. & Pedrosa, R. (2018). From marine origin to therapeutics: the antitumor potential of marine algae-derived compounds. *Frontiers in Pharmacology, 9*, 777. https://doi.org/10.3389/fphar.2018.00777

American Institute for Cancer Research (AICR). (2021). Pulses: dry beans, peas and lentils (legumes). *American Institute for Cancer Research.* https://www.aicr.org/cancer-prevention/food-facts/dry-beans-and-peas-legumes/

Anand, P., Kunnumakkara, A.B., Sundaram, C., Harikumar, K.B., Tharakan, S.T., Lai, O.S., Sung, B. & Aggarwal, B.B. (2008). Cancer is a preventable disease that requires major lifestyle changes. *Pharmaceutical Research, 25*(9), 2097–2116. https://link.springer.com/article/10.1007%2Fs11095-008-9661-9

Arsyad, A., Idris, I. Rasyid, A.A., Usman, R.A., Faradillah, K.R., Lataif, W.O.U., Lubis, Z.I., Aminuddin, A., Yustisia, I. & Djabir, Y.Y. (2020). Long-term ketogenic diet induces metabolic acidosis, anemia, and oxidative stress in healthy Wistar rats. *Journal of Nutrition and Metabolilsm, 2020.* https://doi.org/10.1155/2020/3642035

Ayeka, P.A. (2018). Potential of mushroom compounds as immunomodulators in cancer immunotherapy: a review. *Evidence-Based Complementary and Alternative Medicine,* 7271509. https://pubmed.ncbi.nlm.nih.gov/29849725/

Bank, I.M., Shemie, S.D., Rosenblatt, B., Bernard, C. & Mackie, A.S. (2008). Sudden cardiac death in association with the ketogenic diet. *Pediatric Neurology, 39*(6), 429–431. https://doi.org/10.1016/j.pediatrneurol.2008.08.013

Bansal, M., Singh, N., Pal, S., Dev, I. & Mahmood Ansari, K. (2018). Chapter Three - Chemopreventive role of dietary phytochemicals in colorectal cancer. [Editors: Fishbein, J.C. & Heilman, J.M.]. *Advances in Molecular Toxicology,* Elsevier, *12,* 69–121, https://doi.org/10.1016/B978-0-444-64199-1.00004-X

Bergqvist, A.G., Schall, J.I., Stallings, V.A. & Zemel, B. S. (2008). Progressive bone mineral content loss in children with intractable epilepsy treated with the ketogenic diet. *The American Journal of Clinical Nutrition, 88*(6), 1678–1684. https://doi.org/10.3945/ajcn.2008.26099

Blackburn, K.B. (2018). The keto diet and cancer: what patients should know. *MD Anderson Cancer Center*. https://www.mdanderson.org/cancerwise/the-keto-diet-and-cancer--what-patients-should-know.h00-159223356.html

Boivin, D., Lamy, S., Lord-Dufour, S., Jackson, J., Beaulieu, E., Côté, M., Moghrabi, A., Barrette, S., Gingras, D. & Béliveau, R. (2009). Antiproliferative and antioxidant activities of common vegetables: a comparative study. *Food Chemistry, 112*(2), 374–380. https://www.sciencedirect.com/science/article/pii/S0308814608006419

Bosetti, C., Filomeno, M., Riso, P., Negri, E., Franceschi, S. & La Vecchia, C. (2012). Cruciferous vegetables and cancer risk in a network of case-control studies. *Annals of Oncology, 23*(8), 2198–2203. https://doi.org/10.1093/annonc/mdr604

Brown, E.S., Allsopp, P.J., Magee, P.J., Gill, C.I., Nitecki, S., Strain, C.R. & McSorley, E.M. (2014). Seaweed and human health. *Nutrition Reviews, 72*(3), 205–216. https://pubmed.ncbi.nlm.nih.gov/24697280/

Buehring, G.C., Philpott, S.M. & Choi, K.Y. (2003). Humans have antibodies reactive with Bovine leukemia virus. *AIDS Research and Human Retroviruses, 19*(12), 1105–1113. https://pubmed.ncbi.nlm.nih.gov/14709247/

Buehring, G.C., DeLaney, A., Shen, H., Chu, D.L., Razavian, N., Schwartz, D.A., Demkovich, Z.R. & Bates, M.N. (2019). Bovine leukemia virus discovered in human blood. *BMC Infectious Diseases, 19*. https://doi.org/10.1186/s12879-019-3891-9

Cardona, F., Andrés-Lacueva, C., Tulipani, S., Tinahones, F.J. & Queipo-Ortuño, M.I. (2013). Benefits of polyphenols on gut microbiota and implications in human health. *The Journal of Nutrition Biochemistry, 24*(8), 1415–22. https://pubmed.ncbi.nlm.nih.gov/23849454/

ChartsBin. (2011). Current worldwide total milk consumption per capita. *ChartsBin*. chartsbin.com/view/1491

Chen, L., Jiang, B., Zhong, C., Guo, J., Zhang, L., Mu, T., Zhang, Q. & Bi, X. (2018). Chemoprevention of colorectal cancer by black raspberry anthocyanins involved the modulation of gut microbiota and SFRP2 demethylation. *Carcinogenesis, 39*(3), 471–481. https://doi.org/10.1093/carcin/bgy009

Choi, J.N., Song, J.E., Shin, J.I., Kim, H.D., Kim, M.J. & Lee, J.S. (2010). Renal stone associated with the ketogenic diet in a 5-year-old girl with intractable epilepsy. *Yonsei medical journal, 51*(3), 457–459. https://doi.org/10.3349/ymj.2010.51.3.457

Cimino-Brown, D. & Reetz, J. (2012). Single agent polysaccharopeptide delays metastases and improves survival in naturally occurring hemangiosarcoma. *Evidence-Based Complementary and Alternative Medicine, 12,* 1–8. https://doi.org/10.1155/2012/384301

Cohen, J.H., Kristal, A.R. & Stanford, J.L. (2000). Fruit and vegetable intakes and prostate cancer risk. *Journal of the National Cancer Institute, 92*(1), 61–68. https://pubmed.ncbi.nlm.nih.gov/10620635/

Compound Interest. (2017). Broccoli color changes and cancer-fighting compounds. *Compound Interest.* https://www.compoundchem.com/2017/10/19/broccoli/

Cotas, J., Pacheco, D., Gonçalves, A.M.M., Silva, P., Carvalho, L.G. & Pereira, L. (2021). Seaweeds' nutraceutical and biomedical potential in cancer therapy: a concise review. *Journal of Cancer Metastasis and Treatment, 7*(13). http://dx.doi.org/10.20517/2394-4722.2020.134

Czerwonka, M. & Tokarz, A. (2017). Iron in red meat–friend or foe. *Journal of Meat Science, 123,* 157–165. https://doi.org/10.1016/j.meatsci.2016.09.012

Danahy, A. (2020). How do black raspberries and blackberries differ? *Healthline.* https://www.healthline.com/nutrition/black-raspberry-vs-blackberry

Donaldson, M. (2004). Nutrition and cancer: a review of the evidence for an anti-cancer diet. *Nutrition Journal, 3.* https://nutritionj.biomedcentral.com/articles/10.1186/1475-2891-3-19

Environmental Defense Fund (EDF). (n.d.). PCBs in fish and shellfish. *Environmental Defense Fund.* https://seafood.edf.org/pcbs-fish-and-shellfish

Environmental Protection Agency (EPA). (2020). Learn about dioxin. *Environmental Protection Agency.* https://www.epa.gov/dioxin/learn-about-dioxin#:~:text= Although%20 environmental%20levels%20of%20dioxins,and%20break%20down%20very%20slowly

Environmental Protection Agency (EPA). (2021). Glyphosate. *Environmental Protection Agency.* https://www.epa.gov/ingredients-used-pesticide-products/glyphosate

Environmental Working Group (EWG). (2009). Dog food contaminated with levels of fluoride above EPA's legal limit for humans. *Environmental Working Group.* https://www.ewg.org/news-insights/news-release/dog-food-contaminated-levels-fluoride-above-epas-legal-limit-humans

Erickson, N., Boscheri, A., Linke, B. & Huebner, J. (2017). Systematic review: isocaloric ketogenic dietary regimes for cancer patients. *Medical Oncology, 34*(5), 72. https://doi.org/10.1007/s12032-017-0930-5

Ettinger, J. (2018). Should you be eating seaweed? *Organic Authority.* https://www.organicauthority.com/health/should-you-be-eating-seaweed

FETCH a Cure. (2021). Facts. *FETCH a Cure.* https://fetchacure.org/resource-library/facts/#:~:text=Similar%20to%20humans%2C%20our%20pets,diagnosed%20with%20cancer%20this%20year

Fuhrman, J. (2016). Why a nutritarian diet is superior to the ketogenic diet in the fight against cancer. *Dr. Fuhrman.* https://www.drfuhrman.com/blog/124/why-a-nutritarian-diet-is-superior-to-the-ketogenic-diet-in-the-fight-against-cancer

Fuhrman, J. (2016a). Optimal IGF-1 levels for longevity. *Dr. Fuhrman.* https://www.drfuhrman.com/blog/60/igf-1s-link-to-cancer

Gautam, A.K., Sharma, D., Sharma, J. & Saini, K.C. (2020). Legume lectins: potential use as a diagnostics and therapeutics against the cancer. *International Journal of Biological Macromolecules, 142*, 474–483. https://doi.org/10.1016/j.ijbiomac.2019.09.119

Graham, S. (2005). Carrot compound shows promise for slowing cancer. *Scientific American.* https://www.scientificamerican.com/article/carrot-compound-shows-pro/

Greger, M. & Stone, G. (2015). *How Not to Die.* New York, NY: Flatiron Books

Gu, D., Neuman, Z.L., Modiano, J.F. & Turesky, R.J. (2012). Biomonitoring the cooked meat carcinogen 2-Amino-1-methyl-6-phenylimidazo[4,5-b]pyridine in canine fur. *Journal of Agricultural and Food Chemistry, 60*(36), 9371–9375. https://pubs.acs.org/doi/full/10.1021/jf302969h

Gupta, S.C., Patchva, S. & Aggarwal, B.B. (2013). Therapeutic roles of curcumin: lessons learned from clinical trials. *The AAPS Journal, 15*(1), 195–218. https://doi.org/10.1208/s12248-012-9432-8

Hansen, S.L., Purup, S. & Christensen, L.P. (2003). Bioactivity of falcarinol and the influence of processing and storage on its content in carrots (*Daucus carota* L). *Journal of the Science of Food and Agriculture, 83*(10), 1010–1017. https://doi.org/10.1002/jsfa.1442

Hansen-Møller, J., Hansen, S.L., Christensen, L.P., Jespersen, L., Brandt, K. & Haraldsdóttir, J. (2002). Quantification of polyacetylenes by LC-MS in human plasma after intake of fresh carrot juice (Daucus carota L.). In *DIAS Report, Horticulture: Health promoting compounds in vegetables and fruit.* [Brandt, K. & Åkesson, B., Editors]. Proceedings of workshop in Karrebæksminde, Denmark, 6-8 Nov., *29*, 137–138. http://web.agrsci.dk/djfpublikation/djfpdf/djfh29.pdf

Hardy, C. (2020). Bone cancer in dogs. *Colorado State University: Flint Animal Cancer Center.* https://www.csuanimalcancercenter.org/2020/07/09/bone-cancer-in-dogs/

Harvard T.H. Chan School of Public Health. (2021). Diet review: ketogenic diet for weight loss. *Harvard T.H. Chan School of Public Health.* https://www.hsph.harvard.edu/nutritionsource/healthy-weight/diet-reviews/ketogenic-diet/#:~:text=Generally%2C%20popular%20ketogenic%20resources%20suggest,carbohydrate%2C%20and%2075%20grams%20protein

Hiskey, D. (2014). Pretty much all carrots used to be purple. *Insider.* https://www.businessinsider.com/carrots-used-to-be-purple-before-17th-century-2014-6

Holmer, B. (2019). Acetoacetate or AcAc: all you need to know. *HVMN.* https://hvmn.com/blogs/blog/ketosis-acetoacetate-or-acac-all-you-need-to-know

Hooda, J., Shah, A. & Zhang, L. (2014). Heme, an essential nutrient from dietary proteins, critically impacts diverse physiological and pathological processes. *Nutrients, 6*(3), 1080–1102. https://doi.org/10.3390/nu6031080

Iqbal, J., Abbasi, B.A., Mahmood, T., Kanwal, S., Ali, B., Shah, S.A. & Khalil, A.T. (2017). Plant-derived anticancer agents: a green anticancer approach. *Asian Pacific Journal of Tropical Biomedicine, 7*(12), 1129–1150. https://doi.org/10.1016/j.apjtb.2017.10.016

Ishikawa, T., Nakatsuru, Y., Zarkovic, M. & Shamsuddin, A.M. (1999). Inhibition of skin cancer by IP6 in vivo: initiation-promotion model. *Anticancer Research, 19*(5A), 3749–3752. https://pubmed.ncbi.nlm.nih.gov/10625952/

Iso, H. & Kubota, Y. (2007). Japan collaborative cohort study for evaluation of cancer. Nutrition and disease in the Japan collaborative cohort study for evaluation of cancer (JACC). *Asian Pacific Journal of Cancer Prevention, 8*(Suppl), 35–80. https://pubmed.ncbi.nlm.nih.gov/18260705/

Ivanova, T.S., Krupodorova, T.A., Varshteyn, V.Y., Artamonova, A.B. & Shlyakhovenko, V.A. (2014). Anticancer substances of mushroom origin. *Experimental Oncology, 36*(2). 58–66. http://dspace.nbuv.gov.ua/bitstream/handle/123456789/145333/01-Ivanova.pdf?sequence=1

Johnson, J.L. (2009). Effect of black raspberry extracts on colon cancer cell proliferation. [Master's thesis]. Columbus, OH: The Ohio State University

Johnson, J.L., Bomser, J.A., Scheerens, J.C. & Giusti, M.M. (2011). Effect of black raspberry (*Rubus occidentalis* L.) extract variation conditioned by cultivar, production site, and fruit maturity stage on colon cancer cell proliferation. *Journal of Agriculture and Food Chemistry, 59(5)*, 1638–1645. https://doi.org/10.1021/jf1023388

Jubert, C., Mata, J., Bench, G., Dashwood, R., Pereira, C., Tracewell, W., Turteltaub, K., Williams, D. & Bailey, G. (2009). Effects of chlorophyll and chlorophyllin on low-dose aflatoxin B(1) pharmacokinetics in human volunteers. *Cancer Prevention Research, 2*(12), 1015–1022. https://doi.org/10.1158/1940-6207.CAPR-09-0099

Kahn, J. (2017). Green foods may power your cells like plants. *HuffPost.* https://www.huffpost.com/entry/green-foods-may-power-you_b_10100340

Khader, M. & Eckl, P.M. (2014). Thymoquinone: an emerging natural drug with a wide range of medical applications. *Iranian Journal of Basic Medical Sciences, 17*(12), 950–957. https://www.ncbi.nlm.nih.gov/pmc/articles/PMC4387230/

Khazaei, S., Rezaeian, S., Khazaei, Z., Molaeipoor, L., Nematollahi, S., Lak, P. & Khazaei, S. (2016). National breast cancer mortality and incidence rates according to the human development index: an ecological study. *Advances in Breast Cancer Research, 5*(1). https://doi.org/10.4236/abcr.2016.51003

Kolonel, L.N., Hankin, J.H., Whittemore, A.S., Wu, A.H., Gallagher, R.P., Wilkens, L.R., John, E.M., Howe, G.R., Dreon, D.M., West, D.W. & Paffenbarger Jr, R.S. (2000). Vegetables, fruits, legumes and prostate cancer: a multiethnic case-control study. *Cancer Epidemiology, Biomarkers & Prevention, 9*(8), 795–804. https://pubmed.ncbi.nlm.nih.gov/10952096/

Kresty, L.A., Mallery, S.R. & Stoner, G.D. (2016). Black raspberries in cancer clinical trials: past, present and future. *Journal of Berry Research*, 6(2), 251–261. https://doi.org/10.3233/JBR-160125

Lam, T.K., Gallicchio, L., Lindsley, K., Shiels, M., Hammond, E., Tao, X., Chen, L., Robinson, K.A., Caulfield, L.E., Herman, J.G., Guallar, E. & Alberg, A.J. (2009). Cruciferous vegetable consumption and lung cancer risk: a systematic review. *Cancer Epidemiology, Biomarkers & Prevention*, 18(1), 184–195. https://cebp.aacrjournals.org/content/18/1/184

Lin, B.W., Gong, C.C., Song, H.F. & Cui, Y.Y. (2017). Effects of anthocyanins on the prevention and treatment of cancer. *British Journal of Pharmacology*, 174(11), 1226–1243. https://doi.org/10.1111/bph.13627

Lipi, G., Mattiuzzi, C. & Cervellin, G. (2016). Meat consumption and cancer risk: a critical review of published meta-analyses. *Critical Reviews in Oncology/Hematology*, 97, 1–14. https://www.sciencedirect.com/science/article/abs/pii/S1040842815300780?via%3Dihub

Main Coast Sea Vegetables. (n.d.). https://seaveg.com/

Majdalawieh, A.F. & Fayyad, M.W. (2016). Recent advances on the anti-cancer properties of Nigella sativa, a widely used food additive. *Journal of Ayurveda and Integrative Medicine*, 7(3), 173–180. https://doi.org/10.1016/j.jaim.2016.07.004

Martinez-Outschoorn, U.E., Lin, Z., Whitaker-Menezes, D., Howell, A., Sotgia, F. & Lisanti, M.P. (2012). Ketone body utilization drives tumor growth and metastasis. *Cell Cycle*, 11(21), 3964–3971. https://doi.org/10.4161/cc.22137

McKenzie, B. (2020). Is keto kind to pets? *Veterinary Practice News*. https://www.veterinarypracticenews.com/ketogenic-february-2020/

Medical Xpress. (2009). Carrots cooked whole contain more anti-cancer compound. *Medical Xpress*. https://medicalxpress.com/news/2009-06-carrots-cooked-anti-cancer-compound.html

Memorial Sloan Kettering Cancer Center. (2021). Turmeric. *Memorial Sloan Kettering Cancer Center*. https://www.mskcc.org/cancer-care/integrative-medicine/herbs/turmeric

Michaud, D.S., Spiegelman, D., Clinton, S.K., Rimm, E.B., Willett, W.C. & Giovannucci, E.L. (1999). Fruit and vegetable intake and incidence of bladder cancer in a male prospective cohort. *Journal of the National Cancer Institute*, 91(7), 605–13. https://pubmed.ncbi.nlm.nih.gov/10203279/

Michigan Department of Community Health. (n.d.). Eat safe fish. *Michigan Department of Community Health*. https://www.michigan.gov/documents/mdch/Bioaccumulative__Persistent_Chemicals_FINAL_354016_7.pdf

Minami, Y., Kanemura, S., Oikawa, T., Suzuki, S., Hasegawa, Y., Nishino, Y., Fujiya, T. & Miura, K. (2020). Associations of Japanese food intake with survival of stomach and colorectal cancer: a prospective patient cohort study. *Cancer Science, 111*(7), 2558–2569. https://doi.org/10.1111/cas.14459

Mollazadeh, H., Afshari, A.R. & Hosseinzadeh, H. (2017). Review on the potential therapeutic roles of *Nigella sativa* in the treatment of patients with cancer: involvement of apoptosis. *Journal of Pharmacopuncture, 20*(3), 158–172. https://www.ncbi.nlm.nih.gov/pmc/articles/PMC5633668/

Nagini, S., Palitti, F. & Natarajan, A.T. (2015) Chemopreventive potential of chlorophyllin: a review of the mechanisms of action and molecular targets. *Nutrition and Cancer, 67*(2), 203–211. https://doi.org/10.1080/01635581.2015.990573

National Cancer Institute. (n.d.). Comparative oncology program. *National Cancer Institute.* https://ccr.cancer.gov/comparative-oncology-program

National Cancer Institute. (2017). Chemicals in meat cooked at high temperatures and cancer risk. *National Cancer Institute.* https://www.cancer.gov/about-cancer/causes-prevention/risk/diet/cooked-meats-fact-sheet

National Celiac Association. (2018). Do wheat grass and barley grass contain gluten? *National Celiac Association.* https://nationalceliac.org/celiac-disease-questions/do-wheat-grass-and-barley-grass-contain-gluten/

National Institutes of Health (NIH). (2021). Vitamin A: fact sheet for consumers. *NIH Office of Dietary Supplements.* https://ods.od.nih.gov/factsheets/VitaminA-Consumer/

Novío, S., Núñez-Iglesias, M.J. & Freire-Garabal, M. (2019). Chapter 7 - Isothiocyanates, epigenetics, and cancer prevention. In *Translational Epigenetics, Epigenetics of Cancer Prevention.* [Bishayee, A. & Deepak Bhatia, D., Editors], *8*, 149–168. Academic Press. https://doi.org/10.1016/B978-0-12-812494-9.00007-X

NutritionData. (2018). Seaweed, kelp, raw. *NutritionData.* https://nutritiondata.self.com/facts/vegetables-and-vegetable-products/2617/2

Ohio State University. (2008). Black raspberries slow cancer by altering hundreds of genes. *ScienceDaily.* www.sciencedaily.com/releases/2008/08/080827163933.htm

Olaya-Galán, N.N., Corredor-Figueroa, A.P., Guzmán-Garzón, T.C., Ríos-Hernandez, K.S., Salas-Cárdenas, S.P., Patarroyo, M.A. & Gutierrez, M.F. (2017). Bovine leukaemia virus DNA in fresh milk and raw beef for human consumption. *Epidemiology & Infection, 145*(15), 3125-3130. https://pubmed.ncbi.nlm.nih.gov/28956522/

Pascual, G., Avgustinova, A., Mejetta, S., Martín, M., Castellanos, A., Attolini, C.S.O., Berenguer, A., Prats, N., Toll, A., Hueto., J.A., Bescós, C., Di Croce, L. & Benitah, S.A. (2017). Targeting metastasis-initiating cells through the fatty acid receptor CD36. *Nature, 541*, 41–45. https://doi.org/10.1038/nature20791

Pandya, U., Dhuldhaj, U. & Sahay, N.S. (2019). Bioactive mushroom polysaccharides as antitumor: An overview. *Natural Product Research, 33*(18), 2668–2680. https://doi.or g/10.1080/14786419.2018.1466129

Peng, L., Liu, A., Shen, Y., Xu, H.Z., Yang, S.Z., Ying, X.Z., Liao, W., Liu, H.X., Lin, Z.Q., Chen, Q.Y., Cheng, S.W. & Shen, W.D. (2013). Antitumor and anti-angiogenesis effects of thymoquinone on osteosarcoma through the NF-κB pathway. *Oncology Reports, 29*(2), 571–578. https://doi.org/10.3892/or.2012.2165

Petruzzello, M. (2018). Black cumin. *Encyclopedia Britannica.* https://www.britannica. com/plant/black-cumin

Phinney, S. (2020). What are ketones? *Virta Health.* https://www.virtahealth.com/ faq/what-are-ketones-ketogenesis#:~:text=Ketones%20are%20synthesized%20 from%20the,a%20metabolic%20state%20of%20'ketosis

Pietrzak, M., Halicka, H.D., Wieczorek, Z., Wieczorek, J. & Darzynkiewicz, Z. (2008). Attenuation of acridine mutagen ICR-191—DNA interactions and DNA damage by the mutagen interceptor chlorophyllin. *Biophysical Chemistry, 135*(1-3), 69–75. https:// doi.org/10.1016/j.bpc.2008.03.004

Pitcairn, R.H. & Pitcairn, S.H. (2017). *Dr. Pitcairn's Complete Guide to Natural Health for Dogs & Cats (4th ed.).* Emmaus, PA: Rodale

Poff, A.M., Ari, C., Arnold, P., Seyfried, T.N. & D'Agostino, D.P. (2014). Ketone supplementation decreases tumor cell viability and prolongs survival of mice with metastatic cancer. *International Journal of Cancer, 135*(7), 1711–1720. https://doi. org/10.1002/ijc.28809

Polat, M., Takeshima, S. & Aida, Y. (2017). Epidemiology and genetic diversity of bovine leukemia virus. *Virology Journal, 14*(1), 209–24. https://pubmed.ncbi.nlm.nih. gov/29096657/

Raghavan, M., Knapp, D.W., Bonney, P.L., Dawson, M.H. & Glickman, L.T. (2005). Evaluation of the effect of dietary vegetable consumption on reducing risk of transitional cell carcinoma of the urinary bladder in Scottish Terriers. *Journal of the American Veterinary Medical Association, 227*(1), 94–100. https://doi.org/10.2460/ javma.2005.227.94

Rajewski, G. (2020). Improving the odds of surviving lymphoma. *TuftsNow.* https:// now.tufts.edu/articles/improving-odds-surviving-lymphoma

Ravindran, J., Prasad, S. & Aggarwal, B.B. (2009). Curcumin and cancer cells: how many ways can curry kill tumor cells selectively? *The AAPS Journal, 11*(3), 495–510. https://doi.org/10.1208/s12248-009-9128-x

RawNori. (2021). *RawNori.com.* https://rawnori.com/

Robey I.F. (2012). Examining the relationship between diet-induced acidosis and cancer. *Nutrition & Metabolism, 9*(1), 72. https://doi.org/10.1186/1743-7075-9-72

Robbins, O. (2019). The Keto diet explained: what the science really says. *Food Revolution Network*. https://foodrevolution.org/blog/keto-diet-benefits/

Rohrmann, S., Linseisen, J., Jakobsen, M.U., Overvad, K., Raaschou-Nielsen, O., Tjonneland, A., Boutron-Ruault, M.C., Kaaks, R., Becker, N., Bergmann, M., Boeing, H., Khaw, K.-T., Wareham, N.J., Key, T.J., Travis, R., Benetou, V., Naska, A., Trichopoulou, A., Pala, V., Tumino, R., Masala, G., Mattiello, A., Brustad, M., Lund, E., Skeie, G., Bueno-de-Mesquita, H.B., Peeters, P.H., Vermeulen, R.C., Jakszyn, P., Dorronsoro, M., Barricarte, A., Tormo, M.-J., Molina, E., Argüelles, M., Melin, B., Ericson, U., Manjer, J., Rinaldi, S., Slimani, N., Boffetta, P., Vergnaud, A.-C., Khan, A., Norat, T. & Vineis, P. (2011). Consumption of meat and dairy and lymphoma risk in the European Prospective Investigation into Cancer and Nutrition. *International Journal of Cancer, 128*(3), 623–634. https://doi.org/10.1002/ijc.25387

Rover.com. (2021). Can my dog eat seaweed? *Rover.com.* https://www.rover.com/blog/can-my-dog-eat-seaweed/#:~:text=All%20seaweed%20strains%20are%20considered,it%20to%20your%20dog's%20diet

Safer Chemicals, Healthy Families. (2021). Get the facts: persistent, bioaccumulative and toxic chemicals (PBTs). *Safer Chemicals, Healthy Families.* https://saferchemicals.org/get-the-facts/toxic-chemicals/persistent-bioaccumulative-and-toxic-chemicals-pbts/

Sapkota, A.R., Lefferts, L.Y., McKenzie, S. & Walker, P. (2007). What do we feed to food-production animals? A review of animal feed ingredients and their potential impacts on human health. *Environmental Health Perspectives, 115*(5), 663–670. https://doi.org/10.1289/ehp.9760

Seidenberg, C. (2013). Kombu, a nutritional powerhouse from the sea. *The Washington Post.* https://www.washingtonpost.com/lifestyle/wellness/kombu-a-nutritional-powerhouse-from-the-sea/2013/01/29/aa4bb830-4ad4-11e2-a6a6-aabac85e8036_story.html

Sena, S.F. (2010). Beta-hydroxybutyrate: new test for ketoacidosis. *Danbury Hospital—Technically Speaking* [Guidess, C.S., Editor], *4*(8). https://www.ekfdiagnostics.com/res/Beta-Hydroxybutyrate%20-%20New%20Test%20for%20Ketoacidosis%20(Danbury%20Hospital%20article).pdf

Shanmugalingam, T., Bosco, C., Ridley, A.J. & Van Hemelrijck, M. (2016). Is there a role for IGF-1 in the development of second primary cancers? *Cancer Medicine, 5*(11), 3353–3367. https://doi.org/10.1002/cam4.871

Shoba, G., Joy, D., Joseph, T., Majeed, M., Rajendran, R. & Srinivas, P.S. Influence of piperine on the pharmacokinetics of curcumin in animals and human volunteers. (1998). *Planta Medica, 64*(4), 353–356. https://pubmed.ncbi.nlm.nih.gov/9619120/

Shoieb, A.M., Elgayyar, M., Dudrick, P.S., Bell, J.L. & Tithof, P.K. (2003). In vitro inhibition of growth and induction of apoptosis in cancer cell lines by thymoquinone. *International Journal of Oncology, 22*(1), 107–113. https://doi.org/10.3892/ijo.22.1.107

Siruguri, V. & Bhat, R.V. (2015). Assessing intake of spices by pattern of spice use, frequency of consumption and portion size of spices consumed from routinely prepared dishes in southern India. *Nutrition Journal, 14*(7). https://doi.org/10.1186/1475-2891-14-7

Standish, L.J., Wenner, C.A., Sweet, E.S., Bridge, C., Nelson, A., Martzen, M., Novack, J. & Torkelson, C. (2008). Trametes versicolor mushroom immune therapy in breast cancer. *Journal of the Society for Integrative Oncology, 6*(3), 122–128. https://www.ncbi.nlm.nih.gov/pmc/articles/PMC2845472/

Statista. (2021). Share of dogs and cats fed plant-based diets worldwide as of 2019, by type. *Statista.* https://www.statista.com/statistics/1111389/pet-food-cats-and-dogs-on-plant-based-diets-worldwide/

Stefanson, A.L. & Bakovic, M. (2018). Falcarinol is a potent inducer of heme oxygenase-1 and was more effective than sulforaphane in attenuating intestinal inflammation at diet-achievable doses. *Oxidative Medicine and Cellular Longevity, 18.* https://www.hindawi.com/journals/omcl/2018/3153527/

Tan, K.W., Killeen, D.P., Li, Y., Paxton, J.W., Birch, N.P. & Scheepens, A. (2014). Dietary polyacetylenes of the falcarinol type are inhibitors of breast cancer resistance protein (BCRP/ABCG2). *European Journal of Pharmacology, 723*, 346–352. https://doi.org/10.1016/j.ejphar.2013.11.005

Taniguchi, K. & Karin, M. (2018). NF-κB, inflammation, immunity and cancer: coming of age. *Nature Reviews Immunology, 18*, 309–324. https://doi.org/10.1038/nri.2017.142

Teas, J., Pino, S., Critchley, A. & Braverman, L.E. (2004). Variability of iodine content in common commercially available edible seaweeds. *Thyroid, 14*(10), 836–841. http://doi.org/10.1089/thy.2004.14.836

Thomson, J.R. (2017). How to eat seaweed, for those of you who have no idea. HuffPost. https://www.huffpost.com/entry/how-to-eat-seaweed_n_58876c07e4b0e3a7356bc781#:~:text=Seaweed%20has%20long%20been%20used,dishes%20from%20soup%20to%20eggs.&text=Nori%20is%20a%20red%20seaweed,used%20to%20make%20the%20rolls

Udayangani, S. (2020). Difference between macroalgae and microalgae. *DifferenceBetween.com.* https://www.differencebetween.com/difference-between-macroalgae-and-microalgae/#:~:text=The%20key%20difference%20between%20macroalgae,aquatic%20photosynthetic%20plant%2Dlike%20organisms.&text=They%20are%20mostly%20aquatic%20and%20autotrophic%20in%20nature.

United States Department of Agriculture (USDA). (2008). Bovine Leukosis Virus (BLV) on U.S. dairy operations, 2007. *APHIS Veterinary Services: Centers for Epidemiology and Animal Health.* https://www.aphis.usda.gov/animal_health/nahms/dairy/downloads/dairy07/Dairy07_is_BLV.pdf

University Of Newcastle Upon Tyne. (2005). Carrot component reduces cancer risk. *ScienceDaily.* https://www.sciencedaily.com/releases/2005/02/050212184702.htm

U.S. Department of State. (n.d.). Stockholm convention on persistent organic pollutants. *U.S. Department of State.* https://www.state.gov/key-topics-office-of-environmental-quality-and-transboundary-issues/stockholm-convention-on-persistent-organic-pollutants/

Vetvicka, V., Teplyakova, T.V., Shintyapina, A.B. & Korolenko, T.A. (2021). Effects of medicinal fungi-derived β-Glucan on tumor progression. *Journal of Fungi, 7*(4), 250. https://doi.org/10.3390/jof7040250

Vucenik, I. & Shamsuddin, A.M. (2003). Cancer inhibition by inositol hexaphosphate (IP6) and inositol: from laboratory to clinic. *The Journal of Nutrition, 133*(11), 3778S–3784S, https://doi.org/10.1093/jn/133.11.3778S

Vucenik, I., Druzijanic, A. & Druzijanic, N. (2020). Inositol hexaphosphate (IP6) and colon cancer: from concepts and first experiments to clinical application. *Molecules, 25*(24), 5931. https://doi.org/10.3390/molecules25245931

Vucenik, I., Passaniti, A., Vitolo, M.I., Tantivejkul, K., Eggleton, P. & Shamsuddin, A.M. (2004). Anti-angiogenic activity of inositol hexaphosphate (IP6). *Carcinogenesis, 25*(11), 2115–2123. https://doi.org/10.1093/carcin/bgh232

Vucenik, I., Sakamoto, K., Bansal, M. & Shamsuddin, A.M. (1993). Inhibition of rat mammary carcinogenesis by inositol hexaphosphate (phytic acid). A pilot study. *Cancer Letters, 75*(2), 95–102. https://doi.org/10.1016/0304-3835(93)90193-d

Vucenik, I., Tomazic, V.J., Fabian, D. & Shamsuddin, A.M. (1992). Antitumor activity of phytic acid (inositol hexaphosphate) in murine transplanted and metastatic fibrosarcoma, a pilot study. *Cancer Letters, 65*(1), 9–13. https://doi.org/10.1016/0304-3835(92)90206-b

Vucenik, I., Zhang, Z.S. & Shamsuddin, A.M. (1998). IP6 in treatment of liver cancer. II. Intra-tumoral injection of IP6 regresses pre-existing human liver cancer xenotransplanted in nude mice. *Anticancer Research, 18*(6A), 4091–4096. https://pubmed.ncbi.nlm.nih.gov/9891450/

Wada, L. & Ou, B. (2002). Antioxidant activity and phenolic content of Oregon caneberries. *Journal of Agriculture and Food Chemistry, 50*(12), 3495–500. https://pubmed.ncbi.nlm.nih.gov/10691606/

Wali, A.F., Majid, S., Rasool, S., Shehada, S.B., Abdulkareem, S.K., Firdous, A., Beigh, S., Shakeel, S., Mushtaq, S., Akbar, I., Madhkali, H. & Rehman, M.U. (2019). Natural products against cancer: review on phytochemicals from marine sources in preventing cancer. *Saudi Pharmaceutical Journal, 27*(6), 767–777. https://doi.org/10.1016/j.jsps.2019.04.013

Wang, S.Y. & Lin, H.S. (2000). Antioxidant activity in fruits and leaves of blackberry, raspberry, and strawberry varies with cultivar and developmental stage. *Journal of Agriculture and Food Chemistry, 48*(2). https://pubmed.ncbi.nlm.nih.gov/10691606/

Ware, M. (2018). Everything you need to know about turmeric. *Medical News Today.* https://www.medicalnewstoday.com/articles/306981

Warwicker, M. & Taylor, A.L. (2012). Seaweed: should people eat more of it? *BBC News.* https://www.bbc.com/news/magazine-17870743

Willmott, N.S. & Bryan, R.A. (2008). Case report: scurvy in an epileptic child on a ketogenic diet with oral complications. *European Archives of Paediatric Dentistry, 9,* 148–152. https://doi.org/10.1007/BF03262627

World Health Organization (WHO). (2008). Persistent organic pollutants (POPs). *World Health Organization.* https://www.who.int/ceh/capacity/POPs.pdf

Yeh, T.S., Hung, N.H. & Lin, T.Z. (2014). Analysis of iodine content in seaweed by GC-ECD and estimation of iodine intake. *Journal of Food and Drug Analysis, 22*(2), 189–196. https://doi.org/10.1016/j.jfda.2014.01.014

Youm, Y.H., Nguyen, K.Y., Grant, R.W., Goldberg, E.L., Bodogai, M., Kim, D., D'Agostino, D., Planavsky, N., Lupfer, C., Kanneganti, T.D., Kang, S., Horvath, T.L., Fahmy, T.M., Crawford, P.A., Biragyn, A., Alnemri, E. & Dixit, V.D. (2015). The ketone metabolite β-hydroxybutyrate blocks NLRP3 inflammasome-mediated inflammatory disease. *Nature Medicine, 21*(3), 263–269. https://doi.org/10.1038/nm.3804

Zava, T.T. & Zava, D.T. (2011). Assessment of Japanese iodine intake based on seaweed consumption in Japan: a literature-based analysis. *Thyroid Research, 4*(14). https://doi.org/10.1186/1756-6614-4-14

Zhang, S.M., Hunter, D.J., Rosner, B.A., Giovannucci, E.L., Colditz, G.A., Speizer, F.E. & Willett, W.C. (2000). Intakes of fruits, vegetables, and related nutrients and the risk of non-Hodgkin's lymphoma among women. *Cancer Epidemiology, Biomarkers & Prevention, 9*(5), 477–85. https://pubmed.ncbi.nlm.nih.gov/10815692/

Zhang, M., Huang, J., Xie, X. & Holman, C.D. (2009). Dietary intakes of mushrooms and green tea combine to reduce the risk of breast cancer in Chinese women. *International Journal of Cancer, 124*(6), 1404–1408. https://pubmed.ncbi.nlm.nih.gov/19048616/

Zheng, W. & Lee, S.A. (2009). Well-done meat intake, heterocyclic amine exposure, and cancer risk. *Nutrition and Cancer, 61*(4), 437–446. https://doi.org/10.1080/01635580802710741

Zidorn, C., Jöhrer, K., Ganzera, M., Schubert, B., Sigmund, E.M., Mader, J., Greil, R., Ellmerer, E.P. & Stuppner, H. (2005). Polyacetylenes from the Apiaceae vegetables carrot, celery, fennel, parsley, and parsnip and their cytotoxic activities. *Journal of Agriculture and Food Chemistry, 53*(7), 2518–23. https://pubmed.ncbi.nlm.nih.gov/15796588/

Chapter 9: Plant-Based Diet Solutions for Diabetes

Abdelrahman, N., El-Banna, R., Arafa, M.M. & Hady, M.M. (2020). Hypoglycemic efficacy of *Rosmarinus officinalis* and/or *Ocimum basilicum* leaves powder as a promising clinico-nutritional management tool for diabetes mellitus in Rottweiler dogs. *Veterinary World, 13*(1), 73–79. https://doi.org/10.14202/vetworld.2020.73-79

AlEssa, H.B., Bhupathiraju, S.N., Malik, V.S., Wedick, N.M., Campos, H., Rosner, B., Willett, W.C. & Hu, F.B. (2015). Carbohydrate quality and quantity and risk of type 2 diabetes in US women. *The American Journal of Clinical Nutrition, 102*(6), 1543–1553. https://doi.org/10.3945/ajcn.115.116558

Allen, R.W., Schwartzman, E., Baker, W.L., Coleman, C.I. & Phung, O.J. (2013). Cinnamon use in type 2 diabetes: an updated systematic review and meta-analysis. *Annals of Family Medicine, 11*(5), 452–459. https://doi.org/10.1370/afm.1517

Aune, D., Norat, T., Romundstad, P. & Vatten, L.J. (2013). Whole grain and refined grain consumption and the risk of type 2 diabetes: a systematic review and dose-response meta-analysis of cohort studies. *European Journal of Epidemiology, 28*(11), 845–858. https://pubmed.ncbi.nlm.nih.gov/24158434/

Banfield Pet Hospital. (2016). State of Pet Health 2016 Report. *Banfield Pet Hospital.* https://www.banfield.com/banfield/media/pdf/downloads/soph/banfield-state-of-pet-health-report-2016.pdf

BMJ-British Medical Journal. (2010). Green leafy vegetables reduce diabetes risk, study finds. *ScienceDaily.* www.sciencedaily.com/releases/2010/08/100819214607.htm

Canadian Society of Intestinal Research. (2017). Cinnamon: The good, the bad and the tasty. *GI Society.* https://badgut.org/information-centre/health-nutrition/cinnamon/#:~:text=Cinnamomum%20verum%2C%20also%20called%20true,shifted%20favour%20to%20Cassia%20cinnamon

Chandran, M., Phillips, S.A., Ciaraldi, T. & Henry, R.R. (2003). Adiponectin: more than just another fat cell hormone? *Diabetes Care, 26*(8), 2442–2450. https://doi.org/10.2337/diacare.26.8.2442

Cheng, L.J., Jiang, Y., Wu, V.X. & Wang, W. (2019). A systematic review and meta-analysis: vinegar consumption on glycaemic control in adults with type 2 diabetes mellitus. *Journal of Advanced Nursing, 76*(2), 459–474. https://pubmed.ncbi.nlm.nih.gov/31667860/

Cleveland Clinic. (2020). Can taking cinnamon supplements lower your blood sugar? Some studies find benefits for people with diabetes. *Health Essentials.* https://health.clevelandclinic.org/can-taking-cinnamon-lower-your-blood-sugar/

Czerwonka, M. & Tokarz, A. (2017). Iron in red meat–friend or foe. *Journal of Meat Science, 123*, 157-165. https://doi.org/10.1016/j.meatsci.2016.09.012

de Oliveira Otto, M.C., Alonso, A., Lee, D.H., Delclos, G.L., Bertoni, A.G., Jiang, R., Lima, J. A., Symanski, E., Jacobs Jr, D.R. & Nettleton, J.A. (2012). Dietary intakes of zinc and heme iron from red meat, but not from other sources, are associated with greater risk of metabolic syndrome and cardiovascular disease. *The Journal of Nutrition, 142*(3), 526–533. https://doi.org/10.3945/jn.111.149781

Edermaniger, L. (2021). Resistant starch in potatoes for gut bacteria and potato starch benefits. *Atlas Blog.* https://atlasbiomed.com/blog/potato-resistant-starch/

FoodStruct. (2021). Glycemic index chart – Complete (300+) list from all sources. *FoodStruct.* https://foodstruct.com/glycemic-index-chart

Forster, G.M., Ollila, C.A., Burton, J.H., Hill, D., Bauer, J.E., Hess, A.M. & Ryan, E.P. (2012). Nutritional weight loss therapy with cooked bean powders regulates serum lipids and biochemical analytes in overweight and obese dogs. *Journal of Obesity & Weight Loss Therapy, 2*(8). http://dx.doi.org/10.4172/2165-7904.1000149

Hannan, J.M.A, Ojo, O.O, Ali, L., Rokeya, B., Khaleque, J., Akhter, M., Flatt, P.R. & Abdel-Wahab, Y.H.A. (2014). Actions underlying antidiabetic effects of *Ocimum sanctum* leaf extracts in animal models of Type 1 and Type 2 diabetes. *European Journal of Medicinal Plants, 5*(1), 1–12

Hariri, M. & Ghiasvand, R. (2016). Cinnamon and chronic diseases. *Advances in Experimental Medicine and Biology, 929*, 1–24. https://pubmed.ncbi.nlm.nih.gov/27771918/

Johnston, C.S., Steplewska, I., Long, C.A., Harris, L.N. & Ryals, R.H. (2010). Examination of the antiglycemic properties of vinegar in healthy adults. *Annals of Nutrition and Metabolism, 56*(1), 74–79. https://pubmed.ncbi.nlm.nih.gov/20068289/

Kawa, J.M., Taylor, C.G. & Przybylski, R. (2003). Buckwheat concentrate reduces serum glucose in streptozotocin-diabetic rats. *Journal of Agricultural and Food Chemistry, 51*(25), 7287–7291. https://doi.org/10.1021/jf0302153

Khan, A., Safdar, M., Khan, M.M.A., Khattak, K.N. & Anderson, R.A. (2003). Cinnamon improves glucose and lipids in people with Type 2 diabetes. *Diabetes Care, 26*(12), 3215–3218. https://doi.org/10.2337/diacare.26.12.3215

Kizilaslan, N. & Erdem, N.Z. (2019). The effect of different amounts of cinnamon consumption on blood glucose in healthy adult individuals. *International Journal of Food Science, 2019.* https://doi.org/10.1155/2019/4138534

Labban, L., Mustafa, U.E. & Ibrahim Y.M. (2014). The effects of rosemary (*Rosmarinus officinalis*) leaves powder on glucose level lipid profile and lipid peroxidation. *International Journal of Clinical Medicine, 5*(6), 297–304. https://www.scirp.org/html/2-2100687_44285.htm

Lund, E.M., Armstrong, P.J., Kirk, C.A. & Klausner, J.S. (2006) Prevalence and risk factors for obesity in adult dogs from private US veterinary practices. *International Journal of Applied Research in Veterinary Medicine, 4*(2), 177–186. https://www.jarvm.com/articles/Vol4Iss2/Lund.pdf

Martin, K. (2017). 10 foods that are banned in the United States. *Healthyway.* https://www.healthyway.com/content/foods-that-are-banned-in-the-united-states/

McMacken, M. & Shah, S. (2017). A plant-based diet for the prevention and treatment of type 2 diabetes. *Journal of Geriatric Cardiology, 14*(5), 342–354. https://www.ncbi.nlm.nih.gov/pmc/articles/PMC5466941/

Mezei, O., Banz, W.J., Steger, R.W., Peluso, M.R., Winters, T.A. & Shay, N. (2003). Soy isoflavones exert antidiabetic and hypolipidemic effects through the PPAR pathways in obese Zucker rats and murine RAW 264.7 cells. *Journal of Nutrition, 133*(5), 1238–1243. https://pubmed.ncbi.nlm.nih.gov/12730403/

Montoya-Alonso, J.A., Bautista-Castaño, I., Peña, C., Suárez, L., Juste, M.C. & Tvarijonaviciute, A. (2017). Prevalence of canine obesity, obesity-related metabolic dysfunction, and relationship with owner obesity in an obesogenic region of Spain. *Frontiers in Veterinary Science, 4.* https://www.frontiersin.org/article/10.3389/fvets.2017.00059

Muraki, I., Imamura, F., Manson, J.E., Hu, F.B., Willett, W.C., van Dam, R.M. & Sun, Q. (2013). Fruit consumption and risk of type 2 diabetes: results from three prospective longitudinal cohort studies. *British Medical Journal, 347,* f5001. https://www.bmj.com/content/347/bmj.f5001

Oldfield, J. (2017). Chia seeds promote weight loss in people with diabetes: study. *University of Toronto.* https://medicine.utoronto.ca/news/chia-seeds-promote-weight-loss-people-diabetes-study#:~:text=Chia%20Seeds%20Promote%20Weight%20Loss%20in%20People%20with%20Diabetes%3A%20Study,-Pinterest&text=University%20of%20Toronto%20researchers%20have,maintaining%20good%20blood%20sugar%20control

Raghavan, M., Knapp, D.W., Bonney, P.L., Dawson, M.H. & Glickman, L.T. (2005). Evaluation of the effect of dietary vegetable consumption on reducing risk of transitional cell carcinoma of the urinary bladder in Scottish Terriers. *Journal of the American Veterinary Medical Association, 227*(1), 94–100. https://doi.org/10.2460/javma.2005.227.94

Ribeiro, É.M., Peixoto, M.C., Putarov, T.C., Monti, M., Pacheco, P., Loureiro, B.A., Pereira, G.T. & Carciofi, A.C. (2019). The effects of age and dietary resistant starch on digestibility, fermentation end products in faeces and postprandial glucose and insulin responses of dogs. *Archives of Animal nutrition, 73*(6), 485–504. https://doi.org/10.1080/1745039X.2019.1652516

The University of Sydney. (2021). Search for the glycemic index. *The University of Sydney.* https://www.glycemicindex.com/foodSearch.php

Tvarijonaviciute, A., Ceron, J.J., Holden, S.L., Cuthbertson, D.J., Biourge, V., Morris, P.J. & German, A.J. (2012). Obesity-related metabolic dysfunction in dogs: a comparison with human metabolic syndrome. *BMC Veterinary Research, 8*(147). https://doi.org/10.1186/1746-6148-8-147

Venn, B.J. & Mann, J.I. (2004). Cereal grains, legumes and diabetes. *European Journal of Clinical Nutrition, 58*(11), 1443–1461. https://pubmed.ncbi.nlm.nih.gov/15162131/

Villegas, R., Gao, Y.T., Yang, G., Li, H.L., Elasy, T.A., Zheng, W. & Shu, X.O. (2008). Legume and soy food intake and the incidence of type 2 diabetes in the Shanghai Women's Health Study. *The American Journal of Clinical Nutrition, 87*(1), 162–167. https://doi.org/10.1093/ajcn/87.1.162

Vuksan, V., Jenkins, A.L., Brissette, C., Choleva, L., Jovanovski, E., Gibbs, A.L., Bazinet, R.P., Au-Yeung, F., Zurbau, A., Ho, H.V.T., Duvnjak, L., Sievenpiper, J.L., Josse, R.G. & Hanna, A. (2016). Salba-chia (*Salvia hispanica* L.) in the treatment of overweight and obese patients with type 2 diabetes: a double-blind randomized controlled trial. *Nutrition, Metabolism & Cardiovascular Diseases.* https://doi.org/10.1016/j.numecd.2016.11.124

White, A.M. & Johnston, C.S. (2007). Vinegar ingestion at bedtime moderates waking glucose concentrations in adults with well-controlled Type 2 diabetes. *Diabetes Care, 30*(11). https://doi.org/10.2337/dc07-1062

Xydakis, A.M., Case, C.C., Jones, P.H., Hoogeveen, R.C., Liu, M.Y., Smith, E.O., Nelson, K.W. & Ballantyne, C.M. (2004). Adiponectin, inflammation, and the expression of the metabolic syndrome in obese individuals: the impact of rapid weight loss through caloric restriction. *Journal of Clinical Endocrinology and Metabolism, 89*(6), 2697–26703. https://pubmed.ncbi.nlm.nih.gov/15181044/

Zaman, S.A. & Sarbini, S.R. (2015). The potential of resistant starch as a prebiotic. *Critical Reviews in Biotechnology, 36*(3), 578–584. https://doi.org/10.3109/07388551.2014.993590

Zibaeenezhad, M., Aghasadeghi, K., Hakimi, H., Yarmohammadi, H. & Nikaein, F. (2016). The effect of walnut oil consumption on blood sugar in patients with diabetes mellitus Type 2. *International Journal of Endocrinology and Metabolism, 14*(3), e34889. https://doi.org/10.5812/ijem.34889

Chapter 10: Plant-Based Diet Solutions for Food Intolerances

Dodds, W.J. (2017/2018). Diagnosis of canine food sensitivity and intolerance using saliva: report of outcomes. *Journal of the American Holistic Veterinary Association, 49*(winter), 32–42

Dodds, W.J. (2018). Diagnosis and management of adverse food reactions. *Biomedical Journal of Scientific & Technical Research, 3*(2). https://biomedres.us/fulltexts/BJSTR. MS.ID.000868.php

Dodds, W.J. (2019). Diagnosis of feline food sensitivity and intolerance using saliva: 1,000 cases. *Animals, 9*(8), 534. https://doi.org/10.3390/ani9080534

Dodds, W.J. (2019a). Food sensitivity and intolerance associated with diet type in Golden Retrievers: a retrospective study. *Journal of the American Holistic Veterinary Association, 56*(fall), 52–57

Dodds, W.J. & Laverdure, D.R. (2015). *Canine Nutrigenomics: The New Science of Feeding Your Dog for Optimum Health.* Wenatchee, WA, US: Dogwise Publishing

Foster, A.P., Knowles, T.G., Hotson-Moore, A., Cousins, P.D., Day, M.J. & Hall, E.J. (2003). Serum IgE and IgG responses to food antigens in normal and atopic dogs, and dogs with gastrointestinal disease. *Veterinary Immunology and Immunopathology, 92*, 113–124

Hemopet. (2021). *Hemopet.* https://hemopet.org/nutriscan

Lee, Y.H. & Wong, D.T. (2009). Saliva: an emerging biofluid for early detection of disease. *American Journal of Dentistry, 22*, 421–428

Miller, C.S., Foley, J.D., Bailey, A.L., Campell, C.L., Humphries, R.L., Christodoulides, N., Floriano, P.N., Simmons, G., Bhagwandin, B., Jacobson, J.W., Redding, S.W., Ebersole, J.L. & McDevitt, J.T. (2010). Current developments in salivary diagnostics. *Biomarkers in Medicine, 4*(1), 171–189. https://doi.org/10.2217/bmm.09.68

Ricci, R., Granato, A., Vascellari, M., Boscarato, M., Palagiano, C., Andrighetto, I. & Mutinelli, F. (2013). Identification of undeclared sources of animal origin in canine dry foods used in dietary elimination trials. *Journal of Animal Physiology and Animal Nutrition, 97*, 32–28.

Rinkinen, M., Teppo, A.M., Harmoinen, J. & Westermark, E. (2003). Relationship between canine mucosal and serum immunoglobulin A (IgA) concentrations: serum IgA does not assess duodenal secretory IgA. *Microbiology and Immunology, 47*, 155–159. https://onlinelibrary.wiley.com/doi/abs/10.1111/j.1348-0421.2003.tb02799.x

Stukus, D. (2014). What you need to know about food allergy testing. *Kids with Food Allergies: A Division of the Asthma and Allergy Foundation of America.* https://www. kidswithfoodallergies.org/food-allergy-test-diagnosis-skin-prick-blood.aspx

Chapter 11: Plant-Based Diet Solutions for Chronic Kidney Disease
Alvi, S. (2021). Can dietary fiber reduce toxins in urine? *Medindia.* https://www.medindia. net/news/healthinfocus/can-dietary-fiber-reduce-toxins-in-urine-200958-1.htm

American Kidney Fund. (2021). Know how to prevent kidney disease. *American Kidney Fund.* https://www.kidneyfund.org/kidney-disease/prevention/

American Society of Veterinary Nephrology and Urology (ASVNU). (n.d.). Hospitals offering advanced renal and urinary treatments. *American Society of Veterinary Nephrology and Urology.* https://www.asvnu.org/facilities

Asif, M. (2015). The impact of dietary fat and polyunsaturated fatty acids on chronic renal diseases. *Clinical Science Perspectives, 1*(2), 51–61. http://www.bosaljournals.com/ csp/images/pdffiles/8CSP.pdf

Bacchetta, J., Bernardor, J., Garnier, C., Naud, C. & Ranchin, B. (2021). Hyperphospatemia and chronic kidney disease: a major daily concern both in adults and in children. *Calcified Tissue International, 108,* 116–127. https://doi.org/10.1007/ s00223-020-00665-8

Bauer, J.E. (2011). Therapeutic use of fish oils in companion animals. *Journal of the American Veterinary Medical Association, 239*(11), 1441–1451

Betz, M. (2021). What is PRAL & how does it affect kidneys? *The Kidney Dietician.* https://www.thekidneydietitian.org/pral/

Brooks, W. (2018). Kidney dialysis: is it for your pet? *Veterinary Information Network, Inc.* https://veterinarypartner.vin.com/default.aspx?pid=19239&catId=102899& id=4952107

Brown, S.A., Brown, C.A., Crowell, W.A., Barsanti, J.A., Allen, T., Cowell, C. & Finco, D.R. (1998). Beneficial effects of chronic administration of dietary omega-3 polyunsaturated fatty acids in dogs with renal insufficiency. *The Journal of Laboratory and Clinical Medicine, 131*(5), 447–455. https://doi.org/10.1016/s0022-2143(98)90146-9

Brown, S.A. (2013). Renal dysfunction in small animals. *Merck Veterinary Manual.* https://www.merckvetmanual.com/urinary-system/noninfectious-diseases-of-the-urinary-system-in-small-animals/renal-dysfunction-in-small-animals

Burke, S.K. (2008). Phosphate is a uremic toxin. *Journal of Renal Nutrition, 18*(1), 27–32. https://doi.org/10.1053/j.jrn.2007.10.007

Byrne, F.N. & Calvo, M.S. (2019). Pulses and chronic kidney disease: potential health benefits from a once forbidden food. In *Health Benefits of Pulses* [Dahl, W.J., Editor]. Springer, Cham. https://link.springer.com/chapter/10.1007/978-3-030-12763-3_6

Cases, A., Cigarrán-Guldrís, S., Mas, S. & Gonzalez-Parra, E. (2019). Vegetable-based diets for chronic kidney disease? It is time to reconsider. *Nutrients, 11*(6), 1263. https://doi.org/10.3390/nu11061263

Chakrabarti, S., Syme, H. & Elliott, J. (2012). Clinicopathological variables predicting progression of azotemia in cats with chronic kidney disease. *Journal of Veterinary Internal Medicine, 26*(2), 275–281. https://doi.org/10.1111/j.1939-1676.2011.00874.x

Chen, C.N., Chou, C.C., Tsai, P. & Lee, Y.J. (2018). Plasma indoxyl sulfate concentration predicts progression of chronic kidney disease in dogs and cats. *Veterinary Journal, 232*, 33–39. https://doi.org/10.1016/j.tvjl.2017.12.011

Chen, X., Wei, G., Jalili, T., Metos, J., Giri, A., Cho, M.E., Boucher, R., Greene, T. & Beddhu, S. (2016). The associations of plant protein intake with all-cause mortality in CKD. *American Journal of Kidney Diseases, 67*(3), 423–430. https://doi.org/10.1053/j.ajkd.2015.10.018

Cheng, F.P., Hsieh, M.J., Chou, C.C., Hsu, W.L. & Lee, Y.J. (2015). Detection of indoxyl sulfate levels in dogs and cats suffering from naturally occurring kidney diseases. *The Veterinary Journal, 205*(3), 399–403. https://doi.org/10.1016/j.tvjl.2015.04.017

Cordain, L. (2018). Nutritional deficiencies of ketogenic diets. *ResearchGate.* https://www.researchgate.net/profile/Loren-Cordain-2/publication/332098774_Nutritional_Deficiencies_of_Ketogenic_Diets/links/5c9f99e2a6fdccd46045868c/Nutritional-Deficiencies-of-Ketogenic-Diets.pdf

Dodds, W.J. (2018). Vaccine issues and the World Small Animal Veterinary Association guidelines (2015-2017). *Israel Journal of Veterinary Medicine, 73*(2), 3–10. http://www.biogal.com/wp-content/uploads/2019/05/Dodds-Israel-Journal.pdf

Dorough, H. & Solman, S. (2021). Vitamin D and chronic kidney disease. *DaVita.* https://www.davita.com/diet-nutrition/articles/basics/vitamin-d-and-chronic-kidney-disease

El Amouri, A., Snauwaert, E., Foulon, A., Vande Moortel, C., Van Dyck, M., Van Hoeck, K., Godefroid, N., Glorieux, G., Van Biesen, W., Vande Walle, J., Raes, A. & Eloot, S. (2021). Dietary fibre intake is associated with serum levels of uraemic toxins in children with chronic kidney disease. *Toxins, 13*(3), 225. https://doi.org/10.3390/toxins13030225

Elliott, P., Stamler, J. & Dyer, A.R. (2006). Association between protein intake and blood pressure. *Archives of Internal Medicine, 166*(1), 79–87. https://www.ncbi.nlm.nih.gov/pmc/articles/PMC6593153/?report=reader#!po=2.63158

Ephraim, E., Jackson, M.I., Yerramilli, M. & Jewell, D. (2020). Soluble fiber and omega-3 fatty acids reduce levels of advanced glycation end products and uremic toxins in senior dogs by modulating the gut microbiome. *Journal of Food Science and Nutrition Research*, *3*(1), 018–033. https://www.fortunejournals.com/articles/soluble-fiber-and-omega3-fatty-acids-reduce-levels-of-advanced-glycation-end-products-and-uremic-toxins-in-senior-dogs-by-modulati.html

Ephraim, E. & Jewell, D. (2020). Effect of added dietary betaine and soluble fiber on metabolites and fecal microbiome in dogs with early renal disease. *Metabolites*, *10*(9), 370. https://doi.org/10.3390/metabo10090370

Fielder, S. (2015). Blood-gas reference ranges. *Merck Veterinary Manual*. https://www.merckvetmanual.com/special-subjects/reference-guides/blood-gas-reference-ranges

Foster, J.D. (2021). Canine chronic kidney disease: current diagnostics and goals for long-term management. *Today's Veterinary Practice*. https://todaysveterinarypractice.com/canine-chronic-kidney-diseasecurrent-diagnostics-goals-long-term-management/

Fresenius Kidney Care. (2020). What is dialysis? *Fresenius Medical Care*. https://www.freseniuskidneycare.com/treatment/dialysis

González-Parra, E., Gracia-Iguacel, C., Egido, J. & Ortiz, A. (2012). Phosphorus and nutrition in chronic kidney disease. *International Journal of Nephrology, 2012*, 597605. https://doi.org/10.1155/2012/597605

Goraya, N., Simoni, J., Jo, C. & Wesson, D.E. (2012). Dietary acid reduction with fruits and vegetables or bicarbonate attenuates kidney injury in patients with a moderately reduced glomerular filtration rate due to hypertensive nephropathy. *Kidney International, 81*(1), 86–93. https://doi.org/10.1038/ki.2011.313

Goraya, N., Simoni, J., Jo, C.H. & Wesson, D.E. (2013). A comparison of treating metabolic acidosis in CKD stage 4 hypertensive kidney disease with fruits and vegetables or sodium bicarbonate. *Clinical journal of the American Society of Nephrology, 8*(3), 371–381. https://doi.org/10.2215/CJN.02430312

Goraya, N., Simoni, J., Jo, C.H. & Wesson, D.E. (2014). Treatment of metabolic acidosis in patients with stage 3 chronic kidney disease with fruits and vegetables or oral bicarbonate reduces urine angiotensinogen and preserves glomerular filtration rate. *Kidney International, 86*(5), 1031–1038. https://doi.org/10.1038/ki.2014.83

Greger, M. & Stone, G. (2015). *How Not to Die*. New York, NY: Flatiron Books

Haring, B., Selvin, E., Liang, M., Coresh, J., Grams, M.E., Petruski-Ivleva, N., Steffen, L.M. & Rebholz, C.M. (2017). Dietary protein sources and risk for incident chronic kidney disease: results from the Atherosclerosis Risk in Communities (ARIC) study. *Journal of Renal Nutrition, 27*(4), 233–242. https://doi.org/10.1053/j.jrn.2016.11.004

Hernandez, J. (2021). PRAL: Understanding Potential Renal Acid Load for kidney disease. *Plant-Powered Kidneys*. https://www.plantpoweredkidneys.com/pral/

Hu, J., Liu, Z. & Zhang, H. (2017). Omega-3 fatty acid supplementation as an adjunctive therapy in the treatment of chronic kidney disease: a meta-analysis. *Clinics*, *72*(1), 58–64. https://doi.org/10.6061/clinics/2017(01)10

Hu, C., Yang, M., Zhu, X., Gao, P., Yang, S., Han, Y., Chen, X., Xiao, L., Yuan, S., Liu, F., Kanwar, Y.S. & Sun, L. (2018). Effects of omega-3 fatty acids on markers of inflammation in patients with chronic kidney disease: a controversial issue. *Therapeutic Apheresis and Dialysis*, *22*(2), 124-132. https://doi.org/10.1111/1744-9987.12611

Jackson, M.I. & Jewell, D.E. (2019). Balance of saccharolysis and proteolysis underpins improvements in stool quality induced by adding a fiber bundle containing bound polyphenols to either hydrolyzed meat or grain-rich foods. *Gut microbes*, *10*(3), 298–320. https://doi.org/10.1080/19490976.2018.1526580

Jacob, F., Polzin, D.J., Osborne, C.A., Allen, T.A., Kirk, C.A., Neaton, J.D., Lekcharoensuk, C. & Swanson, L.L. (2002). Clinical evaluation of dietary modification for treatment of spontaneous chronic renal failure in dogs. *Journal of the American Veterinary Medical Association*, *220*(8), 1163–1170. https://doi.org/10.2460/javma.2002.220.1163

Johns Hopkins Medicine. (2021). Liver: anatomy and functions. *Johns Hopkins Medicine*. https://www.hopkinsmedicine.org/health/conditions-and-diseases/liver-anatomy-and-functions

Kalantar-Zadeh, K. (2013). Patient education for phosphorus management in chronic kidney disease. *Patient Preference and Adherence*, *7*, 379–390. https://doi.org/10.2147/PPA.S43486

Kaur, H., Das, C. & Mande, S.S. (2017). *In silico* analysis of putrefaction pathways in bacteria and its implications in colorectal cancer. *Frontiers in Microbiology*, *8*. https://www.frontiersin.org/article/10.3389/fmicb.2017.02166

Kaur, H., Singla, A., Singh, S., Shilwant, S. & Kaur, R. (2020). Role of omega-3 fatty acids in canine health: a review. *International Journal of Current Microbiology and Applied Sciences*, *9*(3), 2283–2293. https://doi.org/10.20546/ijcmas.2020.903.259

Kidney Research UK. (2006). The kidneys – a basic guide. *Kidney Research UK*. https://www.nhs.uk/Livewell/Kidneyhealth/Documents/kidney%20guide.pdf

Lekawanvijit, S., Kompa, A.R. & Krum, H. (2016). Protein-bound uremic toxins: a long overlooked culprit in cardiorenal syndrome. *American Journal of Renal Physiology*, *311*(1), F52–F62. https://doi.org/10.1152/ajprenal.00348.2015

Lewis, J. (2020). Overview of acid-base balance. *Merck Manual – Consumer Version.* https://www.merckmanuals.com/home/hormonal-and-metabolic-disorders/acid-base-balance/overview-of-acid-base-balance

Lu, L., Huang, Y-F., Want, M-Q., Chen, D-X., Wan, H., Wei, L-B. & X., W. (2017). Dietary fiber intake is associated with chronic kidney disease (CKD) progression and cardiovascular risk, but not protein nutritional status, in adults with CKD. *Asia Pacific Journal of Clinical Nutrition, 26*(4), 598–605. https://apjcn.nhri.org.tw/server/APJCN/26/4/598.pdf

Madell, R. & Kubala, J. (2020). Phosphorus in your diet. *Healthline.* https://www.healthline.com/health/phosphorus-in-diet

MedlinePlus. (n.d.). Phosphorus in diet. *MedlinePlus.* https://medlineplus.gov/ency/article/002424.htm

Meijers, B.K., De Preter, V., Verbeke, K., Vanrenterghem, Y. & Evenepoel, P. (2010). p-Cresyl sulfate serum concentrations in haemodialysis patients are reduced by the prebiotic oligofructose-enriched inulin. *Nephrology Dialysis Transplantation, 25*(1), 219–224. https://doi.org/10.1093/ndt/gfp414

Moe, S.M., Zidehsarai, M.P., Chambers, M.A., Jackman, L.A., Radcliffe, J.S., Trevino, L.L., Donahue, S.E. & Asplin, J.R. (2011). Vegetarian compared with meat dietary protein source and phosphorus homeostasis in chronic kidney disease. *Clinical Journal of the American Society of Nephrology: CJASN, 6*(2), 257–264. https://doi.org/10.2215/CJN.05040610

Moorthi, R.N. & Moe, S.M. (2017). Special nutritional needs of chronic kidney disease and end-stage renal disease patients: rationale for the use of plant-based diets. In *Dietary Phosphorus: Health, Nutrition, and Regulatory Aspects (1st ed.)* (Chapter 18). [Uribarri, J. & Calvo, M., Editors]. CRC Press. https://doi.org/10.1201/9781315119533

Murphy-Gutekunst, L. & Uribarri, J. (2005). Hidden phosphorus-enhanced meats: part 3. *Journal of Renal Nutrition, 15*(4), E1–E4. https://doi.org/10.1053/j.jrn.2005.07.009

National Kidney Foundation. (2019). Facts about metabolic acidosis and chronic kidney disease. *National Kidney Foundation.* https://www.kidney.org/atoz/content/facts-about-metabolic-acidosis-and-chronic-kidney-disease

National Kidney Foundation. (2021). Top 5 jobs kidneys do. *National Kidney Foundation.* https://www.kidney.org/kidneydisease/top-5-jobs-kidneys-do

National Kidney Foundation. (2021a). 7 kidney-friendly superfoods. *National Kidney Foundation.* https://www.kidney.org/content/7-kidney-friendly-superfoods

National Kidney Foundation. (2021b). Phosphorus and your diet. *National Kidney Foundation.* https://www.kidney.org/atoz/content/phosphorus

Nutritiontable.com. (2021). Calculate PRAL value. *Nutritiontable.com.* http://www. foodnutritiontable.com/calculate/pral/

Oxford Languages. (2021). Putrefaction. *Oxford Languages.* https://languages.oup. com/google-dictionary-en/

Passey, C. (2017). Review article—Reducing the dietary acid load: how a more alkaline diet benefits patients with chronic kidney disease. *Journal of Renal Nutrition, 27*(3), 151–160. https://www.jrnjournal.org/article/S1051-2276(16)30188-1/pdf

Persaud, N. (2021). Dietary fiber intake associated with reduced uremic toxins. *Renal & Urology News.* https://www.renalandurologynews.com/home/news/nephrology/ chronic-kidney-disease-ckd/diet-fibers-supplement-regulate-indoxyl-p-cresyl-sulfate-bun-uric-acid-ckd-dialysis/

Raditic, D. & Gaylord, L. (2020). Fish oil dosing in pet diets and supplements. *Today's Veterinary Practice, May/June.* https://todaysveterinarypractice.com/fish-oil-dosing-in-pet-diets-and-supplements/

Salmean, Y.A., Segal, M.S., Palii, S.P. & Dahl, W.J. (2015). Fiber supplementation lowers plasma p-cresol in chronic kidney disease patients. *Journal of Renal Nutrition, 25*(3), 316–320. https://doi.org/10.1053/j.jrn.2014.09.002

Schafer-Evans, R. (2019). 'Gut feeling' on postbiotics. *Hill's.* https://admin.myhillsvet. com.au/blog/gut-feeling-on-postbiotics/

Scialla, J.J. & Anderson, C.A. (2013). Dietary acid load: a novel nutritional target in chronic kidney disease? *Advances in Chronic Kidney Disease, 20*(2), 141–149. https://doi. org/10.1053/j.ackd.2012.11.001

Scialla, J.J., Appel, L.J., Wolf, M., Yang, W., Zhang, X., Sozio, S.M., Miller III E.R., Bazzano, L.A., Cuevas, M., Glenn, M.J., Lustigova, E., Kallem, R.R., Porter, A.C., Townsend, R.R., Weir, M.R. & Anderson, C.A.M. (2012). Plant protein intake is associated with fibroblast growth factor 23 and serum bicarbonate levels in patients with chronic kidney disease: the Chronic Renal Insufficiency Cohort Study. *Journal of Renal Nutrition, 22*(4), 379–388.e1. https://doi.org/10.1053/j.jrn.2012.01.026

Shaman, A.M. & Kowalski, S.R. (2016). Hyperphosphatemia management in patients with chronic kidney disease. *Saudi Pharmaceutical Journal, 24*(4), 494–505. https://doi. org/10.1016/j.jsps.2015.01.009

Valle, P.G., Veado, J.C.C., dos Anjos, T.M., de Tassini, L.E.S., Ferreira, L.F.F & Lucas, L.F. (2015). Effect of the association of diet, omega three, and antioxidants in dogs with chronic kidney disease. *Seminar: Agricultural Sciences, 35*(5). http://www.uel.br/ revistas/uel/index.php/semagrarias/article/view/18017

Webb, M.J. (2021). Dietary fibre supplementation reduces uremic toxins in patients with kidney disease. *Nephrology News & Issues*. https://www.healio.com/news/nephrology/20210325/dietary-fiber-supplementation-reduces-uremic-toxins-in-patients-with-kidney-disease

Yang, H.L., Feng, P., Xu, Y., Hou, Y.Y. Ojo, O. & Wang, X.H. (2021). The role of dietary fibre supplementation in regulating uremic toxins in patients with chronic kidney disease: a meta-analysis of randomized controlled trials. *Journal of Renal Nutrition*. https://doi.org/10.1053/j.jrn.2020.11.008

Ward, E. & Weir, M. (n.d.). Chronic kidney disease in dogs. *VCA Hospitals*. https://vcahospitals.com/know-your-pet/kidney-failure-chronic-in-dogs

Wu, I.W., Hsu, K.H., Lee, C.C., Sun, C.Y., Hsu, H.J., Tsai, C.J., Tzen, C.Y., Wang, Y.C., Lin, C.Y. & Wu, M.S. (2011). *P*-Cresyl sulphate and indoxyl sulphate predict progression of chronic kidney disease. *Nephrology Dialysis Transplantation, 26*(3), 938–947. https://doi.org/10.1093/ndt/gfq580

Chapter 12: Plant-Based Diet Solutions for Gastrointestinal Disorders

Alves, J.C., Santos, A., Jorge, P. & Pitaes, A. (2021). The use of soluble fibre for the management of chronic idiopathic large-bowel diarrhoea in police working dogs. *BMC Veterinary Research, 17*. https://link.springer.com/article/10.1186/s12917-021-02809-w

Carlson, J., Erickson, J.M., Lloyd, B.B. & Slavin, J.L. (2018). Health effects and sources of prebiotic dietary fiber. *Current Developments in Nutrition, 2*(3), nzy005. https://doi.org/10.1093/cdn/nzy005

Cayzeele-Decherf, A., Pélerin, F., Leuillet, S., Douillard, B., Housez, B., Cazaubiel, M., Jacobson, G.K., Jüsten, P. & Desreumaux, P. (2017). *Saccharomyces cerevisiae* CNCM I-3856 in irritable bowel syndrome: an individual subject meta-analysis. *World Journal of Gastroenterology, 23*(2), 336–344. https://www.wjgnet.com/1007-9327/full/v23/i2/336.htm

Coelho, L.P., Kultima, J.R., Costea, P.I., Fournier, C., Pan, Y., Czarnecki-Maulden, G., Hayward, M.R., Forslund, S.K., Benedikt Schmidt, T.S., Descombes, P., Jackson, J.R., Li, Q. & Bork, P. (2018). Similarity of the dog and human gut microbiomes in gene content and response to diet. *Microbiome, 6*(72). https://doi.org/10.1186/s40168-018-0450-3

Dannie, M. (2018). Benefits of psyllium husks vs. psyllium powder. *SFGate*. https://healthyeating.sfgate.com/benefits-psyllium-husks-vs-psyllium-pdr-12242.html

de Jesus Raposo, M.F., de Morais, A.M. & de Morais, R.M. (2016). Emergent sources of prebiotics: seaweeds and microalgae. *Marine Drugs, 14*(2), 27. https://doi.org/10.3390/md14020027

Dickman, R., Feroze, H. & Fass, R. (2006). Gastroesophageal reflux disease and irritable bowel syndrome: a common overlap syndrome. *Current Gastroenterology Reports, 8*(4), 261–265. https://doi.org/10.1007/s11894-006-0045-1

Dodds, W.J. (2018). Vaccine issues and the World Small Animal Veterinary Association guidelines (2015-2017). *Israel Journal of Veterinary Medicine, 73*(2), 3–10. http://www.biogal.com/wp-content/uploads/2019/05/Dodds-Israel-Journal.pdf

Dodds, W.J. (2018a). Diagnosis and management of adverse food reactions. *Biomedical Journal of Scientific & Technical Research, 3*(2). https://biomedres.us/fulltexts/BJSTR.MS.ID.000868.php

Edermaniger, L. (2021). Resistant starch in potatoes for gut bacteria and potato starch benefits. *Atlas Blog*. https://atlasbiomed.com/blog/potato-resistant-starch/

Ephraim, E., Jackson, M.I., Yerramilli, M. & Jewell, D. (2020). Soluble fiber and omega-3 fatty acids reduce levels of advanced glycation end products and uremic toxins in senior dogs by modulating the gut microbiome. *Journal of Food Science and Nutrition Research, 3*(1), 018–033. https://www.fortunejournals.com/articles/soluble-fiber-and-omega3-fatty-acids-reduce-levels-of-advanced-glycation-end-products-and-uremic-toxins-in-senior-dogs-by-modulati.html

Fossmark, R., Martinsen, T.C. & Waldum, H.L. (2019). Adverse effects of proton pump inhibitors—evidence and plausibility. *International Journal of Molecular Sciences, 20*(20), 5203. https://www.ncbi.nlm.nih.gov/pmc/articles/PMC6829383/#__ffn_sectitle

Fritsch, D., Wernimont, S., Jackson, M., Badri, D., Cochrane, C.Y. & Gross, K. (2019). Select dietary fibers alter GI microbiome composition & promote fermentative metabolism in the lower gastrointestinal tract of healthy adult dogs (P20-044-19). *Current Developments in Nutrition, 3*(Supp. 1). https://doi.org/10.1093/cdn/nzz040.P20-044-19

Frossard, C.P., Hauser, C. & Eigenmann, P.A. (2004). Antigen-specific secretory IgA antibodies in the gut are decreased in a mouse model of food allergy. *The Journal of Allergy and Clinical Immunology, 114*(2), 377–382. https://doi.org/10.1016/j.jaci.2004.03.040

Garbarino, J. (2020). History and biochemistry of fermented foods. *The Rockefeller University*. https://rockedu.rockefeller.edu/component/biochemistry-fermented-foods/

Gotteland, M., Riveros, K., Gasaly, N., Carcamo, C., Magne, F., Liabeuf, G., Beattie, A. & Rosenfeld, S. (2020). The pros and cons of using algal polysaccharides as prebiotics. *Frontiers in Nutrition, 7*, 163. https://www.frontiersin.org/article/10.3389/fnut.2020.00163

Hosseini, M., Salari, R., Akbari Rad, M., Salehi, M., Birjandi, B. & Salari, M. (2018). Comparing the effect of psyllium seed on gastroesophageal reflux disease with oral omeprazole in patients with functional constipation. *Journal of Evidence-based Integrative Medicine, 23*, 2515690X18763294. https://doi.org/10.1177/2515690X18763294

Huaman, J.W., Mego, M., Manichanh, C., Cañellas, N., Cañueto, D., Segurola, H., Jansana, M., Malagelada, C., Accarino, A., Vulevic, J., Tzortzis, G., Gibson, G., Saperas, E., Guarner, F. & Azpiroz, F. (2018). Effects of prebiotics vs a diet low in FODMAPs in patients with functional gut disorders. *Gastroenterology, 155*(4), 1004–1007. https://doi.org/10.1053/j.gastro.2018.06.045

Huang, Z., Pan, Z., Yang, R., Bi, Y. & Xiong, X. (2020). The canine gastrointestinal microbiota: early studies and research frontiers, *Gut Microbes*, *11*(4), 635–654. https://doi.org/10.1080/19490976.2019.1704142

Jackson, M.I. & Jewell, D.E. (2019). Balance of saccharolysis and proteolysis underpins improvements in stool quality induced by adding a fiber bundle containing bound polyphenols to either hydrolyzed meat or grain-rich foods. *Gut microbes*, *10*(3), 298–320. https://doi.org/10.1080/19490976.2018.1526580

Jalanka, J., Major, G., Murray, K., Singh, G., Nowak, A., Kurtz, C., Silos-Santiago, I., Johnston, J. M., de Vos, W. M. & Spiller, R. (2019). The effect of psyllium husk on intestinal microbiota in constipated patients and healthy controls. *International Journal of Molecular Sciences*, *20*(2), 433. https://doi.org/10.3390/ijms20020433

Jergens, A.E. & Simpson, K.W. (2012). Inflammatory bowel disease in veterinary medicine. *Frontiers in Bioscience (Elite ed.)*, *4*(4), 1404–1419. https://doi.org/10.2741/470

Kim, M.H., Kang, S.G., Park, J.H., Yanagisawa, M. & Kim, C.H. (2013). Short-chain fatty acids activate GPR41 and GPR43 on intestinal epithelial cells to promote inflammatory responses in mice. *Gastroenterology*, *145*(2). https://doi.org/10.1053/j.gastro.2013.04.056

Lahaye, M. (1991). Marine algae as sources of fibres: determination of soluble and insoluble dietary fibre contents in some 'sea vegetables.' *Journal of the Science of Food and Agriculture*, *54*(4), 587–594. https://doi.org/10.1002/jsfa.2740540410

Leib, M.S. (2000). Treatment of chronic idiopathic large-bowel diarrhea in dogs with a highly digestible diet and soluble fiber: a retrospective review of 37 cases. *Journal of Veterinary Internal Medicine*, *14*(1), 27–32. https://doi.org/10.1892/0891-6640(2000)014<0027:tocilb>2.3.co;2

Lin, C.-Y., Alexander, C., Steelman, A.J., Warzecha, C.M., de Godoy, M.R.C. & Swanson, K.S. (2019). Effects of a *Saccharomyces cerevisiae* fermentation product on fecal characteristics, nutrient digestibility, fecal fermentative end-products, fecal microbial populations, immune function, and diet palatability in adult dogs. *Journal of Animal Science*, *97*(4), 1586–1599. https://doi.org/10.1093/jas/skz064

Lin, C.-Y., Carroll, M.Q., Miller, M.J., Rabot, R. & Swanson, K.S. (2020). Supplementation of yeast cell wall fraction tends to improve gastrointestinal health in adult dogs undergoing an abrupt diet transition. (2020). *Frontiers in Veterinary Science*, *7*. https://www.frontiersin.org/articles/10.3389/fvets.2020.597939/full

Linus Pauling Institute. (2021). Fiber. *Oregon State University*. https://lpi.oregonstate.edu/mic/other-nutrients/fiber

Littler, R.M., Batt, R.M. & Lloyd, D.H. (2006). Total and relative deficiency of gut mucosal IgA in German shepherd dogs demonstrated by faecal analysis. *The Veterinary Record*, *158*(10), 334–341. https://doi.org/10.1136/vr.158.10.334

Lloyd-Price, J., Mahurkar, A., Rahnavard, G., Crabtree, J., Orvis, J., Hall, A.B., Brady, A., Creasy, H.H., McCracken, C., Giglio, M.G., McDonald, D., Franzosa, E.A., Knight, R., White, O. & Huttenhower, C. (2017). Strains, functions and dynamics in the expanded Human Microbiome Project. *Nature, 550*(7674), 61–66. https://doi.org/10.1038/nature23889

Maeda, S., Ohno, K., Uchida, K., Nakashima, K., Fukushima, K., Tsukamoto, A., Nakajima, M., Fujino, Y. & Tsujimoto, H. (2013). Decreased immunoglobulin A concentrations in feces, duodenum, and peripheral blood mononuclear cells of dogs with inflammatory bowel disease. *Journal of Veterinary Internal Medicine, 27*(1), 47–55. https://doi.org/10.1111/jvim.12023

Mansfield, T. (2019). Bilophila bacterial overgrowth – infection and detection. *Byron Herbalist.* https://www.byronherbalist.com.au/bacterial-infection/bilophila-wadsworthia-bacterial-overgrowth/

McRorie Jr, J.W. (2015). Evidence-based approach to fiber supplements and clinically meaningful health benefits, Part 2. *Nutrition Today, 50*(2), 90–97. https://doi.org/10.1097/NT.0000000000000089

Meineri, G., Peiretti, P.G., Vitale, N., Vercelli, A. & Ferraris, R. (2008). Evaluation of gastroesophageal reflux disease and related alimentary factors in dogs and their owners. *Journal of Animal and Veterinary Advances, 7*(10), 1292–1296. http://docsdrive.com/pdfs/medwelljournals/javaa/2008/1292-1296.pdf

Minamoto, Y., Minamoto, T., Isaiah, A., Sattasathuchana, P., Buono, A., Rangachari, V.R., McNeely, I.H., Lidbury, J., Steiner, J.M. & Suchodolski, J.S. (2019). Fecal short-chain fatty acid concentrations and dysbiosis in dogs with chronic enteropathy. *Journal of Veterinary Internal Medicine, 33*, 1608–1618. https://www.ncbi.nlm.nih.gov/pmc/articles/PMC6639498/

Monash University. (2019). More than FODMAPs: fermentable fibers and IBS. *Monash University.* https://www.monashfodmap.com/blog/more-fodmaps-fermentable-fibres-ibs/#:~:text=More%20readily%20fermentable%20fibres%20include,to%20benefit%20health%20(6)

Monash University. (2019a). FODMAPs and irritable bowel syndrome: see how the right food choices can decrease symptoms of IBS. *Monash University.* https://www.monashfodmap.com/about-fodmap-and-ibs/

Morozov, S., Isakov, V. & Konovalova, M. (2018). Fiber-enriched diet helps to control symptoms and improves esophageal motility in patients with non-erosive gastroesophageal reflux disease. *World Journal of Gastroenterology, 24*(21), 2291–2299. https://doi.org/10.3748/wjg.v24.i21.2291

Mount Sinai. (2022). Brewer's yeast. *Mount Sinai Today Blog.* https://www.mountsinai.org/health-library/supplement/brewers-yeast#:~:text=The%20B%2Dcomplex%20vitamins%20in,provide%20the%20body%20with%20energy

Murray, D. (2021). The health benefits of brewer's yeast: an inactive form of yeast may help treat diabetes and IBS. *VeryWellHealth.* https://www.verywellhealth.com/brewers-yeast-benefits-431836

Myint, H., Iwahashi, Y., Koike, S. & Kobayashi, Y. (2017). Effect of soybean husk supplementation on the fecal fermentation metabolites and microbiota of dogs. *Animal Science Journal*, *88*(11), 1730–1736. https://onlinelibrary.wiley.com/doi/abs/10.1111/asj.12817

O'Keefe, S.J., Ou, J., Aufreiter, S., O'Connor, D., Sharma, S., Sepulveda, J., Fukuwatari, T., Shibata, K. & Mawhinney, T. (2009). Products of the colonic microbiota mediate the effects of diet on colon cancer risk. *The Journal of Nutrition*, *139*(11), 2044–2048. https://doi.org/10.3945/jn.109.104380

Pawar, M.M., Pattanaik, A.K., Sinha, D.K., Goswami, T.K. & Sharma, K. (2017). Effect of dietary mannanoligosaccharide supplementation on nutrient digestibility, hindgut fermentation, immune response and antioxidant indices in dogs. *Journal of Animal Science and Technology*, *59*, 11. https://doi.org/10.1186/s40781-017-0136-6

Piche, T., Bruley des Varannes, S., Sacher-Huvelin, S., Juul Holst, J., Cuber, J.C. & Galmiche, J.P. (2003). Colonic fermentation influences lower esophageal sphincter function in gastroesophageal reflux disease. *Gastroenterology*, *124*(4), 894–902. https://doi.org/10.1053/gast.2003.50159

Pilla, R., Gaschen, F.P., Barr, J.W., Olson, E., Honneffer, J., Guard, B.C., Blake, A.B., Villanueva, D., Khattab, M.R., AlShawaqfeh, M.K., Lidbury, J.A., Steiner, J.M. & Suchodolski, J.S. (2020). Effects of metronidazole on the fecal microbiome and metabolome in healthy dogs. *Journal of Veterinary Internal Medicine, 34*(5), 1853–1866. https://doi.org/10.1111/jvim.15871

Pinna, C. & Biagi, G. (2014) The utilisation of prebiotics and synbiotics in dogs. *Italian Journal of Animal Science*, *13*(1), 169–178. https://doi.org/10.4081/ijas.2014.3107

Ribeiro, É.M., Peixoto, M.C., Putarov, T.C., Monti, M., Pacheco, P., Loureiro, B.A., Pereira, G.T. & Carciofi, A.C. (2019). The effects of age and dietary resistant starch on digestibility, fermentation end products in faeces and postprandial glucose and insulin responses of dogs. *Archives of Animal Nutrition*, *73*(6), 485–504. https://doi.org/10.1080/1745039X.2019.1652516

Rosen, R.D. & Winters, R. (2021). Physiology, lower esophageal sphincter. *StatPearls*. https://www.ncbi.nlm.nih.gov/books/NBK557452/

Royal Canin. (2012). German Shepherd Dog nutrition & health needs. *Royal Canin*.

Saldana, J.I. (n.d.). Macrophages. *British Society for Immunology*. https://www.immunology.org/public-information/bitesized-immunology/cells/macrophages

Sanderson, S. (2008). Dietary fiber for optimizing gastrointestinal health [Proceedings]. *DVM360*. https://www.dvm360.com/view/dietary-fiber-optimizing-gastrointestinal-health-proceedings

Sarwar, J. (2021). Metronidazole for dogs: dosage, side effects, and more. *GoodRx*. https://www.goodrx.com/blog/metronidazole-for-dogs/

Satyaraj, E., Reynolds, A., Engler, R., Labuda, J. & Sun, P. (2021). Supplementation of diets with *spirulina* influences immune and gut function in dogs. *Frontiers in Nutrition*, *8*, 667072. https://doi.org/10.3389/fnut.2021.667072

Scientific Wellness. (2018). Prebiotics vs. low-fodmap diet. *Scientific Wellness*. https://www.scientificwellness.com/blog-view/prebiotics-vs-low-fodmap-diet-673

Semeco, A. & Kelly, E. (2021). The 19 best prebiotic foods you should eat. *Healthline*. https://www.healthline.com/nutrition/19-best-prebiotic-foods

Slavin, J.L. (2008). Position of the American Dietetic Association: health implications of dietary fiber. *Journal of the American Dietetic Association*, *108*(10), 1716–1731. https://doi.org/10.1016/j.jada.2008.08.007

Smith, P.M., Howitt, M.R., Panikov, N., Michaud, M., Gallini, C.A., Bohlooly-Y, M., Glickman, J.N. & Garrett, W.S. (2013). The microbial metabolites, short-chain fatty acids, regulate colonic Treg cell homeostasis. *Science*, *341*(6145), 569–573. https://science.sciencemag.org/content/341/6145/569

Strompfová, V., Kubašová, I., Mudroňová, D., Štempelová, L., Takáčová, M., Gąsowski, B., Čobanová, K. & Maďari, A. (2021). Effect of hydrolyzed yeast administration on faecal microbiota, haematology, serum biochemistry and cellular immunity in healthy dogs. *Probiotics and Antimicrobial Proteins*, *13*(5), 1267–1276. https://doi.org/10.1007/s12602-021-09765-9

Suchodolski, J.S., Dowd, S.E., Westermarck, E., Steiner, J.M., Wolcott, R.D., Spillmann, T. & Harmoinen, J.A. (2009). The effect of the macrolide antibiotic tylosin on microbial diversity in the canine small intestine as demonstrated by massive parallel 16S rRNA gene sequencing. *BMC Microbiology*, *9*, 210. https://doi.org/10.1186/1471-2180-9-210

Suchodolski, J. (2020). Probiotics, prebiotics, synbiotics, and intestinal health of dogs and cats. *Today's Veterinary Practice*. https://todaysveterinarypractice.com/probiotics-prebiotics-synbiotics-dogs-cats/

Surawicz, C.M., Elmer, G.W., Speelman, P., McFarland, L.V., Chinn, J. & van Belle, G. (1989). Prevention of antibiotic-associated diarrhea by *Saccharomyces boulardii*: a prospective study. *Gastroenterology*, *96*(4), 981–988. https://doi.org/10.1016/0016-5085(89)91613-2

Swanson, K.S., Grieshop, C.M., Flickinger, E.A., Bauer, L.L., Healy, H-P., Dawson, K.A., Merchen, N.R. & Fahey Jr, G.C. (2002). Supplemental fructooligosaccharides and mannanoligosaccharides influence immune function, ileal and total tract nutrient digestibilities, microbial populations and concentrations of protein catabolites in the large bowel of dogs. *The Journal of Nutrition*, *132*(5), 980–989. https://academic.oup.com/jn/article/132/5/980/4687279

Swanson, K.S., Grieshop, C.M., Flickinger, E.A., Healy, H-P., Dawson, K.A., Merchen, N.R. & Fahey Jr, G.C. (2002a). Effects of supplemental fructooligosaccharides plus mannanoligosaccharides on immune function and ileal and fecal microbial populations in adult dogs. *Archiv für Tierernährung (Archives of Animal Nutrition)*, *56*(4), 309–318. https://doi.org/10.1080/00039420214344

Tanprasertsuk, J., Jha, A.R., Shmalberg, J., Jones, R.B., Perry, L.M., Maughan, H. & Honaker, R.W. (2021). The microbiota of healthy dogs demonstrates individualized responses to synbiotic supplementation in a randomized controlled trial. *Animal Microbiome, 3.* https://doi.org/10.1186/s42523-021-00098-0

Tarantino, O. (2019). Prebiotic foods for your probiotic efforts. *Eat This, Not That!* https://www.eatthis.com/prebiotic-foods/

Tizard, I.R. & Jones, S.W. (2018). The microbiota regulates immunity and immunologic diseases in dogs and cats. *Veterinary Clinics of North America: Small Animal Practice, 48,* 307–322. https://pubmed.ncbi.nlm.nih.gov/29198905/

Vázquez-Baeza, Y., Hyde, E.R., Suchodolski, J.S. & Knight, R. (2016). Dog and human inflammatory bowel disease rely on overlapping yet distinct dysbiosis networks. *Nature Microbiology, 1,* https://www.nature.com/articles/nmicrobiol2016177.epdf?no_publisher_access=1&r3_referer=nature

Villines, Z. & Marengo, K. (2019). What are the best fermented foods? *Medical News Today.* https://www.medicalnewstoday.com/articles/325114

Wang, G-d., Zhai, W., Yang, H-c., Fan, R-x., Cao, X., Zhong, L., Wang, L., Liu, F., Wu, H., Cheng, L-g., Poyarkov, A.D., Poyarkov Jr, N.A., Tang, S-s., Zhao, W-m., Gao, Y., Lv, X-m., Irwin, D.M., Savolainen, P., Wu, C-i. & Zhang, Y-p. (2013). The genomics of selection in dogs and the parallel evolution between dogs and humans. *Nature Communications, 4.* https://doi.org/10.1038/ncomms2814

Wastyk, H.C., Fragiadakis, G.K., Perelman, D., Sonnenburg, E.D., Gardner, C.D. & Sonnenburg, J.L. (2021). Gut-microbiota-targeted diets modulate human immune status. *Cell, 184,* 1–17. https://doi.org/10.1016/j.cell.2021.06.019

Wernimont, S.M., Radosevich, J., Jackson, M.I., Ephraim, E., Badri, D.V., MacLeay, J.M., Jewell, D.E. & Suchodolski, J. S. (2020). The effects of nutrition on the gastrointestinal microbiome of cats and dogs: impact on health and disease. *Frontiers in Microbiology, 11,* 1266. https://doi.org/10.3389/fmicb.2020.01266

Zaman, S.A. & Sarbini, S.R. (2015). The potential of resistant starch as a prebiotic. *Critical Reviews in Biotechnology, 36*(3), 578–584. https://doi.org/10.3109/07388551.2014.993590

Index

Numbers

4Ocean, 135

A

Abdelrahman, N., 221
Abdulkhaleq, L.A., 11
Academy of Nutrition and Dietetics, 252
acid load, 237–240
Ackland, L., 59
Adams, C., 95
age considerations
    chronic kidney disease, 233–234, 245
    dilated cardiomyopathy (DCM), 42
    gastrointestinal disorders, 252, 255
    health assessment, 124–125, 167–168
    recipe building, 161–162
Aggarwal, B.B., 194, 208–209
Ahmad, A., 203
Airedale Terriers, 43
Akramiene, D., 202
Alessa, H.B., 214
Alessandri, G., 21–22, 28
Allen, R.W., 223
allergies, 226–227
Alves, C., 206
Alves, J.C., 257
Alvi, S., 246
Amaya-Farfán, J., 91
American Animal Hospital Association
    (AAHA), 72
American Cocker Spaniels, 43
American Institute for Cancer Research
    (AICA), 99, 201
American Kennel Club, 122
American Pit Bulls, 22

amino acids
    cancer-fighting foods, 205
    ingredients reference chart, 160–161
    overview, 65–67
    requirements of, 27, 32, 43–44
Aminoacid-studies.com, 66
Anand, P., 181, 193–194, 196, 208
Anderson, C.A., 238–239
Anderson, J.W., 35
Angelou, Maya, 268
Animal Equality, 24
Animal Genetics, 27
Annals of Family Medicine, 223
anti-nutrients, 118–122
antioxidants
    diabetes, 214–216
    fruits and berries, 191–192, 194, 214–216
    herbs, 222–223
    legumes, 77
    nuts and seeds, 92, 98–106, 219
    oils, 108, 113
    overview, 58–59, 258
    spirulina, 247, 258
    vegetables, 71, 87–89
    yeast, 116
Arendt, M., 27
arginine, 65–66
Arsyad, A., 192
Arts, I.C., 121
Asif, M., 247
Association for Pet Obesity Prevention
    (APOP), 13, 123–124, 128
Association of American Feed Control Ani-
    mals (AAFCO), 32, 69, 103, 163–164
athletic dogs, 38–41

Aune, D., 35, 214
Awad, A.B., 106
Ayeka, P.A., 202

B
Baboumian, Patrik, 40
Bacchetta, J., 241
Backus, R.C., 43
bacteria
    chronic kidney disease, 244–245
    epigenetic factors, 16–17
    fats and proteins, 65–66
    gastrointestinal disorders, 249–255,
    260–267
    gut microbiome overview, 16–18, 28–29,
    181
    prebiotic fibers, 59–61
    prebiotic foods, 92, 97–99, 106, 195, 218,
    278, 280
    preparation guidelines, 175
    water, 74
Bakovic, M., 198
Ball, R.O., 27
Banfield Pet Hospital, 12–13, 212
Bank, I.M., 191
Bansal, M., 198
BARF (Bones and Raw Food diet), 21, 59
Basenjis, 249
Bauer, J., 74
Baur, Gene, 166
Baur, J.E., 247
Beagles, 28, 30, 125, 254
Bean Institute, The, 86
beans
    cancer-fighting foods, 200–201
    chronic kidney disease, 235
    diabetes, 215
    ingredients reference chart, 155–156
    overview, 77–86
    PB and Chickpea Blondies, 289–290
    purchasing tips, 176
    recipe building, 138
    side effects, 169–172
Bélanger, M.C., 43
Bennink, M.R., 35
Bergqvist, A.G., 191
Bergström, Andres, 28

Bernese Mountian Dogs, 182
berries, 194–196
Betz, M., 238
Bhat, R.V., 209
bioaccumulation
    cancer, 182–185
    chronic kidney disease, 236, 245
    overview, 19–20
    toxins in animal-based protein, 35, 38, 48,
    64–65, 179
Biology Dictionary, 29
Blackburn, K.B., 192
BMC Veterinary Research, 213
Boesler, M., 74
Boivin, D., 194, 196, 198
Border Collies, 125
Borowitzka, M.A., 110
Bosetti, C., 196
Boxers, 43, 249
Bresciani, F., 21
Brissette, C., 171–172
British Journal of Nutrition, 29–30
British Medical Journal, 216
Broaddus, H., 115
Brooks, D., 44
Brown, E.S., 206
Brown, G.D., 93
Brown, M.J., 88, 111, 112
Brown, S., 49
Brown, S.A., 233, 247
Brown, W.Y., 41
Brufau, G., 98
Bruss, M.L., 112
Bryan, R.A., 191
buckwheat, 222
budget considerations, 54
Buehring, G.C., 186–187
Bulldogs, 43
Bulsiewicz, W., 16–18
Burke, S.K., 244
Burnham, T., 174
buying guidelines, 162–166, 174
Byrne, F.N., 235

C
calcium, 69, 70–71
Callewaert, D.M., 11, 59

Calories
    calculation of requirements, 125–129,
    139–141
    overview, 61–62, 123–124
Calvert, C.A., 42
Calvo, M.S., 235
Campbell, Colin, 188
Canadian Society of Intestinal Research, 224
cancer
    anti-nutrients, 120–121
    Cancer-Kicking Broth, 274–275
    dietary triggers, 182–193
    fiber and, 60
    food that prevent and inhibit, 193–211
    phytochemicals and, 59
    red meat consumption, 71–72
    seeds, 106
    soy isoflaones, 80–81
Cancer-Kicking Broth, 274–275
canine history, 26–30
*Canine Nutrigenomics: The New Science of Feeding
    Your Dog for Optimum Health* (Dodds &
    Laverdure), 4, 9, 10, 111, 135, 214
carbohydrates
    diabetes, 214–215, 218
    diet comparisons, 21, 27–36, 40–41,
    189–192
    fiber, 244–245, 251, 254. See also fiber
    food intolerances, 227–228, 231
    overview, 56–61
    recipe building, 124, 129, 136
    starches. See starches
Cardona, F., 195
Cargo-Froom, C.L., 70
Carlson, J., 61, 252
Carob Protein Pancakes, 282–283
Carrington, D., 25
Case, L.P., 27, 32, 56, 58, 62–63, 65–66
Caselato-Sousa, V.M., 91
Cases, A., 240–241
Castle, S., 78
Cayzeele-Decherf, A., 260
CDC (Center for Disease Control), 12, 20, 74
Ceballos, G., 24–25
Cedars Sinai, 42
Center for Disease Control (CDC), 12, 20, 74
Center for Responsive Politics, 30
Chai, W., 120

Chandler, M.L., 63
Chandran, M., 213
Chandrasekara, A., 92
Chang, P., 112
charts
    estimated daily calories, 128
    estimated minimum dietary fat RDA, 134
    ingredients reference chart, 155–158
    minimum protein RDA chart, 132
    multipliers for MER chart, 127
    recipe creation chart, 145–154
ChartsBin, 187
Cheeke, Robert, 39
Chen, C.N., 244–245
Chen, L., 195
Chen, X., 235
Cheng, F.P., 244
Cheng, L.J., 220
Chey, W.D., 60
Chihuahuas, 45–46
Chiorando, M., 80
chlorophyll, 199–200
Choi, J.N., 191
chronic inflammation. See inflammation
chronic kidney disease
    dietary solutions, 236–244
    overview, 233–236
    Proton Pump Inhibitors, 256
Ciftci, O.N., 105
Cimino-Brown, D., 202–203
cinnamon, 223
Clapper, G.M., 37
Cleveland Clinic, 87, 223–224
Coates, J., 127, 132
Cocker Spaniels, 43
Coelho, L., 28–29, 250
Cohen, J.H., 196
Colgrove, K., 85
Colledge, S., 28
Collins, K., 59, 80
commercial plant-based products, 162–166
Compassion Circle, 159
Compound Interest, 96, 197
Conchillo, A., 110
Conolly, J., 28
constipation, 59–61, 171, 255, 257, 263
Consumer Reports, 93
cooking tips. *See also* recipes

beans, 85–86
grains and pseudo grains, 93–94
nuts, 102
preparation guidelines, 142
vegetables, 96–97
winter squashes, 90
Cook's Country, 77
Cooperstone, J.L., 95
Cordain, L., 238
cost considerations, 173–174
Cotas, J., 205–206
Crustless Canine Mini Quiches, 287–288
curcumin, 208–210
Czerwonka, M., 71, 187

D
dairy products, 70–71
Danahy, A., 195
Danby, S.G., 107
Danks, L., 66–67
Dannie, M., 257
Darmadi-Blackberry, I., 35
Davies, R.H., 163
de Jesus Raposo, M.F., 262
de Oliveira Otto, M.C., 72, 214
Deckelbaum, R.J., 63
Del Coro, K., 88
Delany, A., 79
Deng, P., 30
diabetes
    beneficial foods, 214–224
    fiber and, 60–61
    genetic factors, 15
    gut microbiome, 17
    obesity, 212–213, 215, 222
    red meat consumption, 71
dialysis, 235–236
Dickman, R., 257
diet comparisons
    carbohydrates, 40–41
    general health results, 14
    genetic evolution of dogs, 27–28
    gut microbiome and, 20–25
    ketogenic diets, 189–193
    Low FODMAP diet, 263–265
dilated cardiomyopathy (DCM), 45–46
Dillitzer, N., 68
Djokovie, Novak, 39

Dkaka, V., 115
Doberman Pinschers, 42–43
Dodds, Jean, 3–5, 10–11, 13–15, 17, 42, 59,
    63, 119, 227, 229, 236, 249
Dogo Argentino dogs, 118
Dolan, S., 80
Dolson, L., 87
Donadelli, R.A., 61
Donaldson, M., 181
Donsky, A., 103–104
Dorough, H., 240
*Dr. Pitcairn's Complete Guide to Natural Health
    for Dogs & Cats* (Pitcairn), 2, 183
Dudas, Dusan, 39
Dukes-McEwan, J., 43
Dunbar, B.L., 63
dysbiosis
    diet comparisons, 21
    overview, 11, 16–17

E
Eckl, P.M., 204
Edermaniger, L., 218, 252
Egan, S., 57
El Amouri, A., 246
El Khoury, D., 92, 93
Elliott, P., 235
Emerson, Ralph Waldo, 8
Encyclopedia Britannica, 59
energy systems, 40–41
English Cocker Spaniels, 43
Environmental Biology, 21, 28
Environmental Defense Fund, 183–185
environmental impact, 49
Environmental Protection Agency (EPA),
    74, 82, 117, 183
Environmental Working Group (EWG), 74,
    174, 188
Ephraim, E., 32–34, 244, 246, 255
epigenetic factors, 9–10, 14–16
Erickson, N., 193
ESHA Research, 269
essential fatty acids. See fatty acids
essential minerals, 69
estimated daily calories chart, 128
Eswaran, S., 60
Ettinger, J., 206

European Prospective Investigation into Cancer and Nutrition, 186

F

Fahim, A.T., 106
fats
  diet comparisons, 34–36
  dietary requirements of dogs, 133–134
  ingredients reference chart, 157
  ketogenic diets, 191
  nuts, 98
  overview, 61–65
  recipe building, 136–140
fatty acids
  cancer-fighting foods, 204–205
  chronic kidney disease, 243, 244, 247–248
  conversion of linoleic acid, 27
  diet comparisons, 37
  dietary requirements of dogs, 133–134
  gastrointestinal disorders, 251–255
  ingredients reference chart, 158–161
  nuts, 98
  oils, 108–113
  overview, 60–65
  seeds, 103–104
Fayyad, M.W., 203–204
fermentation, defined, 60–61
fermented foods, 78, 265–267
Fernando, W.M., 112
Ferrão-Filho, A.S., 19–20
FETCH a Cure, 12, 181
fiber
  carbohydrates, 59–61
  chronic kidney disease, 245–246
  deficiency of amino acids, 44
  diabetes, 214–215, 218–219
  in fruits, 57–58
  legumes, 77
  seeds, 104
  side effects, 169–172
Fielder, S., 237
Fiesel, A., 121
financial considerations, 173–174
Fincher, M., 79
fish oil, 109–111
flatulence, 86, 169–172, 263–265
Florence, T.M., 59
food allergies, 226–227

Food Chemistry, 194, 196, 198–199
food intolerances
  dietary solutions, 225–232
  prevalence of, 13
  soy, 81–82
  testing for, 52
FoodStruct, 217, 218
Forster, G.M., 35–36, 215
Fossmark, R., 256
Foster, A.P., 226
Foster, J.D., 234
free radicals
  cancer, 194, 199, 204, 208
  chronic kidney disease, 243–244
  diabetes, 214, 221–222
  inflammation and, 11, 13, 59
  protection from foods, 94, 97, 99–100, 106, 113–115
  vitamins, 67
Frontiers in Bioscience, 250
Frontiers in Microbiology, 22
Frontiers in Nutrition, 258
Frontiers in Veterinary Science, 64
frozen produce, 175
fruit juices, 57–58
fruits
  chronic kidney disease, 243
  diabetes, 218–219
  ingredients reference chart, 158–159
  overview, 94–98
  recipe building, 136–140
  recipes, 270–271
Fuhrman, Joel, 64, 189–191
functional food, defined, 36

G

GALT (gut association lymphoid tissue), 16
Game Changer, The (Djokovie), 39
Garbarino, J., 265–266
gastrointestinal disorders
  fermented foods, 265–267
  Low FODMAP diet, 263–265
  nutritional yeast, 259–261
  overview, 249–251
  prebiotic fibers overview, 251–255, 261–263
  psyllium, 255–258
  spirulina, 258–259

Gautam, A.K., 201
Gaylord, L., 247–248
Gaynor, L., 33
Geertsema, C., 79
gene expression, 10, 14–15, 34
genetic factors, 9–10, 14, 27–28, 249–250
Genetic Factors Are Not the Major Causes of Chronic Disease (Rappaport), 9–10
GERD (gastroesophageal reflux disease), 249–250, 255–258, 264
German Shepherd Dogs, 249, 260
Gerster, H., 63
Ghiasvand, R., 223
Gibson, G.R., 61
Gillette, R.L., 40–41
Giménez-Bastida, J.A., 91
Glass, D., 96
glycemic load (GL), 31, 35–36
goitrogens, 119
Golder Retrievers, 43, 182
González-Parra, E., 241
Good Food Institute, The, 4
Goraya, N., 240
Gordon, S., 93
Gotteland, M., 262
Gowda, G.A., 33
Graham, S., 197
grains and pseudo grains
    chronic kidney disease, 235, 239
    food intolerances, 231
    gastrointestinal disorders, 254
    Low FODMAP diet, 265
    overview, 90–94
    preparation guidelines, 138–140, 156
    recipe building, 138
Great Danes, 43
Greger, Michael, 186, 194, 200–201, 203–204, 209–210, 241
Greque de Morais, M., 117
Greyhounds, 41, 182
Gross, T., 110
Gu, D., 188
Gunnars, K., 115
Gupta, S.C., 38, 208–209
Gut Microbes, 254
gut microbiome
    carbohydrates, 58–61
    diet comparisons, 20–25

epigenetic factors, 16–18
gastrointestinal disorders, 249–255
genetic evolution of dogs, 28
side effects of fiber, 169–172
toxins, 18–20
gut-associated lymphoid tissue (GALT), 16

H

Haddad, E.H., 99
Hallberg, L., 120
Halo, J.V., 14
Han, E., 84
Hand, M.S., 61–62, 65, 67, 70, 72–73
Hangen, L., 35
Hanneman, A., 85
Hansen, S.L., 198
Hansen-Møller, J., 198
Hardy, T.M., 95
Haring, B., 235
Hariri, M., 223
Harvard Medical School, 11, 35–36, 58, 98, 99, 175
Harvard School of Public Health, 89, 92
Harvard T.H. Chan School of Public Health, 189
Hasler, C.M., 36
health assessment, 49–51, 124–125, 167–168, 176–177
heart conditions, 41–46, 71–72
heavy metals, 44
Hellberg, R.S., 163
Helmstädter, A., 35
Helpots, 79
Hemopet, 229–330
Henne, B., 88
herbs, 203–205, 220–223
Hermsdorff, H.H., 35
Hernanadez, J., 238–239
Hewings-Martin, Y., 170
Hewitt, A., 49
high performance dogs, 38–41
Hill, R.C., 40–41
Hiskey, D., 197
history of dogs, 26–30
Holmer, B., 190
homeostasis, defined, 11
Hooda, J., 71, 187
Hosseini, M., 257

How Not to Die (Greger), 186
Hu, C., 247
Hu, Frank, 99
Hu, J., 247
Huaman, J.W., 264
Hudthagosol, C., 99
Huffstetler, E., 85
Hughes, J.S., 35
Huskies, 41, 258
Hwang, E.S., 119
hypothyroidism, 82–83

I

immune cells, 10–11
inflammation
    carbohydrates, 59
    diabetes, 212
    essential fatty acids, 63
    high protein foods and, 33
    nuts, 99
    oils, 108
    overview, 10—14
inflammatory bowel disease (IBD), 133, 226
InformedHealth.org, 10–11
ingredients reference chart, 155–158
International Agency for Research on
    Cancer (IARC), 82
International Journal of Food Science, 224
International Journal of Oncology, 204
iodine, 83
Iqbal, J., 193–194
iron, 71–72
Irritable Bowel Syndrome (IBS), 61,
    171, 249–251. *See also* gastrointestinal
    disorders
Ishikawa, T., 201
Iso, H., 206
Ivanova, T.S., 202

J

Jack Russell Terriers, 125
Jackson, M.I., 245, 252, 253
Jacob, F., 237
Jalali-Khanabadi, B.A., 98–99
Jalanka, J., 262
Jergens, A.E., 249–250
Jewell, D.E., 245–246, 252, 253
Jiang, L., 117

Jiménez-Cruz, A., 35
Johns Hopkins Medicine, 233
Johnson, J.L., 195
Johnston, C.S., 220
Johnston, J., 43
Jones, S.W., 252–253
Journal of Animal Science, 36, 70
Journal of British Nutrition, 41
Journal of Food Composition and Analysis, 175
Journal of Food Science and Technology, 84
Journal of Meat Science, 214
Journal of Obesity & Weight Loss Therapy, 34, 215
Journal of the American College of Nutrition, 68
*Journal of the American Veterinary Medical
    Association*, 200
Journal of Veterinary Internal Medicine, 21, 251
Jubert, C., 200
Julson, E., 116

K

Kahn, J., 200
Kalantar-Zadeh, K., 241–242
Kang, J.X., 110
Karin, M., 204, 208–209
Kaur, H., 244, 247
Kavli Foundation, 16
Kawa, J.M., 222
Kelly, E., 262
Kerr, K.R., 37–38
ketogenic diets, 189–193
Key, T.J., 35
Khader, M., 204
Khan, A., 223
Khazaei, S., 187
kidney disease
    dietary solutions, 236–244
    overview, 223–236
    Proton Pump Inhibitors, 256
Kidney Research, 234
Kim, G.H., 119
Kim, J., 20
Kim, M.H., 253
King, J.C., 88
Kite-Powell, J., 111
Kladna, A., 121
Knight, Andrew, 1–2, 5, 14
Kolonel, L.N., 196
Kondal, A., 117

Kopustinskiene, D.M., 81, 97
Kowalski, S.R., 240
Kozisek, F., 74
Kozlowsky-Suzuki, B., 19–20
Kresty, L.A., 195
Krill Facts, 110
Kroll Settlement Administration, 163
Kubala, J., 115, 240
Kumari, S., 101

L
Labrador Retrievers, 28, 125, 246
Lahaye, M., 262
Lam, T.K., 196
Lappano, R., 112
Laverdure, Diana, 14–15, 17, 119, 229
leaky gut, 17, 119–120, 230, 259, 263. *See also* gastrointestinal disorders
Lee, S.A., 188
Lee, S.H., 121
Lee, Y.H., 227
legumes
    cancer-fighting foods, 200–201
    chronic kidney disease, 235
    diabetes, 215
    ingredients reference chart, 155–156
    overview, 77–86
    PB and Chickpea Blondies, 289–290
    purchasing tips, 176
    recipe building, 138
    side effects, 169–172
Leib, M.S., 257
Lekawanvijit, S., 245
Lelley, T., 106
lentils, 78–80
Lestari, B., 105
Lestienne, I., 120
Lewis, Carl, 39
Lewis, J., 234, 237
Lewis, L., 27
Li, R., 11, 95, 175
Liebman, M., 120
life expectancy, 5
lifestyle considerations, 52
lignans, 104, 121, 193, 201, 215
Lin, B.W., 195
Lin, C.Y., 260
Lin, H.S., 195

Linder, D.E., 162
Link, R., 112
Linus Pauling Institute, 251
Lipi, G., 187
Lloyd-Price, J., 252
Low FODMAP diet, 263–265
Lu, L., 246
Lund, E.M., 213
Luntz, S., 28

M
macronutrients
    carbohydrates, 56–61
    overview, 20–21
    recipe building, 124
Madell, R., 240
Magee, E., 95
maintenance energy requirement (MER), 126–129
Majdalawich, A.F., 203–204
Major, A.W., 35
Malik, V., 112
Mandal, A., 62
Mann, J.I., 38, 214
Mansfield, T., 263
Marengo, K., 267
Marks, J.W., 170
Maron, D.F., 24
Marsden, S., 61, 62–63, 160
Martin, K., 224
Martin, M.W., 42
Martín, R., 33
Martinez-Outschoorn, U.E., 192
Mayo Clinic, 99
McCartney, Paul, 4
McCauley, S.R., 42–43
McClees, H., 92
McDonald, P., 27, 56
McDougall, J., 19
McKenzie, B., 191
McMacken, M., 214–215
McRorie Jr., J.W., 252
MD Anderson Cancer Center, 192
measurements of ingredients, 138, 155–158
meat diet comparisons. *See* diet comparisons
Meat Science! 72
Medical News Today (MNT), 73
Medical Oncology, 193

Medical Xpress, 198
medicinal herbs, 203–205
Medline Plus, 66–67, 240
Meijers, B.K., 246
Meineri, G., 255–256
Meiyanto, E., 105
Melgar, D., 82
Memorial Sloan Kettering Cancer Center, 210
Mendel, M., 95
Messonnier, S., 160
metabolic syndrome, 213
metabolites, 17, 33–34, 37, 60–61, 254
Meurs, K.M., 43
Mezei, O., 215
Michaud, D.S., 196
Michigan Department of Community Health, 184
microalgae oil, 109–111
microbiomes. *See* gut microbiome
Miller, C.S., 227
Minami, Y., 206
Minamoto, Y., 253
Mineralogical Society of America, 70
minerals
    cancer-fighting foods, 205
    deficiency of, 44
    ingredients reference chart, 158–161
    legumes, 77
    nuts, 98–99
    overview, 68–72
    recipe building, 124
    seeds, 103
Minich, D.M., 118120
Moe, S.M., 235, 241
Moinard, A., 64
Mollazadeh, H., 203–204
Monash University, 262, 263–265
Montoya-Alonso, J.A., 13, 212–213
Moorthi, R.N., 235
Morgane, O., 28
Mori-Nu, 83
Morozov, S., 256
Morris, J.G., 66
Moss, D., 68
Mount Sinai, 261
Muir, J., 60
Mullis, E., 14
multipliers for MER chart, 127

Muraki, I., 218–219
Murphy-Guekunst, L., 242
Murray, D., 260–261
Murugkar, D.A., 84
Mushroom Medley Gravy, 276–277
mushrooms, 61, 72, 201–203, 276–277
MyFoodData, 71, 109, 116–117, 117
Myint, H., 255
MyNetDiary, 109, 155

N

Nagini, S., 199
Nandha, R., 106
National Cancer Institute, 181, 188
National Cancer Institute (NCA), 72
National Celiac Association, 200
National Human Genome Research Institute, 9, 15
National Institute of Health (NIH), 89
National Kidney Foundation, 234, 237–238, 240, 243
National Milk Producers Federation (NMPF), 80
National Research Council, 63, 69
National Research Council (US) Committee on Drug Use in Animals, 19
Nemecek, T., 24–25
Newfoundlands, 43
Nissar, J., 120
non-starchy vegetables, 94–98, 136–140, 156–157
Novío, S., 196
Nugent, A.P., 92
Nutrients, 71
nutrigenomics, defined, 10
NutriScan food intolerance test, 13, 53, 81–82, 225, 229–330
Nutrition, Metabolism and Cardiovascular Diseases, 222
Nutrition and Cancer, 198
nutritional yeast, 116, 143–144, 158, 172, 259–261
NutritionData, 31, 207
nuts
    diabetes, 219–220
    ingredients reference chart, 157
    overview, 98–102
    preparation guidelines, 178, 270

O

obesity
  diabetes, 212–213, 215, 222
  diet comparisons, 34–36
  fats and, 61–65
  gut microbiome, 18
  inflammation, 10–13
  oils, 112, 114–115
  recipe building, 123–125
  seeds, 105
  testing for, 53
O'Hara, A.M., 16
Ohio State University, 196
Ohio State University Veterinary Medical
  Center, 32, 127–128
oils, 61–63, 76, 97, 107–116, 157
O'Keefe, S.J., 253
Okparanta, S., 115
Okuma, T.A., 163
Olaya-Galán, N.N., 187
Oldfield, J., 105, 222
Oliver, J., 90
omega fatty acids. *See* fatty acids
oncogenic viruses, 186–187
Oncology Reports, 204
Ou, B., 195
Oxford Languages, 244
Oxford Learner's Dictionary, 29
Oxford University Museum of Natural
  History, 69

P

Pahwa, R., 11–12
Pandya, U., 202
Pascual, G., 115, 192
Passey, C., 238
Pasteur, Louis, 266
Pate, K.M., 97
Patel, A., 92
Patience, S., 48
Pauling, Linus, 180
Pawar, M.M., 260
PB and Chickpea Blondies, 289–290
peas, 77–86
Pedrinelli, V., 68
Persaud, N., 245, 246
Persistent Organic Pollutants (POPs),
  183–185, 233

pesticides
  carcigens, 183–185
  food intolerances, 225–226
  gut microbiome, 18–19
  seeds, 107
  soy, 82
  in water, 74
PetFoodIndustry.com, 81
Petroski, W., 118–121
Petruzzello, M., 204
Phillips, K.M., 106
Phinney, S., 189
phosphorus, 240–243
phytochemicals
  benefits of, 58–59, 113, 121–122
  cancer, 191–197
  chronic kidney disease, 243
  fruits, 218
  legumes, 77
  nuts, 108
  vegetables, 87, 89, 94–98
phytoestrogens, 121
phytoplanton, 109–111
Piche, T., 264
Pilla, R., 20, 251
Pit Bulls, 22, 246
Pitcairn, Richard, 2, 19, 64
Pitcairn, Susan, 2, 19, 64, 183
Plantasic Life, 40
Plant-Powered Dog Food Summit, 2
Poff, A.M., 190
Pointing, C., 26
Polat, M., 187
Poodles, 219
Poore, J., 24–25
postbiotics
  benefits of, 60–61, 65, 218, 251–254
  chronic kidney disease, 244
  flatulence, 264
  high protein foods and, 33
Prebiotic Potato Salad, 280–281
prebiotics. *See also* gut microbiome
  diet comparisons, 263–264
  gastrointestinal disorders, 251–262
  overview, 57, 60–61
  Prebiotic Potato Salad, 280–281
Proceedings of the National Academy of Sciences, 24

proteins
    chronic kidney disease, 235, 239
    diabetes, 214
    dietary requirements of dogs, 30–34, 43, 129–132
    ingredients reference chart, 155–156
    legumes, 77–86
    nutritional yeast, 116
    overview, 65–67
    recipe building, 136–140
    recipes, 270–271, 282–283
    seeds, 103
pseudo-grains. *See* grains and pseudo grains
psyllium, 60–61, 251, 255–258, 262
Pugs, 262
purchasing tips, 162–166, 174
putrefaction, 244–246

Q
Qin, Y., 16–18
Quest, B.W., 44
Quilliam, C., 38

R
Raditic, D., 247–248
Raghavan, M., 200, 216
Rajilic-Stojaniovic, M., 33
Ramprasath, V.R., 106
Randall, D., 110
Rappaport, S.M., 9–10
Ravindran, J., 208–209
raw food diet, 21–22, 59
RawNori, 207
recipe creation chart, 145–154
Recipe-Builder Pie, 136–137. *See also* recipes
recipes
    Cancer-Kicking Broth, 274–275
    Carob Protein Pancakes, 282–283
    Crustless Canine Mini Quiches, 287–288
    Mushroom Medley Gravy, 276–277
    PB and Chickpea Blondies, 289–290
    Prebiotic Potato Salad, 280–281
    Protein Superfood Smoothie, 270–271
    Super Seaweed Salad, 278–279
    Sweet Potato and Hemp "Cheese" Enchiladas, 269, 284–286
record keeping, 49–51, 129, 137, 170
Reese, C.A., 104, 107

Reetz, J., 202–203
Reilly, L.M., 37
Research and Markets, 4
resistance to diet change, 172–173
resistant starch, 61, 218, 252
resting energy requirement (RER), 126–129
Ribeiro, E.M., 218, 252
Rinkinen, M., 227
RMBD (Raw Meat and Bones diet). *See* BARF (Bones and Raw Food diet)
Robbins, John, 81, 83
Robbins, O., 88, 189
Robb-Nicholson, C., 83
Robey, I.F., 192
Rogers, K., 78
Rohromann, S., 186
root vegetables, 87–89
Rosen, R.S., 256
Round Up, 82, 183, 225–226
Rover.com, 207
Royal Canin, 260

S
Safer Chemicals, Healthy Families, 185
Saint Bernards, 43
Saldana, J.I., 253
Salmean, Y.A., 246
sample nutrient composition chart, 31
Sanders, B., 24
Sanderson, S., 253
Sandri, M., 20
Sapkota, A.R., 188
Sarbini, S.R., 218, 252
Sarita, E., 92
Sarwar, J., 251
Satchell, L., 5
saturated fats, 62
Satyaraj, E., 117, 258–259
Schafer-Evans, R., 244–245, 245
Schauf, S., 64
Scheer, R., 68
Schmidt, M., 20
Schnauzers, 219
Schwartz, S.J., 95
Scialla, J.J., 238–240
Science Learning Hub, 9
ScienceDaily, 34
Scientific Wellness, 264

Scottish Deerhounds, 43
Scottish Terriers, 200
seaweed, 90, 158, 200, 205–208, 278–279
seeds
    diabetes, 222–223
    ingredients reference chart, 157
    overview, 102–109
Seidenberg, C., 207
Self Nutritional Data, 155
Semeco, A., 262
Sena, S.F., 190
Sennebogen, E., 117
Shah, S., 214–215
Shahidi, F., 92
Shaman, A.M., 240
Shamsuddin, A.M., 201
Shanahan, F., 16
Shanghai Women's Health Study, 215
Shanmugalingam, T., 190
Shen, W., 63
Shi, J., 38
Shiba Inu Dogs, 254
Shishodia, S., 194
Shoba, G., 210
Shoieb, A.M., 204
Shoppers Guide to Pesticides in Produce, 174
Shryock, T.R., 20
Siberian Huskies, 41
Silk, D.B., 61
Silva-Sánchez, C., 91
Simply-Healthy, 79
Simpson, J.M., 16
Simpson, K.W., 249–250
Singh, E., 92
Siruguri, V., 209
size considerations, 132
Slagle, A., 106
Slavin, J., 60, 88
Slavin, J.L., 252
Slow Food, 24
Smeriglio, A., 121
Smith, C.E., 42
Smith, J., 78
Smith, P.M., 253
Soft-Coated Wheaten Terriers, 249
Sokol, H., 33
Solman, S., 240
Solomon, S.M., 42, 45

Sorrells, A., 78
soy
    amino acids, 32
    anti-nutrients, 121
    overview, 80–84
    recipes, 287–288
    textured vegetable protein, 117–118
spices, 208–210
spirulina, 117, 144, 205, 258–259, 272–273
Spirulina Energy Balls, 272–273
Sriskantharajah, S., 27
Standish, L.J., 203
starches. See also carbohydrates
    diabetes, 216–218
    overview, 86–94
    recipe building, 136–140
Statista, 190
Staughton, J., 88
Stefanson, A.L., 198
stem cells, 14–15
Stevenson, D.G., 106
Stoeckel, K., 63
Stone, Gene, 186, 194, 200–201, 203–204,
    209–210, 241
Strompfová, V., 260
Subramanyam, R., 115
Suchodolski, J.S., 20, 33, 61, 251, 252
sugars, 57–58
Super Seaweed Salad, 278–279
Swanson, K., 30
Swanson, K.S., 260
Sweet Potato and Hemp "Cheese"
    Enchiladas, 269, 284–286

T
Tan, J., 61
Tan, K.W., 197
Taniguchi, K., 204, 208
tannins, 121–122
Tarantino, O., 262
taurine
    ingredients reference chart, 160
    requirements of, 27, 43–44, 164
Taylor, A.L., 205, 207
Taylor, H., 101, 122
Teas, J., 208
Terriers, 219
textured vegetable protein, 117–118

The China Study (Campbell), 188
The Guardian, 25
Thompson, M.D., 35
Thompson, M.D., 35
Thomson, J.R., 205
time considerations, 177–178
Tizard, I.R., 252–253
tofu, 83–84
Tokarz, A., 71, 187
Tollefsbol, T.O., 95
toxins. *See also* pesticides
    bioaccumulation in fats, 64–65
    carcigens, 188
    chronic kidney disease, 233, 236–237,
        244–247
    commercial plant-based products, 163
    dilated cardiomyopathy (DCM), 42
    dog specific, 122
    gut microbiome, 18–20
    high protein foods and, 33
    nuts, 98, 100, 102
    spirulina, 117
Toxins, 33
Toy Poodles, 254
tumeric, 208–210
Turner, H., 63
Tvarijonaviciute, A., 213
Tweed, V., 116

U
Udayangani, S., 205
United States Department of Agriculture
    (USDA), 186
University of Arizona, 65–66
University of Newcastle Upon Tyne, 87, 198
University of Sidney, 217
unsaturated fats, 62–63
Uribarri, J., 242
U.S. Department of State, 185
U.S. Food & Drug Administration (FDA)
    Center of Veterinary Medicine, 41–42
Uttara, B., 59

V
vaccinations, 18, 236
Vázquez-Baeza, Y., 249
Vegan Calculator, 25
VegeDog, 159, 269

vegetable protein, 117–118
vegetables
    cancer-fighting foods, 196–200
    diabetes, 215–216
    ingredients reference chart, 156–157
    introduction of, 170
    overview, 94–98
    recipes, 280–281, 284–286
Venkata, R.P., 115
Venn, B.J., 38, 214
Vervicka, V., 202–203
Veterinary Cancer Society, 12, 72
*Veterinary Clinics of North America: Small
    animal Practice,* 253
Villegas, R., 38, 215
Villines, Z., 267
vinegars, 220
viruses, 186–187
vitamins
    cancer-fighting foods, 205
    deficiency of, 44
    health assessment, 168
    ingredients reference chart, 158–161
    legumes, 77
    minerals and, 70
    nutritional yeast, 116
    nuts, 98–99
    overview, 67–68
    recipe building, 124
    root vegetables, 87–89
    seeds, 103
Vollmar, A., 43
Vucenik, I., 201
Vuksan, V., 105, 222

W
Wada, L., 195
Wade, P.A., 16–18
Wali, A.F., 206
Wang, G., 250
Wang, Q., 103
Wang, S.Y., 195
Warburg, Otto, 189
Ward, E., 233–234
Ware, M., 210
Warwicker, M., 205, 207
Wastyk, H.C., 266
water, 72–75

Watson, M., 85
Webb, M.J., 244
Webber, J., 26
WebMD, 88
Weese, J.S., 163
Weg, A., 79
Weir, M., 233–234
Wells, S., 28
Wernimont, S.M., 22, 61, 64, 252
Wess, G., 42
Westcott, P., 87
Whitbread, D., 74
White, A.M., 220
WHO (World Health Organization), 11–12,
    82, 183
Wilks, James Lightning, 39
Willett, W.C., 111
Willmott, N.S., 191
winter squashes, 89–90
Winters, R., 256
Winwood, R.J., 111
wolves, 1, 27–28
Wong, D.T., 227
Woodford, K., 71
working dogs, 38–41
Worldometer, 24
Wynn, S., 160

X

Xanthopoulou, M.N., 106
Xiong, Y., 92, 103
Xu, W., 111
Xydakis, A.M., 213

Y

Yamada, M., 65
Yamka, R., 42, 44
Yan, L., 95
Yang, H.L., 245, 246
yeast, 116, 143–144, 158, 172, 259–261
Youm, Y.H., 190

Z

Zaman, S.A., 218, 252
Zampa, M., 24
Zava, D.T., 207
Zava, T.T., 207
Zeratsky, K., 79–80

Zhang, M., 196, 203
Zheng, W., 188
Zhou, Z., 38
Zibaeenezhad, M., 219
Zidorn, C., 197
Zielinski, H., 91
Zimmer, C., 14

About the Authors

Diana Laverdure-Dunetz, MS, holds a Master of Animal Science degree and is a multi-award-winning dog health writer, vegan canine nutritionist and passionate animal advocate. She has specialized in formulating fresh-food diets for dogs all over the world for more than a decade, using nutritional therapies to help her canine clients overcome a myriad of chronic inflammatory diseases and achieve their best possible health.

Diana became vegetarian in 2007 and vegan in 2017, at which time she transformed her canine nutrition practice to creating solely whole-food plant-based diets for dogs. Through her website Plant-Powered Dog (https://www.plantpowereddog.com/) and her formulation consultancy, Diana empowers dog lovers to raise thriving plant-based dogs.

In 2019, Diana created the Plant-Powered Dog Food Summit, which featured 17 global leaders in the fields of veterinary nutrition, science and animal activism. The summit was the first of its kind to reveal the scientific facts about plant-based vs. animal-based diets for dogs. Thousands of people signed up to watch this ground-breaking event.

Diana is the co-author (with Dr. Jean Dodds) of the double-award-winning book *The Canine Thyroid Epidemic: Answers You Need for Your Dog* (Dogwise Publishing, 2011) and *Canine Nutrigenomics: The New Science of Feeding Your Dog for Optimum Health* (Dogwise Publishing, 2015). As these were written prior to her personal and nutritional evolution to veganism, she is thrilled that this current book showcases the latest scientific research on the benefits of a whole-food plant-based diet for modern companion dogs.

Diana and her husband, Dr. Rodney Dunetz, support many animal rights organizations. In 2019, they adopted their dog, Moo, from Vietnam. He resides with them in South Florida, where he enjoys basking in the sunshine and thrives on a whole-food plant-based diet.

W. Jean Dodds, DVM, earned her veterinary degree with honors and distinction in 1964 from the Ontario Veterinary College, becoming one of only a handful of women to enter what was the male-dominated veterinary field.

Jean has published more than 175 research papers and holds 27 patents. In 1986, she founded Hemopet, the first non-profit national animal blood bank. Today, Hemopet's range of nonprofit services and educational activities includes providing canine blood components and related services; adopting retired Greyhound blood donors as companions; and the Hemolife diagnostic division focused on hematology and blood banking, immunology, endocrinology, nutrition and holistic medicine (www.hemopet.org).

Throughout her career, Jean has pioneered many innovative new testing procedures and natural therapies to improve the health of animal companions. The patented NutriScan saliva-based food sensitivity test for dogs, cats and horses has revolutionized early detection and treatment of food intolerances and related gastrointestinal disorders. CellBio, a saliva-based test for oxidative stress, is the only clinically predictable diagnostic test for dogs to identify the presence of or predisposition to oxidative stress damage to cells caused by chronic inflammation, infection, periodontal disease, obesity and cancer.

Jean has a longstanding association and committee membership with the American Holistic Veterinary Medical Association (AHVMA) and the American Holistic Veterinary Medical Foundation (AHVMF). She has dedicated her life to animal welfare and well-being within the scientific community, including helping promulgate the National Institutes of Health (NIH) Guide to the Care & Use of Laboratory Animals.

She is the co-author (with Diana Laverdure-Dunetz, MS) of the double-award-winning book *The Canine Thyroid Epidemic: Answers You Need for Your Dog* (Dogwise Publishing, 2011) and *Canine Nutrigenomics: The New Science of Feeding Your Dog for Optimum Health* (Dogwise Publishing, 2015). Jean and her husband, Charles, have been vegetarian for more than 40 years. When not traveling the globe educating on a variety of animal health topics, they reside in Southern California.